KARAKORAM
The Ascent of Gasherbrum IV

FOSCO MARAINI

KARAKORAM

The Ascent of Gasherbrum IV

Translated from the Italian by James Cadell

NEW YORK

THE VIKING PRESS

'Ahead was the object that riveted our attention—the great mass of Gusherbrum, butt end towards us. Zurbriggen curtly pronounced the nearest peak (26,016 feet) utterly inaccessible, as far as could be seen. . . .'

SIR MARTIN CONWAY
Climbing and Exploration in the Karakoram-Himalayas
London 1894

'The whole of this range, centred round the slim, pyramidal peak of Gasherbrum, is one of the most rugged in the entire Baltoro. Soaring, gleaming walls which appear to give the ice no chance of a proper grip; sharp edges of singular outline; and a series of jagged teeth—these are the dominant features. We freely confess that we were unable to find any likely looking route by which Gasherbrum and the surrounding peaks might one day be climbed.'

ARDITO DESIO
La Spedizione Geografica Italiana nel Karakoram
Milan-Rome 1936

'Gasherbrum IV (26,180 feet) perhaps sets the most difficult problem of all. This masterpiece of a mountain, visible from a great distance, must have attracted many a questioning look. I have looked carefully at this superb peak from every possible angle; but I must admit that I know no really recommendable route. It might be worth considering whether access can be gained to the Col between Gasherbrum III and IV by an exceedingly steep and repulsive icefall. If that could be done there would "only" be the three or four thousand feet of the East Ridge to climb, for one would be at its foot: but it is fearsomely steep and, again owing to its precipitous stratification—for it is the actual reverse of the Baltoro Face—very difficult to climb. So it seems to me that Gasherbrum IV is one of the Karakorum Peaks whose Summit is unlikely to be disturbed for a very long time to come.'

G. O. DYHRENFURTH
To the Third Pole, A History of the High Himalaya
Translated from the German by Hugh Merrick
Werner Laurie, London 1955

Contents

THE GOLDEN ROAD TO THE SEVEN GIANTS

A MOUNTAIN—OR A NIGHTMARE?

DAYS OF SUCCESS

FLOWERS ON THE GLACIER— APRICOTS IN THE VALLEY

Author's Note

Climbers in Italy have been interested in the Karakoram since 1909, when the Duke of the Abruzzi led an expedition there to attempt the ascent of K2, the second-highest mountain in the world. The major goal was soon abandoned—the time was not yet ripe for the conquest of such a high peak—but the Duke and his guides nearly reached the summit of Chogolisa (25,110 feet), touching the height of 24,425 feet, an altitude record which held good for thirteen years. The expedition was also memorable for its scientific results, due to researches in the field by Filippo de Filippi and others, for the maps of Marchese Negrotto and for the superb mountain photography of Vittorio Sella.

A few years later Filippo de Filippi led another very large expedition to the same part of the world. This was mainly scientific in character, and little mountaineering was done. The geological, topographical and anthropological work of Professor G. Dainelli was monumental and is still basic for our knowledge of a good part of the Karakoram region.

Another name we must associate with the further exploration of these mountains is that of Professor Ardito Desio, the geologist from Milan. He accompanied the Duke of Spoleto on an expedition in 1929; he then returned to the Karakoram in 1953; and finally led the successful Italian Expedition to K2 in 1954. The eastern Karakoram had been explored since 1930 by Professor G. Dainelli, who discovered and named the Italia Col, at the head of the Rimu Glacier.

Other projects had been discussed from time to time, but for some reason or other had never been carried out. Since 1928 Professor Dainelli had been carefully planning the ascent of Broad Peak, but this mountain was not to be conquered until 1957, by the courageous Austrian Expedition.

By 1954 or 1955 important unscaled peaks were getting rarer and rarer in the Karakoram. Hence it was only natural that the Italian Alpine Club (the C.A.I.), then under the ambitious and very active leadership of Dr. Giovanni Ardenti-Morini, should plan to return again to this familiar area, before the harvest of major peaks was brought to an end. It should be remembered that the Italian Alpine Club, like many other such organizations on the Continent, is a powerful body with over 80,000 members and a very considerable yearly budget. Important sums are allocated for exploration and for expeditions overseas, in the great mountain ranges of the world.

I happened to act as intermediary between the Italian Alpine Club and the Government of Pakistan, in Karachi, at the beginning of 1958. The hopes of the Alpine Club were originally pinned on Gasherbrum I (or Hidden Peak, or K5, as it has otherwise been known at various times), a splendid *Ottomila* (i.e. 8,000-metre peak), which had been attempted twice before, by an international expedition in 1934 and by a French one in 1936. As a second choice we asked for Masherbrum, as a third for Chogolisa. It soon turned out that Gasherbrum I had been given, shortly before, to the Americans; Chogolisa to the Japanese; and that Masherbrum was to be 'reserved', for some unknown reason, to some unknown expedition of the future.

We were offered Gasherbrum IV (26,180 feet), the original Gusherbrum of Sir Martin Conway, the mountain which gives its name to the whole Gasherbrum family, with its six peaks. Gasherbrum IV was well known as an ugly enough beast! The quotations which preface this book will give the reader an idea of the fame which surrounded the 'Splendid Peak' (as its name can be translated). The offer was however accepted with very high spirits, and preparations started in earnest for an expedition which was to be as strong, as light and as well-equipped as possible.

Riccardo Cassin, the doyen of Italian mountaineers, a name made famous on some of the most horrid north faces of Alpine peaks (Jorasses, Badile, Lavaredo West), was chosen as leader; Toni Gobbi acted as his deputy and took charge of the actual organization. The strongest Italian climbers were invited to a meeting in Milan, where they underwent special medical examinations to evaluate their fitness. Finally Walter Bonatti, Carlo Mauri, Giuseppe De Francesch and Giuseppe Oberto were chosen and added to the list. Only one first-rate man had been left out: Cesare Maestri. This was to the regret of all. But he had always been known as a supreme individualist (he is famous for his exploits as a lone climber), and it was feared that he would not fit into a Himalayan team, which must always act as a tightly knit group.

Dr. Donato Zeni, a formidable rock climber, joined the Expedition as medical officer, and I was asked to act as photographer, interpreter and keeper of the records.

After the usual scamper to get everything ready, some of us left Genoa by boat on 30th April, while others departed from Rome by air on 11th May. At the middle of May we all gathered in Rawalpindi, where we met our liaison officer, Captain Abdul Karim Dar.

From there on we abandoned the beaten track and our adventure started.

FOSCO MARAINI

Foreword

by the PRESIDENT OF THE
CLUB ALPINO ITALIANO

Every bureaucracy puts a thousand obstacles in the way of the man who wants to do anything new. For more than a year my guide through this stormy sea had been His Excellency Delhavi, Ambassador to Italy of the Islamic Republic of Pakistan. But when all the finesse of his Oriental diplomacy had failed to avail me of his Government's permission for a small party of Italian climbers to visit a deserted region disputed between India and Pakistan, he advised me to pay a personal visit to Karachi to see how matters stood.

' "He who wants to go—let him!" ' he told me, quoting an old German proverb.

I received this advice on a February afternoon in 1958. In a thoughtful frame of mind, I sought out my friend Datti at the Club Alpino's premises in Rome. Datti had been pressing our case with the Minister for Foreign Affairs, and I wanted his views.

Time was getting short. It had been amply proved by experience that once July was out you could not hope for favourable climatic conditions in the Upper Baltoro: the monsoon put mountaineering out of the question. And no enterprise could get under way at any period earlier than ten weeks before the monsoon; up till that time, the snow was far too heavy at high altitudes.

One factor besides this time-limit had to be taken into consideration. Five hundred Balti porters could not be enrolled, provisioned and instructed in five minutes, and they all had to be marched 250 kilometres on foot before the approaches to the mountain could be reached. A complicated business— and one rendered more complicated still by the fact that Mr. Clinch and his Americans had applied for the same mountain: G.I. (Hidden Peak). What if we were assigned another peak? More time still would be needed for its special study before we could venture—venture is most certainly the word—on to a mountain we had no idea of!

13

All this was food for thought indeed. But there had been others in the same boat, and I drew a certain amount of comfort from this reflection. Had not Eric Shipton described in *The Mount Everest Reconnaissance* how he had fitted out his 1951 expedition in less than a month? Why couldn't Italian climbers, with the help of their Club, do likewise?

In the Via Gregoriana I chanced upon Fosco Maraini, of the open smile. He was trying to make up a party to go off to the Gran Sasso for a few days' ski-training. This was a lucky break for me. I asked him to plead our case directly in Karachi. Four days later I received a first letter from our special envoy. Another ten and the longed-for permit was ours. It was not for an '8,000-metre peak'. But it was for a 26,000-footer, Gasherbrum IV.[1] Of this mountain it had been written that judging from its forbidding aspect it was likely to remain for a very long time unclimbed.

So the race against time really began, and at the Club Alpino we should be able to test the organizing capacity of the Commission for Extra-European Expeditions: expeditions which focussed the interest of mountain men all over the world. The machine ran sweetly and infallibly into action.

At Genoa, Antonio Buscaglione began, and brilliantly completed, his Gasherbrum studies, profiting from all the various international sources which, with his long-standing enthusiasm, he was able to draw on.

At Monza, Riccardo Cassin and Toni Gobbi paid a visit to the Fossati Bellani stores, and with meticulous care fitted up the Expedition with everything likely to be needed by eight Italians and six Hunzas for a sojourn of not less than three months in an uninhabited region, and with all the most modern mountaineering equipment. The gear filled 280 cases and weighed seven metric tons.

At the Club's central premises in Milan the legal experts arranged insurance policies (no easy matter) for Expedition members. Questions of publicity, payments, exchange, sea and air travel arrangements all received attention. The entire Expedition was covered from all angles for every hour of its life, Swiss, French and German societies all pooling their help and experience towards this end, so that the enterprise could start with its members free from all those little worries they had felt on former occasions.

On Mont Blanc, not far from the Rifugio Torino, the men picked for this arduous exercise got into training and tried out equipment of every type, rigorously selected from all over Europe. Public relations were in the tactful and highly enthusiastic hands of Elvezio Bozzoli Parasacchi, whose name has

---

1. 8,000 metres = 26,247 feet. The height of Gasherbrum IV is 26,180 feet.

always been synonymous with mountaineering and the Club Alpino Italiano, and Amedeo Costa—another champion of only yesterday.

The great day came. On a memorable 30th April the eight men sailed, taking with them, along with a pennant, all the hopes, the fears and the prayers of 80,000 members of the C.A.I. The name of the Italian ship augured well for them: it was *Vittoria*. The eight men were to show how faith, courage, skill, and discipline gladly undergone, are ever the greatest guarantee of success.

GIOVANNI ARDENTI MORINI

Parma *Presidente Generale del C.A.I.*

Members of the Expedition

WALTER BONATTI, born at Bergamo, 22nd June 1930; Alpine guide; lives at Courmayeur. Since boyhood has displayed extraordinary qualities of physical resistance, courage and enterprise. His introduction to climbing was provided by the Grigna pinnacles. From there, he very soon graduated to the trickiest routes in the Alps, his skill in the end surpassing his masters' and winning him a place in the very front rank of European climbers.

Of his achievements, we will quote here only the following: Le Grand Capucin (Mont Blanc) by the East Wall; Le Petit Dru (Mont Blanc) by the South-West Ridge, solo; Mont Blanc by the Grand Pilier d'Angle route. Member of the 1954 K2 Expedition; was with the De Agostini Expedition to Tierra del Fuego (climbing Sarmiento); and in Patagonia (for the attempt on Cerro Torre).

RICCARDO CASSIN, born at San Vito, Tagliamento, 2nd January 1909, leader of the Expedition. His name is linked to some of the major Alpine achievements of this century. His routes, which have become classics in the most fitting sense of the word, show not only a supreme boldness of execution but a most intuitive flair, accompanied by perfect logic, in the plan of attack. It will be enough to mention: Torre Trieste (Dolomites), South-East Ridge (1935); West Peak of Lavaredo (Dolomites), North Wall (1935); Pizzo Badile (Rhaetian Alps), North-East Wall (1937); Walker Point (Grandes Jorasses, Mont Blanc), North Spur (1938).

In 1953 Riccardo Cassin accompanied Professor A. Desio in a reconnaissance visit to the Karakoram in preparation for the K2 attempt.

Born into a Friuli (a Venetian province) family, Cassin is what the Americans call a 'self-made man'. Today, after a life of hard and intelligent work, he owns and directs an active sporting-equipment business at Lecco, and has settled there. Cassin is married and has three sons: Valentino (18), Pierantonio (16) and Guido (13).

Riccardo Cassin has belonged to the Club Alpino Accademico Italiano since 1934; member of the Groupe Haute Montagne, Paris; President of the National Commission for Alpine Training Schools.

GIUSEPPE DE FRANCESCH, born at Cugnan, Ponte delle Alpi (Belluno), 6th March 1924. Chief Climbing Instructor at the Public Security's Alpine School at Moena. National Instructor and Alpine guide. Honorary member, Order of the Thistle; prizewinner and silver medallist, Carnegie Foundation (for rescue work). Between 1952 and 1957 made over 380 climbs, which included twenty-two new routes, nearly all in the Dolomites. Married; lives in Moena.

Some of his chief new routes are: Mugoni (Catinaccio), South Wall; North Forepeak of Catinaccio, South-East Wall; Fungo d'Ombretta; Emma Point (Catinaccio), East Wall.

Among his best-known climbs on established routes are: Marmolada di Rocca, by the Vinatzer-Castiglioni route; Marmolada through the Solda-Conforto route; Sassolungo, Esposito route (the first time this climb had been repeated); Catinaccio, Steger route, East Wall (first solo climb).

TONI GOBBI, born at Pavia, 18th June 1914, the Expedition's second-in-command. A graduate in Law, has indulged a passion for mountaineering since his student days. A dedicated climber, devoting his entire energies to it. Alpine guide and ski instructor; lives at Courmayeur; married the daughter of A. Berthollier, a very well-known Mont Blanc guide; now entitled to call himself a Valdostano too. His organizational gifts have enabled him to found the very-well-known Alpine Ski Expeditions, which take place every year under the auspices of the Club Alpino Italiano. His Libreria Alpina is a centre for mountain climbers from all over the world. T. Gobbi belongs to the Groupe Haute Montagne, Paris. Has several times been Director of the Special Instruction Courses for Guides, held every two years in the Val d'Aosta. Is at the moment President of the Committee of Guides of the Valley of Aosta.

The Gobbis have two children: Gioacchino (14) and Maria Barbara (10).

Among his more important climbs we may cite: Arête des Hirondelles (Grandes Jorasses, Mont Blanc) in winter (1940); Mont Blanc, via Major, winter (1953); Mont Blanc by the Pilier d'Angle (1957), with Walter Bonatti; Mount Paine (Chile) with the Monzino Expedition (1957).

FOSCO MARAINI, born at Florence, 15th November 1912. Graduated in Natural Science: specialized in ethnography. He spent eight years in Japan; sometime Reader in Italian at Kyoto University. He made two journeys to Tibet with Giuseppe Tucci. Author of *Secret Tibet* (1953) and *Meeting with*

Japan (1959). Contributor to numerous papers and magazines; has made over twenty documentary films.

Most of his climbing was done in the Dolomites; a number of first ascents with Emilio Comici, Tita Piaz, Sandro del Torso. Knows the Sikkim Himalaya, the Hindu-kush, and Japanese mountains. Keen skier for many years. A devotee of underwater fishing and photography (Mediterranean, Red Sea, Pacific).

Has three daughters: Dacia (22), Yuki (20) and Antonella (18). Active member of Club Alpino Accademico Italiano, Alpine Club, and Japanese Alpine Club.

CARLO MAURI, born at Rancio (Como), 25th March 1930. Pupil of Riccardo Cassin and one of the most redoubtable climbers of the new generation. Has business interests, but is also an Alpine guide and National Instructor in climbing. Member of the Club Alpino Accademico Italiano and the Groupe Haute Montagne. Among his most notable achievements are: winter ascent of the North Wall, Cima Overt of Lavaredo; winter ascent of the North Wall, Cima Grande of Lavaredo; winter ascent of North Wall, Breithorn; the South-West arête, Petit Dru; winter ascent, South Wall, Dent du Géant.

Has taken part in the De Agostini Expedition to Tierra del Fuego (1955), climbing the Sarmiento; also an expedition to Patagonia, climbing Cerros Moreno, Adele and Luca (1957–8).

Recently married; one son: Luca (1).

GIUSEPPE OBERTO, born at Macugnaga, 14th September 1923, professional Alpine guide. No one knows Monte Rosa better. Lives at Macugnaga, where he married a local girl, Clementina Corsi. They have two children: Alessandra (7) and Alberto (13).

Giuseppe Oberto has made repeated climbs of the Rosa by all the classic routes (Marinelli couloir, seventeen times; the Brioschi route, East Wall, Nordend, six times) and has established several new routes.

DONATO ZENI, born at St. Michele all'Adige (Trento) 11th December 1925. Neurological specialist. Doctor to the Expedition.

Has done most of the trickiest rock climbs in the Dolomites, with at least thirty in the Sixth Grade class. The direttissima on the North Ridge of the Cimon della Pala; the South-East Ridge of the Torre di Roces; a new direttissima on the Cinque Dita (Fünffinger-Spitze) bear his name. He has also repeated the Comici route on the North Face of the Cima Grande of Lavaredo;

the Vinatzer route on the North-West Wall of Catinaccio (Rosengarten); the Soldà route on Marmolada's South-West Wall: and the Buhl-weg on the Red Face of Roda di Vaèl.

Dr. Zeni is National Instructor in rock climbing. He lives and practises at Vigo di Fassa (Trento).

Calendar for the Expedition

1958

30th April	Departure from Genoa
12th May	Arrival at Karachi
15th May	Arrival at Rawalpindi
18th–27th May	Flight from Rawalpindi to Skardu, in groups
30th May	Departure of caravan from Skardu
30th May	Skardu–Shigar
31st May	Shigar–Kashumal
1st June	Kashumal–Dasso
2nd June	Dasso–Chakpo
3rd June	Chakpo–Chongo
4th June	Chongo–Askole
5th June	Askole (second party, 5–8th June, Askole–Urdukass)
6th June	Askole–Korophon
7th June	Korophon–Bardumal
8th June	Bardumal–Payù
9th June	Payù
10th June	Payù–Liligo
11th June	Liligo–Urdukass
12th June	Urdukass
13th June	Urdukass–Biange
14th June	Biange–Gore
15th June	Gore–Concordia
15th–21st June	Concordia (first ascent to Base Camp, 17th June)
22nd June	Concordia–Upper Baltoro
23rd June	Upper Baltoro–Base Camp (all at Base Camp)

FIRST ASSAULT

22nd June	Camp I (18,300 feet)
25th June	Camp II (20,000 feet)
29th June	Camp III (20,300 feet)
6th July	Camp IV (22,800 feet)
9th July	Camp V (23,600 feet)
10th July	First attempt on Summit
14th July	Second attempt on Summit
15th July	Change in the weather (monsoon)
19th July	Return to Base Camp

SECOND ASSAULT

24th July	Camp I
25th July	Camp II
27th July	Camp III
29th July	Camp IV
2nd August	Camp V
3rd August	Camp VI
4th August	Third attempt on Summit
6th August	Fourth and final attempt. Summit reached
9th August	Everyone at Base Camp again
13th August	Departure from Base Camp
24th August	Arrival at Skardu on return journey
3rd September	Arrival back in Italy

(The two assaults on the mountain took fifty-one days in all)

CLIMBING ACHIEVEMENTS

6th August   Summit of Gasherbrum IV (26,180 feet) Bonatti-Mauri. The Summit pair were supported up to 24,700 feet (Camp VI) by Toni Gobbi, Bepi De Francesch and Donato Zeni

5th August	Reconnaissance on Gasherbrum III (26,090 feet) up to about 24,100 feet Riccardo Cassin, solo
6th August	Climb to Gasherbrum-la (*c.* 21,600 feet) Oberto-Maraini
5th August	Reconnaissance of Col 22,139 feet, Oberto-Maraini

All members of the Expedition reached 23,000 feet.
Captain A. K. Dar climbed to Camp IV (22,800 feet)

PHOTOGRAPHIC RECORDS OF THE EXPEDITION

Negatives in black and white (catalogued): 2,510
Colour transparencies (catalogued): 1,000

OTHER DETAILS

Weight of supplies transported from Italy: 15,150 lb.
Maximum number of caravan porters: 514

Publisher's Note

ALL temperature references in this book are in Centigrade. Many heights are necessarily tentative and have been given in round figures. It must also be pointed out that opinions among experts vary, within a few feet, regarding the heights of many of the best-known peaks, e.g. K2 and Nanga Parbat.

Baltistan: Land of Encounter

Nanga Parbat from the air

THERE is a kind of thrill about a plane with no seats. To climb up into a fuselage as bare as a garret, to be welcomed by nothing but a collection of bags, packing-cases, drums of wire, bundles and parcels—it all gives one the feeling that this is the real thing. One is being made free of the arcane mysteries of the upper air, with none of those barriers which so carefully preserve them from a profane public! And, to cap all that, the DC3 in which we were to make this trans-Himalayan flight, from Rawalpindi to Skardu, could not fail to strike the traveller with a certain sly humour as a real old galleon of the skies, whose navigations among the clouds could already be numbered in decades. Not only was she dependent upon pieces of wire to hold her together: some trouble with the combustion gave the engines a most asthmatic splutter as they started up. Thus, as if it was not enough to be really one of the family where the mysteries of the air were concerned, the traveller was also at the mercy of some dubious mechanism. A disintegrating screw, a collapsing tube, an overheated wire—what then?

It was a splendid morning; if it had not been our flight would have been cancelled, for planes will take off from that particular field only under a flawless sky. The usual procedure, once the Met. Department has given the word go, is for the pilot first to make the Gilgit flight towards 5.30 a.m. The Gilgit Valley is farther off, but it is a good deal easier to reach than Skardu; on the return journey the plane veers off its outward course a little, so that the pilot can have a look at conditions over the Indus gorges. Cloud can form in that region, and the only way to know whether flying conditions are possible or not is to go and see! For the flight to Skardu may be highly dangerous, and best called off.

25

This information is not available until about eight o'clock and it is then—if at all—that the Skardu flight takes place.

'Everything's fine today,' I was told by the pilot—a little smiling Bengali whom you would take for something more like a post-office clerk than a navigator of the skies. Yet, as he spoke, there was just that serene self-assurance in his eyes which marks out the man used to danger, and used to facing it untroubled. Cassin had come to the airfield to see me off. 'Goodbye, old boy. Be seeing you soon.'

I got up into the plane with a group of young passengers conspicuous for their 'ten-gallon' Texas hats. They were accompanied by a Pakistani officer in an aloha shirt, Hawaiian style. These were some of the members of the American Expedition to Gasherbrum I (26,470 feet). We'd first met at Karachi, in the gardens of that international institution the Metropole Hotel, and from then on it had been a race, half in joke, half in earnest, to see which of the parties would be first to make Skardu. Now it was clear that the Americans were in the lead. 'The all-important thing is that they're Americans,' said Cassin, with heavy fatalism. 'And we are just poor Europeans, third class.' A factor in their favour, certainly, but one that didn't always carry such positive advantages. It could weigh on the other side. Not a few bureaucrats, bending backwards lest they should appear to be treating the sons of the United States as their favourites, began to favour the others with special treatment! The others, in this case, were ourselves. The fact of the matter was that the Americans formed a smaller group than we did, and one less loaded up with baggage. And last but not least, they had Captain Rizvi. Such was the name of the young officer of the Hawaiian shirt. He had a smiling, roguish resourcefulness which could cope with all comers.

Soon we were airborne, and we made a fair load—six passengers and four tons of equipment and baggage. I don't know why, but weight always seems more concentrated in a packing-case than in a human frame. Our air-galleon none the less purred merrily on its way over a mountain landscape, half wooded, half bare rock. In the distance we saw the slate-coloured roofs of Murree, a well-known summer station some 6,000 feet above sea level. Not long after, the real mountains began. At first the slopes were forested. Then they were barer. Then came snow. At the start we had had the impression of flying very high, but slowly the earth was rising up to us, and now it seemed to want to touch the plane. When we looked straight ahead—not an easy business with those miniatures of windows—we saw colossal chains of mountain peaks, still coloured with the blue of distance; they were much higher than we were.

RAKHIOT
PEAK

SILVER
TEETH

N. PARBAT
26,658

DIAMIR
VALLEY

Rakhiot Valley

The great massif of Nanga Parbat (26,658 feet) as seen from the plane flying between
Rawalpindi and Skardu

From summer in Rawalpindi we had passed to spring in these first out-crops of the Himalaya: now came the perennial winter of the mountains themselves. We were climbing from an Alpine territory to what Dyhrenfurth has called, in his book *To the Third Pole*, a super-Alpine one. I was sitting next to Pete Schoening, the American Expedition's strongest climber, and both of us had our noses glued to the window, to miss nothing of the spectacular world encircling us. Glaciers rushed down towards valleys still dark with shadow, and on every side towered peaks of all shapes and sizes. So far as we could judge, we were flying in a sort of funnel. Very soon, we should be right up against an insurmountable barrier. We knew we were following a well-established route, or we might have been uneasy. A perfect day had begun:

27

our wings slipped through air that was free from the slightest turbulence, and we felt not the slightest vibration. Far off towards the west we could see Haramosh (24,270 feet) and Rakaposhi (25,550 feet)—majestic pyramids of ice rising clear of a regular forest—there is no other word—of smaller peaks. And, suddenly, there was Captain Rizvi beckoning us to the other side of the plane with the cry: 'Nanga Parbat! A wonderful view, too—clear of everything.'

We rushed over to the opposite windows—to the east of us a fortress of ice and a cathedral of mountain peaks moved slowly and solemnly by. They were beside us, above us, beneath us; and in the sharp morning light every detail of their structure stood revealed. We're flying at just above 16,500 feet, ran my thoughts. The summit of Nanga Parbat (26,658 feet) is every foot as much over our heads as Mont Blanc would be at Courmayeur. The flight was so smooth that we ourselves seemed to remain stationary while with a tremendous majesty this giant mountain marched past us. In theory all glaciers should be identical in composition, but those of the Himalaya do seem to be richer, denser, more sumptuous than even the most striking in the Alps. Often enough, they catch the eye less as the mantles of some invisible underlying structure of rock than as structures in their own right. The mountain might very well be all glacier, down to the very marrow of its bones. And then those stupendous cascades of snow, sweeping down! Eloquent testimony to the gravitational force of Earth! Their line as exquisitely perfect as the folds into which some rich drapery will fall.

In the pure fascination of such a spectacle, we forgot all about our own apprehensions—and they were justified, because the flight certainly had its dangers. Every so often we would skim over some gigantic barrier whose reddish rock and snowy peaks almost touched the undercarriage. Then came whirlpools of air, over valleys prowled by rivers of ice, any one of them bigger than the tongue of the Rakhiot Glacier. A downward glance now brought its memories—intensified a thousandfold—of looking down at the sea-bed in underwater swimming. Once more we were passing over promontories and reefs, followed by a reach of deep water. At one moment the swimmer of the azure air all but grazed rock, covered as it were with seaweed, crystal clear in a wave of light; at the next he hung suspended over nothingness. . . .

Beneath us—Pete was not the only one to recognize Fairy Meadow— that enchanted place, famous in the literature of mountaineering, where the rarest birds chatter their way through the grass and flowers and among the gnarled and twisted trunks of ancient conifers—all at the foot of the Giant of a Thousand Winters, the Father of All Avalanches, the Walls of Frozen

Light. There were other names made famous by the German expeditions —Rakhiot Peak, Silver Saddle, The Moor's Head. Resplendent solitudes! We knew them at once. All were sacred in the epic of Nanga Parbat.

No mountain in the world has had such a share of doom and glory. None can tell a more dramatic tale. It starts in 1895, when a small group of mountaineering Englishmen led by Mummery (one of the great figures of his time: the Matterhorn by the Zmutt Ridge, the Charmoz, the Aiguille Verte, the Aiguille du Plan, the Grépon, Dych-Tau in the Caucasus) were lost, together with two Nepal Ghurkas, somewhere on the precipices of the Diamir Valley. At that early date no one had the faintest idea of what it really implied to climb one of the big Asian mountains. Mummery fought back the heaviest difficulties and got up to 20,000 feet. From this modest height, it seems, he reckoned to reach the summit with just one interim night's bivouac upon the glaciers. We know too well today that at 20,000 feet the real difficulties are only beginning, and that to conquer the last 6,000 plus we need 'four or even five well-furnished camps' (G. O. Dyhrenfurth).

Thirty-seven years later another expedition composed of Germans and Americans took on the giant: Willy Merkl and Fritz Bechtold reached 22,966 feet. They had discovered the right route, but only to be beaten back by unremitting storms. It was a sad business, having to give up, but the mere fact of having got back from such a height on such a mountain seemed a victory in itself. The accounts appeared to be closed. But they were not. Poor Rand Heron, an American who lived at Florence and was a first-class climber, had a go at the Pyramids on the return journey by way of Egypt, and smashed his skull. Brahma had taken his revenge—through the Sphinx!

Now followed the two German tragedies. In 1934 a handful of climbers representing the cream of the Teutonic mountaineering world—Willy Welzenbach, Uli Wieland and a few others whose names stood for the boldest enterprise in the Alps and the Himalaya—all perished in one of those storms which swoop down over Nanga Parbat in the monsoon season. The furies of the entire Indian Ocean seem to charge the clouds around this one solitary peak in Asia's greatest mountain chain. Such was the toll exacted from men of iron: men of common clay would have paid it in the earlier stages of such a storm, succumbing far sooner to the inferno of ice, gale and hunger. Then, three years later, in 1937, something unheard of happened: an entire expedition (with the sole exception of one member, Ulrich Luft) was crushed one night under an avalanche. These can come without warning and bury whole valleys. The dead, sahibs and porters, numbered no fewer than sixteen.

29

One more group of Englishmen—and they were asking for trouble, they were trying the ascent in winter—disappeared in bad weather among the séracs of Rakhiot. This was only a few years ago, in 1950.

A mountain so savage, a killer of thirty-one men (fourteen Europeans and seventeen porters), could yield, in the end, only to a splendid folly. The madcap was a little Innsbruck Austrian called Hermann Buhl. Alone, he reached the summit in 1953. He disobeyed the leader's orders, for forty hours he forced a passage over ridges and cornices—all the time above 26,000 feet. He kept himself alive, like the maniac he was, on a few tablets. He spent the night crouched in a hole in the ice, like a wild beast. Not only had he no sleeping-bag, he had no special kit; visited by strange hallucinations, he just pressed on. His crampons worked loose; no matter, he tied them to his boots with string. Onwards, upwards! Nothing to drink, nothing to draw on but his own stupendous courage, and blessed by one sole clemency from Fate—forty hours of no wind and no cloud. The giant peak was happy to welcome such a man as her own, and to accord him such glorious privileges.

But today—today Nanga Parbat was all serenity and light, light embroidered with blue shade. Nothing at all to remind us of the long delirium of suffering, audacity and death. The very motors of our ancient aircraft seemed to put on an extra spurt. We looked ahead of us to the north, so far as we could do so within the limitations of windows facing only east and west. A circle of white, pitiless walls appeared to be closing in. Some mighty barrier to cross, though we could scarcely see it. The motors roared louder and louder till they almost howled. 'Pistons, do your duty!' Now we were suddenly climbing, we'd gained a few dozen metres in height. And beneath us, perilously close, reared a crest of ice, bristling with rocky teeth. We were through the last pass, the highest and most dangerous. Now began the gradual descent.

Soon, however, it became a swift descent—almost a swoop—into the Indus Valley. There was the river, gleaming with sunlight in its gorge of bare rock. An air-pocket: our wings skimmed the rim of the valley itself. It drew closer and closer. There was just the chance to make out a few poor villages, ringed round with poplar trees. And at last came the Skardu strip, and the landing on the long dusty runway.

'Marvellous!' exclaimed Pete. 'But I'm not sorry to be on terra firma again, I don't mind telling you.'

If Pete could say as much, so could I. For Pete was the man who in the course of the 1953 American attempt on K2 acquitted himself rather well. Poor Gilkey had contracted phlebitis at 25,300 feet (Camp VIII). They were trying to get him down. Something went wrong. Pete, unaided, with his own square shoulders, managed to hold five climbers, on two ropes, when three were sliding away and dragging one another into the abyss. He saved the whole expedition from disaster.

'Perhaps is better not experiment'

One breath of Skardu air is enough to make you exclaim, 'Delicious!' We were 7,300[1] feet up in a wide valley, almost a plain, thronged by mighty mountains—if they were close and of no great height their colour was roughly ochre, but if they were farther off and higher they were blue. Their upper reaches were all snow and ice-wall. The air was fresh, light, dry: the sunlight had a real warmth. A subtly mingled scent of flowering plants was borne from far off on the breeze.

The landing strip was on the deserted edge of the valley, where the ground was almost flat, some fifteen kilometres from Skardu itself. It was marked by a sort of rough wooden barracks divided into offices. With their dust of ages, and their personnel working in shirt-sleeves among furniture that had seen its best days, they had the air of the Administrative Department of some agricultural enterprise lost in the depths of some distant colony. Our welcome was the warmest possible. The rest of the American Expedition to Gasherbrum I were already here, having flown in from Rawalpindi a few days before, while the director of the aerodrome, named Mustaq, was a most sympathetic person. He looked like a country gentleman. His woollen headgear would have been most suitable for playing golf in, his jersey had a horsy look and his fustian trousers would have been excellent for a shoot. He spoke perfect English with an Oxford accent and his conversation had the playful allusiveness of the cultivated man on holiday in the country. A handful of other Pakistanis, all local officials, were with him.

Our problem now was to transport ourselves and our goods and chattels from the landing field into Skardu. In Baltistan there are nearly 200 kilometres of roads, some of them quite good, others scarcely suitable for a farmcart; but the vehicles cannot run to more than a dozen or so. There are jeeps, lorries and ambulances. Private cars and taxis are naturally non-existent. For all transport, therefore, one has to turn to the appropriate section of the Army—after obtaining a special permit from Headquarters in Rawalpindi. As in all such cases, one is inexorably at the mercy of chance: if available vehicles are suddenly required for urgent administrative purposes, visitors to Baltistan have to wait.

But in Asia the traveller must always resign himself to the idea of waiting.

1. See table, p. 77.

The daily programme would be incomplete without it. One can therefore stop, look and learn with a clear conscience. Woe to the man in a hurry who sits there fretting and biting his nails. There might be some justification for it in Europe. Here it is just bad for the health.

I was relieved to note that even that devil Rizvi—I had now given up the rat-race with him and his party—for once failed to wave his wand and evoke out of thin air the two trucks promised for the transportation of the Americans and their equipment, my own six cases of photographic materials, and our eight distinguished persons, from the airport to Skardu. In the end we all went to lunch with Captain Nawaz, the officer responsible for the valley's military supplies. A Pakistani rice dish with curry, highly salted meat and tea: most excellent, all of it. Another rule with no exceptions: in the East, better a thousand times the local fare than the fifth-rate imitation of a small-town European cuisine.

In the end it was only late in the afternoon that we got a very shaky truck to take us into Skardu. The sky was overcast and there was a blustering wind from the south. The air was full of dust, but there was no sign of rain. We were soon to learn that the wind was the 'five o'clock blow-up': it happened nearly every day. Through squall after howling little squall we pressed on through sand-strewn air over scorched plain; there were trees here and there—sturdy willows with silvery leaves (*sarsing*)—but if you want greenery, with a true, fresh, neat and inviting green, you will only find it in places which look very much like oases—in fact they are. They are dotted over the plain and the valleys that slope down to it, a long line of them, stretching away into the distance.

At last, a bend in the road brought us into Skardu: here were its low-pitched earth-structures of houses. For me it had memories of Tibet: I could have imagined myself at Gyantse! The same pedlars, with their wares stacked before them on the ground, the same poor pillars of wood supporting the same poor balconies; the same flat roofs mortared together from nothing but mud beaten up and then dried in the sun.

But the people were a very far cry from Tibetans. We were no longer in the world of the Lama, but in a little corner of Islam. The men went about swathed in the noble Balti toga, almost white in colour and made of wool. For headgear they wore either some style of turban or else the Gilgit cap (*Plates 44, 45, 46*). Of their womenfolk there was not a trace. They must have been at home, under lock and key—the general rule in Islamic countries, or in the regions where Islam has made itself felt for a considerable time (Sicily for one). The human landscape is exclusively masculine.

After the 'street of the shops' we went down a slight hill and now we found ourselves passing through one of the many oases. Running water: some little tributary of the Indus channelled to irrigate the fields. Apricot trees, poplars and willows, all very lush, clustering in gardens and patches of cereal. It was an ugly moment, though, for us to salute these enchantments. The wind was blowing up stronger and stronger, the dust seared our eyes. One more sharp turn and we pulled up at the Rest House. Here we unloaded our gear and got ourselves organized for a few days' stay.

The Rest House proved to be a bungalow with quite a few rooms, in the shade of a line of tall poplar trees. It was a house that gave you a warm welcome, and it quickly brought more memories of Tibet, and Sikkim, where you find the same sort of habitation. The pattern followed the British throughout their Indian empire. Such were the sort of quarters put at the disposal of their officials. India, Pakistan, and Tibet too, have now inherited them.

'*Buongiorno*, how are you?' A little man with a moustache, wearing a military-style shirt—but not the trousers—and a huge Gilgit skull-cap of white wool, greeted me with a smile. It was Ali: from now on (in his own words) 'fine gentlemen's cook'. Twelve years or so before, as a soldier in the Allied armies, he had been posted to Italy, and he still spoke a few words of our language.

'Italy—good place, good place,' he went on, with a heartfelt smile, and a slightly sad one. Then he announced that he was good at spaghetti. But perhaps it was better 'not experiment'—'eat one big curry instead'.

Baltistan and Skardu

Soon I had been a whole week at Skardu. The Expedition was caught up in the sort of conditions one dreads in these parts. The clouds had opened up for that lucky Monday's flight, but now they had closed in again over Nanga Parbat and there was no flying over those high crests and the Indus gorges. Our party was therefore divided into two. I was at Skardu, where at the most I could only make myself useful over a few preliminary chores, such as enrolling the porters. The others were stuck at Rawalpindi, in the 'nauseating sultriness' (the phrase was Cassin's) of the plains. A depressing prospect: not only did I feel irked by the unenviable plight of my companions—time was precious and the days were running out without a chance for us to move one inch forward. On our way back we already ran the risk of those monsoon storms in high-mountain country, and we did not want them to overtake us before the climb had gone through. That devil Rizvi had certainly won the day. His party were now definitely in the lead. And there were we, with our seven and a half tons of gear, divided between two places like a small army of stragglers!

C

The only thing for it, as far as I was concerned, was to have a look at this little country, snuggling under the sky itself, and the sort of people who lived here.

Two or three steps from the door of the Rest House and you were right in the middle of Baltistan, at its most typical and its most panoramic (*Plate 11*). Your first impression was one of grandeur. You breathed freedom. You seemed to feel a sense of flight through space itself. On my arrival in that afternoon squall I had seen nothing of the beauties around me. My eyes had been full of dust and the only colour I could make out was the earth-colour which plastered everything. But this morning—or almost any other—what a wonderful sight Baltistan was! Soon after the sun is up, every single element of nature can be seen in its true colour through the limpid air. Distance, however great, makes no difference. The colour is still undispersed, unfaded, intact. The mountains are stone and sand, rock and cliff, splinters of the earth's crust scorched bare, calcined bones of the earth, lacking the sorriest trace of vegetation; the oases, marked by a long line of poplars waving in the wind like a mane, are by contrast green as jewels, or they are the blood of dragons coiled in serpentine folds. Isolated houses and villages naturally spring up where the vegetation is richest—by virtue of that age-old triple link between Man, plant and water. The view, in its vast scope, puts one in mind of certain Flemish landscapes where there is always some fresh detail to seize upon if one looks long enough: the figure one had not seen, busy at the task or pleasure one had missed; the fresh zone of light or translucency of cloud; the novel aspect of a burgher, or a tree, or a castle, or a ship. Here, every lateral valley had its terraces, its thickets of apricot and poplar, its patches of crops. The impression gained was that the population must be rather more numerous than seemed likely at a quick glance. Up on the heights are the glaciers and ice-walls. And down in the heart of the valley, winding its way through a wide, grey, gravelly trough, is the Indus: a full river, a smooth powerful river, the colour of a ripe harvest or the colour of steel, according to the time of day.

The Indus, whose total length is 1,430 miles, comes twenty-fourth among the great rivers of the earth. But how many of its twenty-three mightier brothers can cast such a spell over us? It is one of those rivers so intimately bound up with Man's story that one can scarcely pronounce its name without an emotional undertone. Indus! The dark civilizations of Mohenjodharo and Harappa; the feats of Alexander the Great; the meeting-ground of Greece and India, of the Hellenic world and Buddhism, of India and China; the Silk Road, the Chinese generals and their conquests in Central Asia; Genghis Khan; the Moghul emperors with their dominions stretching from Kabul to Calcutta:

tides of peoples, civilizations, religions, vaunts of conquerors, wanderings of saints—everything Asian has its well-springs in these waters. They rise in the mightiest mountains, like those of the Nile, and in their downward flow make the desert bloom. Their significance in agriculture, in economics, in the settlements of Man and his kingdoms, goes back to history's dawn. According to one legend (though it need not be taken too seriously, perhaps) the very name Skardu is derived from Iskanderia, the city of Iskander. And Iskander is simply Alexander: Alexander the Great being held to have founded it in the course of his triumphal journey through these lands.

The Greeks (from Escateus of Miletus, in the sixth century B.C.) and the Romans (from the time of Pliny onwards) knew the Indus well ('*Indus ab incolis Sindus appelatus*'), but the actual sources of the river remained a mystery until 1907, when Sven Hedin, in the course of one of his explorations, came upon an insignificant spring in the high plateau of Tibet. It rose among calcareous rocks, and the spot was consecrated by sacred stones and flags inscribed with Lama prayers. The world of the Far East had known the source of the great river for upwards of a thousand years, and their geographers had placed it accurately in their charts.

The Indus is one of the three great rivers of India (the others being the Ganges and the Brahmaputra): the very name of the Asian sub-continent shares the same origins. It is a highly interesting geographical fact that the sources of both the Indus and the Brahmaputra (in Tibetan, Tsang-po) lie relatively close to each other: in the same plateau-zone, at 14,500 feet, is the sacred lake Manasarovar—a sheen of turquoise mirrored among its stones from the sky above. Both rivers, after a long meander beyond the Himalaya, cross the mighty chain, the greatest in Asia, scooping out wild gorges for their passage. Then they flow down to the plains and the Indian Ocean. For both, there is a giant mountain marking the last outpost of the range, and each river must wind its way round it before it is free. In the case of the Indus the towering obstacle is Nanga Parbat (26,658 feet); for the Tsang-po–Dinang–Brahmaputra (such are the river's names at successive stages of its course) it is Namcha Barwa (25,443 feet).

Typical of the Indus throughout its upper course is the alternation of narrow gorge, with walls rising sheer, and wide, hospitable valleys. Some 460 miles above Skardu—at Ladak—occurs the first such basin of any importance. It is 11,000 feet high. For over a thousand years a characteristic outpost of Tibetan civilization has flourished here round the city of Leh.

Below the Leh basin the Indus buries itself once more in wild, lost gorges between the Himalaya and the Karakoram. Then, 3,000 feet lower, it slows down to pass through a less forbidding region: Baltistan. Here too are the valleys of Shigar and Shayok, the basins of Kapalu and Skardu. Then it plunges into the Chilas gorges at the foot of Nanga Parbat—and so, down on to the plain.

Coming back to the Skardu basin, it is interesting to note that Giotto Dainelli has succeeded in finding in it the traces of four ancient periods of glaciation, corresponding with those which have left their mark on the Alps. This spot represents the exact scene of the meeting-ground, in remote times, of the powerful glacier of the Karakoram and that of the Indus. At one of these periods the entire basin, its lower egress blocked by glacier-moraine, formed a lake which pushed back more than a hundred miles along the valley. Evidence of its existence is preserved by the frequent terracings which are to be encountered —the favourite site of today's villages. It is also offered by the great quantities of sand which the wind piles up and subsequently disperses in sandy dunes suggesting the African scene.

On the edge of one of these miniature Saharas stands the district's biggest mosque, lime-washed in white. Very few buildings indeed have the temerity to rise in these arid wastelands, but this is one, and the Skardu fort is another.

This ancient pile is perched like a veritable eyrie on rock of tawny hue rising sheer and to immense height from the Indus. Its site is in effect a massive promontory of rock, 1,300 feet in height, washed by the river at its foot. It is almost an island in the midst of the plain, and its choice as a perch for a fortress by the early inhabitants of the valley is no very puzzling one. Even today its battlemented flanks touch one of the promontory's lesser peaks with the romance of the age of chivalry. The place enjoys the reputation of impregnability, and even in recent times, in the course of the disorders which followed the India-Pakistan partition in 1947, the people of Skardu flocked to it for safety. Today it is the Gilgit Scouts who keep watch there—big, moustached fellows from the little kingdom of Hunza on the far north-west fringes of Pakistan. Be it observed—however much it may cause one to smile in this age of atom bombs and hydrogen bombs—it is strictly forbidden to photograph these venerable walls, and even the crags they rise from!

From this eagles' nest of a fortress it is not too much to say that one can see the whole of Baltistan. From the 'polo-field'—a right royal possession in all these western regions of the Himalaya and the Karakoram, and one that stands for riches and independence—right away to the peaks that crown the farthest valleys.

But who are the Balti people? What ups and downs have they known, this remote and tiny race, in the course of the centuries? Our actual knowledge

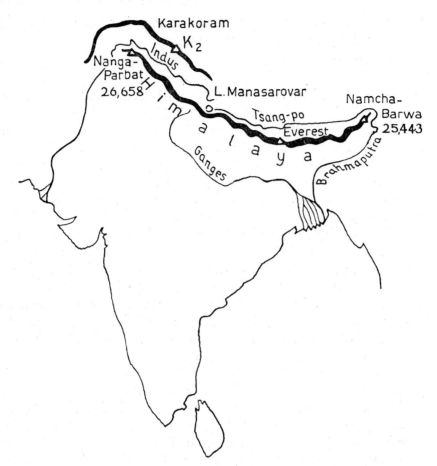

Rivers shown in relation to mountain ranges in Northern India and Pakistan

of them is scanty in the extreme. One school of thought would like to identify this far-off people, perched up in their inaccessible mountains and out of touch with the rest of humanity for the greater part of the year,[1] with the Byltae of Tylomeus. Over the course of the first millennium A.D. a few references to them may be found in Chinese chronicles: Ladak and Baltistan are known as Great Poliu and Lesser Poliu: that is, Great and Lesser Tibet (Pö). For many centuries, certainly, Baltistan must have been under the dominion of Tibet. The language alone proves this: Balti, even as spoken today, remains an archaic Tibetan dialect. There are also recurring traces of Buddhist culture

1. F. de Filippi, *Storia della Spedizione Scientifica Italiana nel Himalaia Caracorum e Turchestan Cinese* (1913–14), Bologna, 1924, p. 50.

37

and the place-names too point to a Tibetan origin. Tibetan chronicles frequently refer to Gilgit (giving it the name of Bru-ja).

Great changes came towards the end of the fourteenth century, and at the outset of the fifteenth the Balti people were converted to Islam. It is not clear why this should have come about. One ancient chronicle of the Buddhist kings of Skardu (endowed by Tibet with the title Gyalpo) appears to have been burned a century ago in the course of the wars of aggression conducted by the Maharaja of Kashmir. If this is so, we have indeed lost a precious document, and one which might have illuminated a very obscure page of history.

Towards the end of the sixteenth century Skardu gained a certain importance from the conquests of its king, Ali Sher Khan. Under him, national frontiers were pushed forward to take in the whole of Ladak, and he founded a local dynasty which persisted through a good many troubles and trials until 1846. Everything of note in Skardu is nowadays put down to the credit of Ali Sher Khan. He it was, so they say, who rebuilt the fortress, while his chief memorial—still to be seen—lies in the great aqueduct, which catches an abundant water supply from the Satpara Mountains and takes it across the valley.

Skardu's last king, Ahmed Shah, had the misfortune to become the enemy of Guleb Singh, the great Sikh conqueror, and the Maharajah of Jammu, who in 1834 turned his forces to the conquest of Kashmir and other territories in the North Indian plains. The subjection of Baltistan proved long and costly, but in the end General Zorawar Singh brought about the capitulation of Ahmed Shah. The formal surrender took place in the old fort of Skardu itself. Baltistan thereupon became part of the Jammu and Kashmir realm, and for a century (1846–1947) her position remained unchanged.

The Dogra kings (so called from their place of origin) seem to have ruled with great harshness, and their name is still hated. I was told by a local schoolmaster—a devoted student of Baltistan's history and traditions—of certain episodes which now took place. They made me shudder. I also learned the story of the revenge the Dogras took on their enemies once they had conquered them. I did not learn it out of a history book. A whole century after the event, it came to me by way of oral tradition. It still lived on people's tongues.

We must bear in mind that we are involved here with what is in Asia a fundamental issue: religion. The Dogra were Hindu, the Balti Moslem. Even today the outlook is the same as it was a hundred years ago. For the masses in India and Pakistan, Kashmir is a burning question. But it has nothing to do with economics or strategy: no, only with the anomaly of a few million Moslems being governed by a narrow aristocratic circle which is Hindu.

38

In 1947 Baltistan became part of Azad Kashmir (liberated Kashmir), which by international convention is reckoned in with Pakistan territory.

From 1840 onwards a great number of European and American travellers, with Vigne as the pioneer, have described Skardu. In 1880 the Marchese Roero di Cortanze made a short stay. The year 1909 saw the Duca degli Abruzzi pass through with the first Italian expedition to the Baltoro Mountains. Then Filippo de Filippi and his eight companions spent a winter there (in 1913). This party of scientists and students were conducting, in the regions between India and Central Asia, one of the most important scientific missions of modern times, the results of which occupy a dozen large volumes.

The Balti people

One glance at a relief-map of Asia is enough to show that the Karakoram chain and the Baltistan valleys at its foot constitute a region of the highest importance. We are not at the geometric centre of the continent, true. But we are very close to what might be called its structural centre. Take one more look at the map: from one single knot, which we can place in Pamir, colossal mountain ranges spread out in every direction: the Tien-Shan ('Mountain of the Sky'), the Kuen-lun, the Karakoram ('the Black Gravel Mountains'), the Tibet highlands, the Himalaya ('Abode of Snows')—and then the Alai, the Transalai, the Hindu-Kush (probably deriving its name from Hindu-Caucasus) . . . they are like the muscles and sinews of a continent tensed, to be seen as it were through the skin.

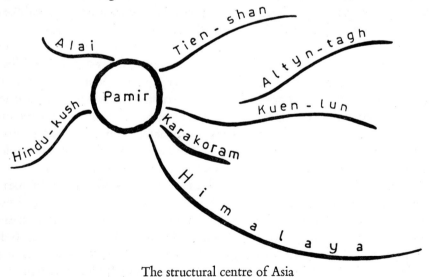

The structural centre of Asia

What movements of peoples, what settlements and clashes and encounters, back through history into prehistory, have taken place around these mountain barriers! This impenetrable mass is like a gigantic rock, shaped into promontories, capes, inlets; and against it, in wave after wave, beats the tide of humanity. The great racial families of the earth, at their farthest outposts, have met here: Mongol Man, European Man, and the darker-skinned dweller of the Indian subcontinent. And here many a great conqueror has set his farthest bourne: Alexander with his Greeks from the west; the T'ang and then the Ming and the Ch'ing emperors from the east; Darius with his Persians; Asoka and Chandragupta with their Indians; Genghis Khan with his Mongol hordes and likewise the armies of Akhbar; Clive with his English soldiers; the Russians of Tsars and of commissars; and now Mao Tse-Tung with his army of Chinese. The waves of religion too have beaten against this rock, the most ancient and glorious known to Man—Islam, Hinduism, Buddhism. Language has mingled no less—Aryan and the Sino-Tibetan group and the Uralo-Altaic. In this region, too, or not far from it, cultures have fused, with some of the happiest outcomes in history: the province of Gandhara, where Hellenic art joins hands with the Buddhist faith, provides one instance.

Baltistan (*stan* in Persian means 'country', 'land': hence 'land of the Balti') is a poor, pastoral region, and anywhere else in the world it would have little of interest to offer the curious traveller. But, just here, we are in privileged latitudes. These valleys have always been channels of communication between one empire and another, one religious sphere and another. From oasis to oasis, from city to city, travellers have met here; speaking different languages, following different customs, stemming from different cultural and artistic streams. Baltistan is a land where all these meet.

From the point of view of physical appearance, the 150,000 inhabitants of the region clearly belong to the 'Europoid group'. This vast anthropological category includes all Europeans (with the exception of the Lapps), a good few North African peoples, and western Asians; here, we are on its extreme eastern fringe. Students have yet to devise a satisfactory name for this important human family. 'Aryan' may be a suitable enough classification for vocables, grammars and syntaxes; it becomes meaningless when applied to heads, hair and eyes. To speak of the 'Aryan' races is like talking about Catholic craniums or polygamous knees: the term represents a 'cross-division', coupling two quite different classificatory features—and that quite apart from the political odium it has gathered over recent decades. 'White race' misses the mark too. It is inexact, and it has too many European connotations. 'Caucasian race' is the feeble offspring of antiquated theories of origin. 'Indo-European' is a cumbrous term, and one now primarily connected with linguistics. And yet a classification is certainly called for: there is a recognizable reality crying out for it, and it is no less recognizable for its complexities and anomalies. If we doubt the reality of these divisions, let us take a look at the Ainu—the inhabitants of those far-off islands to the north of the Japanese archipelago. They impress us immediately as different. The seemingly endless ocean of Mongoloid Man, with the Ainu, has suddenly ended. Here are eyes, hair, hands, beard which need no closer examination: immediately and instinctively we know, whenever we see them, that here is another human family—a species characteristic of a more western sector of the world. No, Europoid Man is a very definitely existent type—and we are forced to stick to that label for him for want of a better.

For a long time it was held that the Balti people were of Tibetan origin, and therefore of the Mongoloid type. Ujfalvy, in 1881, was the first to put this straight. He published a series of anthropological measurements which were later followed up and confirmed by Giotto Dainelli (1913) and Gino Allegri (1929). The confusion arose from the fact that here was a Europoid race, physically the kinsmen of more westerly peoples, speaking a dialect of Tibetan —and, therefore, linguistically linked to more easterly peoples. This is only one of the many instances of race and language proving to be quite unconnected. We need only remember the Normans of the tenth century. Norsemen from Scandinavia they were and they remained; but they came under the influence of more civilized local peoples, and ended by speaking Early French. When they conquered Great Britain in 1066 it was not the language of the Vikings they brought with them: and it is to these Norsemen that the English language owes much of its 'latinization' and its further divergence from northern and Germanic roots.

Then there is one more element of the unexpected: for four centuries now the Balti have been a Moslem people. So that every day, in this little country, one meets men who, judging by appearances, might be just of doughty mountaineering stock or good, decent country folk from the southern peninsulas of Europe—only to find that they express themselves in an archaic dialect of the language of the Tibetan poet Milarepa or the Lama reformer Tsongkapa, and that their names are Mohamet, Hassan, Khasim, Ali—sonorous names, redolent of the Koran and the *Thousand and One Nights*, and the desert and the minaret beneath a slender moon. *Voilà du Baltistan pur!*

But let us get back to the Balti physical type for a moment. I said they belonged to the great Europoid family—but I added a 'fundamentally' which is not without significance. In point of fact, for the most part, the Balti people possess a dolicocephalic cranium, smooth black hair, chestnut-coloured eyes without the Mongol slant to them, and a middling stature—all characteristics which safely permit of their classification under the Indo-Afghan type (Allegri-Biasutti). But side by side with this type, often in the same village, within the self-same family, there are others which could not be more divergent from it. Are we, or are we not, in a land of encounters, of crossed strains? One of our porters (*Plate 15*) from the village of Kapalu had such a pure-bred Nordic appearance that we used to call him 'the Viking'. He had the bearing and the height, and that light skin which in the sun takes on the tawny colour to be seen in Swedish holiday-makers at Capri or Taormina. He had the blue eyes, and his eyebrows had whitened under a tropical sun. In a cultural sense he was the perfect Balti: he spoke, he sang and he dressed like a Balti, and the fervour of his evening prayer when he turned towards Mecca matched that of his Balti brothers. But for all that, in body, in bone formation, skin, iris, hair, he turned one's thoughts at once to ski-champions and navigators of such illustrious names as Hakulinen, Eriksen, Amundsen. And side by side with him there were others who brought to mind, with equal distinctness, Southern India. Then again, we encountered one Balti of pronounced Negro aspect. Others gave proof of the strongest foreign strain one comes up against here—the Mongoloid. And there were the mixed ones. One of the best of the porters, very soon marked out for the photographic team, was a Mongol-Negro type—his smiling old face made me think of a cross between Lao-tse and Uncle Tom. The fact is that the Balti race constitutes a living anthropological museum, and deserves more attention from students than it gets.

In the matter of language the very use of this Tibetan patois commemorates an ancient and troubled page of Balti history, whose details remain obscure. Such divergencies between language and race, religion and culture, the language and the alphabet, and so on and so forth, can always be traced back to contacts and conquests, migrations and influences: in other words, they are in themselves historical documents of the first order. The Tibetans speak in a tongue which has affinities with Chinese: but to write it they borrow characters of Indian origin. The ancestry of the Japanese language is still obscure, but we can be certain at least that it is quite unconnected with Chinese—yet it is written in Chinese characters. The Turks of today read, in Roman lettering, a masterpiece of Arabic literature translated into a tongue of Central Asiatic origin. The great majority of Europeans have adopted a religion from Palestine, they add up their accounts with Indian numerals, they dress in a style whose beginnings go back to the Völkervanderungen—all these constitute phenomena which only history can explain.

In the second half of the first millennium after Christ, Baltistan passed under Tibetan rule. Little is known of this period. But it must have been a long and important one, bringing an appreciably superior civilization to a backward people; no less was necessary if the original Balti language was to be ousted by that of the rulers. Balti as spoken today is an archaic form of Tibetan, the words being still pronounced as, in Tibet itself, they are nowadays only written. Rice, for instance, is in Balti *bras*, and in the Tibetan script it is written as *bras*. But the pronunciation of Lhasa has been capable of some strange evolutions, and today Lhasa knows rice as *dren*! The third person of the present indicative of the verb 'to be' is in Balti *yod*. It is written *yod*. But in Tibet the pronunciation has evolved to '*yö*'. Hundreds of such examples come to mind. Balti grammar and syntax too reveal archaic features.

It stands to reason that the Balti spoken today is not just an archaic Tibetan. It is also a bastard Tibetan. Tibet's cultural ascendancy must have come to an end altogether with the little country's conversion from Buddhism to Islam. From then onwards, there will have been an influx of fresh linguistic elements, brought by the new faith itself, and by fresh cultural affiliations with lands before remote. Not only is aeroplane in Balti *jahaz*, an Urdu word; for book (*kitab*), city (*shar*), doctor (*hakim*), fast (*roza*) and, of course, infidel (*kafir*), Balti resorts to Urdu-Persian.

On a vastly more modest scale all this puts one very much in mind of the evolution of the English language. In English, simple homely words connected with ideas of house, work, family, have remained Anglo-Saxon— pot, hat, dog, cup, hoe. Similarly, in Balti, such words still show the Tibetan roots. But in the same way as in English, *school, evolution, doctrine, master, grammar,* have been adopted from Latin, so, in Balti, words on a similar cultural plane have been borrowed from Urdu, Persian and, in certain cases, Arabic.

From the cultural point of view, too, the Balti panorama is a highly composite one. Eastern elements (Tibetan) mingle with western ones (from Dardia, Afghanistan, Hunza), with southern (Kashmir) and northern (Turk or Kirgiz). Without venturing into a complex field, and still largely an un- explored one, I will mention just one or two facets of Balti life which impress the traveller for their echoes of Tibet: the use of barley flour or washed grain for food, mixed with tea—and often enough, butter too—to make *tsampa*; the preference for tea with butter and salt; the habit of carrying babies on the shoulder (*Plate 13*); the hair-style favoured by the womenfolk, the hair being done up into a large number of minute tresses or plaits (there should be 108, the sacred Buddhist number); the use of cords made of yak-skin strips, alternating black with white, to bind up a package of goods and fix it to one's shoulders; the habit of calculating the passage of the years by the twelve-year cycle (*loskor*)—deriving as it does in the last analysis from China. Thus: 'How old are you?'—'Three cycles plus two years'—that is, 12 plus 12 plus 12 plus 2 equals 38. Finally, Balti jewellery is typically Tibetan-Mongol: turquoise and coral set in silver (*Plate 14*).

The Balti dwelling, exhaustively studied by Giotto Dainelli, is a humbler version of the Ladakhi dwelling; so here again we are confronted with a Tibetan heritage.

A paean in honour of potatoes

On my very first day in Skardu, almost before I had got myself organized in the Rest House, I called on the Political Agent.

Sir Habib-ur-Rhaman Khan turned out to be a retired general and an affable gentleman somewhere between middle age and the age that follows it. He was tall, well set up without being corpulent, fairly dark skinned and rather bald. He had a look of keen intelligence and he wasn't in the least tongue-tied. He was sufficiently at home in English to speak it with humour as well as correctness. The English influence was also plainly apparent about his manners, his clothes, his habits, his very gestures. By day, I generally found him dressed in grey flannels and a chocolate-coloured rough wool jacket. Here was one more official who struck the traveller as a man of independent means and academic culture, and one who might have spent a few years at Oxford or Cambridge. If he was off on a tour through the country, then he was dressed for the occasion: narrow fustian breeches, chessboard shirt, a long jacket, riding switch, coloured scarf. If there were visitors in the evening, then he was ready to receive them in faultless evening dress—and he could play the perfect host, always ready to join in the conversation of his guests and gently steering it. At every other moment some little trait of character would come out, some little trick of gesture or bearing, firmly establishing him as that mixture of countryman and man of the world which is typical of the English gentleman in his happier incarnations.

But on closer acquaintance—we did most of our chatting in the course of a daily constitutional—I found no friend of England but an Anglophobe: and not the lukewarm Anglophobe so common in Pakistan, no, a furious one. What an ironic situation! Why proclaim, by your clothes, your manners, your appearance and your speech, a race you openly detest? Why not come out in your true Moslem and Pakistani colours—and clothes, and headgear, insignia, gestures, everything—and be all of a piece? But nowadays you can find such

44

Sir Habibs all over Africa and Asia, and they need cause the traveller no surprise.

It cannot be said that the General had had a placid life. Born into a family whose links with England go back for generations, he was educated in India's finest military schools. With the Second World War his feelings took a strong anti-English turn. He turned his back on those he considered the enemies of his country and threw in his lot with the famous 'Liberation Army' and its commander, Chandra Bose. Many of my compatriots will recall that name: for obvious reasons it was given a good deal of publicity in Italy during the war years. Soon our General was a Senior Head of State, and in that capacity he went to the Far East in 1944. It was now that he paid his visit to Japan. On his return the following year he found himself involved in an air mishap in the island of Formosa, in which Chandra Bose lost his life.

Sir Habib-ur-Rhaman ('The Well-Beloved of God') spoke at length of Japan: he was delighted to find that I too knew and loved that far-off country. The impression I received was that Japan had really 'got' him; he was still enchanted with the country, its art, its women, its houses and its festivals.

'I like the Japanese,' he told me, 'for their virile nature. And they're always busy at something. They're a young people, that's their secret, and they've a great future to look forward to.'

'Then, General,' I said, 'you will be happy to receive Professor Kuwabara from Kyoto University. He'll be here in a few days with his party. They're coming to climb Chogolisa. I expect we'll be gone by then, but if not we could have a grand gathering one evening for some *sukiyaki*.'

'What a wonderful idea! It would be fine. But we'd want *sakè* to drink too. Who knows, though? Our Japanese visitors may bring some with them. Why, this year the Baltoro will be like the piazza of some big city at the height of the season. Pakistani, English, Italians, Americans, Japanese, perhaps a few Austrians and Germans too. What a commotion it'll be! But that's what we like. It'll be bringing money and work to a derelict race whom we've got to rescue, somehow or other—from poverty and ignorance—however long it takes. I'm decidedly in favour of expeditions. We'll just have to fall in with any requirements the Military might make, that's all. How can you help it? They've got their job to do, everybody has to consider that. . . .'

Without breaking off, the General got up from his armchair and took me out of his little office into the garden. The Residence was a delightful country villa, almost buried beneath climbing plants in flower and the boughs of a few biggish trees. Their leaves murmured in the wind and glittered in the sunlight of that wonderful mountain morning. The house suggested the

45

retreat of a sage—a sage who didn't want to lack for anything, much as he might disdain the superfluous. In every corner of it you were conscious of the touch of those hateful British, who had taken the stones of Baltistan and tried to recreate one of their charming Somerset or Devon cottages.

We stepped out on to a real lawn, perfectly flat and smooth and scented with spring. There were armchairs of wood and wickerwork, a table and an umbrella. There was also a big brown bear, or the skin of one, stuffed with straw and kept standing on its feet by means of wooden splints.

'There's a fine beast for you,' said the General. 'I got him the other day in the mountains round Arandu. That's a valley you ought to see. The finest in the Karakoram, perhaps. There's not only a big glacier of the Baltoro type, and some colossal mountains covered in ice and snow, there's a good bit of vegetation, too. So you get a lot of animal life. Bear, wild goat by the hundred, eagle, snow-leopard. The small game's not worth the cartridges, though.'

'Up in the Baltoro there's wild goat too, they say. Cassin's a good shot, and he's brought a first-class gun. Perhaps we'll be able to eat fresh meat at Urdukass. . . .'

'If you have the time! I know the work involved in these expeditions of yours.'

The General sat down, called a bearer and asked him to bring two orange-ades (alcohol is the forbidden fruit of all forbidden fruits to the Moslem: you never see it; that mention of *sakè* was only a joke, I thought). He crossed his legs, picked up a little stick and rhythmically struck at his boots with it. Then he went on:

'You'll have other things to think about besides shooting! I'm told the peak you're out to climb is a mighty hard one. But I can understand your feelings about it, you know. At one time I couldn't. I couldn't make out what these expeditions were getting at, up there in those God-forsaken places. Now I'm all for it. It's a fine game played between the world's great nations. Ah, if only they could use it to settle international questions, instead of resorting to war! Some international violation? Right. Two teams—and away! Victory to the one who gets there first. But then, perhaps war is something necessary. Home life for the womenfolk—the cooking and the kiddies. The great out-doors for the men—the sabre and the gun. Nothing to be done about it. The All-Powerful so ordered things, and all we can do is bow our heads to them. And then, your expeditions appeal to me for another reason, the main one, I dare say: you set an example to our young men, you give them heart with these bold bids of yours, with no thought of profit behind them. What I'd really like to see up there every year is a couple of Pakistani expeditions. But they don't mean anything to most of our people. Yet we've got some first-class pilots, and we can hold our own with anyone in a good many sports. Did you see we gained second place at Tokyo? [The General was referring to the Olympic Games of Asia, held there a few days before.] The Japanese won, of course, it was a foregone conclusion. But then there's a hundred million of them, and they're a formidable people. But the other Asian countries—oh, we left them behind. Our neighbours—they didn't show up in such glowing colours. . . .'

Inevitably, the talk veered towards India. I felt I already knew what the General was going to say, and his words caused me no surprise. Here was a man of open mind, a man who had travelled quite a lot (though not in Europe) and one who called himself 'very liberal'. Yet towards the Indians he could never overcome a feeling of deep, instinctive, irremediable antagonism. The Hindus, if they are not enemies, are always foreigners, in the most absolute sense of the word. The Moslem point of view seemed to me to be this: 'We are strong, we are honest, we are straight—but very simple. The Hindus on the other hand are weak, but they're crafty, they make learned doctors and quibblers. And there are three times as many of them as there are of us. If we were put together in one state we should end up with our backs to the wall, or the pistol would go off and there'd be civil war. So the best thing is for the subcontinent to stay divided into two: Moslem India (Pakistan) and Hindu India.' The General appeared to be a friend, even a personal one, of Nehru, Patel, Panikkar and others, but while he spoke of them sympathetically enough, his conclusion was always: 'It's stronger than they are, they just hate us. . . .'

The orangeade arrived, brought by a servant in most elaborate headgear. A dog with ingratiating ways came in and rubbed against us. The air was like that of Paradise: fresh, light and touched with the scents of the countryside, stirring in a light breeze, full of sun. In the distance, however, those violet, ice-crowned peaks had already gathered plumes of dark cloud. By afternoon, they would certainly entomb the whole valley. Then the light breeze would become a hot, dry wind, angrier and more lugubrious with every gust. The air would be clean no longer, but charged with dust and fine sand, to invade one's eyes, one's clothes, one's house. The tall poplars, now so serenely elegant, swaying with the liquid rhythms of a zephyr, would creak and grate as if they were made of metal, setting the nerves on edge.

A certain agitation crept into the General's voice. He had come to his many memories of that tragic moment of history when the British Indian Empire was divided into two independent parts, the states of Pakistan and Hindustan (August 1947). They were terrible days, without a doubt. I have

47

heard Indian friends speak of them with the same emotional intensity. Neither side can claim to have kept its hands clean. Just now, circumstances brought me to hear the Moslem side.

'Who will ever reckon up how many trainloads of refugees were left in the middle of the country, purposely abandoned by the authorities? Their fate was to be assaulted by fanatical bands. Men, women and children, they were shown no mercy. At Jammu, hundreds of Moslems were put in trucks and told they would be given safe conduct over the frontier into Pakistan. Instead of that they were set upon in the night, when they were out in the country; they were robbed and killed. There are some things it is hard to forget.'

'General, they speak of a million dead on both sides. Does this figure seem to you an exaggeration?'

'No. No one will ever know just how many were killed. The million mark may well have been reached. Too many of the killings took place at night, far from any beaten track. They're buried for ever in darkness. Ah, the English bear the gravest responsibilities for it all. The original plan was for the transfer of power to take place gradually, over quite a fair period of time, say a year, the idea being to avoid any time-gaps when effectual authority was suspended. But the old masters packed up and went in a matter of days, before the new ones had been able to put their roots down. Then the fanatics, the jackals, the madmen had a clear field, and India just caught fire. . . . Try one of our apples, they're the first to ripen. They're very sweet and fragrant.'

Like the finished man of the world he was, the General knew he was guilty of speaking with too much heat, of betraying almost a personal hatred: so from these overtones of Anglophobia he turned to horticulture, so smoothly that I was scarcely conscious of the break. Fruit growing was one of his favourite occupations. It was clear that the General was not the man to take lightly his duties as the Grand Old Man of Baltistan. He spoke to me at some length on such matters as schools, roads, bridges and water-supply. His tone was serious, and he seemed to have a good grasp on realities.

'Up here there's a host of things waiting to be done. We're heirs to whole millennia of misgovernment. The Dogra! Wild beasts! That's what they were. Their only interest in Baltistan was to send the tax-gatherers from Srinagar. They sucked our villages dry. Have you noticed how mild-mannered our Balti are? You may think it's their nature. Let me tell you that it's centuries of terror. The English did as little for the people as the rest of them, they propped up in power little local bigwigs who were all bigoted reactionaries and ignorant egotists, but at least they gave us the example of an incorruptible administration. Give the devil his due, there was that much to be said for 'em. But now, what's coming back into fashion? The sealed envelope. . . . It's too much. Let's talk about potatoes instead. D'you know they do remarkably well here? I've got a little experimental garden, we'll go along and have a look at it if it interests you: I play about with all kinds of plants to see how they do in this climate and these soils. The potatoes take the prize. But the locals don't care for 'em. There's a superstition that they've got no food value. How stupid! The English, I don't like them one bit, but I've always admired them for their energy. The Germans too. And what do they feed on? Potatoes. Up here a poor harvest means the people go hungry. If your Balti would only plant potatoes he'd be saved a good many thin times.'[1]

This paean in honour of the potato went on for a long time; in the end, exactly how I cannot recall, we started speaking of cameras and films.

When the orangeade had been drunk and the apple tasted and the ingratiating dog patted on the head, we made our way back into the office. Here the Political Agent showed me a long typewritten memorandum listing the rights and duties of porters in mountaineering expeditions. A sort of 'Constitutional Rights for Expedition Personnel', in fact.

The stabilization of porters' wages, and everything to do with their welfare, equipment, rations, set down by a competent authority and accepted by the porters themselves, is an excellent thing, without any doubt. But I was somewhat taken aback all the same, because we had left Italy with other ideas; the K2 Expedition had had quite different experiences, and on these we had based our own plans. Unexpectedly hard conditions were now being imposed on us, and we had no option but to accept. Had we known all about them a few months beforehand, we should have been forewarned and come forearmed. I was afraid Toni Gobbi and Riccardo Cassin would be none too pleased when they arrived, to be confronted by such a document. We could only hope for the best.

With regard to the choice of porters, too, a new condition had come into being. The Political Agent's Office had drawn up a list of fifty 'high-altitude porters'; it was compulsory to choose your men from this list, and then to get your choice approved by the P.A. Again, the idea of listing a picked group was excellent. The only pity of it all was that it was compulsory. You had to limit your choice to the list. If I were to return to Baltistan now, I

---

1. These experiments with potatoes seem to constitute a regular feature of Baltistan history. De Filippi records that in 1835 Hugel despatched from Srinagar, as a present to Ahmed Shah, 'a sack of potatoes, to introduce their culture'. But the experiment must have met with small success; De Filippi observes (in 1913) that he 'saw no trace of the precious root in the country'.

should have my own special list of four or five names. They are the names of 'ordinary' porters who proved more capable and more willing than several of the high-grade, high-altitude gentry. By all means give the Expedition a list, but as a basis for choice not a pistol to be held at one's head.

'The final approval of the men chosen,' the P.A. told me, 'is something I've kept for myself, for the simple reason that the expeditions that get here first tend to collar all the best men. If I see a list that skims the cream, I go over it with the head of the party and try to get him to leave some for later arrivals.'

Having got over this last administrative chapter, we trooped out into the garden again, talking cameras. All at once the silent dog of the ingratiating manner noticed the stuffed bear. He began to prowl round the animal, snarling. But perhaps he was of such high intelligence that he could amuse himself by growling with his tongue in his cheek. I looked him over carefully. Yes, perhaps he was.

The grandfather who could fly

The weather still couldn't make up its mind what it was going to do. Here at Skardu there was often a brilliant sun. But over the mountains towards Nanga Parbat (the giant itself was invisible, but its satellite peaks could be plainly made out) there was a dark mass of cloud. Flying was still too risky. More than once we had heard that a plane had left Rawalpindi. But it always turned out to have gone to Gilgit (an easier flight, even in uncertain weather conditions), or else it had gone back.

'It sometimes happens that we can be isolated here for a month,' said Mustaq.

That was real consolation.

Meanwhile our American friends were all ready to start off for the mountain itself. They had got their band of 120 porters and were already loading them up. That devil Rizvi knew all the answers! He already had one expedition to his credit—the British attempt on Masherbrum (25,660 feet) the year before. He was on home ground. He knew the ropes, and among other things he had got hold of the best high-altitude porters. Some of them had climbed with him before. The party was moving off in two days.

For some time now I had been seeing a good deal of the Americans, and often shared a meal with them. They were a group of young professional men, certainly not the last word in mountaineering as far as technical experience went. In the place of it they brought sincerity, and a touching idealism, to their venture. Nice, quiet, well-mannered, harmless Americans these. Enthusiastic about everything. In radiant spirits at having got here, at being actually ready to start—for the highest mountains in the world. They were quite overawed by them. Great ventures are born of such men as these. Great disasters, too!

My own companions, when I came to think of it, seemed far harder, tougher nuts than these mere youths. The matter of age alone might have had something to do with it. The average age, in the case of the Americans, was twenty-eight. With us, thirty-six. But the really telling factor was this: the Americans, to use the word in its purest sense, were dilettanti; they were doctors, schoolmasters, technicians, agriculturists who had left their desks and offices for a glorious adventure, and a slightly crazy one. Our men were essentially mountaineers, professional climbers: the ice-wall, the glacier, the arête were their whole life, they were career and family, bread and passion.

Something of an exception among the Americans, however, was provided by a smiling colossus from Seattle, in Washington State, called Pete Schoening. If he shook your hand you lost the use of it for three days. Let us not forget a fact that I have already mentioned—that in 1953, in the Houston attempt on K2, Pete succeeded, single-handed, in holding five men who were sliding away into the abyss: at 24,000 feet too! He was chief climber of the expedition, and his companions spoke of him as a group of young enthusiasts of the track might speak of Fangio or Nuvolari. His word was final, absolutely, in all cases.

On the organizational side, the chief was Nick Clinch, a different type altogether. Long, thin and bespectacled, you would have taken him for a butterfly collector or a beetle fancier. At any moment you expected him to go off with a net or a jar and dig himself in beside some irrigation channel to pursue some such hobby. But Nick could spring a good many surprises. He was anything but a feeble young man. We did a bit of a climb one afternoon, and he was one of the first up. And, far from being the absent-minded professor, lost to the world in palaeozoic classifications and speculations, he was a fluent and most entertaining talker. By profession, he was a lawyer after all! Had he been an Italian there would have been nothing in the least odd about this: after India, isn't Italy the country with more lawyers than any other in the world? In America, a country where they do so much and talk so much less, a lawyer is a horse of another colour—something rare. At lunch, one day, there was an exchange which I, the Italian of the party, found most illuminating: 'But, my dear Nick, what on earth persuaded you to go in for Law?' Nick gave his own good reasons. The others seemed to offer him nothing less than their sympathy! Imagine, a nice fellow like that going in for anything so darned dubious! 'I'll bet you end up in politics!' snorted somebody. After which the topic changed.

If Nick can cope with politics as he coped with the organizational side of the expedition, he will certainly succeed. In America, there was no interest in mountain climbing. Everybody said the same thing. The Americans just couldn't make out what the climber was getting at. An exploring expedition had to have some scientific or commercial object, or it didn't make sense. What everybody wanted to know was: '*Is there money in the business?*'[1] If there isn't—well, nobody will discuss it any more. And, in spite of all this, behold Nick, going it alone, with no private means, with nothing but his golden tongue and his passion for high mountains—collecting together the sum of 30,000 dollars necessary for this Gasherbrum venture! Of course, a good many dollars had to come out of the pockets of the party themselves before the total could be made up. One or two had forked out heavily.

'We're in hock up to our eyes,' Nick told me. 'Even if everything goes well, it's still going to take us two or three years of mighty quiet living to foot this bill.'

On top of all this, on top of appearing frail and being strong, Nick came out with a further surprise. He might look as if he went about with his head in the clouds, but he had some real brainwaves. The most brilliant of them (he thought so, too, he admitted) was this: why ask the Pakistani Government for an official to accompany the party, as everybody does? Why not ask them to provide two officials, on the understanding that they shall participate in the expedition on terms of absolute equality and equal rights with the foreign sahibs? Then the party could call itself, at a pinch, an Americano-Pakistani expedition. All doors would be open to it, everything would go on oiled wheels. Pursuing this inspired line of thought, Nick had the name of every member of the party, sahib or not, inscribed on the eight ice-axes. Captain Rizvi's and Captain Akram's were put first. This little gesture had the wildest success: I don't know how many times we poor Italians were reproached by our own accompanying official, Captain Dar, for not doing likewise. But more of that later.

Bob Swift must have been another strong-armed type. A middle-school physics teacher, on the taciturn side, a man who had to be seen in action before his hidden force became evident, he had one arm in plaster. Long before starting for Baltistan, he'd brought his wrist down so heavily on his desk, while trying to keep order in class, that he had broken it.

1. Direct speech italicized between quotation marks is given in its original language in the Italian edition—Transl.

'What a collection!' Nick laughed. 'Here's me can't see two steps forward without my glasses, and there's Bob going to the Karakoram with one arm in a sling. *We're nuts.*'

Nuts indeed described Andy Kauffman ('I'm the grand old man, not a day less than thirty-seven'). To join this expedition in Asia he left—or as he himself said, he deserted—his post as Embassy Secretary in Paris. Lastly, there was Tom Nevison, a young doctor, and there was a rancher from California named Tom McCormack. He was the intellectual of the company. '*I never read the Odyssey,*' he said. '*I thought this would be a good chance.*' And he showed me the copy he'd brought along. It was a cheap cloth-bound edition. He kept it in his pack with his gloves and his snow-glasses. Happy Ulysses, to make this unforeseen journey across seas of ice!

Captain Rizvi and Captain Akram of course were with us all the time. Their presence never meant a moment's constraint. There was always the same effortless atmosphere of camaraderie. I emphasize this because you often hear of racial feeling in America. It exists, certainly, but the two factors necessary for its existence, the mob and the matriarch, were absent from an all-male party whose social grading gave them a certain culture and refinement. Then again, a common language is without doubt a great help. Speak one fluently, and it becomes something more than a passive instrument of communication: word and thought are so profoundly linked that language in common means emotional background and subconscious evocation in common—if not actual ideals too.

Captain Akram was a dark-skinned man with dark hair. For the last few days he had been ailing, and on that account he was to stay in hospital when the Americans went off, coming along with us, when he left Skardu, to join his own team later on. Rizvi I have already spoken of. Here at Skardu, no less than anywhere else, he was his prattling, laughing, joking, no-trouble-at-all self. This was the fellow who'd started by collaring all the air-passage priorities, and then stolen all the H.A.P.s from under our nose. What would he get up to next? Yet I couldn't help liking him. At least, he brought off his various coups with a smile, and that was something.

While we were chatting over a 'Coke' after lunch it came out that Rizvi belonged to one of the families descended from none other than the Prophet himself. In point of fact, he bore the noblest of noble names, Sayad. The fact that Rizvi belonged to aristocracy of some sort—social, intellectual, even financial, no matter, I use the word in the strict etymological sense—was one you couldn't long remain unaware of. He treated other people with an elegant assurance which was out of the common.

'My forbears,' he told us, 'came from Khorassan, which is Russian territory today. After four or five generations of meandering, they finished up at Quetta in Baluchistan. My grandfather seems to have been a big *pir*, a holy man of great fame. He would stand and meditate on a certain wall, and in the course of his meditations he had the power to fly to any place he thought best. At least, he was credited with it by the townspeople, and the nice part is they still believe it! By the way, the wall is still standing, and people make pilgrimages there.'

Rizvi smiled, but the fable did not displease him. After all, wasn't it better to have a grandfather who could fly instead of one who was just president of a bank, for instance, or a salesman of agricultural machinery? Rizvi ended up with a complaint. He voiced it with playful irony, but the underlying seriousness of it wasn't lost on me. He said the world was changing too much these days.

'The time was when to be a Sayad meant that you could live like a lord doing nothing; and all the most beautiful women were yours. Now we just drink Coca-Cola, and no one believes in anything any more. *Another sip?*'

The rajah in the windowless palace

The Political Agent gave a supper-party for the Americans, and invited me along with them. At the Residence we found all the notables of Skardu: Sir Habib-ur-Rhaman with some of his assistants, of course; then the Senior Doctor in charge of the hospital; the Major in command of the Northern Scouts; the Director of the civil airport; the Captain in charge of food stores; and so on and so forth: some twenty altogether. Men only (Islam!) No alcohol (Islam!) Many of the guests were in evening dress, others wore military uniform, the Americans grey suits. It very soon dawned on me that nearly everybody present was from 'outside'—from the Pakistan of the plains—that is to say from the Punjab, Sindh or Bengal. Only two clerks were Balti. They spoke remarkably good English and were cultivated enough in matters of local interest. Conversation stuck to very male topics: hunting, mountaineering, guns and anything mechanical.

Then supper began. The first dish offered by the silent servants, with their bare feet and their whirlpool-turbaned heads, consisted of some very special potatoes, roasted, sliced and sweetened: exquisite. Then, still in the drawing-room, a cup of piquant broth, a light liquid curry almost, was offered round. Soon after that we passed into the dining-room where the table was richly, and very variously, laden. We attacked it standing up. The Political

Agent, as always, was the perfect host. He talked to his guests, offered them food, poured them out drinks free from alcohol and followed the entire proceedings with that meticulous care, disguised beneath an air of absent-mindedness, which is the proud mark of the true gentleman.

There were several *pièces de résistance*: a wild goat Sir Habib had killed three days before, wild geese, a curry to be eaten with rice, of course—rice a creamy white in colour, with a hint of green, and bitter-sweet to the taste: there seems to have been yoghourt in it. Unfortunately no one could give me the exact recipe—a pity, because here was something really first class which it would have been a pleasure to offer one's friends back in Europe. We were all enthusiastic. When it came to the last spoonful, Nick Clinch and I exchanged a quiet smile, and we gallantly left it on our plates to avoid the charge of gluttony. *'It's for Miss Manners.'*

After supper we returned to the drawing-room for a long bout of tea-drinking. The general theme of the conversation was now mountaineering. Everybody in Baltistan follows these expeditions, as *aficionadoes* follow bull-fights. One of the P.A.'s secretaries showed us the album sent by the Austrians after their Broad Peak climb in 1957. There were some fine photographs in it. Another showed us a similar album presented by the Japanese after their long reconnaissance of the glaciers of Baltoro, Biaho and Hispar. The name of Hermann Buhl naturally cropped up. He came to a heroic, Wagnerian end on some blue precipice of Bride Peak—Chogolisa, that is—the peak nobly mantled in ice as a young bride might be veiled for her wedding.

.   .   .   .   .

One afternoon we passed at Mustaq's house. We got to know Mustaq at the airport. Now he was still more affable, more courteous and more amusing. He had a little villa in a beautiful spot—crowning a green hill. It was not on the usual Baltistan pattern—two floors, and the stairs outside. His sitting-room looked very well with its rugs of local craftsmanship.

Against all local custom, we were received by his young wife and her two children—Ainie, aged eight, and Azvi, four. Their mother was very pretty: she had golden skin and there was a touch of mystery to her eyes. When they were looking at something, you could not be sure if they saw it, and when they saw it they didn't appear to be looking. She wore a sari in a black-and-green flower pattern and sandals of red and gold. There were several cluster-rings on her fingers, and a diamond in her nose. She moved with a suggestion of sweet submissiveness, and with that sinuous, slightly feline elegance which is equally characteristic of all Oriental women (with the exception, perhaps, of the Tibetans).

The fact that Mustaq wished us to meet his wife showed how familiar he was with Western ways. The Americans were enthusiastic.

'Mr. Mustaq,' exclaimed one of them, 'your wife is surely charming.'

The ultimate concession to Western ways had been reached, in substance as well as form. Mr. Mustaq, in the matter of expressed sentiments, was probably more accustomed to British reserve than American expansiveness: and he struck me as somewhat disconcerted.

Happily, tea now arrived and tensions were lowered—international tensions, intercontinental tensions, inter-cultural and inter-religious tensions. There was a complicated succession of dishes—little rolls of meat in a sort of fried butter (samosa), a tasty yellow sweet hard as stone, with an egg-and-sugar base (anda halwa), sweet biscuits (shakar para) and the good old platefuls of dried and lightly roasted apricot-kernels.

.   .   .   .   .

Burning sunlight: a few white clouds—a rude and rustic afternoon. We had all been invited by the P.A. to the opening of the new school. A jeep took us for a short ride and set us down on a bare, sandy hill. We climbed up on foot to the new building which rose from its summit—a one-storey building of a dozen rooms and an arcade, all simplicity and good taste, local materials and Balti style. In front there was a triumphal arch with a banner inscribed: 'Happy Greetings!'

In the playground they were all assembled: a platoon of boys dressed in shirts and shorts of khaki, but the white wool beret to be seen at Gilgit. Everything very well ordered. The band—flutes and drums—filling the air with an enchanting music, rather a cross between a Viennese waltz and something composed for the Arabian Nights; two rows of visitors, male; and the notables, with the P.A. in the centre, seated under the arcade.

The ceremony started with some collective gymnastics performed by the boys in uniform to blasts on a whistle from a rather sloppily dressed schoolmaster. Various speeches followed: first the School Warden's, then those of a few Mullahs—Moslem Doctors of Law—men of severe and ascetic appearance, turbaned and bearded—very black beards for the young ones, salt-and-pepper, or just white, for the old. Then a toddler of five or six years gave an address— a long one, too, and fluent: he was loudly cheered. Sir Habib-ur-Rhaman made his reply and declared the school open. The assembly broke up.

Once more, in the course of this little ceremony, and more definitely this time, I had the feeling I'd already become familiar with on other occasions—that the notables, the little powers-that-be of Baltistan, fell into two distinct categories. One we have met already, in the person of the P.A. and his assistants—men from the 'outside', the plains of Pakistan—and in reality complete strangers here, every bit as much as Piedmontese would be in Sicily or Apulians in Alto Adige. These were the men who in a certain sense had simply replaced the British. Then there were the local people—all born here, all closely tied to the valley. First came the Rajah, the descendant of the family which for a very long time had held Skardu in fief in the name of the Maharajah of Kashmir (of the Dogra dynasty). Then came various Mullahs and the heads of the leading families. I would hazard the guess that there was some bad blood between the two groups. The locals, I should imagine, would very much like to paddle their own canoe, while the men from the Pakistan plains, though I may well be mistaken, looked on them as a set of reactionary feudal obscurantists, presumptuous ignoramuses, quite ignorant of every side of modern life.

I got to know the 'Crown Prince'—the Rajah's eldest son—a middle-aged man, rather thin, dressed just like the good Kadi you can see in the pictures of last century's travel books. He had an aristocratic bearing, an imperious beard and a little narrow turban. The Rajah apparently lived in a 'palace', but it was now reduced to a wretched ruin and even the glass in the windows had gone. I saw this 'palace', at some distance, from Mustaq's house. A really tumbledown hovel it looked, too! While we were on the way back to the Rest House, someone told me that the Rajah still received an annual pension, to this day—a subsidy, if you like—of about 13,000 rupees (over £800 or some $2,400), a large sum of money here.

The political programme seems to aim at the gradual deprivation of those classes which have enjoyed centuries of privilege.

'They're ignorant, they're reactionaries,' my informant went on. 'And what do they do with the money they get? At least they could have their windows repaired! It's a scandal in Skardu.'

The curious part is that these notables of local origin represent a caste superimposed on the true Balti population. They are the descendants of small seigneurs, soldiers of fortune, conquerors' favourites and so on—their families have established themselves in a dozen ways. Many appear to have come in the first place from Hunza and Nagar, two famous breeding-grounds of warriors over beyond the Hispar glaciers. The real Baltis have always been held in complete subjection: by everybody. And this, as we shall see, has had a saddening influence on their character.

'My king walks through the streets?'

Giotto Dainelli noticed many years ago that it was rare to find a real village in the oases of Baltistan. There are people and there are dwellings; but these latter come in separate clusters, one here, one there, almost hidden under the apricots, the poplars, the willows and the sorb-apple trees. This is true of Skardu too. I looked at Skardu in the light of Dainelli's old photographs, dating from 1913, and it didn't appear to be greatly changed.

This whole 'city', 'Capital of Baltistan', really comes down to being one vast garden and kitchen garden. Scattered among the trees and the bushes are government offices, residences, hospitals, mosques, the Rajah's palace. The houses form one dismal huddle in the bazaar-and-market quarter: 200 yards of streets lined with miserable shops; humble, jerry-built places run up in essiccated mud bricks, with wooden pillars, balustrades and window frames.

One morning I went to the bazaar to buy some paper and a pencil, and also to see if I could find some little souvenirs of Baltistan to take home. I thought of the bazaars of Tibet, richly laden, often with objects of considerable interest: picturesque curiosities, some of them really beautiful, all made by local craftsmen. But here there was only a terrible dearth of all such things. I had to remember, certainly, that this was the realm of Islam: hence, no pictures, no prints, no statuettes, no images—any talent the people might have possessed for pictorial art had long since gone to waste. And there was also Baltistan's very real poverty to take into account. The main business here was just to survive, to satisfy the five primary needs of life: hunger, thirst, sleep, sex and shelter. Thus the goods offered were the basic things: a few rough clothes to wear, rough shoes and slippers; cord for parcelling up one's burdens; small hampers to take one's few possessions; some agricultural tools; food of various kinds—they were all here. Tobacco, too.

Smoking represents the Balti's one pleasure. Alcohol in any form is, as we have learned, forbidden in no uncertain manner under Moslem law: sex can surely give few satisfactions where it is often so dangerous and, in the strict sense of the word, insalubrious—though by way of compensation there is a good deal of homosexuality. The result is that pleasure is entirely centred on smoking, and smoking alone. Smoking draws the Balti as a spring in a desert draws a man desperate with thirst. Cigarettes are naturally in the greatest possible demand, and there are some quaint varieties of pipe. If the Balti is up in the mountains and has neither he won't be beaten. It is characteristic of him that he will still smoke somehow. He will contrive a 'pipe' out of clay, scraping out a 'bowl' for the tobacco and sucking at a punctured hole for mouthpiece and stem.

But if the bazaar at Skardu offers the traveller almost nothing of the slightest interest to buy, it must not be thought that the human spectacle gives him nothing to see. Since the beginning of time, Baltistan has been the melting-pot of Asia, and this has left its mark everywhere. Take a look at the Balti in his flowing toga of rough wool: he has only to fling it round him and there he is, suddenly invested with all the pride of the patriarch—though he may be nothing but the humblest rustic. Here are the mountain people of Gilgit, Hunza and the Chilas, with their white wool headgear—a style which must be fast spreading eastwards, because in the 1913 photographs taken by the De Filippi Expedition it is scarcely to be seen, while today it is everywhere. The Balti will wear it with pride: it stands for culture, elegance, a higher standard of living. It helps remove the sense of inferiority which the inhabitants of these high valleys have always felt towards the richer and more cultivated peoples of Gilgit. This head-covering is without doubt a thing of beauty—and complete virility. It consists of a 'tube' of wool twirled round and round to a point. In the cold it can be pulled down over the ears. It puts one in mind of the style worn by merchant princes in the paintings of Masolino de Panicale.

But there were other patterns to be seen too: the Chirgiz fur toque; the pith helmet; the little karakul fez, popular with youth; the cap from Shigar and Braldu, often seen on the real countryman. There was the turban, too, and all the subtle variations on its theme—each with its special significance, at least for the knowledgeable in such matters.

I had a look into the shops. Everywhere I found a courteous welcome. One moustachioed shopkeeper, wearing a turban with a badge on it, inquired whether I was German. I told him I wasn't, I came from Rome. At this, with paeans of joy, he showed me an oleograph on the wall: Rome, the Via dell'Impero, the Colosseum, Victor Emmanuel's monument.

'There is my King,' he said, in quite good German. 'Aman Ullah. When he was turned out of Afghanistan I had to flee too. I've been here a good many years. It's a hard life, but at least I'm free, and I'm safe—d'you ever see my King? Does he walk through the streets?'

I had to confess that I did not know his King personally.[1] But I could recall that he was in good health, and Rome gave him nothing to complain about. 'Fine, fine!' cried the moustachioed Afghan, his eyes flashing fire in quite an intimidating fashion. What he really seemed to want to say was: 'Fine, boys, just go on doing your duty. Touch one hair of my King's head and I'll make short work of you!'

The next shop but one was kept by a tall and suave Chinaman, who

1. Ex-King Aman Ullah died on April 25 1960.

spoke almost faultless English. He was a refugee from Sinkiang ('the New Colony'). He'd left there on the arrival of the Communists a few years before. Of his flight across mountain passes, glaciers and deserts he had no wish to speak, but he dropped enough hints, in the course of our conversation, to suggest a real ordeal.

The common bond between all these men, differing as they may in race, culture, origin and language, is the religious one: the great, unifying tradition of Islam. Many were Moslem refugees from Kashmir—which was still 'under the bondage' of Bharat (that is, India); or so they gave me to understand.

The Rock of Buddha

I have already mentioned the fact that a number of Buddhist monuments exist in Baltistan. They testify to a long and important period in the country's history—right up to the fifteenth century, when the unexpected conversion to Islam came about. Graffiti and reliefs of Buddhist origin are to be found both at Shigar and Skardu; Filippo de Filippi has described some of them, and a few photographs form part of his exhaustive studies in these regions.

The most important of these sculptures are to be found near the road to Satpara, a kilometre or two out of Skardu, on the right-hand side just past a stream. A big granite rock, a natural shrine, chrome in colour, is conspicuously visible there; and the entire surface of this narrow wall, twenty-six feet in height and some eighteen in width, is covered with imagery, inscriptions and graffiti. Near its upper edge there is a hole or slot: this will certainly have been used from time to time for slinging a canopy to protect the sacred sculptures; the custom is to be seen in Tibet to this day. On the other surfaces of this piece of rock some interesting inscriptions are also to be seen, and there are a few, later and less inspired, on the stones round about.

The major design has an image of Buddha for its centrepiece. The figure is about life-size and surrounded by twenty others, all similar but on a smaller scale, and placed in a square. To left and right stand two other figures (one of which may be seen in *Plate 18*), the whole group forming what is known in the terminology of Buddhism as a *Mandala*. According to the interpretation of experts, one of the standing figures portrays Maitreya, and the central one Buddha Sakyamuni; the twenty smaller and identical figures represent previous incarnations of Buddha Sakyamuni.

From an artistic point of view it cannot be claimed that we have anything first class here. But historically, and iconographically speaking, the interest is considerable. A. H. Francke claims that these sculptures date back at least to the tenth century A.D. The inscriptions at the foot would appear to have been added when the carvings were already of some antiquity. They urge the pious to look after the sculptures, to revive the colouring (of which hardly a trace now remains) and to see that the space at the foot of the rock, which must have known the prayers of many a pilgrim from the most distant parts, is kept clear.

A crime against photography

On the morning of 25th May, as I was making my way down again from the Rock of Buddha, a small boy came running to meet me with the news that the *jahaz* (the 'airborne') had arrived from Rawalpindi.

Then the fine weather wasn't just a local phenomenon! There had been a real change for the better throughout the whole area.

I rushed back to the Rest House. There I found Cassin, Gobbi, Bonatti, Mauri, Oberto and De Francesch, all in the best of health and bright-eyed with wonder: they could still see Nanga Parbat before their eyes. Cassin and Bonatti had seen such a spectacle already, some years before, but for the others it had come straight out of the blue of the unknown. The most deeply satisfied of them all was Bepi De Francesch: it was his very first flight into the bargain!

'What a Baptism of Air for a climber!' he exclaimed with a laugh.

'My dear Bepi,' I told him, 'make sure you never go anywhere from now on except by train or bus. Because, after the privilege of that flight, any other's going to seem as dull as ditch-water.'

Zeni and Captain Dar had stayed behind at Rawalpindi to see to some baggage we'd had to leave there. The bulk of our stuff, fortunately, had come along with my six companions.

They told me a good deal about the thin time they had had in Rawalpindi. Every single morning it was a case of getting up with the lark, and standing by with everything packed—and then the clouds would gather or the wind would get up too strong, and one more flight would be cancelled. All this uncertainty, this feeling of a jinx on everything—on top of the sweltering heat—got to be too much. It seeped in. It got at the moral fibre. Today's flight was nothing less than a liberation, a rebirth.

No post yet. And I was dismayed to learn that a long telegram I had sent off a few days before to Cassin in Rawalpindi had never reached him. Was it because I had advised my companion to ask the Military Authorities for permission to photograph Nanga Parbat from the air? Had some unknown body of censors held it back? Let me interpolate here a warning to any travellers who may want to get to the Karakoram by way of Skardu: get your permits to take photos from the air in Karachi through your own Embassy. Apparently the permit is given there without any fuss. It is a crime against photography to let Nanga Parbat go by without an attempt to imprison that majestic play of light and gleam and translucency in film. If possible, colour film.

Stifled by red tape—but happy!

Monday, Tuesday, Wednesday—25th to 28th May—what days they were! Not a minute to breathe. One of us would be off to the airport to bring the baggage along in the truck, another going from official to official to get all formalities straight, another would be going through the porters' list, another preparing the packs . . . the Rest House was all bustle and go. It was a Rest House no longer, but rather caravanserai, workshop, barrack-square. We were all ready for the word 'go' now, or almost, but somehow or other we had still to work out the following problem: how to transport seven and a half tons of gear with the aid of 450 porters up 137 miles of track, gravel-bed, stream, moraine and glacier to the Base Camp—that is, from an altitude of 7,500 feet (Skardu) to one of about 19,500 feet.

Gradually, in relays, all our goods and chattels arrived, and our two last members as well—Dr. Zeni and Captain Dar. 27th May saw everybody present and correct. The only thing we still hadn't got was the cylinders of liquid gas. Apparently the pilots had been none too eager to handle them, fearing leaks at the diminished pressure of high altitude. In the end, however, with the last of the baggage, one container was sent as a try-out. Everything went well. It looked as if we should soon have our fuel after all. It was a vital item.

I will not attempt to describe our various activities over the course of those non-stop days. Without graphs, and something like a railway time-table, I couldn't! If I open my diary anywhere between 18th and 25th May, when I was waiting for a break in the weather to enable my companions to fly in, I find entries like this: 'A stroll over the country' or 'Afternoon—writing letters, then up to the fort, copying inscriptions' or else 'Visited Rock of Buddha. Back at 12. A swim in Indus. Sunbathed for an hour.' Now it was anything but inscriptions, swims and cultural research. The tone had changed. 'Spent day between Rest House and airport, jeep and truck to transport cases etc.' (May 26th). 'Enrolling porters—rig for same' (27th). 'Afternoon—organizing gear: calculating expenses' (28th). We got up at dawn, and at night we fell into our beds with hardly a moment to inscribe our diaries even with those telegraphically brief records.

The various jobs we had to do came under several headings. First and foremost there was the transport of all our gear from the airport to the Rest House: it would have been plain sailing if every time we needed a vehicle we hadn't had to run to the Military for it. No one knew when the next plane would be in. Therefore no definite programme could be arranged, and it was clear that the trucks might not always be at our disposal. As a result there were misunderstandings and worse. Often, hours would go by and not one piece of baggage would be moved. When this chore was settled at last, and all our gear had been conveyed to the Rest House, the various cases had to be un-packed, and the contents divided into packs as far as possible identical in weight —down to the last gram: sixty pounds apiece (27 kilos, 240 grams). This was a long, difficult and delicate job. We all took a hand in it, with Toni Gobbi directing operations. He was everywhere at once, with a leather satchel under his arm, full of notebooks, pocket-books and papers; pencils in his pockets, in his hands, or in the bosom of his shirt. These were heavy days' work for him.

While we were thus parcelling out all the gear, we had to see about engaging the porters too. We should need pretty well 450, not to speak of the high-altitude men. Captain Dar dealt with the first category. He went through them one by one, taking particulars of their name, father and village. Sur-names were unknown here, so that a typical entry might run: No. 284, Karim, son of Ghulam, from the village of Parkuta; or No. 361, Ibrahim, son of Rakmat Ullah, from the village of Satpara, and so on, through page after page. Dar took all these details most meticulously. 'You never know, they might turn out to be Indian spies.' What they would be spying on was not clear—ice and rock, perhaps? But this part of the world lives and breathes spies, and one must resign oneself to the fact.

So far as the high-altitude porters went, our misfortunes started at the earliest moment, and haunted us throughout the whole expedition. I had scarcely arrived in Skardu before I was trying to pick out what I thought to be the best men—judging not only by their appearance but by the sort of testimonials which had been given them by well-known climbers, English, German, Austrian or Japanese. Then I learned that, from the moment of enrolling them, I should have to pay them a pretty good wage. So it had seemed better to wait for Cassin. When he came the two of us got down to the job and I made out our first list of picked men; naturally, we consulted Bonatti too: some of them were known to him and from his experience on K2 he was in a position to give us some good tips about them. We engaged a total of fourteen men. There were long talks with the P.A. because one or two names did not appear on the officially approved list, and because the P.A. seemed to think fourteen was rather a high number (perhaps he was right).

These porters were scarcely signed on before they started to make in-sistent demands for special mountain clothes and gear: they wanted to show off the insignia of their new office to the whole country! We had long and animated discussions among ourselves: should we make the concession or not? But then Sir Habib-ur-Rhaman stepped in. He told us that our predecessors had handed over everything to the porters as soon as they were engaged. We decided that it was up to us to go and do likewise. Bonatti, speaking from his own experience on K2, warned us that we risked the early loss of scarce and costly equipment. But the precedent of K2 proved to have no validity here and now!

'Today, everything is changed!' so we were told by both Captain Dar and the P.A. True, Dar made no bones about it, and the P.A. put it gently. But it came to the same thing.

In this way, Skardu was afforded a grand spectacle: lo and behold, Taqi, Mahmud Hussein, Ghulam Rasul and the rest swaggering about its streets, clothed and shod in mountaineering style and brandishing, a little clumsily for the most part, that supreme symbol of caste and valour, the ice-axe. Towards midday the sun grew rather hot (we were in shirt-sleeves and shorts) and there were the chosen few from among the porters sweating as if they were delirious with fever, dripping sweat from their bursting rose-red faces to their toes—yet absolutely refusing to divest themselves of one single woollen stitch of their 'uniform'; wool shirt, wool trousers, wool jerkin, windproof and snowproof jacket, they wore the lot! One of them was even strutting about in his dark glasses. Yet they were in their seventh heaven. 'It's no penance if your heart's in it,' as they say in Tuscany.

The porter who proposed himself, nay, imposed himself, however reticently, as chief porter and therefore chief of the whole caravan, was a certain Taqi, from Satpara. Frankly, none of us was too pleased, and we racked our brains to try to decide what could be done about it. He was a dark, slovenly fellow, and he could give you an ugly look. His voice was strident, and jarred on our ears. He always wore a sort of beggar's cap perched sideways on a head of bristly black hair. We learned that he hailed from one of the best families in Satpara; this, rather than any personal charm, explained the ascendancy he was able to assume over all his fellows. He had already taken part in various expeditions and he showed me a letter from Eric Shipton. It was brief and to the point: 'Taqi makes the worst possible impression down in the valley. But, as higher ground is reached, his qualities of courage, determination, goodwill and good humour come out. For me he has been a good porter.'[1] Thus, we ended by regarding him as one of the party, and for the time being we put him in charge of the ordinary porters.

1. Text of Shipton's letter quoted from memory; actual words may have been different.

Where mosques are like pagodas:
the Shigar mosque

2

Askole: circular dwellings of stone and mud.

An interior, Kashumal.

3

A loom in the shade of the apricot trees (Kashumal).

4

Ploughing at 10,000 feet (Askole).

The Baltistan landscape is one of scorched earth and desert, except in watered regions. Oases glow with a rich and vivid green.

Baltistan - Land of mountains, sun-lit glaciers, wild rivers. Land, too, of fruits, of apricots and slender poplar-trees.

Skardu Valley

12

13

14

Baltistan - a melting-pot of race - and costume - from far and wide in Asia.

Bodhisattva carved in rock near Skardu: traces of a Buddhist past.

An ornamented window in the Shigar mosque: elements of the civilisation of Islam.

19

An interior - Askole.

Supplies for the Balti caravan represented another important question. Judging again by the practice in the K2 Expedition, it was only necessary to supply flour, and then only beyond Askole. But the new regulations laid it down that not only must a variety of foods be provided for the ordinary porters beyond Askole. For the porters extraordinary, they must be provided from Skardu itself. All this meant that we had to revise our ideas drastically. Questions of finance were involved (all supplies could be acquired at the Military Subsistence Stores) as well as those of logistics. Cassin, Gobbi and I spent the entire afternoon of the 28th sitting at a table in the Rest House making, or re-making, the necessary calculations. Our calculations suggested that we should need at least another hundred porters for the transport of 50 sacks of flour, 16 sacks of sugar, 1,200 lb. of condensed milk, 580 lb. of butter, 72 lb. of cigarettes, besides 210 lb. of dahl (a sort of lentil). The caravan would have to start with eleven tons instead of the seven and a half we had reckoned on.

There was still another difficulty: the transport of petty cash. At Rawalpindi we had changed our bank drafts into silver and other coinage (rupees, half-rupees, quarters and so on), but the P.A. had assured us that it was no longer necessary to weight ourselves down with all that metal. So we changed a good proportion of our money into 10-, 5- and 1-rupee notes. It may be worth while putting on record for the benefit of future travellers that the ones and fives are particularly useful. From now on expeditions may cover deserted valleys and plains denuded of life with large sums in a small, light wooden chest. Be it said to the honour of the Balti that with regard to money not one dishonest act marred their record.

One last detail we still had to organize was a courier service for our post. We arranged for a man to leave Skardu every ten days, and to hand over to two others at Askole, who would climb as far as the Base Camp. These also had to be supplied with shoes, uniforms and blankets, not to speak of a stiff financial advance, and, once more, that symbol of authority and distinction, the ice-axe.

That evening we were invited to the Residence by Sir Habib-ur-Rhaman. A most delightful party, just like that given for the Americans. Wishing to show our gratitude to the P.A. for his interest in our venture, we hit on the idea of presenting him with two medicine chests. We knew how difficult it was for him to get hold of certain medical products up here, and we thought that a gift of this nature, representing as it did one tiny step forward in his programme of aid for Baltistan, would be bound to please him. When we presented our gift, he thanked us warmly.

E

With evening the traveller turns towards Mecca,
kneeling among the stones of the river-bed

The evening came to a close with some Alpine songs, Bonatti, Mauri and Gobbi forming a first-class trio.

The name on the ice-axe

A fortnight had now passed since that moment when, in the Rawalpindi Military H.Q., I had met the man in whose company we were to explore the trackless mountain wastes of Baltistan.

All I had known of him, till then, was his name: Abdul Karim Dar.

A young, bronzed colonel had asked me into his office and given me a chair.

'Your liaison officer will be along in a few minutes,' he told me.

We talked of mountains and snow, and the Colonel described a march he had done in some grim country round Nanga Parbat. I looked round the bare, austere office—as one does in such circumstances. It had a big window opening on to the boughs of a tree, where a few birds were somewhat petulantly singing. I confess to a high degree of curiosity as I waited for the name Abdul Karim Dar to take on a face. We were going to live cheek by jowl with this unknown quantity for months together, right outside civilization. The prospect was no joke. Things might go very well, or hopelessly wrong. It was in the hands of Fate.

We heard steps. The door opened. The face—there it was. Should one put one's trust in first impressions? This expedition was to leave me a little hesitant on the point. Be that as it may, however, my first reaction was a secret sigh of relief. Our official companion struck me as a very likeable fellow indeed. He was tall and chestnut-haired, with very regular features. He wore uniform elegantly, yet unfrivolously; in different dress he might have passed for the descendant of one of Alexander's Greeks. I learned soon after that he was the son of a Moslem refugee from that sector of Kashmir which was still under the sovereignty of India. The young Colonel introduced us, hoped we would get on together, reminded us of our reciprocal rights and duties, and then, wishing us good luck, left.

But from that moment it cannot be said that we saw eye to eye with the Captain. In some of his judgments I was soon struck by a certain dourness. Very early in our acquaintance we paid a joint visit to one of the municipal offices, where we had some business. It was about twelve o'clock. The clerks were eating their lunch, which seemed to consist of rice, spice and a few barely perceptible shreds of meat.

'Look at them,' rasped the Captain, turning to me. 'Idlers! Gorgers! They ought to be ashamed of themselves. Instead of thinking of the public

66

they are supposed to serve, and the work they ought to be doing, they are wasting the Government's money devouring every titbit they can lay their hands on. In the Army we eat once in the morning and once in the evening, and that's that.'

His comments on the social situation of Pakistan showed the same acerbity. We were walking along on one occasion when a large, powerful and silent car containing an old man who must have been very important or very rich happened to push us right up against the edge of the road to avoid some other traffic.

'There's a thin time coming for all those parasites,' said the Captain. He laughed, but his tongue had a rough edge to it and I could read what was in his mind. 'It's not fair that a hog like that should go round the town on his perambulating throne, while thousands of pairs of hands are working for him in the country. Starving into the bargain, too.'

Perhaps the Captain was a Communist? Allah forbid! Your puritanical, fanatical military man is a familiar figure—a key figure, one could say—in the psychology and hence in the politics and the achievements of Asia today. He is the very incarnation of Islam here, and the Hindu tradition there: the spirit of Shinto in one city and the inheritance of Tai in the next; always there is this violent urge towards social reform, and, very often, a fascist make-up to go with it; order for order's sake, my country right or wrong, and out with all foreigners. A glance at the map of Asia in 1961 will show that from Egypt to Formosa there are millions of men in the power of generals who have come up from captains, majors and colonels just like Dar. Power, riches, age and new persuasions may then combine to calm down their fierce spirit, but that is another story.

At Skardu we were in continual contact with Dar. Dr. Zeni spoke some English, but most of the interpreting fell on me. It is scarcely sufficient to say that the atmosphere grew more and more strained. Dar had no chance of direct communication with my companions, so that mutual relations of the most cordial antipathy arose. The language bar might not have been the only reason. We were all exhausted and nervy just now. Even the long-suffering Cassin, always so warm and generous-hearted, would go off the deep end at any time, and tell me he had had enough. Then came a very black day. It started even before breakfast. I hadn't got up before the Captain was knocking at my door.

'Good morning, Maraini, I want to speak to you.' (Fortunately English contains only one second person singular, or for two pins Dar would have been addressing us with a lofty 'thou'.)

'Good morning to you. Yes? Well, go ahead.'

The Captain came halfway into the room and stopped.

'What's all this about one party going off before the other? It's absolutely forbidden, you understand? *How can I keep an eye on you if you split your party into minor groups?*'

It was this way: Cassin, with the most understandable wish to pause for a day or two at Urdukass (13,287 feet) to get used to the altitude, wanted to start off with me, and some fifty or sixty porters, two or three days ahead of the main party. Cassin was nearly fifty years old. Could any project seem more reasonable? He and I needed a little more acclimatizing to the height than the youngsters. But no. The regulations said 'Group division forbidden', and the Captain was going to keep to the exact letter of the law.

At eight o'clock we were all at table for the first meal of the day: tea, milk, chupatty cakes, eggs, biscuits, butter—up in mountain country it is as well not to start the day on an empty stomach, and the cook, without realizing it, might have been following the tradition of the English breakfast. The Captain joined us with a scarf round his head, turban fashion, and a very dour face indeed. I don't remember exactly what started the avalanche, but an avalanche it was.

'The very first thing you did, Maraini, was to come here ahead of the rest of the party without one word to me. I said nothing that time, I didn't want to put a spanner in the works. But now I can see you're going on in just the same fashion. You're just not taking me into account. You propose, and you dispose, and you take all your decisions as if I were just a spectator pure and simple. Now, I note that you've done all the picking and choosing of the high-altitude porters off your own bat. It won't do. What if your list included men who, for reasons you're not supposed to know, will get left behind?'

'My dear Dar,' I said, 'there's the list. You have only to strike out what names you want to, and we'll find replacements.'

'And then you had the cheek to present me to the Political Agent last night! It was I who should have presented you. And, on top of that, you made a bad blunder with those medicine chests. I should have made the presentation in your name. I am your link with the Pakistani authorities in any and every circumstance, and I am also your link with the ordinary people. Yet you must act the boss. You've ruined everything. What am I supposed to be? A mere onlooker?'

'My dear Dar, we're here to climb a mountain. Not for a game of diplomatic pat-ball. Don't forget, the important thing about the medicines was

surely that they should get into the hands of people who need them. The
Political Agent isn't such a stickler for form as you are.'

'You don't see him when he's annoyed. Last night he was certainly
annoyed. And then, to add insult to injury and ruin the whole evening, your
party strikes up a song. Don't you know that in the presence of one's superiors
it is not done to sing?'

My companions went on eating in silence. The storm raged in English
over their heads. Little by little I managed to get Dar calmed down. On this
occasion I did not act the interpreter for him. Why raise the tempers around
us by translating his remarks?

Two hours later Cassin, Dar and I went off in a jeep to the Military Stores
to get the porters' food supplies. The Captain's good humour appeared to have
returned. Like all fanatics, he spoke movingly of his family and his home and
his children. He told us something of the wretched life he had endured as the
son of refugees: his parents in 1947, feeling they could not stomach a Hindu
government, being Moslem themselves, had taken up all their roots—leaving
their home, their land, their possessions and their place in the world. Dar had
certainly had a very hard time of it since boyhood. Adversity is a school
which makes some of us all the more deeply human, and gives others a rough
edge. Captain Dar it had transformed into a powerful hater. He hated the
Indians, he hated the rich, he hated the English, he hated the Communists. His
temperament, like a climbing plant, had put out tendrils that eagerly embraced
every sharp and bitter point of the rock they were trained on. Or perhaps
hatred was not the word. Contempt, then? Certainly he did not seem to
invite pity for his lot. Looked at dispassionately, and without rancour, he
struck me as a man who wanted to pay the world back in its own coin, and he
hated the world because it was not to his liking, it didn't come up to his ideals.
The be-all and the end-all of his ideals being the Koran.

It turned chilly. I got a sweater out of the jeep and slipped it on. It happened to be my blue expedition sweater, with the very narrow three-coloured
band round the left sleeve. Dar's face suddenly clouded: I was beginning to
know the signs now. Something had gone wrong.

'Tell me something,' he said, quietly. 'Which is best? A sweater with a
V neck or a polo collar?'

'It's hard to say. Depends on when and where you need it. If it's not too
chilly an open neck is better. If you've got to bivvy somewhere some cold
night, this is the one to have. With a collar.'

'Then I'm not to come up the mountain with you?'

'But how d'you make that out, Captain?'

'You gave me a V-necked one. You're keeping the polo collars for yourselves. Really, you get all the halfpence! What am I supposed to be? A spectator? Or am I a member of the Expedition too? Look at the way the Americans do things! Rizvi and Akram get exactly the same treatment as everybody else—yes, they even get their names on the ice-axe, d'you know that? But I . . . all right. I haven't all your shoes, I've no ice-axe, I haven't got packs like you. But don't think I haven't noticed, oh dear no!'

'My dear Dar, first of all, do understand, it isn't true that you're not equipped on a par with us. There's still some clothing and gear packed up in the cases. You'll lack for nothing, you'll see. As for the peak itself, you're bound to understand that those of us who go on to the top slopes and perhaps the Summit itself will need a variety of special equipment. You're an athlete, anyone can see, but you've never done any climbing at very high altitude, have you?'

'That's true. But you must never forget that I want to be one of you. Don't put me in a position where I feel my technical inferiority, or I might feel forced to vindicate myself in other ways.'

Dar often came out with extraordinarily innocent utterances like this. Had there been just the two of us we might possibly have hit on some modus vivendi. But between him and the rest of the party lay the language barrier, and I was afraid that was going to be the source of endless trouble and mis-understandings.

Ordering the food supplies was a long business. When costs were totalled up in rupees, the figure was surprisingly high—a good deal higher than we had been prepared for. Cassin got me to ask the Captain whether his redoubtable list could serve just as a guide, or whether it had to be followed in every detail. I explained that we bore quite heavy responsibilities with regard to the costs of the Expedition. We couldn't just go spending money as we liked. Our resources constituted no private fortune. They had been advanced to us by a national association—the Alpine Club—and we were answerable for every penny.

'What?' snapped the Captain, in the same split second as my question made sense to him. 'You, with case after case chock-full of all God's good things —you'd deny the porters what is only their due? The Colonial Age is over now! Competent authorities have worked out these rations, and you'll have to provide the porters with everything on the list. If it's going to cost you too much, leave some of your superfluous gear behind and take fewer porters. Then you'll have a smaller bill, for your stuff and ours.'

Slowly, the mournful situation became defined: the Captain took us for slave-drivers, European brutes, litter-borne lordlings, an inhuman weight on the poor Asiatic's back. My companions regarded our official companion as a cross between an agitator and a policeman. The porters, simple country fellows, but blessed with a real countryman's cunning, too, could see that trouble was brewing, and they decided to fish in the troubled waters good and hard. And in the midst of this sea of trouble, behold the poor interpreter, with all its waves beating on him. The Captain, explaining his own point of view, treated him like the mouthpiece of some despicable feudalism. His own companions, if ever he tried to explain to them the hard facts of life just now, called him a hopeless dreamer—or something worse!

No doubt about it. The Gasherbrum bristled with difficulties, even right out here, before the very approaches had been reached.

Eleven Tons on 450 Shoulders

Out of limbo into life

AT LAST came the great day! On 30th May we were off. We were all happy, and not only because the Expedition was stirring to life out of that limbo which had entombed its early stages, not only because we were exchanging that limbo world for a caravan mountain-borne beneath the azure sky, and the hawks that hovered in its heights: we were wearied of Skardu and the petty round, and now we hoped for better times. We had to march, we had to ford rivers, we had to fight fatigue, to build camps, and put our wits to simple, elemental things. That way lay harmony.

We were out of bed round about five o'clock that morning. The rooms of the Rest House were still cluttered up with gear which had yet to be stowed. Some of my companions slept on *charpoi*, the little Indo-Pakistan style beds. Others on rubber mattresses or in sleeping-bags. Some of the special porters, who had come to be personal attendants, soon turned up and helped us with the baggage. It was unbelievable how much of our stuff had to be packed at the last moment!

Each of us had his own personal bag, containing an entire outfit and a small 'skeleton pack' to sling over the shoulders; this covered immediate needs. I myself had a pretty good-sized pack—camera, cinecamera, film, viewfinders, tripod and other accessories to make photography possible at all hours. There is always one last little problem on excursions like this, too: books. That wasn't such a bad idea of McCormack's to bury the Odyssey in his kitbag! We are all of us going to read one of these mammoth works one day: we nearly always fail to because we never have time. But, for once, here was the man who might have time: three days confined to a tent by bad weather,

72

sickness, a broken ankle . . . they were all on the cards. And you can't consider books without considering weight. Hence, the greater the concentration of reading matter the better. In the end, it is largely a matter of chance what you take—for back in Europe before you start you have something else to think about. My own miniature library comprised the Koran, an anthology of English verse from Chaucer to Eliot, a translation of the Tao-Te-Ching, and two books of exploration by Dyhrenfurth and Shipton—and lastly the proof-sheets of one of Dainelli's works on the discovery of the Karakoram. Ah, I was forgetting! I also had something I'd bought at the last minute in a shop in Rawalpindi—*The Theory of the Leisure Class*, by Veblen.

But just now we had anything but *leisure*! We were all occupied, every moment of our time: Cassin and Gobbi had their logistics, Bonatti, Mauri, Oberto and De Francesch were in charge of the 424 porters now arriving, and of all loading problems. Dr. Zeni was giving the finishing touches to his mobile pharmacy. While I dashed hither and thither, still trying to navigate my way through a rough and uncharted sea of words, words, words. 'Maraini, come here, what does this fellow want? Can't understand whether he's suffering from sore feet or whether he's trying to sell us slippers.' 'Fosco, for the Lord's sake tell the Captain that even the porters extraordinary really ought to carry something.' '*Sahib, no take breakfast this morning? All ready, please tell others.*' '*Masahib, dii bakass chogo yod, lechmo med.*' (*This case is too heavy, no go.*) It was all enough to drive me crazy. Shall I last out? I wondered. It would be terrible to collapse halfway!

About half past nine, when confusion was worst confounded, along came Sir Habib-ur-Rhaman to give us his salutations. He was dressed as if he would soon be off on a trip himself: light cap, rough wool jacket, riding breeches, green jerkin—what a sense of time, place and correct wear! He greeted us with great affability; I would go so far as to say I even caught the light of envy in his eyes, and I heard a note of it in his little speech. He would be not displeased to be starting off for the high peaks—leaving his office and his files and turning his thoughts to the true, simple little things that fill a pioneer's day. Before taking his leave he called me aside with an exhortation to do my utmost to preserve harmonious relations between our group and Captain Dar.

'My dear friend,' he said to me, in that suave brand of English of his, rich in long, literary-sounding words such as 'rationalize' and 'comprehension', 'I appreciate the fact that the position is going to be highly difficult. The Captain's a fine person, but—how should I say?—a little incisive, and all of a piece. Then perhaps you're a little beyond him, he's used to the formalities of

73

garrison life, with its rules and regulations, while you are all men more used to combating the difficulties of nature rather than those of bureaucracy. Ah yes, I understand well enough, you're all the more sympathetic to me for that! Perhaps Captain Dar will come to see the point as well. Try to meet him half-way, give him no chance to intervene in the affairs of the caravan. Then everything will go smoothly, you'll see. You yourself can do a great deal, you speak both languages: nearly everything depends on you. Let me know how you get on, send me a letter by courier. Goodbye—goodbye. . . .'

At last we made our way down to the Indus. A hundred metres below the Rest House it is a silent and powerful stream, flowing between a steep, sandy bank on one side and a flat, empty gravel-bed on the other. We now had to transport our four-hundred-odd souls across the river by means of an ancient wooden ferry: fifty of us at a time. The pilots were in high spirits, and singing. An expedition didn't come their way every day of the week, believe me! And, so far as I could gather from Cassin, they had demanded, with a little encouragement from Captain Dar, quite an exorbitant ferry-fare. We were beginning to see the force of a general rule at work; the Captain claimed to stand up for Justice and Justice for him meant one thing—tapping Cassin's pockets with as big a hole as possible, and irrigating the earth of Baltistan with every available lira of Italian cash! Beneficence is a virtue . . . but more of that later!

Eleven o'clock saw us finally gathered on the bare gravel-bed on the far side of the Indus. A moving sight we made, too: 424 porters ordinary, 15 porters extraordinary, 10 sahibs (ourselves and Captains Dar and Akram), a policeman and a cook. Total, some 451. Cases by the hundred, other baggage, all those sacks of food which brought the weight up from seven and a half metric tons to eleven—they were strewn over the gravel beach in most orderly fashion. The next item was to get the porters loaded up; and it had to be done with all the care in the world to keep the weights identical, or later we should be faced with a lot of grumbling at equal pay for unequal avoirdupois. For Toni Gobbi, this was another heavy day's work in itself. A born organizer, it came naturally to him to keep everything under control and to bring a maximum spirit of efficiency and precision to his three dimensions—men, objects and movement. Sadiq was a great help, too. He was a dark, emaciated Balti with almost a Tibetan air, with a fuzzy little goatee on his chin and a white Gilgit beret on his head. Sadiq might have been forty years of age, and he had been caravan chief to the K2 Expedition. He was one of those men who make an excellent first impression: intelligent, willing and a member of that sacred fraternity of Simplifiers of Things. (Dar, of course, belonged to the doubtless still more sacred genus of Complicators.) But Sadiq's very virtues had found him out. He was no longer a caravan chief. He was under contract to the Government for certain construction jobs, and naturally could not leave steady work for the adventures and uncertainties of a trip like this. Today, however, he had managed to down tools. He had come to help give us a start on our long road to glory. It was he who gave out the identity discs, which not only carried the porter's number but furnished him with a guarantee of payment when the day of reckoning came.

The sun was burning hot: it blistered the very stones on the beach and the air streamed with its glitter. A dip in the ice-cold waters of the Indus would have been very welcome! But there wasn't even time to think of it. What with the crowd, the baggage, the colour and the commotion, the gravel stretch took on the appearance of a fairground. Fortunately the baggage had nearly all been weighed out into pretty well equal parts, to avoid trouble among the porters. Even so, there were cases and kit-bags that might be a few ounces underweight, to judge by the number of cunning hands that stretched out for them so eagerly. More than once Hassan, the policeman, had to intervene between two, or even more, before they came to blows.

The porters started off as soon as they were loaded up. Cassin, Gobbi and I were the last on the beach, and it was past one o'clock when we were finally able to start the great trek. We left behind us one solitary figure—an old man who'd spent the whole morning watching us, sitting on a pile of stones and spinning some grey wool. 'Salaam! Salaam!' he croaked, as we started at last for the north.

Across the bed of an old lake

Once we had left Skardu, our way lay across a sandy desert—a real Sahara! We were, in fact, crossing the bed of a very large lake of the glacial epoch. Its underlying surface consisted of an immense moraine, whose first discovery and description we owe to Giotto Dainelli. Every now and then we ran into clay formations, curiously formed of sheet upon wafer-thin sheet of the most contorted shapes—rather like a *mille-feuille* that had been run over! Dainelli has a most ingenious and persuasive explanation for this phenomenon. During the last ice-age but one, he claims, several glaciers crept their way into the Skardu Valley basin. 'For some time, the tongues floated in the waters of the lake. In the end, they melted, to let fall their moraine-content. This, sinking to the bottom, caused the disturbance in the lake clay.' Now that the lake had disappeared, only the geological puzzle remained.

Only the presence of those immense mountains that closed in the valley—

75

Marshala (16,902 feet) right opposite us, and the peaks beyond Shigar towards Koser Gang (20,997 feet), reminded us that we were anywhere near the roof of the world. The sand was the finest possible, just like the best our own beaches could show. We joked about it with Toni Gobbi: 'Where's your bathing cabin, old boy? They must have given you one miles from the sea, we'll never get there. . . .'

That feeling of 'never getting there' deserves a word or two. Here, for the first time, we were experiencing something which we were going to become very familiar with as the days went on. These mountains and valleys are so well proportioned in their very vastness that only by dint of footing it across them, with puny, human footsteps, can one get any real idea of the scale of creation they represent. You get the same phenomenon in Tibet. In Italy, on the other hand, or in Japan, you often get the very reverse: the valleys and mountains which appear so vast turn out to be nothing of the kind, and the scale something which mere humans can encompass quite well.

Often we passed beneath walls of red rock; every now and again a gnarled and twisted stump of a tree. Forlorn, scorched-earth places, not without a certain primordial beauty. The Balti porters kept up a very fair pace, but they would make frequent stops. For the most part, they went forward in chance formations of ten or twenty. They would be slogging along when one suddenly cried '*Chavaz*' or '*Dika-Duk*', and every man would come to a halt, hanging his pack on his *matu*—a stick shaped like an ice-axe which they were never without.

After a time we came to a spring. A real marvel it was, too. Imagine the roughest and rawest place in the world, the very abode of desolation, where the rocks crumbled away under the action of sun and wind—and there, all of a sudden, out of a mountainside, gushed a torrent, a torrent of icy limpid water. We made a long stop, and highly welcome it was. We ate and drank our fill. A good few of the porters took a sluice, their bare brown bodies glistening with water and sun. Song and cheerful voices filled the air.

Towards three we took to the road again. A twist in the track turned the whole caravan into a long snake-like formation—a human serpent coiled across the plain. The white C.A.I. cases glittered like the scales of some monster in slow, silent, sinuous movement. Such was the suggestion visually. From the human point of view, the caravan appeared rather to be the migration of a whole people. There was something tragic and wonderful about it. It was as if history had put the clock back to the time of the Eruli and the Visigoths (*Plate 28*).

All over the northern and western reaches of the sky dark heavy clouds

76

were gathering. The light was almost violet. At eye level, an infinity of sand and rock, still glinting in the sun, seemed the very scene of Judgment Day, ready to receive the boundless multitude come to judgment. The afternoon squall was blowing up harder and harder. A few poor withered leaves whirled round and round.

Onward, onward! We were making a fair pace now over the vast plain. From Skardu to Shigar—fifteen miles. Quite an accomplishment for the first day out. The scene once more put me in mind of Tibet—the stretch of country between Phari Dzong and Gyantse, for example. But in Tibet there was no green isle like the oasis of Shigar, which we were now approaching. A green isle in a wide, wide sea of dun-coloured rock.

Memories of Tibet came back to me too when we met with a merchant on the march. He had a little white horse, with the short legs and thick hide that are typical of Central Asia, loaded with stuffs of every colour; he was off to the villages in the valley to sell them. The horse had a little harness-bell round his neck. Its monotonous tinkle was with us for a long time, till at last it died away into the distance.

The following table shows the various *parao* or stages between Skardu and the Base Camp. Distances are approximate, based on figures we were given in Skardu. Altitude, in most cases, is also approximate.

Expedition stage				Milage covered			Height climbed in feet
Skardu–Shigar ..	..	..	..	15	..	..	7,260– 7,600
Shigar–Kashumal	..	..	..	12	..	..	7,600– 7,800
Kashumal–Dasso	..	..	..	13½	..	..	7,800– 8,150
Dasso–Chagpo	..	..	..	12	..	..	8,150– 8,600
Chagpo–Chongo	..	..	..	9½	..	..	8,600– 9,400
Chongo–Askole	..	..	..	5½	..	..	9,400– 9,750
Askole–Korophon	..	..	..	7½	..	..	9,750–10,400
Korophon–Bardumal ..	..	..	..	5½	..	..	10,400–10,750
Bardumal–Payu	..	..	..	9½	..	..	10,750–11,050
Payu–Liligo ..	..	..	..	6	..	..	11,050–12,190
Liligo–Urdukass	..	..	..	7½	..	..	12,190–13,160
Urdukass–Biange	..	..	..	5½	..	..	13,160–13,600
Biange–Gore ..	..	..	..	6	..	..	13,600–14,300
Gore–Concordia	..	..	..	5½	..	..	14,300–14,900
Concordia–Upper Baltoro	..	..	..	6	..	..	14,900–15,900
Upper Baltoro–Base Camp ..	..	..	..	5½	..	..	15,900–16,750

Total 132

A meal on the polo-field

We reached Shigar about half past five in the evening of 29th May. The weather had considerably worsened and we marched through a drizzle of rain in a fading light. There was a nip to the dank air, too. We went on for a stretch past our green isle. The track lay beneath *byer-pa* (poplars), *sarsing* (willows) and *chuli* (apricots) across well-watered fields full of fine fresh grain. Every now and then we came across dwellings made with those humble mud bricks which turn grey with damp and sweat with the odours of a sink. Men greeted us, women usually fled or hid their faces, children tagged on to us like a comet's tail, and the tail grew thicker and thicker. By the time we reached the polo-ground we had a whole little crowd of them with us, all silence and wonderment. The polo-field is the 'village green' of all the villages in this part of the world—a stretch of grass quite level and well-kept, say a hundred yards long and thirty wide. The boys studied us intently for some time, then they grew bold and started playing polo, but it was poor man's polo, without ponies. They employ a ball and sticks, no more than the Valdostani for their Sunday *fiollet* games.

The porters straggled up in dribs and drabs. We soon put up our own tents. Gobbi had all the loads stacked up in piles, one for every locality the porters hailed from. Slowly, mournfully and very still, night came down on us, among the trees of the Shigar oasis. We lit the fire. Mauri and Oberto cooked our meal, trying at the same time to impress the principles of the operation on Murad, the cook.

Murad, Murad the Mournful, was a tall, studious-looking fellow with the slow and measured movements of an ecclesiastic. A figure of great dignity. Every single act of his life, one would have thought, was part of a ritual in which he had a weighty role to play. He was the last person one would ever have reckoned on finding in such an expedition. Who put us in touch with him? I can't remember. At Skardu we had a long and fruitless hunt for a cook. At one moment it looked as if Ali might come along with us. This would have been a stroke of luck indeed! Quite apart from the fact that he spoke very fair English, and had his smattering of Italian, he was quick, he was honest, he would have knuckled down to all the troubles and trials of caravan life, and we liked him. But unfortunately he held a Government post: he was chow-kidar at the Rest House. It came out that the P.A. had told him he could tag along with us, certainly—but, alas, when he came back to Skardu he'd find someone else in his job. Of course Ali had no answer to that one. He had to give up all ideas of the Expedition. We lost a precious addition to it that time.

78

Murad was Hobson's choice. I'll learn, he told us, and I'll go wherever you take me. He appeared to have been some small Skardu innkeeper, head over heels in debt—business troubles. The Expedition proved his salvation: it would enable him, if not to pay off his debts, at least to keep up the interest on them. All this I learned from Captain Dar, in one of his kinder moments.

These, unfortunately, had soon grown to be very few and far between. From Shigar onwards, the Captain was to leave us with anything but happy memories.

The first night out with a big caravan is always a tricky business. Too many little things haven't yet settled down into a system. We had scarcely got the gear sorted before we had to start giving out the porters' rations. It was dark. It was drizzling. In the flickering light of a small lamp we had to calculate how many times seventeen went into four ounces, or how many ounces there were in 424 at a fifth of an ounce per head—and all this on soggy paper with a pencil that wouldn't write. Or else we had to improvise various devices for opening tins, or closing up sacks, or extracting small portions of butter, or measuring out spoonfuls of tea. An hour had pretty well gone by before we got through these chores. My companions had finished their supper. Oberto, bless him, had heated up a portion for me, and at last I sat down by the fire, hungry as a hunter, to devour it. Captain Dar was eating late, too, delayed by some self-imposed surveillance of our organizational powers. Both of us were getting to the end of our tether.

I was savouring the first spoonful when along came one of the porters extraordinary with a saucepan in his hand. He asked me for the condiments. In the general confusion I must have forgotten to give them out with the rest of the food.

'Half a mo',' I said. 'Just let me finish this, and I'll be with you.'

It would only mean two or three minutes' wait for him, at the most. But the Captain, who was also eating, came over to me with a jeer on his face.

'You,' he observed, 'haven't you got condiments on your plate? Or am I mistaken?'

'Well, what of it?'

'There speaks the real slave-driver! He can eat, he can stuff his belly full. The porters can starve. Hasn't it dawned on you they want the condiments?'

'Ah, my dear Captain,' I told him. 'There speaks a noble soul! A perfect, generous heart! But what have you to do with us? We're but poor human-kind, sadly imperfect—so I'm just finishing off these few spoonfuls before I go and see to the porters.'

'You're not finishing——'

'Yes, I'm finishing them all right.'

We were really being as silly as two children wrangling over a toy horse. But there are moments when the very mildest of us will see red. Suddenly I didn't want another mouthful. I hurled my plate, and what was left on it, down to the ground. The Captain had a piece of bread or something in his hand, and he did likewise with that. For one moment—or so my companions said later—it looked as if we were coming to blows. My memory of the incident is a little confused, but I do remember growling: 'This isn't an expedition, it's a perambulating concentration-camp. D'you know what you're behaving like? Some poke-nose policeman! For God's sake let us have a little peace.'

Riccardo, the nicest of fellows, and Captain Akram, a peaceable youngster with his head screwed on the right way, tried to persuade us to make it up, and once I had stopped seeing red I held my hand out to the Captain, inviting him to forget the whole childish scene and bury the hatchet. But he refused. We withdrew to our tents in a huff. The evening was dank, nasty and black. But we felt blacker.

Half an hour later, however, I got a tardy laugh out of the silly business. I could feel a hand gently prowling the outside of my tent for the flap. It was Taqi:

'Sahib . . . the condiments . . . ?'

It was the 'poor porters' who'd suffered. I was sorry.

The great serpent between two banks of eyes: Shigar

Shigar is not only a rare beauty-spot. It interests the traveller on various grounds. It was a pity we had to hurry on. Its oasis may well be the richest and best cared for in all Baltistan. Some figures alone give a striking idea of it: fifteen kilometres long, it has some 20,000 inhabitants. Village succeeds village—every one of them lost in the thickest clusters of trees that one can imagine.

From the earliest times Shigar has been ruled by a Rajah. One legend which I heard several times on the spot, and which was not lost upon Giotto Dainelli, tells how in the beginning an eagle flew from Gilgit carrying in its claws a boy, an upstanding smiling boy. The shepherds took him and looked after him. Soon he became a young man of exceptional strength and beauty, and the people wanted him for their Rajah.

The legend had its core of truth as legends often have. Those who know this part of the world claim that there is a good deal of local evidence pointing to the fact that the aristocracy was drawn from Gilgit and Hunza. The route from Hunza to Shigar, across the Hispar glaciers, the Nushik Pass (16,339 feet) and the Arandu Valley was naturally known from the most ancient times. Shigar is not only richer than Skardu, it may well be more ancient. Clearly men found perfect living conditions here—height 7,800 feet, southerly aspect and abundant water. At Skardu, the probability is that there was nothing but the fortress on the rock near the confluence of the Shigar and the Indus—a meeting-place of valleys, caravans and passes. At Shigar there are a number of old houses, some of great beauty. There is a Rajah's 'palace' and, although I had no time to see them, there are apparently Buddhist remains and several mosques, some of them quite richly adorned.

We woke to splendid sun, whose shafts speared the greenery high over the polo-ground with gleams of gold and shadows of green. Some rain had fallen in the night. Everything was fresh and smelt of new-washed earth. After breakfast (fire, smoke and curses!) the porters took up their loads, 'hurling themselves on to their packs like so many beasts', as one of us noted in his diary. The high-altitude porters tried to get things ship-shape, but it was a wearing business, and nearly drove them to their wits' end. The poor Balti 'pack-horses', for centuries only too used to lying low and keeping quiet, would not co-operate. If ever they are to be led back to the human dignity of independent beings, it will be a long and difficult road. At last the caravan moved off.

Once more the giant serpent was threading its way through the valley and on either side, like the banks of a river, were two banks of curious eyes. We were one of the sights of the year. Hundreds of men and youngsters and children lined the polo-ground to give us a cheer, to take stock of us, to stare at all our strange accoutrements, to hear the strange and incomprehensible tongues we spoke. We were the mysterious men from the Great Outside—the magicians of the pill-box and the machines. We had boxes that could talk and pieces of glass that could see, medicine bottles that could cure and—money, money, rivers of money. Where did we hail from, where were we going—and why all this? But perhaps their thoughts didn't run in those channels after all; perhaps, to these crowds, we were just a phenomenon of nature like a comet, a tempest, or a bird never seen before.

The Shigar children were fascinating. A few words of Balti, and you could count on a reply and a laugh every time. No silly shyness, no gawking. Yet the women we saw hardly at all. They had but to glimpse us in the distance and they would either cover their faces or run miles. Odd! In this little corner of the world there is such a warm welcome waiting for you in the very air, in the sun, in the mighty mountains sheeted with ice—and in the men

F

with their peaceful talk, in the serene and bearded patriarchs, in the healthy laughing boys with flowers stuck under their hats—there's such a welcome in all this, in nature and humanity alike, that it strikes cold and heavy to see the womenfolk run away and hide, as if we had brought pestilence or plague. The men sit out in the sun, smoking and talking of this and that, while their wives and sisters and daughters are working in the fields, nothing but bent backs in the long grass—cowering like scalded cats and dressed in hazy violet or a rusty brown. Such is the vague wan colouring of the rags they wear, and their mood matches it. They show not the slightest desire to sing or smile.

How hard it must have been for them, I thought, that transition from the liberty they enjoyed under the Buddhist cult to the serf-status of the Moslem era. True, the Koran need not be interpreted so rigidly in this direction —look at Turkey. But in this remote backwater what could you expect but bigotry? What a difference in the women of Tibet! There, they hold their heads high, just like their menfolk. They will greet you with assurance, they laugh when they want to, they take charge when they have to, they buy and sell and travel—all without let or hindrance. And yet the Tibetan women remain superbly womanly. Even the old tough ones still do up their hair in the 108 little plaits or coils and take endless trouble with the rancid butter, their cosmetic and their safeguard from the sun. . . .

Soon after we had left the polo-ground we came upon the mosque of Shigar, in part quite recently renovated (*Plate 1*). It was of great interest. I am speaking without the book, but I don't think I am far wrong in saying that it suggests a Buddhist temple adapted to Allah. First and foremost, there is the general form of the edifice: in substance it is one chamber, rectangular in shape. Surrounding it is an arcade whose roof is supported by wooden pillars some twenty-five feet high, with capitals of the characteristic form that is found right across Eurasia, from Macedonia to Japan. Most striking of all, the pinnacle on the tower vividly recalls the *chorten*—pagodas—of all those Buddhist structures to be seen throughout Asia, which are at the same time reliquaries and symbolic representations of the Universe. This particular pinnacle, it turned out, was very new indeed, dating only from the previous year: it had been modelled on a larger and more ancient version crowning the mosque of Shah Hamadan at Srinagar. If we bear in mind the history of these countries, we can accept without astonishment the fact of an architectural conception passing from one religion into another. Even ritual can do the same. For that matter has not Christianity sometimes adapted its churches—at Syracuse and Rome, to give only two examples—from the temples of the classical world?

And was not the Basilica the Tribunal, the Chamber, and perhaps also the money-market, of Ancient Rome?

I paused for some time in this mosque. With a sympathetic guide, most eager to show me everything, I examined the carved wood panelling around the door and windows—peasant craftsmanship at its best. The decorative motifs were a rich mixture of Indian elements from the plains (today's Pakistan) and traces of a more distant world of Chinese culture. Typically Buddhist is the linked cross pattern shown in *Plate 19*.

After leaving the mosque we trekked for some hours through the villages and the gardens of the Shigar oasis. Every now and again, over beyond the river, or through a gap in the branches of the trees, we caught a glimpse of those great snow-mantled heights and the glaciers and ice-walls linking peak to peak. They were the last outcrop of the chain that begins with Rakaposhi (25,550 feet) over between Gilgit and Hunza, continues with the Haramosh (24,270 feet) and ends at last in the precipices of rock that tower over the River Shigar.

Smiles, rupees and growls

The next stage of our trek, from Shigar to Kashumal, was quite a lengthy one, but it was pleasant going, pretty well on the flat all the time, and much of it through garden and orchard. At times the greenery broke off and we were crossing desert again: stone, sand and a few wretched stumps of trees.

On our left (that is to say, on the right bank of the River Shigar as it flows roughly southwards) we saw a stupendous chain of mountains covered with snow and ice. They were not the real giants, but their outline was rugged and striking, and the rock of their lower slopes was full of beautiful, warm hues. Bonatti, Mauri and I were now walking in a group, and for a long stretch we mulled over a project, reserved for some dim future, of conducting climbing campaigns to these peaks. They were high enough and difficult enough to offer a challenge of the highest class, and yet just near enough to civilization, and sufficiently out of the colossus class, to make a full-scale expedition unnecessary. To our right we caught glimpse after fleeting glimpse of the Koser Gang Peak (20,997 feet)—climbed as long ago as 1899 by the American Bullock-Workmans, husband and wife, with Mattia Zurbriggen as guide. We also saw the valley giving access to the Skoro-La, a pass 16,749 feet in height, leading straight into Askole. It was crossed by the Duke of the Abruzzi's Expedition in 1909, by some sections of the Duke of Spoleto's party in 1929, and by the K2 climbers of 1954. Umberto Balestrieri also climbed a peak to the west of the pass—the Cheri-Chor (17,881 feet). Just here, we were on classic Italian mountaineering territory. Some such echo from the past is always welcome. But then, might it not be a better thing to seek out some virgin territory for a goal? Thousands of kilometres of immense mountains stretch out towards Nepal or Bhutan—unknown, mysterious, mesmeric.

At various points in our march we passed low square or rectangular structures; often the stone was worn away and sometimes a carpet of grass or wild flowers covered it. These were *mazar*, the tombs of *pir* (holy Moslems). Some were obviously tended with veneration. Little coloured flags were planted by them. Others suffered from oblivion and neglect. Here was a clear pointer to the fact that we were crossing country inhabited by the faithful of the Shiite cult. For most Moslems veneration of saints is tantamount to idolatry; here the proud relentless granite monotheism of Islam makes generous allowances, for once, to the human need to worship not the Supreme alone but also the exceptional being in whom His light shines most resplendently.

Then, between two villages, on the flat roof of a house whose outer wall marked the boundary of the track, we saw a girl: a pretty one with—at last—a smile. But I had scarcely pointed the view-finder in her direction before she disappeared, and a chorus of old ladies began to growl at us. We were just going on again when the really unexpected happened. The girl called us back with a movement of her fingers (familiar to us in Europe too!) which made it plain that for a good baksheesh we would get a good photograph. The chorus of old ladies calmed down at this and began to smile. So we offered a rupee. Oh, no! One wasn't enough. Two? Never! Five? All right then, five.

Late that afternoon the sky became overcast. An air of gloom began to weigh down over the valley. We stopped for a mouthful under a group of poplars. Then I hung behind for a while; I had met a little man with a flute. A fat and dirty-looking vagabond he was, too, but his playing charmed the whole countryside. I was lucky enough to get hold of the porter who had our tape-recording machine inside his pack, and, by offering the flautist a small sum, I was able to record part of his thin, enchanting little tune.

I was giving my whole attention to the business in hand, inside the court-yard of some rustic dwelling, when Captain Dar suddenly appeared. He stopped at the gate, as if he was going to spring on me! There was such a scowl on his face that not only did the poor musician abandon his playing; a handful of humble folk had gathered to watch the fun and they took to their heels.

'Maraini,' said Dar, 'today you've done a most terrible thing!'

'Oh?' I answered. 'What?'

'You have dared to photograph a woman. D'you think we're in your country? In this one women are not seen, they are not approached, they are not photographed. . . .'

Dar's complaint was grotesque, all the more so because the bargain— a mighty dear one for us—had been of the girl's own proposing. She it was who had suggested selling us her cover-girl smile. I tried to reason with the Captain. I told him he ought to be pleased that when we went back home we should at least have this one happy, healthy face to show for our trip (*Plate 14*); we had plenty of dismal ones. Sad, often diseased, they lined the route to stare at us as we passed.

'Besides, Captain,' I went on, 'in our country too there are plenty of places where cameras aren't too popular. I remember once I was at Pente-dattilo, in Calabria. I'd seen a face in a window, a perfect incarnation of Mediterranean beauty. I was just going to take the picture when out came a man with a ferocious moustache. He banged the gate in my face and rasped, "You dare start photographing here!" You'd have thought from his expression that he was warning me against robbery with violence.'

This little story helped to calm the Captain's alarm. I think he was pleased to know that such irrational antics were not the monopoly of Baltistan. Well, let's hope he was. Let's hope I was beginning to see what made him tick, and even feel a certain friendliness towards the fellow. The impression we had to avoid at all costs was that of looking down our noses at him. He'd rear up at us like a cobra. But let him realize all humanity had its foibles—and that nobody dare cast the first stone—and all might be well.

For the rest of the day, as far as Kashumal, we kept together. Very slowly, talking of all sorts of different things, we seemed to reach a better understanding. Just before we reached Kashumal, something happened which couldn't have been more welcome: we shook hands, and the hatchet was buried.

Saucepans, and that mythical being—the Expedition

Kashumal means 'the place of the apple trees'[1] but in the spot where we pitched our tents there was only a handful of dried-up apricot trees in the middle of a sandy plain. We were close to the huge gravel-bed of the River Shigar: the stream itself just now was a mere trickle, a long way out. The sun was brilliant again, without a cloud any longer. The colours of evening made the mountains an enchanting sight. The air was still. The sand had the dry smell of powdered rock. In the great desert silence, voices, laughter, curses,

1. W. Kick, 'Place Names in Northern Baltistan', *The Mountain World*, 1956–7, p. 195 Kick gives the spelling KUSHUMAL. The local pronunciation seemed to me better indicated by KASHUMAL.

and the songs the porters sang as they made their evening meal, all had a strange sound-effect. Rather than break the silence, they seemed to underline it.

The men split up into groups of twenty or thirty. After they had piled their cases and their kit-bags, they lit a fire from wood they had collected and began heating up the water for their tea in an iron pot. Others were mixing flour and water and rolling out the paste thus obtained on a smooth stone. When it reached the desired consistency, they would take a lump and shape it into a 'bread bun' with their fingers. Then they would pat it between the palms of their hands to make the texture uniformly soft and light. A *chupatty* was then ready for the hot metal 'bakestone'. A tastier and more extravagant form of *chupatty* is called *paranta*. This is fried in butter (*ghee*) of the type seen all over India and Pakistan and up among these mountains too. Others made sauce for the *chupatty* with curry and *dahl* (lentils). The general rule was for one group of men all to come from the same village.

All this time, the high-altitude porters would be helping us get our tents up. In every expedition these porters extraordinary turn their hands to a little personal service for the sahibs, and each of us had by now picked the man of his choice from the pool. Cassin, for instance, had Haji Ali, a distinguished and emaciated old fellow with a salt-and-pepper beard who followed him about everywhere. They had already explored a good many highlands, valleys and glaciers together in the Desio Expedition of 1953. The two men were full of mutual esteem and got on well, though one spoke a Northern Italian dialect and the other Urdu. The trick was in the intonation of the voice and the accompanying expression. It made much better sense than the mutually incomprehensible spoken word.

I myself found a porter who, when it came to the simpler forms of photography, proved an intelligent assistant. Haji Ismael would tag along with me on the march with a case full of gear—cameras, film, tripods. He was very small and very thin—all sinew, muscle and bone: not very strong, I should have said, but intelligent, willing and good-natured. From his appearance you would have put him down as being somewhere between forty and fifty. He had whitening hair, networks of wrinkles and a little grey beard. Yet he swore he was only twenty-six. I got several of us, including Dar, to try and catch him out. Impossible: he always gave the same figure. Well, life was a bitterly hard business in the remote villages, and thirty gave everyone quite an elderly look. Haji Ismael might have anticipated a general fate by four or five years. Both he and Cassin's Ali were 'Hajis'—a style to which no one has the right until he has made the pilgrimage to Mecca. But members of the Shiite sect

86

need not go so far. They have a Mecca of their own: the object of their pilgrimage is the tomb of Hussein, Mahomet's luckless nephew, at Karbala in Iraq. A visit there will make a man a rightful 'Haji'. Like Ali again, Ismael appeared to have done his bit of travelling (soldiering for the Allied armies, during the war and after). Their experience of the outside world had broadened their minds, and gave them a halo of glory in the eyes of their fellow countrymen.

We ourselves had paired off, two to a tent. Our original idea had been to keep moving round. In this way we had felt we should get to know one another better, and we should be all one clan instead of a number of fixed groups. In the end, however, instinct got the upper hand. Mutual attractions, in the way of similar tastes and habits, won the day. It may not seem so, but the intimacies of tent life run deep. For instance, one man may want to read for a few minutes when he goes to bed. The other might want the light out straight away. One will get through the night, or long spells of it, without moving. Another may not be able to keep half so still. There is the neat and tidy man with a place for everything: it can be torture for him to share a tent with the type that throws his clothes all over the place and leaves everything just where it falls. Bonatti made a pair with Mauri, quite naturally. They were the babies of the party, fast friends who had done great things together in the Alps and the Andes. Cassin and De Francesch, Gobbi and Oberto made two other pairs who got on well together. Dr. Zeni and I were the best of friends and shared for a long time, till all my photographer's gear began to take up too much space and forced me into a 'Pamir' tent of my own. Captain Dar naturally had his own tent, and for the moment he shared it with Captain Akram.

Our camp was a Tower of Babel. Balti, Italian, English, Urdu and the dialect of Lombardy made one glorious jumble from morning till night. Translation was vitally necessary to progress and the onus of it nearly always fell on my shoulders. I was always one of the last to be able to sit down to a meal, or go to bed. I couldn't spend ten minutes taking photographs or turning film without having to explain to some interrupter that '*thrommo-chu*' meant 'hot water' or that '*vai al diavolo*' could be rendered 'go to hell'. It was too much of a burden. I hoped I could stay the pace. The main thing was the film. I certainly didn't want that to suffer. The truth is that the camera-man, in any expedition, should be free to do his job, and his job only. I would go further and say that taking photographs and taking moving film are two distinct métiers, and there should be one man to each. Seeing things with a photographic eye and seeing them with a 'cinema' eye is quite different. It is the static opposed to the dynamic. Each brings a totally distinct viewpoint to bear on panorama, persons and events.

Then again, interpreting for the most part means something rather more complicated than taking simple statements from one tongue and putting them in another. With such phrases as '*thrommo-chu*' and '*vai al diavolo*', of course, it is plain sailing. But more often than not the matter to be rendered is more complex, the personalities engaged in the argument may be at daggers drawn, and in such cases it is difficult for the interpreter to remain a mere uninvolved and passive instrument. I found myself on a battle-ground: on one side were the porters, given full support by Captain Dar, and sometimes, if the truth were known, egged on by him; and on the other side my companions, whose very reasonable wish it was to go ahead as fast as possible, and give the Italian Alpine Club good value for the money they had provided us with.

Today for example (31st May) up came the question of the saucepans. The porters, ordinary and extraordinary, had an ugly habit of making their requests not once and for all but in little dribs and drabs. Today our high-altitude men, plus the policeman and the cook, seventeen persons altogether, informed us that they had no pots and pans for their cooking. 'The Expedition' (that mythical being, as mythical as the robbers of a 'robber government') should provide. If the Expedition didn't provide, they might see about going home again.

The problem would not, indeed, appear at first sight to be a transcendental one, though the proportions it took on within our international, inter-linguistic, inter-cultural and inter-religious society were grave, nay, momentous. Those there were who maintained that the applicants should learn the hard way. Others were in favour of gentle persuasion. The Captain was always coming out with some little taunt which I thought might just as well be left untranslated; while the porters, who knew all the answers, were determined to ram home all their demands good and hard. The business was settled at last when we accepted the offer made by a porter ordinary; he was to go down to Skardu at full speed, buy the pots and pans and catch up with us a few stages higher.

In the general way the common-or-garden porters, simple rustics and herdsmen, whether they came from Satpara or Kapalu or Hushe or Shigar or Askole, were much—ah, how much—better than their exalted brethren, the porters extraordinary. The latter were full of pretensions out of all proportion to their real worth. The ordinary porters drew less money, asked for neither rations nor blankets (for the moment they found places to sleep in the villages we passed through), they carried twice the weight and they were fine fellows, modest in their demands and nearly always in a good humour. At most, if they passed you or caught you up on the march, they would ask for *shikre*—a cigarette.

I was lucky to have a smattering of Balti. With the help of Haji Ismael (*nge ushtad*, my teacher) I made my daily effort to increase my vocabulary and to grasp something of the grammar. As I have already said, what we had here was a Tibetan dialect, and very often I came across vocables and items of grammar to remind me of the great language of the Asian highlands which I had studied and spoken a few years previously. Very often, when none too sure of a word, I would resort to the Tibetan equivalent, pronouncing it according to the script—and nearly always with good results. One morning, for example, I was beaten by the all-important verb 'to do, to execute'. In Tibetan, it is *che* by pronunciation, but it is written *byed*. Pronounced thus, it was instantly understood by Haji Ismael, though the Balti pronunciation is closer to *bed*. Balti has some words, however, which seem quite innovatory, and I have failed to see where they come from. Turkish or Arabic? It might help to know these languages. *Bustring*, woman, is one such word. *Astana*, tomb, is another.

However, this was not the most propitious moment for philological research! Nor was it exactly an unadulterated thirst for knowledge which spurred me on. My object was simply communication: to break through the language barrier which can so cruelly isolate men, especially when they belong to different civilizations. Clearly I lacked the verbal resources to enter into philosophic discussion, and it is doubtful if our Balti friends would have appreciated it in any case. They were simple souls, rude, rustic, unveneered; fundamentally good men, lovers of peace and a sight more honest than most human beings on the multiform face of this planet, Earth.

It was incredible how great a gap one could bridge with a few words. To be able to ask one of the porters, while sitting over the fire with him, or taking a rest at the side of the track: 'What village d'you come from? How many sons have you got? Have you been in these parts before? What are you going to do with the money you earn?' To be able to understand his answer; to satisfy his curiosity about us; to crack a joke about the hard work, the sun, the long trek and life's little ironies—this was a pleasure indeed. Some such little touch will put two human beings into communication, and bring down that absurd barrier between the 'mysterious Sahib' and the 'inscrutable Man from the East'.

Slowly the sun sank down over the distant mountain crags beyond Arandu. Within that circle lay the Hispar Glacier. Night fell over the valley. Firelight from our camp took on a deep, vivid, dancing orange sheen. It wasn't cold, only fresh. All of us knew well enough that before long we should be up against nature in a rougher, more implacable form. So we made the most of

89

this moment with an almost sensuous pleasure. We enjoyed the colour, the breeze, and some music too—one of the porters had brought out a flute!

The men gathered round in a circle as if for some festival. Each district came out with one of its traditional songs: some twenty or thirty voices would sing, while one did an age-old dance to their accompaniment. We went the rounds of them all: it might have been a competition between the various villages. Mauri took a very careful tape-recording of these songs. They begin very slowly, with one solo voice; then the rhythm gains in pace, accompanied by a clapping of the hands. This becomes rapid to the point of frenzy. The dancer follows the song, at first limiting his movements to his hands and head. But then come small steps, and, at last, complete self-abandonment to an intricate pattern of gestures and whirlwind motions—till he falls to the ground, faint and dizzy. Every village seemed to know its songs and dances. The differences between them were sometimes slight. One of the favourite motifs had a refrain which was itself an endless repetition of the word *men-dok*, flower (*Plates 44, 45, 46, 47*).

Soon we had finished our usual evening pasta and meat gravy. We took it in turns to be communal cook (Murad the Mournful clearly had no great culinary gifts, and then his services had been practically requisitioned by the Captain, who needed a Pakistani diet to remain in good health). We joined the porters, and stayed with them a long time over the songs and dances. The Captain came up to me.

'So you see what fine things I can organize? Just have a little faith in me . . .' he said.

At bottom he was a great big boy, and he loved to feel important. Possibly we were all making a gigantic mistake? What we should have done was to give him complete command of the caravan, handing over all our money and responsibility with it. He would be in his element appointed to command, and we should reach our goal with no vexations. Once or twice I pointed out the possible advantages of this arrangement; but the relations that reigned between Captain Dar and my companions were so full of nervous tension that it could not really be even contemplated. Such a solution would need harmony and mutual trust. Both these qualities, I might add, were lacking.

Let us have another look at the Balti dancing. They were transformed. The very same men who, a couple of hours before, had appeared nothing but poor, wretched pack-horses were now dancing with a pride, an elegance, a lightness of step and an absolute sureness of gesture which made us marvel. One of the finest was the Viking, the very tall 'Nordic blond' from Kaphalu (*Plate 15*). The dances we were watching had clearly been learned in earliest childhood, and they represent a rich Balti heritage. A fascinating theme to study! The whole region between the Pakistan plain and Afghanistan—right across Kafiristan and Sinkiang—is the home of these virile dances. For the most part they are war-dances: sword and shield play their part in a good many. Towards the east of the region, in Ladak, one passes into a zone of influence of the religious dances of the Lama and the sacred themes (*cham*), but several of the movements remain the same—for example, a characteristic pirouette in which the dancer jumps up and whirls round in the air at a slanting angle.

One wonders also if it is legitimate to recognize the influence of the *dervish* dance in the self-induced stupefaction of the finale. But all this is the vague speculation of the poor dilettante! Real students today have all the time in the world to get down to the subject, they pursue their ruthless inquiries everywhere, with all the modern means of research at their disposal—cinematograph, tape-recorder, the transcription and investigation of ancient texts, and so on. We were just simple mountaineers, out to climb a mountain—a mighty difficult one into the bargain. We had to put aside all thought of scientific curiosity and just abandon ourselves to the spectacle and the music.

We had only to take a few paces into the night, and the dark plain, and we could see the whole gathering as a single entity, a crowd by lamplight and firelight. The voices, the handclapping, the song itself were borne on the breeze in wave after wave, mingling with the scent of aromatic plants.

Kashumal: peace and misery

On the next night we pitched camp a fair way from Kashumal. The following morning a mere half-hour's trek brought us to the vegetation and the dwellings of the oasis. Toni Gobbi and I stayed behind to have a look round. Habitations of any sort were few and far between, scattered among apricots, poplars, willows and mulberries, on the slope of a little cone-shaped hill watered by a torrent coming down from Koser Gang (20,997 feet). Some of the houses were poor in the extreme, others of fairly solid construction: the system of interlocking beams for the walls, the framework filled in with dried clay bricks, was everywhere the same. The stairway was outside, and generally made of wood.

The people seemed very friendly. Naturally, we only saw men going about (but if we looked hard we could make out the inquisitive eyes of little girls, the sad eyes of their mothers, the bedevilled eyes of old women, peering at us out of tiny windows, or from a roof, or from the transom of a door). The men really seemed to have a flair for enjoying life. The old bodies were sitting out in the sun smoking their complicated and picturesque pipes, and those who were not quite so old worked at a primitive loom in the shade of a mulberry, or spun wool with that sureness of touch and measured gesture which comes from a lifetime's experience, for they had been at it since boyhood. Two boys, sitting by themselves, were removing their lice with tender and meticulous care. We breathed an air of utter satisfaction, of eternal peace.

'All this gives rise to a question, my dear Toni,' I observed, 'and one we have flirted with often enough, but without diminishing its underlying seriousness. Isn't it better to live in ignorance of everything—asphalt and macadam, vehicles, telephones, television, the seven or the seventy deadly machines— to live in bliss without knowing it? Or is it better to wear oneself out in the wake of fantasies and chimeras, pursuing an ever-elusive happiness?'

Toni seemed to be all for running water, and h. and c.

'Besides, even they will wake up from this torpor in the end, believe me. . . .' Then he went on: 'What should we have been, you and I, two or three centuries ago? Two brave burgesses, maybe, in some little provincial town of Europe, with a mental horizon that hardly stretched beyond it. It's exactly because of all our stirring and all our efforts that today we can know and see and comprehend such an infinity of things. Planes and telegrams and cameras and international credits, and the things that make life possible in places where once there'd have been no question of life—all those things are the fruits of the chimera-hunt. Don't you agree?'

'I suppose you're right,' I answered.

Yet what was the secret of the peace we found here?

We said a word or two to an old man. With great courtesy, he asked us into his home. We went up a steep wooden stairway and found ourselves in the typical courtyard of the Balti house. I saw a tub for rainwater, sacks of vegetables, one or two bits of gardening gear, a pile of chopped wood and a saddle. It all made me think of the fields and the seasons, of long journeys along stony mule-tracks and high mountain-passes in the wind. The sun's heat was now coming down with a vengeance. The old fellow took us into a room off the yard, a sort of living-room and kitchen, a low-pitched, smoky place. With four or five others, we sat down by the dying embers of a fire (*Plate 3*). Our host offered us some apricot-kernels. They were exquisite: like peanuts to look at, but hazel-nuts to taste. (By the way, they are one of Baltistan's chief products: large quantities are exported.) We drank tea, joined in some family chatter, and talked about our trip. The grave old fellow greeted our every phrase with a long murmur of approval. The others looked at us with wide-eyed wonder.

If this was one of the better homes of the oasis, as seemed likely from its appearance, then we were certainly in a land of paupers, or else in one that had been stripped bare for centuries. When you looked round at the lush fields, and the orchards whose yield, even without the help of an improving hand, was already so great—you were tempted to think the second theory the more likely one.

'The rule of the Dogra here,' the Captain told me, 'was a curse. Their tax-gatherers were like leeches. They would take the shirts off the people's back.'

And it was a fact that neither in this house nor in any other that I saw did we come across the slightest sign of that ancient countryman's prosperity which greets the traveller at once in Tibet. Not one object of value, not one piece of wrought metal: no arms, no rich stuffs, nothing but the bare minimum to cater for the humblest needs. Even the jewellery of the womenfolk was just a pauper's trinkets, whose interest lay in their design and colour alone. The artistic influence was that of Tibet or Mongolia rather than the Punjab or Kashmir.

Even in the people's expression you can often see that needless humility which comes from long misrule by greedy and pitiless rulers. They have no pride, the poor Balti. Certainly it might prove dangerous to treat them too badly, but their very anger would be only that of the beaten dog, who bites all and sundry indiscriminately. You would never risk the proud rejoinder from them, still less a slap in the face. As a nation, they have borne with a long, long sickness. I was beginning to understand now why the porters asked for so few things at a time. They were so used to having their backs against the wall. It was second nature to them to feel their way carefully, stealthily. What else could you expect from the weak and the maltreated? What other weapon had they, these people for whom power had always been something hated, lodged elsewhere?

When we left, we gave our host a rupee. He thanked us for it again and again—this humble sum (1s. 6d. or 20¢) is something in a country where a workman will earn three in a day, and probably no more. Common currency is extremely rare still. It is only in the last few years that it has come into the hands of the ordinary people at all. Yet Baltistan is not poor; fruit, for instance, could be grown on an intensive scale. You get a combination of conditions which is very rare, except in really good seasons, elsewhere: excellent soil, enriched by a sun that is always shining, and all the water you want, from the glaciers.

'In the end there'll be another thing, too,' smiled Toni. 'One day there'll be tourism!'

93

'Yes, by 2058, perhaps. Then it will be possible to stretch out in your chair at the Koser Gang Hotel, while they recharge your atomic motor. Then it'll be off again along the Baltoro motor-road to Payù-Kulm.'

Tandara: small paradise in a large desert

We left the Kashumal oasis to find ourselves in real desert. Every so often, a little stone cairn—a *burji*—would keep us from straying off the track. The sun was very powerful. It was time to try and take some measures against it, or we should have been roasted. We had to remember that we were 8,000 feet up, and at the same latitude as Malta. On our right, now, we never lost sight of the glacier of Koser Gang (20,997 feet).

The Bullock-Workmans are some of the most important travellers to have explored this part of the world, and it is impossible to pass this way without feeling beholden to them (envious, too, perhaps!) for their venture. They were an American couple, evidently not without private means, whose first idea was to tour Asia by bicycle. But having reached Kashmir they wanted to have a look at Baltistan, and when they saw it they came under the spell of these huge mountains. From then on (1898) they lived for this region, dedicating to it years of travel, study and research. They were first in the field at the glaciers of Chogo-Lungma ('The Great Mother of the Country') and among the very first to cross the Hispar, the Biaho and Siachen. They reached the higher slopes of Nun Kun (23,458 feet) and traversed almost all the principal valleys of the Karakoram, recording their travels in a number of books.

Neither of them had received a really scientific training in preparation for their travels, but they often took topographers and naturalists along with them. In 1908, and again in 1911, one of their companions was Count Cesare Calciati, who surveyed the best part of the Hispar Glacier and the valleys adjacent to the Masherbrum range. Their guides—the Zurbriggens, the Savoyes, the Reys, Meligas and Chenoz—were men from the Italian Alps, from Macugnaga or Courmayeur.

After some hours' march, we all joined up for a haversack lunch at a tiny oasis which really did seem to belong to Paradise: Tandara. We were besieged on all sides by a sun-scorched wilderness, an expanse without a shadow or a blade of grass. But just here were trees, greenery, grass, flowers and a stream of fresh, limpid, laughing water. There were some ten houses in Tandara, and five families. Some of the inhabitants turned out to come and smoke a pipe with us, and offered us dried apricots. We ate our lunch, then we sat back and enjoyed the rest and the song of the water among the stones, and the murmur of the wind in the poplars. Beyond the valley rose mountain peaks we did not know, crowned with still, translucent clouds (*Plate 10*).

All of us generally started off together on these marches, but everybody had his own pace, and in the end we all split up. The Captain was capable of some great feats. We would see him disappear over the horizon and he was nearly always the first to reach the day's stopping-point. A very fine walker. Circumstances saw to it that Haji Ismael and I, however, were always last of the line; I made many stops to take stills or film. Not only that, but we often met travellers and we would stop for a word with them, always glad to learn anything we could about the path we were following, or the district we were going through.

Once we had left Tandara behind we marched for hour upon hour in the heat of a tropical afternoon and found nothing that could be called an oasis. We saw only one sign of men, too: a tiny mill, working cheerfully all on its own. The motive power was supplied by a waterfall, adapted on the same ingenious system as can be found anywhere from here to the Caucasus, as Vittorio Sella had discovered.

Onward, onward. Every so often I would catch up with Gobbi, and we finished together that day. It had seemed one of the longest. A journey without end. Still one more sandy plain to traverse, one more stretch of sloping and shifty ground, one more dry gravel-bed. We passed the place where the Braldu joins up with the Shigar, and we left to westward the Basha Valley, with its hot springs and its track through to Arandu (9,678 feet)—one of the highest villages in Baltistan, opposite Chogo-Lungma. At long last we crossed the Braldu by raft and by the time we reached Dasso the daylight had gone.

The Braldu gorges: jewels—and goitres

Up in the mountains above Dasso, we learned, precious stones were to be found. But the village turned out to be a poverty-stricken place, the very opposite of what you might expect from a 'jewel-market'. We camped in a meadow near the river, and the *lambardar*—the mayor—came to pay us a welcoming visit. He was a man who clearly hadn't starved, most respectful in manner. He wore a little turban and an old Allied-armies battledress blouse, and he was never without a riding switch. He had brought us eggs and chickens, the former exceedingly small and the latter exceedingly tough. Yet it was a pleasant change to see fresh food. Even after a few days, we were beginning to get tired of tins.

We were well into the Braldu Valley here. It was a far cry indeed from the broad, straight, gently sloping valley of Shigar which we had left behind

95

us. Here, glaciers and torrents had scooped out the rock; the river ran a tortuous, crashing course between huge crags that had come tumbling down the
steep mountainside. The mountains hemmed us in. It was like being in a narrow
ditch. The high peaks glistening with ice were out of our range down here.
The track very soon became hard going. As far as Dasso, one could have
done it on horseback, had one had a mind to. From here on, it was a footpath
and no more.

We left Dasso next morning in dazzling sunlight. The sky, where we
could see it for light cloud, mountain peaks and the ramparts of our valley,
was a vivid blue. The shadows in the valley, by contrast, seemed mysterious
things that might have stolen out of grottoes. Before long, we were doing a
stiff climb up to a plain some 2,000 feet higher. Apparently there was some
barrier ahead of us, a stretch of sheer cliff which could not be climbed. Hence
the deviation; only in winter when the river was frozen could the route follow
it without veering off for a while. At last we came down to the gravel-bed
again, making our descent through the unstable masses and the loose sand of an
ancient moraine deposit.

Coming to the nearest point in our route to the river, I found the two
captains, Dar and Akram, taking a dip—plunging like thunderbolts into the
icy, whirling, mud-coloured waters of the Braldu. I joined in. But I had to
admit that the water felt like ice that had hardly had time to melt. (This was
actually the case!) One second of it, up to the neck, was like being held in a
jaw of a million teeth. On the bank once again, however, the sun soon seeped
in, warm and comforting.

For some days the two captains had been keeping each other company
on the march. An excellent thing, because Akram was the opposite of rough
and rude, his personality had balance and he was full of common sense. Naturally their conversation was bound to turn again and again to the 'problem of
those Italians'. The influence of Akram on Dar could only be for good. Actually,
after his outburst at Kashumal and the resulting peace, there had been a few
days of splendid isolation on Dar's part. But now I saw that he was trying to
make advances to us with a cordiality hitherto unknown: relations were to
assume a new and friendly basis. I hoped so! Today, while we were sunning
ourselves on a boulder, Cassin, Bonatti and Mauri happened to pass by. Said
Dar:

'It seems your friends are real sportsmen. I really do believe by now that
you haven't come here for questionable motives.'

'You thought we were spies?' I asked.

'Don't forget that we're at war,' came the reply—the reference being to the state of permanent 'half-war' between Pakistan and India, over Kashmir. 'And in times like these you've got to keep your eyes open.'

'Well, I'm very glad that's off your mind. There's always a bond between sportsmen of every country, isn't there? That's what ought to give us a team spirit in this bid for the mountain. Besides, the porters have only to tell there's some sort of tension between us and they'll get everything they can out of it. The going will get more difficult every day. . . .'

'Agreed, you're perfectly right. Those cursed bastards have got no idea of making a pact and keeping to it. They want a kick in the behind. You pay them up to the hilt of the contract, so it's up to them to do their part.'

'Yes, Captain. But they're good chaps at heart. . . .'

This was a sudden change of attitudes and a comic one! Here was the Captain going for the Balti while I took up their defence. I liked this role much better. The Balti had many faults I wasn't blind to, but I had always had a great liking for them. I could never quite forget that their negative side was the heritage of centuries of misrule. Where everything is forbidden, and where everybody is treated like a slave from the cradle to the grave, the arts of subtle substitution and evasion are soon learned if the Government is to be outwitted —the Mafia provides a conspicuous example from our own history. No one working for a certain end ever ventures to declare it, for fear of being frustrated from the start. To go from A to B, you proceed via a mythical unknown, C. This distracts the attention of the onlooker from your real goal.

But the Balti people have some fine qualities too. They are honest, they serve you faithfully and they are high-spirited. Physically they are strong; above all in the show of resistance they can put up to hardship and fatigue. You can see thin little men with legs like storks', shouldering weights of thirty or even forty kilos for day after day, along tracks that would make the stranger think twice before he ventured on them carrying nothing at all. No one can pretend, of course, that they can learn the art of mountaineering or coping with an ice-overhang in forty-eight hours. You have to be patient with them, and you have to show understanding and deal with them on a warm and human plane; you must respect their needs and customs, and keep a decent time-table which allows for proper stops. They have been crossing the mountains for a long, long time; they have learned how to confront all their moods.

In the afternoon we came to a place where the Braldu Gorge widened out considerably. On our left now was a whole range of alluvial terracings, split up by little streams running in ravines, and well covered with vegetation.

This was the Biano oasis. The horizon was closed off by colossal snow-covered mountains. A little short of them, still to our left, the Braldu Valley opened into another. In 1903 the Bullock-Workmans had climbed to this point in the course of their exploration of the Soshum glaciers. Very close to this meeting-place of the valleys, in a little meadow, I found our camp already pitched, among fruit trees and rows of poplars. The bags had already been unpacked.

Chakpo (or Chokpiong) is one of the smallest oases in a region which the traveller may well find a somewhat forbidding one. The wretched conditions of life here are at once evident in the inhabitants of the district, a surprising number of whom are afflicted with goitre, while an equally surprising number are cretins. Goitre (which is due to a chronic lack of iodine) is to be seen throughout Baltistan. But in these lost villages, cut off from the centre of things, it looms frighteningly large in the human landscape. There are the modest sufferers content with an apple or an orange in the throat—and there are the goitre champions, pompously wearing a whole crop of gourds round their necks. Although the conspicuously affected are, to say the least of it, mentally retarded, poor simpletons who can only be entrusted with some such humble task as winding wool, the medium range of the begoitred ones make first-class porters. The affliction seems to have no ill effect upon their life-force. In the matter of the cretins, a few are quite unaffected by goitre. Here, at Chakpo, we had one who would make the rounds of the camp, a figure black with filth and full of lice, dressed in a few scarecrow rags. When you saw him, something plucked at your heart.

Besides the goitre-sufferers and the cretins, I saw some fearful cases of trachoma and heard more than one catarrh that sounded like a death-rattle. What a heartrending contrast between Man and Nature in these valleys! The limpid torrents, the crags halfway up the sky, suggested some legendary people, a race of heroes of an age of gold; here was the reality, a wretched sub-race: the humiliated ones.

From this point on, it was very heavy going for Dr. Zeni. We had to set aside a definite hour—five to six—for his clinic. Otherwise he would never have had a moment to eat, so great were the numbers that sought his aid for maladies of every sort.

The satellites of Jupiter

I had no real appetite that night, and it was plain that my companions too were weighed down by these sorrowful sights—and by the catarrh concert which had echoed mournfully in our ears since our arrival. But, when the darkness fell, the porters struck up a song and the whole area of the camp with its orchards and its dry walls presented the spectacle of a piazza during festival-time. Fires, cups of tea, bowls of steaming broth, chupatty cakes with their rich smell of roasting grain. . . . Mauri and I stayed there a long time, now with one group, now with another, taking photographs and recording songs. For the Balti, a big-scale expedition like this means a lot of things: there is the hard work of the porterage itself, but there is the prospect of sure wages too, while the transmigration of peoples (for that is almost what it comes to) turns into a series of kermesses or rustic fairs—tribal encounters in the glade! Among the men of every village there is always some leading spirit. He is the one who leads the songs, who will pull a flute out of his knapsack. He knows all the jokes and the games, and cocks a snoot at every rival village. The Kaphalu party (Kaphalu is near the foot of Masherbrum, towards the south) was full of appeal. One of them sang the praises of his village for us: Come to Kaphalu you must—Skardu's dry and full of dust . . . But Kaphalu is calling you . . . with apricots and beauty spots and pretty girls . . . yes, pretty girls, *ragsha bustring*: and his eyes shone as if he had been singing 'Cherry Ripe'.

When we got back to our tents we found all the others asleep, or at any rate deep in their sleeping-bags. Only Bepi De Francesch was still on his feet—and motionless. With a big pair of binoculars, whose magnification I did not know, he was giving all his attention to the starry sky.

'What have you discovered, Bepi?' I asked him.

'Come and have a look at the satellites of Jupiter. They're wonderfully clear tonight.'

Just at that moment I was pleased to discover the satellites of Jupiter, but I was still more pleased to discover that a police-school climbing instructor, who was already a first-class climber, should also turn out to be a devotee of the stars. Rough and ready in appearance, with heavy hands and a fine spirit, gentle, generous-hearted, his curiosity about things ever awake—that was Bepi.

Jula: the triumph of a people's technique

Today was *Jula* Day. So we got off to an early start. The sun was up with us. This year it seemed to be a benign sun all the time, with no wish to play tricks on us.

Jula is the name given to those suspension bridges made from three cables of plaited branches and tree-roots. You have one for your feet and the other two to grip with your hands. The stout cables, which we might call swaying girders, are held together by a network of frailer 'wires' of the same material:

the whole forming a rudimentary and rather unstable bridge. In the high valleys of the Karakoram range, and round about, very many of these *jula* are to be seen. The Balti has an endearing habit of informing you, just as you are about to entrust your life to these contraptions, that *jula* are never repaired till they collapse. It follows, therefore, that they are unlikely to collapse except beneath the weight of someone crossing them.

A *jula* in the path of a sizeable caravan means a hold-up for hours and hours: hundreds of people cannot get across in a matter of minutes. That was why we started so early in the day. Before we reached the *jula* we had just about four hours' hard going, four hours of the narrow and sometimes alarming Braldu Valley—all stones, landslips and ravine, shut in by great buttresses of bare and lowering rock.

Half an hour out from Chakpo, on our right, we saw baleful evidence of the power of water to scoop out rock. The river, until that point of a fair width, narrowed to a mere thread buried in a deep ravine, whose sheer sides almost touched. Grey, compact rock, chiselled away under the action of the flowing water, has been most curiously wrought by it. Here was the very swirl of a torrent inscribed in rock for your hands to touch; while your eye marvelled at a colouration which seemed some fantasy of the mineral world. You found the same bands of colour as in the eye of a peacock's tail: concentric circles of crystallization in the hues of an agate. And down there in the depths roared the fury of the river, a thread the colour of earth.

Vegetation was very sparse here, and flowers rarely come by: a wild bean with red flowers; a few shaggy ciperaceae (in places which could store up a water-supply from the rains); a few rose bushes, all thorn and pale flower. Once we passed a veritable mountain torrent of trees; they wound their way down the mountainside from one chrome terrace of parched detritus to the next, keeping faithfully to a little mountain torrent of water: willows, poplars, sorb-apples. Then came what might have been the ruins of a city, abandoned for thousands of years. But it was only the curious effect of erosion among ancient glacial deposits, which had remained suspended on the flanks of the valley. The recent geological history of this region amounts to a continuous alternation between deposit and excavation over the four ice-ages. It is written here as clearly as it might be in a book.

Before we got to the *jula* we made one crossing of the Braldu by a more ordinary sort of bridge—two tree-trunks lodged in the banks. This was one more of the places where I lived in fear and trembling for all our brand-new camera and cinecamera gear. It was spread over nine cases. Fortunately I had a hand-picked group of men to carry them, and I had put Karim, from

Parkuta, one of our most senior porters (and one of the cleanest) in charge. Whenever I passed them on the march I was delighted to see the care with which they had put the cases down in the shade to protect them from possible damage from the sun's rays, should they have fallen out for a halt. If you want good results, especially in colour, you must take infinite care of all your photographic material from the day you set out to the day the film can be safely despatched for developing.

By the time I reached the *jula* myself it was very nearly afternoon. The valley at this point was narrow and winding, and a striking scene greeted me: a huge crowd, not one member of it still, shrieking and howling as they followed the antics of the men crossing; they might have been watching a game of polo. The wretched *jula* was loaded up as it had never been before, and it swayed in an intimidating manner; time and time again you could count as many as eighteen porters crossing at a time, all with kit-bags or cases on their shoulders: no less than a ton and a half suspended over the icy yellow waters of the swirling river. A fall meant pretty well certain death: if the current failed to ensure it, the intense cold would mean the finish. A few of the high-altitude men stood on the bridge holding the 'hand-rails' apart. These always have a tendency to swing together and hold up one's passage. All in all it was a complicated way of getting to the other side of a river, and it was heavy work.

But, when you pause to consider it, a *jula* is a triumph of primitive techniques and an extremely ingenious affair. Who knows what centuries of trial and error have not gone into it? Calculating the optimum diameter for the three principal cables alone is an art in itself. How does one compromise between safety (thick cables and reliable ones) and lightness (thin cables and dangerous ones)? Technically, the structure may have a rough-and-ready look, but it is put together with great skill. Whole kilometres of supple branches or roots of equal thickness, plaited like the strands of a rope, go to the making of both 'girders' and cables. The bridge itself is anchored to the mountain by two tower-like structures thirty feet high, one on each side, and heavy stones are brought up too to make the rooting of each cable still more secure.

The crossing went on throughout the whole afternoon. The sun was setting by the time the last of the men went over. The village of Chongo, where we were making our stop for the night, was perched upon a natural terrace 600 feet or so from the heart of the valley.

Chongo: home of the rotting men

Chongo! Smelly old tumbledown Chongo—we shan't forget you in a hurry!

The camp was pitched among the apricots of a very dank little glade. A stream flowed round it, bringing down all manner of filth from a handful of the humblest hovels, which stood at the foot of lofty, forbidding crags.

We were getting supper when some men put down a stretcher in front of us. On it lay a poor, grey-faced, filthy relic of a man, still quite young, his foot bound with a bandage the colour of congealed vomit. Dr. Zeni got down to an examination at once. When he had stripped off the bandage, and a second covering of birch-bark, he found the foot plastered with cow-dung, which in many places is credited with healing properties; anyone who has ever looked at some ancient treatise on medicine will be familiar with the part played by excrement and urine, even among us Europeans. And to think that this was the perfect way to make a bacillus culture! . . .

Zeni at last cleared the foot of cow-dung too, and laid bare a perfectly frightening festering sore. Half of the heel had gone, eaten away by the degenerative processes of suppuration. What remained was a foul blotch whose colours, from blood-red at the centre, went through a spectrum of yellow and green round the edges of the sore to black on its dirty fringes, where the skin was encrusted with a sort of dry scale formation. Zeni gallantly cleaned up the huge wound while the poor devil, held down by two of his companions, cried out to some Shiite saint. Then he applied strong antibiotics and gave a morphine injection, and bound up the foot. He told those who had brought the man that the best thing they could do, in two or three days at the latest, was to get him on a stretcher to Skardu.

'If you don't, he'll die, I can tell you that,' he concluded. Captain Dar, deeply moved himself, interpreted this verdict.

We had got under way with our nightly chores again when another member of this rotting human species was brought along by two relatives. This time it was a hand. Once more our gallant Zeni sent a patient on his way, full of lamentations, true, but properly bound up and full of antibiotics as well.

That evening, finding myself alone with the Captain for a moment, I was maliciously tempted to ask him how it came about that the new Government never gave these poor remote people a thought, once it had slipped into the place of their old and despised foreign administrators. But he had broached the subject himself before I uttered a word.

'It's a scandal,' he declared, 'that there's not even one mobile pharmacy in this valley. I don't say a fully qualified doctor, but anybody at all.... I can begin to see what an enormous task lies in front of us. But we must succeed.

I swear I'll hide nothing when I send in my report. I'm ashamed for you visitors to our country to see such things.'[1]

At such times as this there was nothing to be said. The Captain came in for all our sympathy. At bottom, he was honest and he was sincere. He was quick to see both his own faults and those of the system he believed in. He didn't try and get out of it.

Bathing à la belle étoile

The sky was full of grey, full of gloom, even, when we left this district where humanity was left to rot. This was the first time the weather had looked dubious since we had started. From Chongo onwards, we kept to the heights of the valley—the alluvial terraces, cracked into block formations by deep ravines. We had to go down these and up again the other side: stiff work. Soon we reached the valley of the hot springs: *Chongo les bains*.

The valley itself was a shallow one, the colour of dried leaves, and the springs were veritable, if rough-hewn, fonts in the rock—a whole line of them, full of very hot and sulphurous water. It was a treat to get one's clothes off and take a bath. My companions were all plunging in. Some were shaving, others exchanging a commentary on people and events—just like worthy Japanese in the *o-furo* (honourable bath). What echoes of Japanese mountains there were in this spot! In Japan too there were *noten-buro*—'baths à la belle étoile'—where mountaineers sought refreshment after a stiff climb.

Askole, the Valley of Legend

On the third day out from Dasso, the valley broadened again. Once more we saw the beautiful poplars of Baltistan, proudly lifting their light green laughter to the skies. Where there are poplars there are men and fields and dwellings. We were 10,000 feet up, at Askole, the last village in the valley. For the previous two days we had been hemmed in by rock, we had made our way through a land full of bleak ravines and the rushing of a river that swirled and crashed and carried away the sand and ate up the very rock as it passed. All this had the apparent effect of isolating us from the rest of the world. So that now it was as if we had come to some magic Shangri-la, floating in time and space. The inhabitants here were a far cry from those wretched relics who lived, like some human larvae, in the last two villages we had passed through.

1. Incredible as it may seem, both these afflicted men turned up again, fit and well and smiling, when we passed through Chongo on our way back, three months later. They came along to the camp with a present of chickens. Naturally the one with the bad foot had not been taken to Skardu. Oh, the power of penicillin in the virgin organism!

But everything here had the air of legend, and in a certain sense enchantment too. The mountains were colossi: even above them towered the great hooked beak of Mango Gusor (20,632 feet). Millennium upon millennium of raging torrents had scooped out these valleys. Everything in nature had a primordial strength, everything was sculptured in master-strokes, everything in earth and sky was implacability and disdain. The very rock seemed to writhe in torture beneath the weight and majesty of the glaciers. On the flat stretches, the boulders that some landslip had sent crashing down the mountain-side were as big as houses. The trees themselves, encountered here and there, gnarled and knotted, seemed charged with power. It was a place that gave you a sense of peace, but, at the same time, a sense of some terrible force lying in ambush, a monster in a doze, or sleeping.

The men themselves proved to be true sons of their own soil. One of them, out with a plough, hailed us loudly (*Plate 5*) and an old fellow came up to us with his little son in his arms (*Plate 21*). While we were going into Askole itself we met quite a number of worthy peasants, draped in their togas and either barefoot or wearing a sort of slipper made of goatskin (*Plate 24*), often with riding switches in their hands. The people of this remote region, Balti though they might be, had a prouder bearing than the inhabitants of Shigar or Skardu. Perhaps there was a time when they eked out their few poor harvests with a little highway robbery? We were always coming across a face which might have belonged—well, if not to the brigand himself, at least to the brigand's kin! And brigands, if you are not their actual victim, strike a peculiarly sympathetic note in us, don't they? These were men who cultivated a spirit of liberty without bounds (*Plate 26*).

The houses here, no less than the inhabitants, were different. Far more primitive, in fact. Except in a few that had been recently built, there was no sign of the old gracious pattern of Shigar or Skardu—square or rectangular, ultimately deriving from Ladakh and Tibet, a pattern in which a spiritual concept, as well as technical skill, played its part—a type of dwelling whose carved wood panels and little arcades showed a hankering after form and elegance. No, the houses here were the real primitive shape—round, a wall encircling the fireplace; and the walls were just patched up out of any old pebbles from the stream, barely cemented together with mud. The stairway in all cases was outside, windows were all but non-existent. In fact, they were not so much houses as just dens. The dens of men used from childhood to roam about the mountains, like wolves or snow-leopards (*Plate 2*).

At Askole, the 'green' was a little enclosure set apart in a place where there was quite a huddle of these huts. It was marked by a handful of big poplars and around it, in constant danger of collapse, was a dry-wall of stones. Here, every expedition for decades, from the time of Conway or the Duke of the Abruzzi onwards, must have pitched camp. Toni Gobbi, Beppe Oberto, Captain Dar and I stayed for two days, as we had some reorganizing to do. Cassin, Bonatti, Mauri, De Francesch and Zeni went on ahead with a group of forty men. They wanted to get the camp ready at Urdukass, halfway along the Baltoro Glacier. We were faced from now on with a good many complex tasks. With villages and houses at an end, the porters would be provided with overnight quarters no longer. From this point we carried our own bed and board on our backs. Askole was like a port from which, after coasting from harbour to harbour, we were at last putting out into the open sea.

Organizing a caravan to traverse uninhabited regions is a real headache. Ardito Desio has stated the problem in the clearest terms:

Every porter will consume say one kilogram of food per day, and in favourable conditions can be expected to take a pack of up to thirty kilograms. Therefore, to ensure that he shall carry twenty kilograms of expedition gear, his total absence from the camp base must not exceed ten days [10 kilos of food], which is to say, speaking in practical terms, five outgoing days and five days for the return journey. If the expedition-gear weight can be reduced to ten kilos, the porter's availability can be extended to twenty days [ten days out and ten days in]. But that will mean doubling the number of porters. The maximum self-sufficiency period for a light caravan cannot generally exceed twenty days—or a ten days' outward journey. However much study has gone into the detail of the organization, and however well trained the personnel at the expedition's disposal, it will be found very difficult to exceed this figure. For a heavy caravan it will be lower.[1]

Our own problem was certainly to calculate for a ten-days-out availability period: we should need this to reach the Base Camp. But we should not be following Professor Desio's system, excellent as it may be for small caravans in which every porter's pack consists of both Expedition gear and his own food. Instead, we should be adding to the expedition a number of men, X, carrying exclusively food for the rest (and for themselves). The figure reached in our calculations for the additional number of packs was 118. With every day there would be the weight reduction from food consumption, and a number of the porters, no longer needed, would return to Askole. This whole administrative question, as if it was not sufficiently complicated in itself, was inextricably mixed up with others: pay-rates, rationing, ground-sheet issues and the provision of snow-glasses. The whole headache was Toni Gobbi's,

1. *Alpinismo Italiano nel Mondo*, Milan, 1953, p. 17.

and once more it meant a couple of days when the poor fellow didn't know whether he was on his head or his heels. Captain Dar now took a major part on the operational side and it must be admitted that once he appreciated and understood the innocent spirit of our enterprise he did his best to be of help to us. The language barrier meant that I had to be there all the time, but I confess that the role of mathematical calculus held no temptations for me. I attended as nothing more than an itinerant vocabulary! All the time my eyes were following the scene around us, and my mind was trying to grasp it. I wanted to preserve it on film. My heart was in my cameras, not the calculations.

The weather was worsening. One would no longer have thought it was June, the month of flowers and the solstice. The sky was overcast, grey, forbidding. The leaves of the poplar trees quivered in the dark and icy breezes. The humidity often smudged with a cold sweat the long lists of names in our notebooks—Mohamed Ghulam, Karim Ismael, Hassan Ali . . . and the place-names denoting their origins—Satpara, Parkuta, Shigar, Kaphalu, Hushe. . . .

The crowd of Balti made a fine spectacle: you could have gazed for hours at those patriarchal figures, those shepherds and bandits and the rest, all swathed in their flowing togas, waiting in silence to be put on the pay-roll. In the rather dismal, greyish light of a day entombed by cloud, these figures looked far more at home than they would have done in brilliant sunshine, decked out in all the colours of the fair. I strolled among the crowd on the field, and up and down the lanes through the houses close at hand, trying to catch the essence of these mountain men, in a head-and-shoulders here, a group there, a piece of human statuary farther on. . . . But the groans of poor Toni, from under his weight of work, caught up with me. 'Hey—*vieni qua*—tell these chaps they'll get their sun-glasses at the Baltoro. . . .' Or else it was the Captain: 'Explain to Gobbi that these men were paid eight annas less upon release, we must now make an account of the sum due to them and then we'll hand it out to the P.A. on our return.' On top of it all, the Balti: '*Sahib, biango nga kyong set-pa, mul chōngas.*' ('Sahib, five chicken here, cost fifteen rupees.')

All the more welcome for all this was the supper Beppe Oberto was preparing for us—cheese pastries, minestrone fit for a cleric on a feast day and roast chicken—the chicken dry and stringy enough to defeat even the cook: the general poverty and barrenness of the land came out in anything reared on it. But if we were 10,000 feet up we were still in the world of men, and we still had an appetite. We could sleep o' nights, too.

In the afternoon we made a purchase of the highest importance: 118 sacks of flour (*atta* in Urdu; *pe* in Balti). I should point out that at Askole there were Government supplies and that through the Military Authorities at Skardu we had obtained permission to draw some of our quota here. The Captain told us that we would have done better to purchase the whole quantity at Skardu, the grade here being far inferior. The cost would have been about the same, for better flour; here we were paying transport charges to a remote spot into the bargain. However, we hadn't got our flour, so we went to the stores to draw it.

The stores! What a grand, high-sounding name. All we found was a typical Askole dwelling, a den a little bigger than most, at the bottom of a lane. The lane wound its way down a hill, and in the middle was a rivulet of liquids and excrement. Everything curves in Askole. The houses curve, the streets curve like the twists in a maze, the very stones and pebbles in the walls are round or oval. The sacks themselves, when we found them, turned out to be ancient affairs like wineskins—they were goatskins patched together, and filled with a greyish *pe* that smelt mouldy ... so many things in Baltistan can conjure up what life must have been like for our own wild and redoubtable ancestors of the Apennine forests—the sort of life you can scent in certain passages of Latin authors when they speak of the Marsi or the Sanniti.

At last, on Friday, 6th June, we were definitely ready to leave Askole behind us. The last morning was a real inferno! We were up with the lark at half past five, with the sky as grey as ever (*Plate 23*). Cases, personal baggage, tents, sacks of food, the skin-sacks of flour—everything stood ready in mighty piles under the trees. All that remained was to divide it among 482 porters. That 'all'! What a pallid euphemism for a labour which began round about seven o'clock and was hardly completed by one! By the time we saw the loaded back of the 482nd porter vanishing into the blue, Toni Gobbi, the Captain and I were absolutely done, and we had no voice left. Once more we had had to make a full register of all our men, with name, paternity, birthplace, identity-disc number and description of load—and all in the midst of fearful hubbub and confusion. For a people so divinely capable of behaving like speechless hermits, lost in meditation by the hour, it is absolutely incredible how the Balti can be suddenly transformed into a howling, seething mob. Every manjack of them was shoving his neighbour out of the way and rushing up to us, the sahibs and the martyrs, to tug at our sleeves with the most insistent demands for the most useless things, or the most absurd ones. We did our best to get the packs absolutely equal in weight, but some little differences would inevitably remain, and if they saw a case that was a few ounces less than the next one, or a pack that looked more manageable, they would swoop for it, they would struggle for it, they would come to blows for it.

'Who wouldn't come climbing in the Karakoram?' sighed Toni, when at last we got the chance of a word with one another.

'The climbing part is just incidental to these expeditions,' someone answered. 'It's like a sort of consolation prize.'

The *lambardar* of Askole, accompanied by his sons, came to see us off and wish us well. And at last we left our pitch (full of scraps of paper, empty boxes and fragments of cases) to a dismal crowd of cretins, goitre-sufferers and old bleary-eyed men; for even here, eking out their wretched lives in the shadow of those legendary togaed supermen, these unfortunates were to be found.

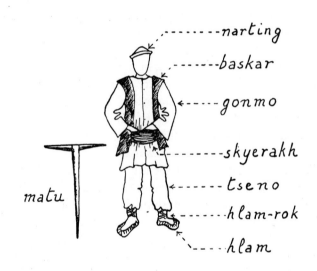

The Golden Road to the Seven Giants[1]

Korophon: the tent of the sheikh

THE day was grey and cold; the farthest tongue of the Biaho, one of the great glaciers of the Karakoram range,[2] resembled, at a distance, some enormous coal-heap to feed a factory. Ice? There was no visible sign of it. We could make out only what seemed to be shapeless hillocks of gravel and stone and moraine, covering pretty well the whole bed of the valley. The snout of the Biaho Glacier came down from a lateral valley forma-tion merging into our own broader valley at an acute angle. It stuck out like a mass of dark molten metal, obstructing our path.

Glaciers, as everyone knows, may be described as rivers—peaceful, solemn rivers—of solid water. Now lengthening in their course, now contracting, they mirror, some years after the event, the cyclic variations of rainfall and temperature, or, in other words, climate, local and general. At some periods the forward end of the Biaho seems to have pushed right across the Braldu Valley, forming a lake in its higher reaches. Lakes of similar formation (i.e. by glacier obstruction) have been frequently noted, and the collapse of the natural dyke has often produced disastrous floods, sudden, unforeseen cataclysms indeed. Just now, the forward end of the glacier-snout was some distance away from the left side of the valley. It was probably the case with this particular glacier, as with nearly every other in the world at the present time, that it was in a contracting or retreating phase. This would be borne out, too, from descriptions we have of it in 1915, in 1929 and in 1953, from Giotto Dainelli and Ardito Desio.

1. They are: Muztagh Tower, Masherbrum, K2, Broad Peak, Gasherbrum, Chogolisa and Golden Throne
2. The others are: Hispar, Chogo Lungma, Baltoro, Siachen and Rimu.

We got up on to the glacier, to be lost in an ocean of hillocks, ridges and sudden troughs. 'The surface,' wrote Dainelli, describing his 1913 explorations, 'gave the impression of a great storm-tossed sea, suddenly immobilized, and in crossing it we would find ourselves now in the trough of a wave, unable to see anything at all except the advancing one, and now on the crest of a wave from which the whole infinitude of this ocean was visible.'[1]

Over to our left lay the entrance to one of the great highways of the Karakoram; eleven days' march—I was told by Haji Ismael—and you reached Hunza. The majesty of these seemingly boundless tracks, with their palaces of ice and their cathedrals of rock, is enough to take one's breath away. It was by this route that the Braldu Valley was reached for the first time by Sir Martin Conway and his companions in 1892, and the Bullock-Workmans passed this way, too, with their guides from the Valley of Aosta (in 1899 and 1908). Still others were Eric Shipton (1939) and some members of the Italian K2 Expedition in 1954 and the Japanese in a 1956 venture; and one could quote still more names.

A little higher up, on our left again, another valley formation of some importance opened up with the River Dumordu. Crossing rivers and streams in the Himalaya and the Karakoram is quite a problem, and it can be a highly dangerous game. The number of explorers and climbers who have lost their lives at it is quite high. In inhabited sectors of the valleys there are always rafts (*zak*) or suspension bridges—the *jula*; higher up, and in barren territory, the traveller is left to his own devices. Here, to be sure, there was a small *jula* over the Dumordu, but to reach it we should have had to go several kilometres up the valley. At the moment, however, the water was low and the summer thaw had scarcely begun: the porters decided to ford their way across the river, which at this point split up into numbers of quite narrow channels.

So I, just like the rest, took off my trousers and my shoes and waded in. The cold was frightful. A few steps, and all feeling vanished from my lower limbs. When I got to the opposite bank, my legs could have been amputated without an anaesthetic. The flesh was red as fire, but utterly insensitive.

By a stroke of luck, the dry part of the gravel-bed on to which we finally emerged from the water was covered with a woody, aromatic plant which went by the Balti name of *burtse*. It grew in dry tufts a few inches high. We gathered some sizeable heaps of it and got a fire going to bring back some life into our poor numbed selves. In the end, we put the tents up here too, or a little farther on. Oberto, as usual, cooked us a supper which smelt heavenly

1. G. Dainelli, *Esploratori e Alpinisti nel Caracorum*, Turin, 1959, p. 211.

after the day's hard labour. Toni and I meanwhile got on with the job of doling out the rations. Doing this for 500 mouths takes hours. How bitterly at such moments we regretted the loss of Sadiq, the Desio Expedition caravan chief! Here was a task on a scale quite outside most people's power of conception. But we had no one to help us out. Taqi soon proved quite useless when it came to taking command—or any sort of responsibility. Hours might go by with no real cause for complaint, but every time we gave him a job for which he needed to show a little authority over the men, he let us down; he behaved like a mischief-maker and produced a lot of noise to no effect whatever. That rough, grating voice of his; that hired-ruffian air; and those operatic and quite unavailing gestures, tore all our nerves to pieces—Balti nerves and Pakistani nerves, not only European ones.

Luckily for us, the Captain was doing his best to pull his weight now, and he was really making himself useful. The men felt his authority and showed every sign of a healthy respect. Dar now represented the Supreme Court of Appeal whenever there was a clash of wills in the caravan. In fact his prestige was now so firmly established that the day came when even Riccardo Cassin— the best of chiefs, so warm-hearted, so understanding, always the man to set an example by shouldering the heaviest pack, first up and last to bed and never given to getting up on the high horse of his authority—even this same Riccardo Cassin, when I went to see him about something one day, gave me an answer with undertones of bitterness beneath the jest: 'Don't ask me! Go and see the Blue Prince about it, inquire the nature of his august desires on the point. He's the chief of this expedition.'

That was what it had come to: the Captain proposed and disposed. The trick was to make his august desires correspond with ours. One thing I did discover: he was success-mad by now. 'His' Expedition, 'his' Italians had to make a better showing than the Americans and the Japanese. Of course, I resorted to all manner of means to ram one point home in his head: success meant speed. It meant getting to the Base Camp before the monsoon storms.

Dar's prestige among the men depended on several factors. First and foremost, he represented the powers-that-be, and in the minds of the simple Balti souls there was only the haziest of distinctions, if that, between the Civil Power and the Military Power. Then he spoke, or more often shouted, in Urdu—the tongue of the metropolis—and it must be admitted that he had an energetic and magisterial style. Then again, he was one of those men who take a real delight in disposing and deciding and keeping all the reins in their hands. By now he had a regular little court. Murad the Mournful, with his sad and serious eyes—like those of a philosopher heavily in debt—now cooked for him alone. Ali, a young fellow still disfigured by the mark of a burn he had suffered from as a child, acted as his personal attendant, his valet and his general factotum. The Captain had his own tent and his own kitchen, in fact his own miniature General Staff, and a great deal of coming and going there was there, too, among seekers of favours, justice and advice. It might have been the tent of a sheikh.

Mercifully, as I have already said, the Captain's manner towards us and the Expedition had undergone a radical change; and one had to make allowances for the fact that everything was such a complete novelty to him that he just couldn't grasp it.

'I was with my unit in the Kashmir hills,' he told me, 'when one fine spring day I was just seconded for duty with an "Expedition to the Karakoram Range". Why, I had no idea what an expedition was! True, I'd seen bits about the Everest climb and so on in the papers, but I hadn't the vaguest notion how they set about it. And I'd never so much as set eyes on an Italian. I'd heard about them in the war, and not given them a thought since. What you've got to understand'—Dar was in an expansive mood—'is that I had to find out everything for myself. They just said "Keep an eye on things, you never know, this isn't exactly peace-time." It took me quite a few days to get the gist. I see now that you're just sportsmen, and we've got a tough nut to crack—but naturally it took me some time to get the hang of it, and get into the spirit of things. I'm sorry your companions don't seem to consider me one of themselves. I'd like to be just one of you. The Americans, now, here's one thing they've done, they've had the names of their accompanying officers put on the ice-axes. . . .'

Ah, those American ice-axes! They were famous, they'd become a symbol, a banner with a strange device . . . and every now and then I would pause to bless the name of old Nick, who'd thought of the idea. If ever those blessings had reached him, would his ears have been red.

Bardumal: a prayer among the stones
Bardumal: rock and wind, iron-hard earth, and solitude.

Up here, where the valley split into two, where there were thus two vast corridors to invite the frozen air—up here, for the first time, we really felt we had penetrated into the mountains. The wind smelt of snow. The sky was fringed with sharp peaks, or else it seemed to loll against the mighty flanks of some great buttress. The men were prepared for a grim night. Bardumal had little to recommend it as a stopping-place. It was no valley with a wind-shield of trees, like Payù, it had no giant boulders that had come tumbling

Men - and their burdens! A chilly June morning at Askole.

Lham - Balti slippers.

25

A Balti *porter.*

The Balti - men of the mountain.

26

Conversation goes on, deep into the night.

Caravan across the desert.

29

31

Onwards to the Base Camp with five hundred men, through more than a hundred and twenty miles of rock, river and glacier. Adventure - expedition politics - a people in migration.

A flame in the solitude.

With night comes cold.

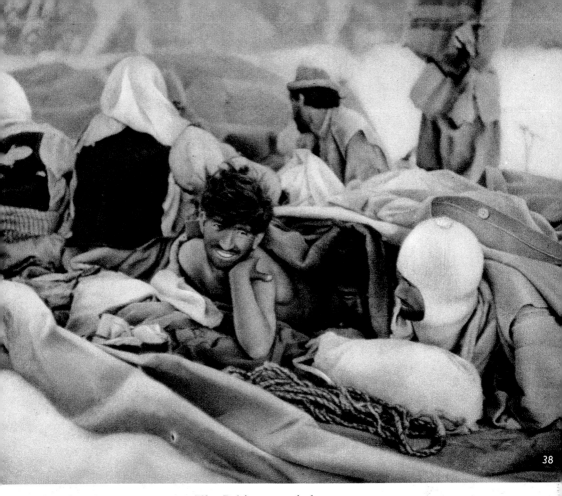

38

The Balti - sons of the snows.

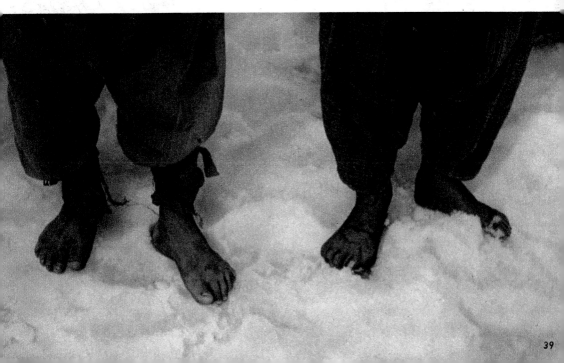

40   41   42

A red-hot stone is used for making tok cakes.

43

Song and dance in the night.

down the mountain; at Urdukass, these had provided us with ready-made shelter. There were none at Bardumal. Perhaps it had been chosen simply because it was the place where two valleys met. Be that as it may, up on an open flank above the river there were a number of dry-walls, roughly made— heaven knew when or by whom! Each group of porters settled for one. Then they set to. A few men got to work on their wall, to try and make it a bit more solid, others scoured the ground for *burtse*, or the twisted boughs of some pitiable cypress; the older porters made the fire with them and then got on with the dough for the 'bread' or fetched water for the broth.

Many, too, found among the stones from the river-bed a seclusion convenient for prayer: they knelt among them, turning towards Mecca (*Plate 22*). Islamic prayer calls for a whole ritual of gesture, bowing and genuflexion— the porters acquitted themselves of it with the self-same grace and naturalness as they had shown in their nightly dances, performed in firelight. The piety of these men—and the same is true for all I have ever met of the Moslem faith —might be a little showy in its manifestations, but it was absolutely sincere and spontaneous.

Religion and life itself are bound together with far closer ties in Islamic countries than in Christian ones. The reasons are twofold. Firstly, the religion itself is more tolerant; less sublime, perhaps, but closer to the realities of human nature: religion therefore is not something remote from daily existence. And then again, spiritual life, in territory where Islam prevails, is less profoundly penetrated by those demons of study, criticism and learning which are the glory of the West and its cross. As a result, life does not become remote from religion. The faith is one the human spirit clings to, without the slightest need for compulsion.

A little later in the day—it was dark, in fact—Bardumal offered a wonderful spectacle. The sun had set in one of those bleak skies, driven by the winds of a high valley, which hold endlessly a gleam of greenish blue over to the west, while the vault overhead is already dark and pin-pricked with stars. Little fires, devouring what wood and plants the men had gleaned, were burning everywhere. The mountain seemed to be on fire, and the flames crackled upwards into smoke, which caught mischievous shafts of light as they twirled and fluttered. The men were figures of sculptured dark against that precious pallor, that fleeting, sad translucency, in the west. Voices could be heard . . . louder voices . . . then the songs began, borne on the wind in waves that carried with them the strong scent of aromatic plants.

This was one of those moments when one could abandon oneself to the breathtaking beauty of the scene. They were rare; in the general way

H   113

On a raft in the rushing Shigar river

we tramped these mountains as if we were off to the wars, head down and jaws set, our one dour object being to defy the force of gravity and the force of human idleness, to make a torrent of heavy expedition gear flow uphill instead of down dale!

I forget when I first began to suffer from mountain sickness. One or two of us were none too well at Bardumal. I think somebody had the idea of penning a ballad, but no one felt in sufficient high spirits to have a go at it. The Captain stood it worse than anyone. He showed up for a moment with his face a spectral green. Then, definitely, he retired to his tent. And, at the supreme command, all was silent.

Spring in Payù

Payù in Balti means salt. The district that bears this name is indeed one where, in many places, the steep mountain slopes are white with a sort of light saline incrustation. At Payù the valley really begins to open up and the traveller is on the very threshold of great mountain country, and quite close to the forward end of the great Baltoro Glacier.

In this district we began to make out the first of the giants. Still down in the valley, eastwards of us and towards the Baltoro, was a whole line of red castles, granite and ice: the Cathedrals of the Baltoro. Ahead of us too, but towards the opposite side of the valley, we saw our first glaciers and a series of peaks we did not know, wild and magnificent. At one point, coming to the top of a rise, Toni and I both gave a real shout: we saw the Aiguille de la République. A feathery peak ending in a needle—just like the Aiguille de la République seen from the Mer de Glace. But it is an old game, finding familiar names for the pinnacles and peaks towering over one. I have come across the mention of it in Dainelli's books, and I imagine that everyone who has come this way must have played it; the attraction is an imaginary claim to possession, a signing and sealing of friendship between that silent rock-mass and the tiny heart of Man—Man venturing with trepidation in this measureless world. Look —the Vaiolet Towers! Look—the Grivola! Look—the Dent du Géant!

Unlike Bardumal—and Korophon too—Payù makes a natural overnight stop. There is a wide, flat stretch, a sort of terrace perched over the valley and dotted with ancient granite masses. In the course of thousands of years they have assumed strange forms, reminiscent of Henry Moore's sculptures. Or else one might picture them as wrought by some strange and colossal machine, the dream of some mad king who set them there, imagining he could bewitch the stars. They are those bones of a mountain, that wreckage of the mountain gale which in Corsica men call *taffoni*.

Just short of this terrace, and just beyond it, were two enchanted valleys. Two tiny freshets of streams ran there with water crystal clear. All round grew poplars which seemed a thousand years old. The poplar is a tall and beautiful tree, but everywhere, till now, I had seen it as the very essence of youth, a delicate embroidery in green. In this spot, however, the poplars looked like olives—those gnarled, rugged, twisted old trees known in Sicily as 'Saracens' —presumably because they go back to the time of the Arabs. If they grow to no great height here, it may be because of the snow and the wind and the general severity of the climate, but to make up for it they expand at the base, taking on that mythological aspect of strength and antiquity; the gnarls and whorls chiselled into the bark seem the very engravings of eternity. In the second valley—the one a little higher up—the poplars were not the only reminders of the forest we had left behind; there were other trees too, the most conspicuous being birches, virginal as ever. Higher still, scattered here and there as if part of a plan to assault a fortress, were some sturdy cypresses, dark green in colour, often half crushed to pieces by an avalanche—each one of them a survivor; a hero of the green, still world; torn, gashed and splintered, their dead branches raised heavenwards in a dying spasm.

It was 8th June. Spring in Payù. The branches of ancient poplar and dainty birch alike were sprouting with a frail green tracery—pure enchantment in this grim world where everything was so male, so forceful. There were a few humble flowers. Granite castle and ice castle were pictures often framed within blossoming boughs! A place for lovers of myth and saga. An alcove for Tristan and Yseult.

'Dawn—Moslem chants and roaring streams,' says one of the diaries. The reference was still to Bardumal. On the morning of the previous day, before sunrise in fact, with the first pale gleams of dawn itself, one of the porters had stirred, and somewhere or other was chanting a long, long prayer. It was a modulated wailing, born of the nothingness of night, swording the nothingness of sleep; it rolled like a great breaker of ineffable thanksgiving through the space-seas of a sky full of ecstasies and stars. A little later—hark to the sounds of good, ancient, dusty Mother Earth! Hens chattering like a clutch of old women at their tittle-tattle! At last we came out of our tents. Sun-up. The purest breath of morning in our lungs.

We got off in really fine style for once, with everything organized. Toni Gobbi was like a conductor, giving the signal for his squadrons to depart in their appointed order as if he was calling forth the violins or the horns with his magic baton. The Captain, in form once more and no longer green, gave his assistance from the top of a knoll.

The march was really a short one, with one or two tricky places for the porters. The Balti has a perfect sense of balance. I have never seen a man put a foot wrong or hang back in a dangerous passage. Some of the men were carrying bigger and heavier loads than the rest, but there was not one fall. The going was precarious sometimes, too. Slippery patches, sand and mica, then a very good score of metres across yellowish river that flowed fast and furious. By now, we saw no more of the wooden sandals popular round Shigar: many of the porters wore *hlam*—'slippers' of goatskin, first rate for the snow. A good many others went barefoot. The sole of the Balti foot has a protective layer of skin hardened like horn, the thickness of a rubber sole and equally tough. At the junction of this 'rubber sole' and the normal skin, however, little cracks can form—often quite deep—and they can harbour infections. The pain sometimes becomes acute. I have seen Dr. Zeni deal with a good many of these cases, but it seemed that apart from dressing with emollients for the worst of them, little could be done.

Here at Payù we got the camp into really good shape—on the flat among the *taffoni* and the thorny bush, right in the sun. The porters, wilier than ourselves, and blessed with a weather-eye, went up to the second little valley where there was a rude and humble hut—for shelter in case of need. Operation Dole-Out lasted from 1600 hours to 1900 hours, with everybody running round in circles—not silent circles, either. Then night came—very cold, but still and full of stars. After supper Toni, Oberto and I stayed up for a long time round a fire of dry stumps and roots. Thus ended what had been, all in all, a perfect day.

The next, however, proved an inferno. It marked the lowest ebb in the whole excursion. From morning till night, nothing but squabbling and bawling and laying down the law. At seven o'clock we embarked upon Operation Dole-Out once more—which was never anything else but a headache without end. The simplest act becomes a burden when it has to be repeated 400 times. Just try and give out 400 bread rolls, 400 apples and 400 napkins to a disorderly crowd in a field, and tell me if it isn't past a joke! Here we weren't giving out anything so simple and straightforward, and we were haunted at every step by unforeseen technical difficulties. The trouble we had with the tea, for instance! Tea weighs light and our scales hadn't been made to measure out minute quantities. We had other problems to cope with too. That morning, every single pair of eyes stared downwards.

'They've got more than we have . . . this isn't enough . . . we're supposed to get equal. . . .'

But our first chore that morning was Operation Pay-Off. The porters who were going back had to be paid. Every day food stocks for transport dwindled with consumption, so that a certain percentage of hands became superfluous. The accounting was a long job: not all the men had been taken on the same day, and not all had carried the same weight. All this had to be allowed for. Some had drawn advances. Others had, after engagement, changed places with friends or relatives so that questions of identity were somewhat difficult to sort out. For the most part, it was the Captain who kept the tally. Toni counted out the cash. He handed it over to me, and I did the actual paying.

Another problem confronting us now concerned a specialized branch of the porterage—firewood. From this point on, nature would cease to provide us with anything combustible. A certain number of men would therefore have to carry sizeable faggots of wood for the nightly fire and the cooking of the chupatty or *tok*. The pity of it was that we had failed to come to an agreement either on the quantity of wood to be transported or on the number of men to be detailed for the job. The whole problem was one we hadn't foreseen in Skardu, so that it was totally uncatered for in our preparations. As a result, once we were far from the base, our porters found blackmail to get their own way a sore temptation.

'You do as we want—or back we go.'

We found this, to say the least of it, distressing.

Our third problem, and the one that took longest to solve, was to rearrange the whole caravan. Four hundred men had to be split up into groups of thirty, each with a head porter. This was the only way of simplifying things, and they needed simplifying, now that we were on the verge of glacier country and the going would be altogether harder. Dar saw to all this, and, to give the devil his due, it was his great day.

For a start he assembled our army on the 'terrace' of Payù (*Plate 35*). This in itself was an enormously long business. It must not be forgotten that with a few exceptions the Balti have never done any military service, and that they have all the psychological characteristics of the most down-trodden lumpenproletariat: deep in their make-up, fear of authority goes hand in hand with the irresistible urge to outwit it. Hence their lack of discipline—a lack in substance as well as form.

There were moments when my heart almost bled for poor Dar. Imagine one man, with two hands, trying to seize and hold 400 blackbirds. He would form one group, and set it aside, telling the thirty men to sit down. As soon as he went off to get another group together, two or three members of the group already formed would calmly get up, leave their unit, call their special friends over from every quarter . . . and so on.

Hassan, the Urdu-speaking Balti policeman who looked like a Mongol and belonged to the Hunza Scouts, gave the Captain all possible aid. They looked like a shepherd and his dog trying to keep a flock together when it was frightened by a train. We were at the end of our tether. I summoned up the last of my flagging energies to try and get some of it into a few photographs.

It was dividing the men into groups of thirty that was the difficult part. It sounds so simple! It would have been—without a whole invisible network of sympathies, interests, affinities which drew some men together, and inter-district rivalries thanks to which they wouldn't form part of the same group with others at any price. Possibly they were afraid that somehow or other this redivision was going to do them out of some of their rations. Had each village or district been able to muster exactly thirty souls, the problem would have been solved. But, of course, there was no such nicety in the numbers. The sun was at its zenith, or very nearly, veiled with a few very high pearly clouds —and we were still at it, bawling, arguing, running here, there and everywhere, weary and worn and getting nowhere at all. Dust started to fill the air. It got into our throats and our eyes. Sometimes, Captain Dar put one in mind of a sort of Alexander the Great among his armies, in some desert plain of Persia. At other moments he would turn to me with his eyes nearly out of his head, with nothing left of his voice but a gurgle. 'These bastards, these sons of good women, these dopes—they don't see anything . . . I can't do any more. . . .'

At one point it came to violence. The head of one little village really had his knife into the Captain and the rest of us. At his latest trick we saw Dar explode with fury. He started in on the rebel—always one of the least helpful of the porters—who went down beneath his attack.

Our lunch? Oberto had made a minestrone—it would have put some heart into us again—but we hadn't even time to taste it. The sun grew dimmer. Then it started down the sky. The rabble was at long last looking something like an army. Captain Dar, one has to admit, was giving the Expedition sterling service. He was looking pretty done. His hair was flopping down outside his cap on to his sweaty forehead, his voice was reduced to a croak, his eyes were bloodshot. But he had got things ship-shape: thirteen groups of thirty, each with a chief. Records were duly made in the notebooks.

Ah, we thought, now! Now we can have a mouthful to eat. Then we can get going again, and make Liligo before dark. The thirteen 'corporals' had been called for their first briefing. They had received their rations and got their marching orders for three o'clock in the afternoon. It looked as if the day would end in peace after all.

Five minutes later, all hell broke loose. All that grouping, the result of such toil and trouble—it just collapsed. The units lost all identity. The clamour began once more. Dar, Toni and myself, and the corporals too, were besieged by a howling and ferocious mob of porters. What had happened? It must not be forgotten that all these differences of opinion went on to the accompaniment of a real Babel of languages—Urdu, Balti, English, Italian . . . superhuman efforts were often necessary over a mere word or two. At first we hadn't a clue as to what it was all about. Then the issue became crystal clear: the corporals were ready and willing to start today. The porters wouldn't hear of it.

'Today—stop here!' yelled one begoitred demagogue, appointed by force of circumstances in five minutes. 'Today, too late to start!' he continued, hoarse with ferocity. 'Today, must cook *chupatty*. You don't want? Don't want, then! We go back.'

Without giving us any time to reach an understanding, our army—or rather the rabble that remained of it, a howling, cursing mob, brandishing sticks and *matu*—began to melt away under our very noses, going back the way they had come. It was an ugly moment. Apart from the fact that for a minute or two we really didn't know whether they were just going to run out on us, or whether they were going to give us a rough-house into the bargain, one thing seemed certain: we were going to be abandoned in this wild and incomparable spot, we were going to be left high and dry with our seven and a half tons of baggage, like the captains of steamers stranded on a sandbank and deserted by the crew. We soon saw that, luckily, what looked like the great run-out was merely the gesture of a few hot-heads: the calmer ones knew which side their bread was buttered. By deserting now, they would be forgoing their daily pay; no one was really crazy enough to resort to violence. The end of it was that the runners, after a hundred metres or so, began to trickle back. They had had to think twice: it was understandable. In any case, it was now too late to go on. As soon as the word went round—'We're stopping here overnight'—spirits soared again.

After supper, once more I made my round among the porters, stopping first at one fireside then at another, and exchanging a few words. The songs tonight were wilder and more passionate than on other nights. On all sides voices of defiance—looks of defiance. The peasants of Askole were hymning victory. There was no doubt about it, these brigands of the lonely pass, these ruffians of the rocks, these haughty buccaneers of Baltistan, these wretches—there was a certain charm to them! Bearded hooligans, they would split up a dried cypress-trunk for the fire as if they were at work on an enemy carcase; they went about it with great crashing laughs. Cave-men of old, with a mammoth caught in a trap! Sometimes they really struck fear into you. It was like playing with a snarling wild beast: all very well to admire his expression of primeval strength. One also feared his capacity for attack. The only way to look at the situation, really, was to imagine oneself the head of a business concern, under Trades Union fire.

I turned back to my tent, racked with the strains and stresses of the day. I caught a glimpse of towering peaks, mysterious under a moon which seemed to spear the earth with shafts of silver, scattering light and shadow of almost chemical hardness. Ah, the mountains, nature, the Secrets of the Universe. ... How misguided of us to think that a great expedition brought us up against those things, that we should be engaged in a struggle of Man against the bulwarks of rock, and ice, and altitude—that we were a spearhead into the realm of cosmic secrets! For all I know, small-scale expeditions may be a different matter, but these big, cumbrous affairs are first and foremost—at any rate until Base Camp is reached—a struggle against human obstacles: now, a symphony of human strength, now a pitting of wills one against another, a dire battle of needs, a clash of human ambitions.

Jottings from a diary—2058!

'Got to the Grand Baltoro Hotel yesterday about five in the afternoon, after a most pleasant run on the new scenic road Baltistan–Braldu. Just to think that only a hundred years ago climbers came up here on foot, with those impossible caravans! And at that time they hadn't even got tetracon pills. Everything's so simple now: two tetras a day for a week, and the red-corpuscle oxygen content is stepped up to cope with the high-altitude shortage. You can step on to the highest mountains in the world feeling fine, no need for those acclimatization periods that bothered our ancestors! I like this hotel. It's on a sort of terrace high up over the valley, with some very pretty trees all round. There's a very fine observation gallery where you find men and women from everywhere in the world, taking the sun. There's a big swimming-pool with plastic roofing. When it's not too cold you can be out in the open, other times you're in a nice warm transparent bubble that gives complete protection from the elements. Baltistan is one of the great touring centres of the world nowadays. Our great cities, with life getting more artificial every day, have got unendurable, people feel a more and more urgent need to get as far away from them as possible for their vacations—right into the very heart of nature, in fact. And what place could be lovelier than Baltistan? Tropical suns, almost; snow and ice to your taste; oases green as jade; and so many sweet little villages still unspoiled by the atomic cooker and a lot of folks worried stiff about radiation. "How many rays did I absorb today? What was my intake for yesterday? Let's add it up"—and so on. The World Alpine Club did a good thing when it gave this enterprise its whole-hearted support. They pressed a little booklet into my hand the minute I got here; there seem to be at least eight huts in the Baltoro and you can get to them by helicopter. The one at Concordia is the biggest of the lot.

'John and Ivan want to do some serious climbing. But I think I'll be happier just admiring the view with Michiko. We haven't been married long, and this could still count as our honeymoon. John was on about some new mountain venture he wants to start all yesterday. There's very little that's new round these peaks now. Those virgin peaks, they got round to climbing them a hundred years ago when they came up here by primitive methods. Then, when they opened the road to Askole and made the first shelter in Concordia, you got the epoch of the great ice-walls—K2 North Side, Muztagh Tower North-East, Gasherbrum West, Masherbrum North. Big stuff for the times. Today, all that's left is a few crazy arêtes and some traverses. Very fashionable today, the 'round-tour' climbs. It seems that K2 can be done like this, keeping exactly to the 24,000 feet altitude all the way round. John and Ivan want to do it at 26,000 feet. A great novelty. Must wish them luck. What marvellous mountains! What sun! How nice to enjoy a week's holiday at the expense of the World Federation of Disintegrating-Integrators, on the Roof of the World!'

Baltoro: 'Saluad' to the All-Powerful

Let us turn back a hundred years. No Grand Hotel, Baltoro. No helicopter service to range the colossi. No 'round-tour' climbs of K2. Let us take up our burdens and get on our way again, on foot, like our ancestors for thousands of years. Today the caravan went off in grand style: all punctuality and no squabbling. Tempers were perfect. What a contrast to the day before. Does it just possibly do some good, a tussle on these lines every so often?

When we left Payù, Toni, Oberto and I bade a last farewell to everything that grew there—the leaves, the grass, the tiny flowers of these enchanted valleys. We were well aware that for weeks now we should see nothing but rock and ice. Vegetation, in the life of ordinary people, is something taken so much for granted, something so trivial, in fact, that it is never given a second thought. But, when you know that you are going to leave it behind you for good, you say goodbye to it as you would to a friend, or a nice old dog you feel particularly tied to.

For a long while the track stuck to the left flank of the valley (the right, orographically speaking, to anyone descending). The going was high, over terrace and hillocks. Time after time the track plunged down, where some stream had cut itself a gorge in that incoherent mass of stone and gravel, and climbed up again on the other side. We were now facing the Baltoro Glacier. The monster choked the whole valley—ancient and grey and wrinkled and surly. Its gate wept a milky-white stream which split up into a hundred rivulets hurrying through the gravel-bed.

When the porters had all but actually set foot on the glacier, at the very edge of the snout, something striking happened. Every group had stopped in serried ranks. Then, in louder and louder tones but always on the same note, there rose a prayer to Allah, the All-Powerful. The hymn filled the vast valley; was lost; came back; died again and was born again on echoes in the wind. Haji Ismael told me that this was called a '*saluad*'. 'Whoever sets foot on a glacier,' he explained, 'never knows if he will be spared to come back; it is the moment to cry on the protection of the Omnipotent—no?'

While the caravan was slowly making its way up the first moraine, I took two porters, Haji Ismael and Shukur, with me and went down to the glacier's gate to photograph it from close at hand. The 'gate' is the opening through which the stream or river, formed in the inner heart of the glacier, emerges. Everything took on gigantic dimensions. This little descent had looked nothing: it proved long and difficult enough. The gate at this actual moment was very small, nothing much more than a horizontal slot, and it was at the bottom of a sinister-looking amphitheatre of black ice-cliffs stained with sand and gravel, a hundred metres in height. Our only way to the gate lay along a narrow gravel tongue, bombarded every now and again by stones falling from the heights. Big stone blocks clattered down around us with a great uproar; ricocheting from precipice to ice precipice, they finished up in the water, splashing it sky-high. Haji Ismael followed me lightly and nimbly enough, but his greenish face might have been that of a Sancho Panza boldly following his Don Quixote to a profitless death. Shukur had stopped to crouch in the shadow of a boulder; he trembled as he chanted his prayers in a high voice. The curious thing was that Haji Ismael was small and none too strong. Shukur was big enough to fight a bear, and his very walk was a strut of defiance: you would have thought he could grab a dozen devils by the scruff of the neck.

During the last 15,000 years, so geologists tell us, the earth's glaciers have, generally speaking, retreated, but there have been alternating rates of progress in their retreat. Historical evidence points to the fact—to give one example—that well back in medieval times the glaciers were in marked retreat. Then began an advance which reached its peak about the middle of the last century.

Today, all over the world, glaciers are contracting. The Baltoro, no less than the Biaho, follows the rule. In these cases, we have precise data back to 1909 and 1913 (the Duke of the Abruzzi's Expedition, and Dainelli's); Ardito Desio, in 1929 and 1953, added to it.

Not far from the forward end of the glacier is a big rock, which we can take to be unmovable. This gives us a measuring-rod. In 1892 (at the time of Sir Martin Conway's exploration) this mass was some distance from the end of the glacier 'several dozen yards, perhaps more, say a hundred yards'— such was Desio's verdict after examining a photograph. In 1913 the rock was 260 feet from the forward end (Dainelli). In 1929 the glacier reached right to it (Desio). Now it has receded perceptibly.

At the time of my own visit to the Baltoro, I didn't fully appreciate the importance of this boundary mark, but, from the photographs I took, I should judge it to be 262–328 feet from the glacier's snout. We are therefore back in 1913, perhaps in 1892. It may also be noted that Ardito Desio in 1929 found the glacier, in spite of its frontal advance, to be taken as a whole 'in diminution'.[1]

'Of the world's great glaciers,' Desio wrote, 'the Baltoro is one of the largest, and also the best known.' It actually belongs to the aristocracy of the six giants of the Karakoram and constitutes one of the most notable ice-masses to be found outside the polar regions. It is highly regular in shape—a model glacier one might well call it. At its higher level it takes the form of a reservoir-pool which opens like a fan; in its lower reaches it is an ice-tongue thinning out progressively till it finishes at 11,224 feet, not far from Payù. The effective length has been variously calculated, but it may be taken as approximately fifty-eight kilometres. It has some thirty tributaries, of which a few—the Duke of the Abruzzi, the Godwin Austen and the Vigne—are of considerable dimensions. The whole surface area of the Baltoro glaciers amounts to 471 square miles. They can therefore be said to occupy 54 per cent of the entire basin.

The name Baltoro, according to Burard, is generally believed to derive from *dPal-gTor-po*—composed of two Tibetan words meaning 'abundance', 'riches' (*dPal*) and 'giver, distributor, disseminator' (*gTor-po*).[2]

I confess, however, that this derivation seems to me altogether too literary. All very fine and poetic, but too recherché. It must be borne in mind that not all the names in this region are of Balti and therefore Tibetan origin. There

---

1. A. Desio, op. cit., p. 396.
2. S. G. Burrard and H. H. Hayden, *A Sketch of the Geography and Geology of the Himalaya and Tibet*, Delhi, 1933, 2nd Ed., p. 49.

are traces, by no means negligible, of other linguistic strata. Nor must we forget that the name Baltoro is to be found in the region at least three times; besides being the name of the glacier it is also that of a little village on the Talla, a small river, and, again, it attaches to a valley joining the Basha above Shigar. It may well be that 'Giver and Distributor of Fertility' suits well enough a glacier forming the well-springs of a river which fecundates the land, but the name still seems to me not pre-eminently applicable to a group of rustic dwellings. In place-names, as good a rule as any is to look for the simple explanation. If we leave the question of the 'tor' hanging in the air, we find that the first syllable is a Burushaski word: *pal, bal*—wall or crag, high rock—to be found in Baltar, Baltit, Bualtar, Balchish[1] . . . which well describes this extraordinary valley's most conspicuous feature. It may also be noted that the name 'Balti' itself has been pronounced as not necessarily of Tibetan origin. It may derive from the Burushaski root, and mean, though we cannot be sure without further philological research, simply: 'Those of the rocks, of the steep-sided mountains'—a telling description, surely, and an apt one.

The road to Liligo: the towering splendours

Talking of place-names—the two that marked the start and the finish of that day's march are really delicious—Payù and Liligo.

I can never forget the good Ettore Zapparoli, poet and musician of the heights, who disappeared mysteriously among the crags of the Monte Rosa— a symbolic end, a touch of final glory, and a ruthlessly fitting one on Destiny's part. I can never forget him saying to me: 'I'm looking for names for two ballet roles. In this ballet I'm trying to express the magic of glaciers under the moon.' Dear Zapparoli! If you were alive today and faced me with this same problem, wouldn't it be natural to suggest Liligo and Payù?

Payù, we could say, loves Liligo tenderly, but an evil spell was cast over him, and he was imprisoned in a birch-trunk. Liligo, the daughter of the King of the Glacier, can only free Payù from his wood prison by sacrificing herself. Thus, in the moment when Payù regains his freedom, Liligo dies. Payù, who cannot live through his sorrow, hurls himself from a crag, down into the Baltoro Glacier, and that is why the Baltoro is always weeping: a river formed of that ever-welling sorrow flows down to the valleys of Baltistan, and those tears become the little blossoms on the apricot trees. . . .

It was very right and proper for the porters to greet the Baltoro with their *saluad* to the All-Highest. What a mournful world is a glacier's! There may be no dangers to it in the true sense, but the very aspect of that landscape

1. W. Kick, 'Place-names in Baltistan', *The Mountain World*, London, 1957.

conjures up cosmic upheaval, catastrophe on a titanic scale. Our track climbed up and down, swung this way and that among dip and hillock, land-slip and rock-mass, stone-heap and sand-heap, all scattered to confound confusion. Here was the great distinction between fluvial deposit and moraine—that very confusion. Running water can discriminate among the stone it carries down according to mass and weight. But the glacier cannot. It takes everything along; with infinite patience it turns everything over, it kneads, pounds, mixes, crushes everything together, and at long last regurgitates its burden.

Often we passed small lakes: funnels, they looked like, funnels stopped up at the bottom. The water might be bright, limpid blue, or it might be milky, or muddy. Some of these lakes had shores of ice, and lumps of ice floated on the surface: a polar touch. Sometimes the track skirted dark bluffs of ice, a few score metres in height. Ice old and grey and almost black with age, decomposing, dead: limbs of a mastodon which saw the world begin.

How old could this glacier be? A difficult question to answer. According to certain measurements taken by the Marchese Negrotto, during the expedition of the Duke of the Abruzzi, a stone marker opposite Urdukass was displaced by 390 feet in sixty-two days. Roughly calculated, this would mean a rate of 2,132 feet a year. It must not be forgotten, however, that in winter the glacier's movement is perceptibly slower, at any rate in its lower reaches: in the middle stretch movement speeds up in winter. From these factors it may be hazarded that the ice at the forward end of the Baltoro is probably two centuries old.

The caravan went slowly on. When, from the crest of some hillock, the whole panorama of the 'storm-tossed sea suddenly frozen still' came into view, it could be seen stretching for miles, winding its way among the rocks. The cases, all lettered in red with 'Club Alpino Italiano Gasherbrum IV', passed so close that you could have almost touched them, and then dwindled and faded, only rescued from the blur of distance by their movement and their red paint. The men were beginning to puff and blow: they too were now feeling the altitude. They often stopped for a break. If we passed, they never failed to ask for cigarettes. This request was such a standing order that on one occasion when I reversed the procedure and anticipated it, putting out my own hand with the words 'Give me a cigarette', I got a good hearty laugh from everybody.

We were now well inside the Kingdom of the Baltoro. On our right (the orographic left) the mountain barrier was anything but unique; on the opposite side, however, what a spectacle! We were passing a regular forest of peaks and towers and pinnacles; the world does not contain a more striking throng, all in granite that ranged from tawny brown to terracotta red—colours that blended wonderfully with the white of the snows and the frozen bluish hues of hanging glaciers, séracs and crystal-still cascades. The valley sloped gently eastwards, and soon we found ourselves, so to speak, in a gallery: in the first hall of the world's most spectacular museum of Shape and Form.

20,528

20,226

Nameless Tower (20,528 feet)

Exhibit One: Nameless Tower (20,528 feet), a superb shaft rising between the First Cathedral of the Baltoro and the Trango Peaks. Not only is it still unclimbed: no one has ever got near it. At one time it would have been pronounced 'inaccessible'; nowadays we use that word with great caution. Perhaps there is not a mountain in the world that is really inaccessible. What is its height from the base? Toni and I gave it a lot of thought. In a world where everything is so perfectly proportioned it is very easy to miscalculate. These mountains are like the Parthenon: seen from a square in Athens it looks small.

126

But climb the Acropolis and it takes on giant size; and when at last you reach its fabled stones you are conscious of your own pigmy stature beneath columns of the mightiest girth and entablatures of dizzy height. We could rest assured that Nameless Tower could not be less than 3,000 feet in height from its base.

Exhibits Two and Three: The Cathedrals of the Baltoro—mighty buttresses detaching themselves from the principal watershed to the north of the Baltoro and running southwards in a cavalcade of turreted crests; pinnacled, terraced, knife-edged, plumed and toothed, they reach the 'Grand Canal' of the Baltoro in cusp-crowned walls, magnificent of scale and construction, solemn, serene, Doric. We might indeed be looking at some great palace or cathedral (*Plates 50, 51*). The first is the more imposing. There is a sense of splendid order about the way the pyramids rise, one on top of the other, one melting into the other. Parallels from music spring to the mind. At last they all merge in one supreme bastioned tower. There is a matchless majesty here: how few edifices built by human hands can even suggest it! Here again (and one could say so on every page of this book) the dimensions must not be forgotten. The bastion's peak is at least 6,500 feet above the glacier. Six thousand five hundred clear feet of precipice carved in granite!

Exhibit Four: most beautiful of all and—along with the Matterhorn, Siniolchu, Alpamayo and Fuji—one of the world's mountain splendours— Payù Peak (21,654 feet). This mountain rises at the far end of the last buttress which, at a lower level, drops towards the Baltoro and has the effect of closing in the valley (*Plate 49*). While the Towers of Trango and the Cathedrals are in essence rocks, here we have a true, full-scale mountain, with its own glaciers, crests and buttresses. What strikes the eye at once is their perfect unity in a symphony of highly divergent elements. When you stop to look at the mountain, you realize that the total effect is a matter of valley and tower, gendarme and pinnacle, couloir, pass and shoulder; but no single element, colossal though its scale may be, obtrudes upon the general impression. This is an indescribable one of eruption, of a jet-like force of vertical form ejected from the earth, endowing weight and mass in granite with a dynamic defiance of gravity itself—with veritable wings of stone. And it is an awesome, evil, bristling, horrific mass: impossible to contemplate without that mixture of enchantment and uneasiness which every sovereign mountain inspires.

Liligo: courtesy visits

Liligo is the name of a flat, sandy stretch at the foot of a high smooth wall, of regular formation, running westwards. It is quite flat, and the perfect terrace: you might think it had been specially constructed for a camp. All round, the mountain-mass swoops down steeply on the 'storm-tossed sea, suddenly frozen still' of the moraine covering the Baltoro. And up there, beyond the glacier, you can enjoy the sublime and dramatic spectacles of snow and ice—the Towers of Trango, the Cathedrals, above all Payù Peak. One has only to add that the strong, rich afternoon sun keeps the rock warm till the very last moment of daylight, and it will be seen that Liligo is the perfect pitch.

The moment Toni, Oberto and I got there, we sat down on some stones for a breather. The porters were coming along in their groups, talking, shouting, singing. I can't quite think why, but, what with the sand, the voices and the fury of the sunlight pouring down on the valley, I almost had the impression of being at the seaside one Sunday in August. But not long after, pausing only to put a bit of order into all the clutter they had been carrying, sometimes singly, sometimes in a group, the porters went down to the sand-dunes that stretched towards the glacier, and kneeling towards Mecca began to pray there; and then, with the shadows lengthening fantastically, we seemed to be on an August beach no longer, but rather somewhere in that desert strip which runs round the world from Morocco to Takla Makan, in the sandy lands of Islam. At last, in a baroque splendour of ray and colour and cloud that filled the empyrean, the sun dropped down, beyond a farther valley, among the distant peaks.

Not a murmur of dissent at the camp that night. The porters had found a few stumps of wood after all, among the rocks, and had a cheerful blaze going here and there: the flicker of the flames lit up their faces in sudden reddish spurts (*Plate 27*). With the Captain in tow, we paid our courtesy visits, just as if we were at some International Rally of Lovers of Camp Life, who in the normal way were solid citizens of consequence. A pity I felt so done: I couldn't even muster enough spirits to enjoy the peace of the evening. A case of nervous exhaustion rather than physical. The days that really took it out of you were those like yesterday, with its 'Revolt at Payù'—they took a heavier toll than all the marching and the altitude and the hard going put together.

Almost before the sun had gone down, a really stiff, silent cold set in—just like that. This was the first warning of that 'oven to ice-box' change which we were going to suffer from a good deal now. By day the ray of the tropical sun came down without mercy, a machine-gun barrage of rays, scorching skin, eyes, brain itself, drying up the air, parching the throat. By night—intense, wintry cold. And not even five minutes' grace between the one and the other.

All together again at Urdukass

The going between Liligo and Urdukass seemed to me very wearing indeed—

the worst in the whole expedition, I should say. In every venture worth the name there comes a moment when your reserve strength seems to reach rock bottom. For me, this was that particular stretch. Yet my companions, judging by their comments, didn't seem to think that it was anything out of the ordinary. But for every minute of it I had to go plodding on with the feeling of dragging my body after me—and my body wanted none of this exertion, it only wanted to lie down. At every halt I envied the very stones. Nothing urged the stones on and on, nothing disturbed their place in the sun. Then some porters would pass by, so much more loaded than I was, and a feeling of guilt would spur the old war-horse on once more.

It seemed one of those endless treks. There was always one more mound of stony stuff to climb or circumnavigate. Not a hundred metres' plain sailing. No peace for your feet and your legs. It was one long climb, with stepping-stones thrown in—huge block-like stepping-stones, and stream after stream between them. There were crevasses to be on the look-out for, and shifting sand that you tried to grab at with your feet. Sometimes there were long, stiff climbs. But when you got to the top it was only the top of some puny hillock, though you thought you had gained a great height. Then on the other side you had to go down, down once more, to the bottom of the trough. Measured in actual foot-slogging, I think this particular day's march would show twice the mileage one would infer from the map.

On the other bank of the Baltoro, the parade of marvels continued in a miraculous play of light, colour, reflections and perspectives. But I had no energy left to enjoy it. For me, the march had become a forced-march. Head down, I plodded on, driven by the last glimmer of a sense of duty. I was making for a place, whatever it might turn out to be, where I could fling down this useless bundle of poor aching bones. It must have been plain from my face that I was at the end of my tether. When I finally arrived, I heard Cassin growl out a greeting, 'You don't look too happy, old boy.' At all events, it was a good feeling to join up once more with the men who'd gone three days ahead of us—and had begun to be a little worried at not seeing us before: we had been delayed by that 'Revolt at Payù'.

At Urdukass—we got in at about 1400 hours—we found the camp all ready, with a big tent to hold us all for meetings, a properly organized kitchen —a whole village in miniature. We could get our second wind here, and rest for a spell in the splendid afternoon sun.

Urdukass is the name of a wide but steep slope, grassy at the top, down to the 'Grand Canal' of the Baltoro. The name, in Balti, means 'Fallen Stones', and in point of fact that whole sweep is covered with blocks which look like houses or small forts. The stone is an ancient granite smoothed by time: its natural reddish tone is enhanced here and there by lichen growths. Many of these blocks, piled on top of one another or leaning on their neighbours like men worn out and dizzy after too rapid a descent of the mountain, form grottoes or snug, wind-proof dens—a welcome refuge from the open when it comes to passing the night. Urdukass is one of the last places where vegetation is still to be seen. There is a good deal of grass; bushes, too, and a small stream. We were 13,310 feet above sea level.

Urdukass has become a compulsory stopping-place for all expeditions. Conway and the Duke of the Abruzzi chose it for their Base Camp. More recent climbers have inscribed a souvenir of their stay on the stones; we, no less, found one with a projecting 'roof' and wrote on it: 'C.A.I. G.IV. 1958.' We also left a message of greeting for the Japanese who were following in our tracks at a week's interval: 'Chogolisa San-do' (Mountain-road to Chogolisa).

Urdukass must have been known to the Balti for a very long time. It probably provided a stopping-place for the caravans which, up till the last century, went up the Baltoro to venture across the Karakoram chain by the Muztagh Pass. This was the road to Turkestan ('Land of Turks')—known today by the Chinese name Sinkiang ('New Colony, New Dominion').

Wild goat goulash à la Baltoro

That evening, all together in the communal tent, we listened to a recital of adventures from our friends: up here on their own for a few days, they had been shooting for the pot.

'Just before we got to the Biaho Glacier,' began Cassin, 'I had a look with the glasses to see if there was anything moving in the mountains. Couldn't see a thing. Nor could De Francesch. It was Haji Ali who spotted them when I gave him the binoculars—a herd of wild goat. What a sharp eye he's got, that old fellow, we couldn't make out anything at all. "They're there, over there, a whole herd of them," he said. Well, we knew Haji Ali, so we got going. If he sees wild goat, I said to myself, it means they're somewhere about. After we'd crossed a stream and got a few hundred metres nearer, I saw them myself, far off—a herd of animals a bit bigger than our chamois, a sort of reddish colour. Good camouflage. . . .'

(Carlo Mauri was cook tonight. From some sauce he had made came a most tempting smell. Outside the tent there was the usual hubbub of the porters. Every so often one of them would come in to ask for something: administration in this battalion of ours was a job that never finished! First they wanted this, then that—sugar, cigarettes, shoelaces, blankets. . . .)

'Well,' Cassin went on, 'I loaded up and we continued to climb along a couloir, but we were still 500 yards short of the herd. I tried to get them in my telescopic, but could hardly see anything at all. We were so far off that the sights covered half the biggest goat. We got closer. I tried again. The lenses gave a magnification by ten. I fixed the biggest buck, half by guesswork because I still couldn't really see him, and fired high. The herd went off raising a great dust. But one goat was left. Got him! It needed a second shot to finish him. Then Haji Ali got his knife and ran ahead to cut his throat, turning the head towards Mecca—or he couldn't have eaten any. He was a fine beast, eighty pounds, I should say. We had a royal meal of roast goat liver, eh, Walter? You could believe it when you saw it, couldn't you? Real wild goat— we had it next day, and the day after that too.'

(One porter more showed up: 'Sahib—*Tarpal*'—the *Tarpal*, from the English tarpaulin, were the groundsheets we had brought from Italy—just one more thing we never seemed to have enough of.

'But what do they do with the *tarpals*?' asked someone. 'Eat them?'

There was no escape. I had to get up and solve, once more, the eternal problem of the *tarpals*. When I got back to the tent, Riccardo was telling the story of his second time out with the guns—with Haji Ali again, on the rocky foot of the second Cathedral of the Baltoro. There was more to it this time. The two men had gone off rather late in the afternoon. They were planning to make it short and get back before dark.)

'As usual,' went the tale, 'it was that darned Haji who found first. I couldn't make out a thing, even with the glasses. He swore he'd spotted a dozen goats up on a ledge. Right. We moved off and there they were, grazing. Five or six of 'em. As they got wind of us, they slowly started making their way off. I waited downhill, then I loaded up with seven seventy-twos—I had the Driling with the telescopics—I got the biggest billy in my sights and fired. A hit! He gave an enormous bound. The rest of the animals came forward a few dozen metres and then stopped for a look-see. It was a regular battle of wits between us from now on, and I thought it was never going to stop. I fired two more shots. The old goat vanished. I took aim at another of the beasts who was still there, and hit him too. But the cartridges were all wrong. What we wanted was two-point-fives for a target this size. They were too far off too, into the bargain. Haji Ali was hard on my heels, giving signs of jubilation. 'Sahib— two *kaput*!' I lost them. Then, there they were again, on the rock wall, one on top of the other, at twenty-five or thirty yards. The she-goats were with the other billy now 600 feet higher. I wanted to fire again, but I was in an awkward position. Then Haji Ali told me not to finish them off. He had to do

131

that, turning the head to Mecca and slitting the throat—otherwise none of them could touch the flesh. . . .'

('Boys, the pasta's ready!' In came Mauri with a pan flying a white cloud of savoury steam. The altitude was already beginning to give us jaded appetites, and a nice tasty, tempting dish was a real pleasure. We filled our tin plates and set to. After a while, Riccardo picked up the threads of his tale again.)

'Well, the problem now was to catch up with the two wounded goats. It was no joke. A mighty risky business with that wall rising practically sheer. Haji Ali found a way up, though, a pretty roundabout one, and we got to within 250 yards of the animals at their level. I fired again. They made off. I took another shot. One slumped down. Two more bullets. The other one finally gave me the slip along a ledge. Curse it! Now I'd got no cartridges left, only the very small ones. Not big enough to blow 'em a kiss, animals that size. Well, there we were: Haji Ali on one ledge, me a bit lower on another, both trying to get nearer. We saw traces of blood. Must have been getting warm. Then Haji Ali got to the smaller of the two I'd shot. He was just going to finish him when he took an acrobatic leap and got away again, down. I thought I'd got the other by now, but he leapt off the second I came close to him, and ran for it. I put some small shot into him this time, but it didn't make any difference. The goat was dragging on one leg, but he got down nimbly enough, on the sort of rock I didn't like the look of myself—it was too tricky. The only thing we could do was to go down to the glacier again. We couldn't see the wood for the trees up there. When we'd got down, we saw one of our goats cowering by a sharp turn in the wall, about 250 metres over our heads. And then, imagine it, I found three more cartridges in the reserve in the butt of the gun. I could easily have finished off both of them while I'd been within a few metres' range! Now it was practically night. What was to be done about that, Haji Ali? Bivvy up. We had no option. Wandering across the Baltoro in the dark would have been madness. Haji Ali got hold of some sticks and we lit a fire. I built up a bit of wall to keep the draughts out. We had hardly a bite to eat with us, and we were dressed for an afternoon stroll, not a night at 13,000 feet, over a glacier too. In mountains you want a hide like an elephant and the patience of Job. We didn't want you others to start getting worried, so we lit a second fire too, higher up, on a ledge in the rock. Didn't you see it? I had a bar of chocolate and a few Mou caramels. Haji Ali had a few dried apricots—the flyblown sort you see drying on the walls in Baltistan. They were good, though! What a frightful night it was! Enough to freeze a brass monkey. Those stones were sharp, too, and we had to screw ourselves up not to get jabbed. The hours went by somehow. Daybreak came at last. Opposite us we had a perfectly wonderful view of Gasherbrum, and the Masherbrum never looked finer. What a pity I had no camera! But you don't carry one on afternoon strolls. And the weather was cloudy when we left Urdukass. . . .'

'Eat up, Riccardo,' we said. 'You don't want it to get cold and spoiled.' But Cassin, between one mouthful and the next, kept going with his story: he seemed to be living once more through those hours, so foul in fact, so fair in memory!

'As soon as we could see, we started scanning the heights. One of our goats at any rate was still up there on his perch. But it would have been too dangerous for us to try and get him. By a stroke of luck, round about seven, Haji Ali's son turned up, with another of the porters. They'd brought us something to eat. Then they gave us a hand with the goats. We went off after them again the minute we'd had something to put some life back into us. I gave the gun to Haji Ali. He got up to within seventy or eighty feet of the one we'd sighted. All three of them did. Then they saw that the animal was not only alive, it was still on its legs. It leapt off. They fired, but I daresay they'd never had a gun in their hands before and the bullets went wide. Haji Ali's son was closing in to finish him off by hand when he gave a sudden jump for a terrace. He slipped and never made it. Down he went, right on to the glacier 600 feet below. That did finish him. I ran up with the knife, but when Haji Ali and the others got there they said it was no good. The animal had already been killed. They couldn't eat it. They helped me skin him. A pretty big one, he was, 260 or 280 pounds. The horns are nearly a metre long—here they are—with eighteen bosses. Eighteen years old! A potent elder in the republic of the goats! . . .'

The end of the adventure Riccardo left to the others: he was too busy himself eating in a hurry to make up for lost time.

'Riccardo's keeping quiet now,' exclaimed one of us, 'because his conscience is black!' The fact was that Bonatti, Mauri, Zeni and De Francesch had had to spend a horrible night with no news of their leader. With the first light they had started off across the Baltoro to try and find the missing men and give them a helping hand if they needed one. At one point they had heard noises. A little while afterwards they came upon the smashed carcase of the second goat—the one killed the night before. In the end, they got up on a hillock and from there—some distance off and in shadow—saw two figures bent over what appeared to be a dead form or a badly wounded one. There was a moment of bewilderment and dismay: something must have happened to Riccardo! Not till they had got down again did they get the picture clear: the dead form was no human one, it was the carcase of the big goat. And one of the men bent over it, in the act of skinning it, was—Riccardo Cassin.

Mauri appeared.

'Now prepare yourselves for the next course,' he announced. 'Wild goat goulash à la Baltoro!'·

Wills stiffen, tongues loosen, greed grows wings

But peaceful moments are rare ones in an expedition on the big, heavy, complicated scale of this one. You look round at a world of marvels, but . . . mountains, gentle and most beautiful mountains, forgive me my words . . . there is scarcely a moment free to pay homage to them or to seize their image. All the time it is: 'Come on now, dole out the cigarettes to the porters. What'll they say? What are you doing there with that tearful expression?' That, or some such request. And one's last reserves of energy, which one would dearly like to devote to a cinecamera, are swallowed up in administrative detail.

Two very heavy days came for us now. Our whole organization collapsed and we had to start afresh. Happily, we were in Dar's good graces now. He was giving us every help. Dar had become more likeable, too. He was trying to pick up a few words of Italian, and full of eager curiosity over climbing and mountains. And yet he still remained a complete martinet. Rules were rules, and they had to be obeyed to the last comma. What we found ourselves up against, as often happens in human affairs, was not so much a question of the law as of the correct interpretation of the law . . . and that meant a solemn saraband of English, Italian, Urdu and Balti.

Toni Gobbi's idea, and a very good one from the general point of view, was to start off again on 12th June. But the porters had made up their minds already, on the previous day, not to fall in with his wishes. They had to cook chupatty and *tok*, some needed four days' supply (those going as far as Concordia) and some needed seven days'—these were the Base Camp group. To reach an agreement on this one point alone several hours of polyglot discussion was necessary. On the 11th June, however, Cassin made one or two other decisions. The caravan must be lightened. With this object in view, 100 porters ordinary must be sent down, and the number of porters extraordinary—whose demands were daily becoming more impossible—must be thinned out. What they had asked for now—a little at a time of course, but the sum total of their demands was none the less startling for that—was nothing less than a complete set of climbing equipment, just the same as we had, for every one of themselves, otherwise goodbye! This too, as the reader may well guess, was the subject of long discussion, with plenty of voices raised in recrimination, accusation, violent pleading and highly involved misunderstandings. The men who wanted to make concessions were taxed with being defeatist and subversive:

their iron-hard opposites, however, risked being put down as slave-drivers. However, there was a very real limit here, imposed by strictly practical considerations. Whatever our wishes to meet, or not to meet, the requests of the high-altitude porters, we had only six sets of complete equipment to dispose of. Therefore let them decide: all go off except for six men who would be completely equipped. Or the whole lot stay and share out six men's gear. More discussions. Contradictions, imprecations, threats, bumbledum and comic relief. At last, Cassin—Riccardo Cassin, who was always so good, so brotherly of manner, not only with his own companions but with the most exacerbating of the porters, too—Cassin grew really angry.

'Let all go except six,' he snapped.

Later that day, when darkness had long fallen, the tent of the chosen porters was like a saucepan of water, boiling furiously. You could hear it galloping away for hours in the silence of the night.

Next morning—sky clear, but more than a nip in the air. The precipices beyond the 'Grand Canal' of the Baltoro, gold in the translucent light of the first sun, looked like spiring Italian palaces—the Signoria, the Regione, the Bargello, the Doge's—all beflagged for some official procession of barges and gondolas along the glacier. Several groups of porters had camped on the moraine-piles a hundred metres below us; the smoke of their fires of *burtse* and undergrowth floated blue in the air above the *tarpals*, which were green— spread out to dry they looked like lizard-skins. Some groups had settled themselves in 'dens' or under natural roofs or in fissures in the *urdoa* (rocks) of Urdukass. They were all cooking their first meal, which was eaten at half past six or seven. This was always one of the quietest and most serene moments of the day. Everybody was getting on with his own affairs and the sun poured down its blessing.

But all too soon the air was full of bargaining once more. Wills stiffened, tongues were loosened, greed grew wings. An invisible tracer-fire was going off all round us, its lines crossed and recrossed, merged and concentrated and at last directed on to our tents, the place where Cassin, the Captain, Gobbi and I myself were once more pondering the problem of how to loosen our heavy caravan chains. Operation One, for Action, Immediate: pay off ninety-six porters returning to base. The job took hours, of course. Not all came from the same place of origin. There were bonuses for special services rendered and even deductions for punishment (each case decided on its own individual merits by the Captain). When the departing porters at last had their money, we had to give them their rations. After all that, the remaining men had to be regrouped into eleven units of thirty, each with its corporal, of course. Here,

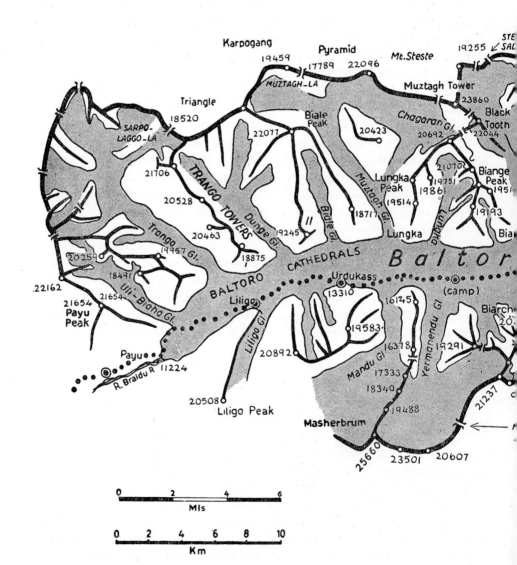

Karpogang
19459
17789   22096
MUZTAGH-LA
Pyramid
Mt.Steste

STE
19255 ↙ SAL

Triangle
18520

Biale
Peak
22077

Muztagh Tower
23860

Chagaran Gl
20692   22044

Black
Tooth

20423

SARPO-
LAGGO-LA

21706

TRANGO TOWERS

20528

Dunge Gl

19245

Biale Gl

Muztagh Gl

18717

Lungka
Peak   19751
1986
19514
Lungka

21070

Biange
Peak
1951

19193   Bia

Lungka Gl

20259

Trango
19957 Gl

20463

18875

BALTORO CATHEDRALS

B a l t o r

18491

.22162   21654

21654   Uli-Braha Gl

Payu
Peak

Liligo

Urdukass
13310

16145

(camp)

Biarch
20.

Payu
19583

Biarchi

Liligo Gl

20892

Mandu Gl   16378   19291

Yermanendu Gl

R. Braldu R 11224

20508

Liligo Peak

17333

18340

25660   23501

19488

20607

Masherbrum

21237

0   2   4   6
Mls

0   2   4   6   8   10
Km

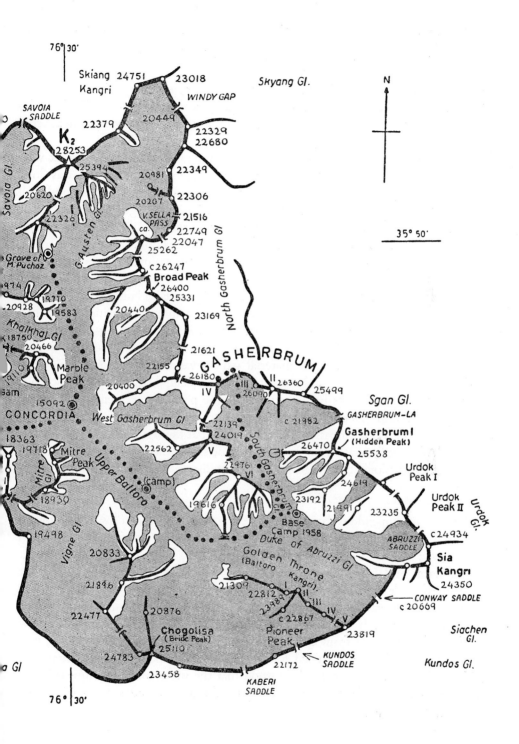

we hadn't so much space at our disposal as at Payù: we needed more room for such large-scale manœuvres. Then we had to dole out to these 350 men rations for a matter of days. Even this wasn't plain sailing. Some would be four days on the march, others seven; hence, a whole notebook full of calculations and sliding-scales, complicated from time to time by the unexpected factor.

Then we had to deal with the high-altitude porters, keeping the six who inspired most confidence and paying off the others. But at last this was done too, and they went with God. At the very last moment, however, a bombshell burst, and it took us completely by surprise. The privileged ones took it for granted that they could keep the equipment issued at Skardu, ice-axes and blankets included. Heavens alive! This wasn't in the book. We hadn't foreseen it and we had no ruling for it. All sorts of interpretations were possible. Not even the most intricate affairs in the Kingdom of the Two Sicilies had released such torrents of argument between *avvocati* as this! Naturally the Captain sided with the porters, thus destroying the harmonious relations that had reigned between us now for days past. Supporters of the strong-arm methods were suddenly proved right, in a manner that boded no good. The result? We were stripped of a lot of material which was very valuable down below because it cost so much—and absolutely invaluable up here, being irreplaceable. That evening, relations between the supreme powers were tense once more. Captain Akram alone poured oil on these troubled waters. He said little, but what he said was unimpassioned, and he said it at the right time.

'Afternoon, weather not holding—some snow; then sun again. Wonderful sunset. Discussions at length, on, with and by the porters. Getting a nightmare.'[1]

Biange: the ancient bones of the glacier in motion

Two more stupendous days now; our eyes galloping from colossus to colossus, lost in admiration of fresh masterpieces in mountain and ice. Four of them we saw: Broad Peak (26,400 feet) shortly after leaving Urdukass, and our Gasherbrum IV (26,180 feet). They were so distant, however, that their vastness made little immediate impact: one got used to it gradually, in which process these giants lost something, no doubt about it. Masherbrum (25,660 feet) and Muztagh Tower (23,860 feet) on the other hand, swung into view quite abruptly, and from comparatively close at hand. Muztagh Tower, in a certain sense, has been ruined for ever by Vittorio Sella's famous telephoto. That demon photographer understood that the mountain spires upwards like some monolith of awesome proportions, far beyond our reach—*only* when

1. From a diary.

seen from the high reaches of the Baltoro, and in the subtly misleading space of a telescope field at that! The admirer of the photograph, all unawares, has no idea that he is looking at a spectacle which scarcely exists in nature at all. Looking at the Muztagh Tower from the point at which the photograph was taken, but with the naked eye instead of a telescopic lens, we see simply a little bump on the horizon.

Masherbrum, however, does dominate the whole middle stretch of the Baltoro: from precipice to hanging glacier, it pyramids to a snowy plume. This gives it an air of vaunting, evil power belied by its lower bastions, majestic as their measurements are.

The start from Urdukass was rather a confused affair. At the last moment we were forced to leave forty-four cases hidden in the moraine, the remaining number of porters being too few to take them along with the caravan.

Once we had gone down the grassy slope of Urdukass to the glacier we marched for hours and hours along the ridges of the moraine hills, much more regular and easier going than the tossing waves of the lower Baltoro. Here, too, however, there were often tortuous stretches where the ice was uncovered, with little lakes, real rivers that scooped their meandering way through the ice, ravines, whirlpools and places which could have been no less fatal than quicksands. Here and there, too, we came across pyramids of *nevé*, hard and compact, fifty or sixty feet high. These formations, which have been called the 'Sails of the Baltoro', crown the stony stratum (superficial moraine) which covers the ice and probably marked the last outposts of powerful spring avalanches.

This particular part of the journey was of course one long photographer's field-day. Haji Ismael and Shukur followed me with the kit-bags full of gear. (Every so often, for some reason or other, they would halt: the two of them could take up their perches on a stone in the sun and fall straight asleep, bless them!) So far as I could, I tried to get my pictures at dawn or sunset. All the world by now must know what the mountains here look like when the sun is high; the remarkable light-changes, however, are to be seen only when night is passing into day, or day into night. And those were what I wanted to capture.

We stopped the first night at a place called Biange—a flat stretch, cold and exposed to the wind, between two moraine hills. The porters were in good spirits, however, and we spent a cheerful evening and had some singing. The setting sun touched Masherbrum with light-shafts of fiery rose and flung bright flames of green on to the Trango Towers, the Baltoro Cathedrals and Payù, pausing itself, like some cosmic reflection, over the peak of Gasherbrum. This triumphal pyramid of a mountain marked the very end of the Baltoro,

139

now a mighty avenue sombre with the shades of night. We sang too this evening. But for the last time! From now on who would have the heart to sing, with the whole weight of the Expedition on his mind?

At Biange we slept for the first time on ice. Against the intense cold we had first-rate equipment and our sleeping-bags were very snug. From beneath our mattresses, as we slept, came sinister creaking noises; bursts of sound that were deep, distant and mysterious; metallic sounds of rending. What we heard was the ancient bones of the glacier stirring. It was a grim thought; here were millions of tons of water-rock prowling with inexorable slowness over a bed of smooth stones, while up above new deposits of snow were for ever gathering.

Climbers of Muztagh Tower and Masherbrum

Muztagh Tower, after half a century and more of forbidding fame as a symbol of absolute inaccessibility, was unexpectedly conquered by two independent expeditions—one English and one French—in 1956, which is not to say, by any manner of means, that Irving's description, 'Nature's last fortress', suddenly proved meaningless. The mountain capitulated, true, but only to the grimmest of assaults. It was scarcely a case of 'How easy it turned out after all those awful warnings!' Muztagh Tower was conquered only because its assailants were men of resolution, men of great ventures, and because the technique of the attack on the Giants of the Earth had by then really come into its own.

The first men to get anywhere near the mountain were four Englishmen: J. M. Hartog, I. MacNaught-Davis, J. Brown and T. Patey, with a Pakistani officer. They set up their Base Camp on Muztagh Glacier on 28th May 1956. After some recce work, they decided to take the West Col, ascending the Chagaran Glacier to attack the peak which crowns the North-West Crest. They did the climb to the col and then looked up, a little awe-struck, at the tricky pyramid itself. Then they had to go down to Base Camp to wait for a spell of bad weather to pass. Some days later, on 26th June, they met the French party, whose guide was Guido Magnone, one of the foremost climbers of our time.

'After five minutes of rather formal conversation,' J. M. Hartog tells us, 'we got cosy in the tent. And we had a real pow-wow about climbing in general and the problems of the Baltoro in particular. Somebody passed round tea, biscuits, butter, honey, cheese and cakes. . . .'

In fact, the rivals soon found themselves close comrades and everything went off in the best possible fashion. The English party decided to keep on trying for the North-West Crest, the French started getting ready for an attack on the South-East Crest.

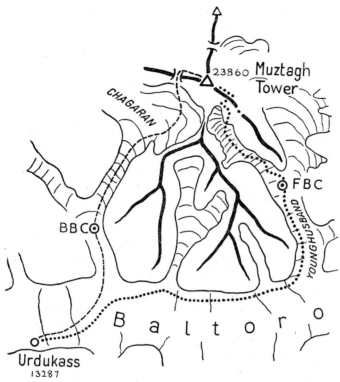

Route of the British Expedition (1956), first up the Muztagh Tower.

Route of the French Expedition (1956), with camps.

BBC (British Base Camp), FBC (French Base Camp)

Muztagh Tower is a curious mountain; in form a tetrahedron, it can show a totally different outline according to your viewpoint. Look at it from the Upper Baltoro and it seems a big tower, but the reality is a mighty rump which assumes such an aspect only when looked at obliquely. From the west it appears to be a pyramid, and one whose ridges do not impress as impossibly steep. But this too is an optical illusion: the actual ridges are not indeed sheer but they rise from between two imposing walls which are extremely steep and anything but reassuring. The final climb bristles with irregularities, razor-edges and other dangers.

In the face of great difficulties the English managed to get a Camp III pitched on the West Col (20,276 feet) and a Camp IV high up on the ridge (5th July), and in the course of the next two days all four members of the expedition, as two separate sections, managed to reach the summit; Brown and MacNaught-Davis on the 6th July, Hartog and Patey on the 7th. The Karakoram had seen, for the first time, climbing of a class which would have done credit to any mountain man even 9,000 feet or more lower, on the shoulders and peaks of the Alps.

'It was open-face work all the time,' wrote Hartog. 'The South Wall plunged into an abyss, with nothing to stop one's fall. Any falling body would have gone straight down to the glacier 4,000 feet below.'

At Camp IV, Hartog, chancing to look for some small object which had got under his mattress, found himself peering straight down a precipice through a tear in the flooring of his tent. Rock-manœuvres of Grade Three (it is difficult to preserve an accurate record of what happens 7,000 metres up) and very steep ice-slopes at maximum exposure came one on top of the other.

The 1,000-foot ridge joining the West Peak and the East Peak (almost equal in altitude) proved razor-sharp and unstable. As if that were not enough, it was interrupted by a gendarme, which meant a Grade Five passage.

From the summit the English could make out the French down at their own Camp IV (v. *figure*, p. 143) 2,000 feet below them. 'We could see one little dot just by the tent,' said Hartog. 'Vague shouts, quite unintelligible, were coming up from below.' The description of this moment from the French side runs: 'On 7th July, R. Parangot made out two small points moving against the sky on the terminal ridge; the British were getting to the summit. It was a foregone conclusion that they would make it. *En Avant!*'

The French party (A. Condamine; P. Keller; R. Parangot; a doctor, F. Florence; a Pakistani liaison officer, Captain Ali Usman; and Guido Magnone as their guide) needed all the enthusiasm they could muster. They were on one of the most formidable faces of the Baltoro, opening up a route to the top still more difficult, more dangerous and more exposed than the English were attempting. The South-East Ridge, above Camp IV, is a very tall order indeed. The French found that 820 feet took two days to climb. Ribs of rock and ice-couloirs alternate with slabs covered by *verglas*. Then the weather let them down badly and the four men were forced to spend days imprisoned in the tents of Camp IV.

On the 10th July the weather improved and on the 11th they started for the heights. It was easier going this time: in their previous tentative bid for the summit they had at least been able to fix ropes. But the ridge brought one long succession of difficult treacherous passages, with maximum exposure. At 1600 hours the men had touched a bare 22,400 foot level. They had to resign themselves and bivouac for the night. The cold was cruel and glacial.

Next morning they pressed on again, making painful progress through

MUZTAGH
TOWER

BLACK
TOOTH

IV

III

II

I

Muztagh Tower, showing the route taken by the French in 1956
as seen from Baltoro Glacier

soft snow and losing their breath in the effort. 'The trail-maker would grope thirty steps, forty at the most, then, without a word, go to one side and leave a clear field for the next man of the rope.' It was only as late as 1300 hours that the four men reached the summit, where a fearful north-easter was blowing. The sky had been clear for some time. Now it started to snow. The party made frantic efforts to shorten the interminable descent in order to escape the storm that was coming up, and reach Camp IV before dark. When they finally gained the safety of the tents, it was night.

At Urdukass, these two parties, English and French, joined up and with the utmost warmth celebrated a joint victory. Hartog, however, had one foot badly frost-bitten. The expeditions combined forces and took him down. Hartog concludes his account with these words: 'The generous aid given by the French remains for me one of the noblest acts in the history of international climbing. What might have been a spirit of rivalry was transformed into one of warmth and friendship.'

.   .   .   .   .

Masherbrum, in 1958, had already been the object of three unsuccessful attempts. The British tried it in 1935, the New Zealanders in 1955, and the British again in 1957. All these attacks were on the South Face (from Hushe)—that is, on the opposite side to the one visible from the Baltoro: grand-scale ascents with ice practically all the way; only with the peak itself comes rock.

In the 1957 bid Walmsley and Whillans got within just short of 100 metres of the summit. What stopped them was a rib of ice-covered rock. It rose more and more sheer, and more and more like glass, all the way. To go on meant a bivouac for the night in impossible conditions. With victory so close, the pair had to turn their backs on it.

It must not be forgotten that these climbers, by this point, were at the very end of their tether, physical and nervous. The battle for Masherbrum had been one of terrible severity. The Base Camp had been pitched as early as 15th June. It was 15th July when Smith and Whillans made a first attempt on the summit, but deep, soft snow slowed their progress down to a few yards an hour and soon halted them altogether. They bivouacked at 24,803 feet, but the next day bad weather forced them back.

On 19th July, with no warning at all, came a death: that of Robert Downes at Camp VI. As can well be imagined, this struck a bad blow at morale, and, not only that, precious days and precious physical resources were sacrificed to get the body down the mountain. The next attempt took the advance party

Masherbrum

25660

Showing the route followed in the
British attempt of 1957

right up under the peak, but by now it was 15th August—two months since
the expedition had come to grips with the mountain. No climber's strength
can hold out for ever against the relentless demands of high altitude. The time
comes when you are acclimatized no longer. You are spent.[1] Had Walmsley
and Whillans reached their 15th August station on 15th July, there is a good
possibility that they would have done it. Masherbrum, to this very day, remains
one of the great goals of the international climbing world.[2]

1. 'If you believe that excessive prolongation of effort will result in the human organism
developing a corresponding increase in resistance, you believe in a pure illusion. What you
really get is rather the reverse, and it does not take so long to develop to a quite intensive degree.
Once the progress of adaptability to extra effort comes to a stop, a general slackening sets in,
possibly with grave consequences, and that is why I would still give this advice to expeditions,
especially climbing expeditions aiming for the real heights, even today: avoid that over-long
and strenuous period which is often devoted to "acclimatization", so called. Once you have got
to the real field of your activities, take a short rest and then get going as rapidly as you can,
within the limits imposed by weather conditions and snow. Do not rely on one team to reach
the summit. Form two or more. One fails? Right; there is your replacement, all ready to go.'—
G. Dainelli, *Esploratori et Alpinisti nel Caracorum*, Turin, 1959, p. 339.

2. Masherbrum was finally climbed by an American expedition during the summer of
1960. The summit was reached on 6th July by George Bell and Willi Unsoeld, then again on
the 8th by Nick Clinch and Captain Javed Akhtar.

K

The retreat from Berezina

Who will ever forget the evening of 14th June—the 'retreat from Berezina'?

We had the weather on our side. It was still splendid. In a storm, I dread to think what might have happened. That morning we left Biange very early: by 7.30 we were on the march in intense cold. Then the sun came out and 'oven conditions' began.

This may need a word of explanation. The air in itself is not hot, it gives no discomfort: in the shade the thermometer is five or six degrees above zero. It is the rays of the sun which, what with the latitude, the height and the reflecting power of the snow, reach the intensity of an infernal bombardment. Our 'oven' was quite unlike the sort of oven you get in summer in Italy. The phenomenon is not an easy one to describe. It is something like being in front of a very powerful source of pure light and heat, or an electric arc of tens of thousands of candlepower, or, again, a crucible full of molten metal.

I have mentioned the snow. We encountered the first stretches of it soon after the start. They soon became more numerous. Then we reached a level where they covered practically the whole area; there were only a few bare, stony patches where the sun had had any effect. The going grew harder, and exhausting. We kept leading the way, but the porters tagged along at a snail's pace, often sinking in under the weight of their packs. At three that afternoon the caravan halted on a little saddle which afforded fair shelter: there was a big patch of moraine with no snow.

'We'll stop here for the night,' the men announced.

Farewell, fair hopes of making Concordia in one day! But we laid down the law so successfully that we got the porters moving once more. Toni Gobbi marched ahead as trail-maker—if 'march' was the right word! The form of locomotion one had to resort to was sometimes more like swimming, and at others it resembled a half-crawl, head down, on shifting sand. The snow was getting worse all the time—deeper and less firm. We now took turns in making the trail—or clearing a passage, for that was what it came to; every so often the leader had to change places with another of us to get his breath back. The porters followed as best they could, with loud grumbles.

An hour and a half of this, and we were obliged to rest up for a while. We had come to an area of moraine hillocks, with little islands clear of snow scattered here and there. It was getting late now, and the sun was well on the way down. The men, sunk deep in the snow, some of them almost smothered, stretched out in a line you could measure in kilometres.

'Anyone would think it was the retreat from the Berezina!' said Carlo

Mauri, and the expression hit the mark so well that we used it to describe the present stage of operations from then on.

Very soon we came to realize that the spectacle we were watching was pregnant with disaster. It only needed a change in the weather. The men were not making any progress at all. They had stopped where they were in small groups. That was how they were going to spend the night. And it was already clear that the cold would be intense—worse than anything yet.

While the high-altitude porters were giving my companions a hand with the tents—we had pitched camp on an ice-covered glacis—and while Oberto, or it may have been Bonatti, I don't remember too well, was getting the supper behind a few groundsheets rigged up to keep out the bitter wind, I turned back, to give out *tarpals* to the porters and to try and urge the stragglers to hurry along so that they could take a turn with them too and get some protection. But I soon realized that these would be vain exertions on my part. Tonight I saw with my own eyes how extraordinarily self-sufficient the Balti could be when up against conditions which were not just tough, but tremendous. Here were these men, naturally tired out after a long—and heavy—day. Their legs and feet were all wet after the afternoon's march through soft snow; they had nothing but hot tea and a few dry, insipid buns to put some life into them. Everything around them was in the grip of a stiff, stark frost. The air turned to iron, to glass; a silent, bitter wind blew down from the mountain. The very colours of this world of snow went from the gold of sunset to the cruel, hard, livid hues of deep winter. Yet the Balti—full of groans and grumbles demanding extra cigarettes (which I hadn't got), and with an occasional curse—were not just resigning themselves to the worst. Some were putting up stone walls; some had improvised a field-kitchen in the shelter of the larger rocks; some had put down a rug between two piles of cases and lay on it covered with a *tarpal* or their thick woollen garments and furs they had brought with them —but not singly: they slept in packs, tight together, snuggled right down and scarcely visible. The Balti knew a thing or two; they had known for a long, long time, ever since they had been drawn across these mountains by the hunt, by their stock-breeding, by commerce. . . . And what did an expedition amount to for these men? Only commerce in one of its more curious forms. It was a caravan that instead of avoiding the mountain heights sought them out. The caravans of commerce went over a mountain range to reach a distant valley. An expedition went through the valleys to reach the distant peaks.

When I got back to the camp it was to find that my companions had already slipped into their sleeping-bags. They were right. In cold like this, the sleeping-bag is the one place where you can feel comfortable. Haji Ismael came out of the first-class-porters' tent and got me a bowl of broth. Of course it took the skin off my tongue. What else could I expect? In these wonderful and terrible places there is always a close conspiracy between fire and ice.

Today, Concordia!

We were on the very brink of some sublime sanctuary of nature; no one who was conscious of nature's fascination, no one with half an ear for her hidden and awful secrets could reach this spot and not feel that sense of imminent revelation to come. In a very short while now we should find ourselves right up against K2, at the foot of Broad Peak and the Gasherbrum; we should be encircled by a veritable forest of giants, giants in stone and ice, thronging us, in their unassailable might, at the behest of the Divine Power. It may be argued that, for anyone endowed with this religious sense of nature, even a vase of flowers becomes an altar; a simple field, a bare hill, can be the very flesh and blood of the world. True. And yet these places remain unique. Supreme landscape. Lands of inspired stone. Imprisoned within this rock is the quint-essence of all those cosmic forces, those secret powers, those oceanic wastes of Time; elsewhere, their presence may be felt, but only more dimly, bereft of the splendid significance which enriches them here. It is only meet and right, therefore, that we should advance with reverent steps and a sense of awe.

Once more that morning, waking and putting my head out of the tent, rubbing my eyes open and trying to get some warmth into my face, I looked up at those peaks, as yet scarcely touched by the earliest rays of an unclouded sun in an untroubled sky, and I felt a sense of deep thankfulness for the privilege that was mine.

It may be that any good pilgrim in such moments lives through emotions not far different from these. The pilgrim to Rome reaching the city of St. Peter after weeks of travel, and seeing from afar—from the Cassia Hills or the solitudes of the Via Aurelia—that cherished dome; the faithful followers of the Dalai Lama, making out from some hill-top between *chorten* and *lung-ta* the wall of the Potala, seat of the Incarnation of Celestial Benevolence, after a journey through mountain wasteland and windswept pass; the voyager to Mecca, braving the fury of the seas and the thirst and fire of the desert to purify himself in the holy places of the Prophet; the youth reaching at long last that colonnade of mighty cypresses at Ise in Japan, at the end of the *Ise-Mairi*—the 'Going to Ise' to pay homage to that little dwelling in the depths of a wood which houses the symbol of the Sun-God—is there some sort of magic bond between us all?

'Don't daydream so much—get on with the job.' Such seemed to be the unspoken advice of a handful of porters who had suddenly appeared from nowhere to ask for something. They were all talking at once and I couldn't immediately make out what they wanted: then I caught the keyword, *razi*—cord. This is another thing the Balti seem to eat. Every morning, cord by the dozen yards had to be issued, to enable the porters to tie their packs on their back. All in all, the Balti struck me as extremely honest. *Razi* for them, however, must be just one of those things, like ski-sticks among students on vacation, which change hands with no questions asked. And there must be some really talented collectors of *razi*, some real hoarders of *razi*. Every day three, four, six, eight men would turn up without any *razi* and I would have to supply them.

'Don't forget,' said Gobbi, 'when they "lose" maybe a few lengths of that goat's hair stuff, or yak—what they get is first-quality nylon, indestructible. . . .'

We wanted to start for Concordia as early as possible, and Cassin, Gobbi and I had made all the necessary arrangements to do so. We wanted to get to our destination while the snow was still hard from the overnight frost.

Everyone considered this an excellent plan. Even the porters fell in with it. Yet the cold of the night was so tremendous that we had to wait for sun-up and the gladdening effect of a few minutes' warmth before the caravan could start moving. It was June, and five o'clock brought daylight. But it was half past six before we were under way. This was a short stage, however, a bare two hours, and the snow held up very well. The weather was perfect: a blue sky, and not a breath of wind.

Concordia is the name given by Sir Martin Conway to that vast plain in which two rivers of ice join up to form a straight down-flow—the 'Grand Canal' of the Baltoro. The name was suggested by the other Concorde in the upper part of the Aletsch, Europe's largest glacier, in the Bernese Oberland, and this, in its turn, seems to have been inspired by memories of the greatest and most spectacular *place* in Paris. Aptest and most sonorous name, full of poetry, rich in its evocations—geographic, historic, semantic. But Conway had a magic touch when it came to finding names for these trackless regions, which might as easily belong to some unpeopled star. Looking upwards now, to our right we saw the Upper Baltoro, which geographers justly claim to represent the principal channel of the great ice-river. To our left, the Godwin Austen came down to form a royal highway straight to the foot of K2.

K2! This supreme monarch of the whole region came into view, very rightly, only at the last moment. It had been hidden by the rocks of Crystal Peak. It came out suddenly from behind the scenes, alone, unmarred, framed in the perfect picture; impossible to imagine a more spectacular scene, or one more graphically presented. It took our breath away. It was a true colossus, yet such were its proportions that it took quite some little time to establish any reality of relationship between it up there, and that mere dot, man, down here! In fact, that whole itinerary along the Baltoro seemed to have been devised by some prince-poet who had used his genius to hand down to posterity a work whose like was never seen. The Overture—for Towers, Pinnacles, and Precipice, between Payù and Urdukass; then the Parade of the First Giants— Masherbrum, Biarchedi and Muztagh Tower. And then, already half-heard as a recurring motif, the Pillar of Gasherbrum, glorious finale to the Golden Road. But now comes the supreme moment of all: after a breathless wait, behold at last the very Patriarch of the Mountains, regal, serene; a mountain conceived on a giant scale, given the space and setting that are meet and right for a giant. In the mighty mass of the whole, each single part seems so finely wrought, each one a telling note in a mighty chord; and in the patterning of ridge, couloir, rock-face and ice-fall, thrusting inexorably upwards to the peak, there is the logic of a Bach fugue.

By the side of K2, Broad Peak, although it has the distinction of being over the 26,000-foot mark, looks just a gallant old mountain-mass, thrown up by chance. K2 is architecture. Broad Peak is simply geology. K2 is construction, definition, form. Broad Peak is one more storm-tossed wave, higher than the rest, of a land-mass in upheaval.

Gasherbrum IV, by contrast, now towering over us, is the mountain of youth, of elegance, of inspiration. Let K2 be Emperor and crown; Broad Peak a Queen Mother so greedy for the cream cakes at her glacial ceremonies that thrones crack beneath her august avoirdupois; Gasherbrum is sword and hero, lover and cavalier, swan-white grace.

In the distance, to the east and the south, rises a whole populace of mountains, togaed in ice: the Golden Throne, Chogolisa and all their Court Chamberlains as yet unnamed in the annals of the Baltoro. Nearest of them all, the Mitre Peak, all hooked and crooked; beyond, a sea of arrogant white flames.

Mountain names of the Baltoro

Of all the uninhabited or barely inhabited stretches of the earth's surface, the Karakoram is one of the most vast—outside the Arctic and the Antarctic regions. It is also one of the least penetrable and the least hospitable. Small wonder then that local names for mountains, passes, valleys and glaciers are few and far between. Nor must it be forgotten that the Karakoram has in its surrounding valleys populations speaking languages which differ radically —even in the linguistic group they belong to—a factor which has often led to misunderstandings, duplications and misinterpretations. These are only some of the reasons why nomenclature—or, as the specialists would call it, toponomy—is complex, controversial and in a continual state of flux.

The northern side of the range is populated by Turki-speaking races. Two of the principal names are Turki: Karakoram and Muztagh. The first means 'Black Gravel'. It was originally applied to a pass, 18,287 feet, affording (to this day) communication between Ladakh and Central Asia. The second means simply 'Mountain of Snow', 'High Mountain', and corresponds to the Tibetan *Kangri*. These two names have certainly changed in significance.

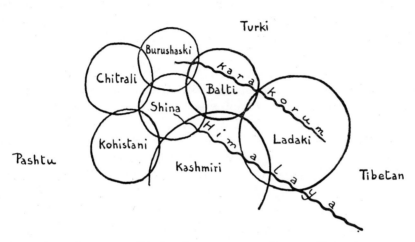

Key diagram indicating languages prevalent in the Karakoram. Pashtu, Kohistani, Kashmiri and Shina belong to the Indo-European group; Balti, Ladaki and Tibetan to the Chinese-Tibetan group; Turki to the Uralo-Altaic group. Burushaski is an isolated language of unknown origin.

'Black Gravel' has expanded to denote a whole mountain range: the generic term Muztagh, fitting enough for a whole host of mountains, has narrowed to describe only one peak—the Muztagh Tower (23,860 feet), and two passes, the Old Muztagh (17,782 feet) and the New Muztagh (18,373 feet).

The populations on the south side belong, linguistically, mainly to the Tibetan Group (they are the Ladakhi, of Mongol origin, the Balti, Europoid), and we owe to them the majority of the place-names here. I have already mentioned 'Baltoro'. Two other highly important names (almost the only two indigenous ones in our present pitch) are Gasherbrum and Masherbrum. Paired names on this pattern are to be met with in various parts of the Karakoram and the Kashmir sector of the Himalaya. Sometimes they comprise only one actual designation (e.g. Nobande-Sobande, Nun-Kun), sometimes they indicate two neighbouring places, the one being in some sense complementary to the other—e.g. Bilafon and Lolofon, Baltoro and Saltoro. In our present pair, the 'brum' stands for top, summit, 'isolated peak rising suddenly from the surrounding earth'. *Rgasha* (with the initial 'r' almost silent) is a very common Balti word, meaning 'beautiful, splendid'. It is one of the first words the student of the language comes to learn; *rgasha stak-ji* (beautiful tree), *rgasha phru* (fine child), *rgasha nang-po* (beautiful house) are the sort of elementary expressions one soon learns to exchange with the porters on the march. Hence *rgasha-brum* stands clearly for 'splendid summit', 'beautiful peak'. *Masha-brum* appears to mean 'snowy mountain', but the etymology in this case is obscure.[1]

So far as transcription goes, we may note that these names were originally 'registered' by Montgomerie, about 1860. At this time, transcription was a somewhat haphazard business, and only later was the golden rule adopted: consonants to be rendered in the English style, vowels in the Italian. The whole name was in this case transcribed in English style; and in English the sound *a*, especially if not too open, is best rendered by *er*. The spelling Gasherbrum therefore renders phonetically, accepting this English peculiarity, what would later have been written 'Gashabrum'. 'Gasherbrum' read aloud in the Italian or Continental style contains a syllable which does not exist in Balti. It is too late to change things now: the toponym is in common usage.

Some other peoples to the south (and more especially the south-west) of the Karakoram speak languages belonging to the great Indo-European family: I refer to those known to many authors as the Dardi, one small group of them (the Machnopa) living in isolation from the rest along the Indus. The main language, for our present toponymic purpose, is Shina. But its use is not sufficiently widespread to touch the central region of the chain, and the Baltoro, at any point.

On the west side of the Karakoram one more race remains to be taken into account; they are few enough in number, but mettlesome, even aggressive folk, known from time immemorial for the dash they have displayed in crossing high and tricky passes, often with rapine or some short-lived conquest in mind. I mean the Hunza. Their language is Burushaski, and it is one which philologists have so far failed to classify.[2] It may be, however, that the ancient

1. N. Clinch thinks that the name means 'Day of Judgement', or 'Doomsday Mountain', but does not give any special reason for this interpretation (*see* N. Clinch, *We Scaled Doomsday Mountain*, 'The Saturday Evening Post,' 25th March, 1961).

2. D. L. R. Lorimer, *The Burushaski Language*, 3 vols. Oslo, 1935.

substratum of names in the Western Karakoram is of Burushaski origin. This, at least, would seem to be the possible truth of the *Bal* of Baltoro, and the quite-probable truth of the *mal* of Bardumal and Kashumal.

In the valleys, names are quite frequent, for there are villages, caravan-stops, rivers and so on to be denoted. But up in the heights, particularly around the Baltoro, indigenous names are very rare indeed. As we have seen, Kara-koram and Muztagh are of local origin, but it has taken the study, sympathy and caprice of European and American explorers to narrow them down to any precise signification. The same might be said for Payù (in Payù Peak). Truly local designations remain only three in number: Baltoro, Gasherbrum and Masherbrum. Clearly, however, as exploration proceeds, so all those blank spaces on the map will have to be filled up. And here, various methods come into play.

One method of procedure, as old as Man and perhaps the best, is to call the place after its chief characteristic. The master of this elusive art was Sir Martin Conway. He was more than a climber: he was an art historian, a critic and a genuine poet. The names he awarded to the Baltoro valleys show a rare sensitivity. They are nearly always apt, euphonious and evocative. Concordia I have already mentioned. Sir Martin is also to be credited with Crystal Peak, Marble Peak and Mitre Peak, all girding Concordia to the west. The names are richly descriptive for the first two of these peaks: mineral, august and all agleam; for the third, liturgical and light-hearted at the same time, but not irreverent. Conway it was too who baptized 'Golden Throne', thus making mythology itself of a mountain mantled in ice, a thing of splendour and grandeur, solemn and baroque; and 'Bride Peak' is his too. Fitting poetry for that proud maiden veiled in eternal snows. The name has taken on a still more terrible sweetness for those who know her latest secret—the loss of Hermann Buhl, the hero buried somewhere on the bosom of that white solitude. The last on Conway's list is Hidden Peak—Gasherbrum I—true mountain of mystery hidden by the mightiest ramparts till the last second of the last minute: only the traveller who has made the ascent of the entire Baltoro sees it suddenly unveiled.

A second method, which has been followed in the Himalaya too, consists simply in numbering the mountains: for example, Peak 13, which became K2 when the number was preceded by an initial denoting the range. There are many Ks, one of the best known being K36 (25,400 feet), or Saltoro Kangri, a worthy goal for some bold expedition of the future. Another K was K5, which became Hidden Peak, and subsequently Gasherbrum I.

'K2' itself came to be regarded as merely a temporary designation. For a more permanent style many names were proposed, among them Waugh,

Albert, Montgomerie, Godwin Austen, Akhbar and Babur. As recently as 1958, actually while we were in Karachi, the local papers (*Dawn*, the *Pakistan Times* and so on) were full of articles and readers' letters to the effect that a suitable name must be found for K2. What a sorely mistaken idea! 'K2' may owe its origin to chance, but it is a name in itself, and one of striking originality. Sybilline, magical, with a slight touch of fantasy. A short name, but one that is pure and peremptory, so charged with evocation that it threatens to break through its bleak syllabic bonds. And at the same time a name instinct with mystery and suggestion; a name that scraps race, religion, history and past. No country claims it, no latitudes and longitudes and geography, no dictionary words. No, just the bare bones of a name, all rock and ice and storm and abyss. It makes no attempt to sound human. It is atoms and stars. It has the nakedness of the world before the first man—or of the cindered planet after the last. And if the great mountain gleams with a light seen on no other, it is that letter and that number which shed it. What a disaster it would be to exchange them for some insipid bureaucratic choice! That happened to Everest. May K2 be spared. One thinks of the toponymic squalor of the new areas in our cities— all those Via Cavours and Garibaldis and Romas and Nazionales: dykes of grandiloquence built to hold back the tide of all those homely and haphazard names bravely borne by an ancient, unplanned medieval core of streets—the Via Palla, Torchio, Olmetto (Milan); the Via degli Agli, del Giglio, dell'Amorino (Florence), della Ciambella, the Pozzo delle Cornacchie (Rome); the Settimo Cielo, the Cinquesanti, the Donnaregina (Naples). Let these haphazard Karakoram names be safeguarded in the same way. If 'K2' is due to chance, then chance has been kind to the second mountain of the world. Chance can take its place with all the forethought and planning of the geographers and name-devisers, a laureate *honoris causa*. For once it amounts to a touch of genius.

What is more, the name is well established by now: almost proof against the attacks still made by men of poor and arid spirit. It has also given rise to a curious phenomenon. The Balti have taken it into their own tongue, slightly adapting it to their own pronunciation so that it becomes *Keitu*. Not only that, but I should say it is acquiring a generic connotation of 'peak', 'summit'. At the climax of our Expedition, when everyone was waiting for Bonatti and Mauri to come down from the Summit of Gasherbrum IV, the porters asked, 'You finish your *keitu*?' Once, too, when we were looking at an unnamed peak near Chogolisa, one of the porters said to me, 'What a fine *keitu*, Sahib!' The strange destiny of words! They are like rolling stones, moraine-stones on the glacier. Never still, never fixed. Speak of K2 and you will sometimes hear the names Chogo-ri (Balti), meaning simply 'Big Mountain' or Lamba pahar

(Urdu), whose meaning is almost the same. Both of them poor, generic, pseudo-indigenous names.

The third method is to name places after people. The system scarcely wins the approval of geographers. Why should it? May not the sublime valleys of the Baltoro, and like places, be spared such suburban squalor? Yet some names have stuck, especially in the case of glaciers. We have the Godwin Austen Glacier, the Duke of the Abruzzi Glacier and others—the Young-husband, the De Filippi, the Savoia. There are further toponyms which lead one to reflect on the destiny to which some names are heir. Most typical of all is the Vittoria Sella Saddle—in Italian the *Sella Vittorio Sella*, which reminds one of a botanical treatise written by Professor Fiori (Flowers), the well-known theological tract by Monsignor Chiesa (Church) . . . and the best tailor in Florence, Maltagliati, which might be anglicized to Misfit.

But let us pass on to the fourth and last system—which goes to the language spoken on the spot for the name it seeks. This is a far happier state of affairs, and one that has, in general, endeared itself to the hearts of geographers. In the case of the Baltoro, true, there might be some hesitation over which language to choose, the region being uninhabited; but at least for the eastern and central reaches Balti is usually accepted, with some allowance for Buru-shaski towards the west. Professor G. O. Dyhrenfurth and Professor A. Desio have added many new names to the map, using Balti sources. The first-named has extended the term Gasherbrum to cover the whole family of mountains surrounding and enclosing the South Gasherbrum Glacier, and he has re-christened, or, in more exact terms, substituted a redesignation for Sia-Kangri (formerly Queen Mary Peak); Baltoro Kangri (Golden Throne); Chogolisa (Bride Peak) and some others. To Professor Desio we owe a whole list of new names to be encountered on the map between the Khalkhal Glacier and the Mandu Glacier. Often an existing toponym has been extended to cover some additional feature of the landscape: for example, the name Biange, from being that of a mere stopping-place, is now given to a glacier above it. Then again, names of the descriptive type have been devised, but in Balti: for instance, Biarchedi, meaning forked, or curved. Some names, originally composed in European languages, have by the same token been translated into Balti: thus Broad Peak becomes Phalchan-Kangri (never Falcan-Kangri; Balti, like Tibetan, knows no F).

To recapitulate, Baltoro names belong to five different categories: the indi-genous, the cypher-type (initial and number), the names commemorating per-sons, the descriptive names in European languages and similar ones in the local language. Let us consider briefly the whole question as it stands at the moment.

Indigenous names virtually do not exist. The cypher-type are there, but are unlikely to be added to: the series is closed. Names commemorating persons win approval from no one: exceptional cases are rare. Let us hope that these suburban baptisms have now ceased altogether; these mountains are a far cry from the over-spill areas of our great cities, where life is a weary and overwrought business indeed.

There remain the two master systems: the descriptive name in the European tongue, and in the local tongue. There is a good side and a not-so-good side to both. The golden rule is to respect the language spoken on the spot. But it must not be forgotten that just here we are dealing with an uninhabited region. Nomenclature is at its best when it mirrors the vicissitudes of the men who have lived in the place it is desired to name; who have suffered there, toiled there, fought their battles and left something of themselves. Now, in these lost valleys and up on these ridges of ice, the stuff of life and death, weariness and fear and hope and joy and the emotions of the human heart, belongs to the explorer from afar—the European, the American, the Japanese. The Balti may be almost as old as their mountains themselves—so may the Kashmiri, the Ladakhi, the Sherpa, the Hunza and others—but for them the mountains have always represented just the merchant's bane.

Many times I asked the porters about them, hoping to discover new names and check old ones. But their answers were as exasperating as the peasant's reply to the botanist: 'What's this plant called?'—'It's a flower.'—'And this one?'—'A flower'! The mountains were all Chogo-ri (Big Mountain) or Kang-ri (Snowy Mountain) or Kang-chen (Mountain of the Big Snows). The one physical feature of the region which seems to have made any appeal to their imagination is the contorted pinnacle of rock in the first Cathedral of the Baltoro—Belché Kurik—'Hooked Finger'. The Baltoro belongs to Baltistan, but it also belongs to the world; in that sense, it is like the Arctic or the Antarctic. Was there not a time when the Alps, for all their total lack of political connection with England, were more English than Swiss, French, Italian or Austrian? The Tyndall Peaks, Walker Points and Tuckett Passes all bear testimony to the last half of the last century when all the major conquests were made by the gentlemen from across the Channel. For such reasons, descriptive names in European languages, if they are proposed and accepted with great caution, need not be banned merely as such: some of the names bequeathed by Conway are stupendous, and they command respect; when I see the insipid style Baltoro-Kangri (Mount Baltoro) taking the place of 'Golden Throne'—which describes a great mountain to poetic perfection—I am inclined to think we are following an abstract principle too far, to a point, in fact, where it merely impoverishes

'Hooked Finger' (Belché Kurik), a high point on the
first Cathedral of the Baltoro—probably 200–260 feet.
(*From a telephoto*)

and banalizes a splendid reality. And all this quite apart from the fact that this
procedure needs a certain knowledge of the language in question before it can
be resorted to. It is all too easy, in one's zeal, to create names that are pseudo-
Tibetan, pseudo-Balti, pseudo-everything.

Today, after nearly a century of exploration in the Baltoro zone, the
nomenclature of mountain, glacier, pass and valley can therefore be put down
as complex and heterogeneous. But why should this be a drawback? Does it not
mirror life and reality—all the diverse origins of the men who have explored,
studied, loved these places? All their various temperaments and outlooks? It has
been observed, and rightly, that toponomy must develop like a healthy child,
following its own nature. Here, as in language, use is everything. Here, for
what it is worth, is my own opinion on this question of Baltoro names.

157

Point one: hands off K2! It is a jewel of a name. No change could ever be for the better. Respect and preserve Conway's fascinating names—Crystal Peak, Marble Peak, Mitre Peak, Golden Throne and, naturally, Pioneer Peak which he himself climbed. Broad Peak is certainly not an original name, but it is in use now, and, anyway, much better than the pseudo-exotic Phalchan-Kangri—a bit of Academic neo-Balti. On the other hand, keep the substitution Sia-Kangri for Queen Mary Peak—let us do everything in our power to stop these mountains from being cluttered up with the names of kings, queens, presidents, guardian angels, popes or wives left at home. Frail fame of mortals signifying nothing; why enshrine it in the immortality—or at least the longevity—of snow and ice? In the case of Bride Peak/Chogolisa it has to be admitted that both are exquisite names—the one for sense, the other for sound. Chogolisa would seem to be the one more common in modern usage. Let us accept it with a good grace.

In this whole matter, nothing is worse than systematization. System is the catalogue, the tags and labels; it is a museum, death; and place-names are too important, too charged with spiritual magnetism, to be left in the hands of bureaucrats and commissions. They need the touch of life!

K2 and Broad Peak: disaster and success

The first attempt to climb K2 was made in 1902 by a big-scale international expedition under the leadership of O. Eckenstein (the Eckenstein of those famous crampons!) There were a lot of the big names of the time in it. I can recall G. Knowles and A. C. E. Crowley (British); H. Pfanni and V. Wessely (Austrian); J. Jacot-Guillarmod (Swiss). At the time—it was a few years after Mummery's attempt on Nanga Parbat—no one had any real idea of what it involved to climb these 8,000-metre (26,250 foot) giants, and the expedition naturally had to return with its object unfulfilled.

Seven years later (1909) the Duke of the Abruzzi, fresh from his conquests at the Pole, in America (St. Elias) and in Africa (Ruwenzori) selected K2 as his latest objective. The team of mountaineers and explorers he took with him included the Marchese F. Negrotto, F. de Filippi, Vittorio Sella, G. Botta and the guides—G. Petigax and the brothers Alessio and Enrico Brocherel—and three porters, all from Courmayeur. Leaving Srinagar on the 25th April, they were at Urdukass on 25th May. Reconnaissance of the mountain decided the Duke to attack first on the South-Eastern Ridge. This became the approach of all expeditions, including the one that was finally victorious in 1954. In Desio's nomenclature it is marked by the letter *Delta*, but it came to be known to all mountaineers, everywhere, as the 'Abruzzi Ridge'. The time was not yet ripe, however. As yet, there was no special equipment. We lacked experience of conditions at great altitude and there were no trained local porters. The Duke had to abandon his main objective; but with the aid of his guides the team did manage to reach the 19,685-foot mark, in spite of the many difficulties encountered.

The Duke's wise decision to give up the peak itself did not mean, however, abandoning the pitch. Abruzzi and his team, often facing periods of appalling weather, explored all the great mountain's faces (except, by force of circumstances, the north side): they were the first to climb to the Savoia Ridge and they reached Skyang-la, not to speak of the Windy Gap. They then turned to the opposite end of the Baltoro and tackled Chogolisa. The Duke, together with Giuseppe Petigax and the Brocherel brothers, got within 450 feet of the summit, only to be caught in a storm which forced them down. On this occasion, Abruzzi and his guides set up the climbing record of 24,606 feet—and this stood for thirteen years, right up to the time when the English began their attacks on Everest.

This Abruzzi Expedition of 1909, although it failed to achieve its main objective, will always remain a model enterprise by virtue of the quantity and the quality of the achievements made in every field. The Marchese Negrotto made the first 1:100,000 map of the region. Vittorio Sella brought back a peerless set of photographs, still unexcelled to this day. De Filippi embarked upon the sort of geographical research which later made him an eminent figure among the specialists on Central Asian questions.

The subsequent expedition (1929) of the Duke of Spoleto deliberately refused to raise its sights to the big peaks, concentrating its attention on scientific exploring. Ardito Desio's monumental description of the mountains, valleys, glaciers and passes of the Karakoram, which sets the international standard for all studies of the Panmah, Baltoro and Shaksgam basins, was one of its fruits.

There have been other expeditions in fairly recent years, all returning with photographs and a store of scientific knowledge. I can recall that of Professor G. O. Dyhrenfurth, in 1934, whose team included the Italian Ghiglione; the French Expedition of 1936, directed by H. de Ségogne, which attempted Gasherbrum I; and, lastly, the Shaksgam Valley exploration venture of Eric Shipton (1947)—the first to explore the north face of the giant.

In 1938 the unexpected happened. K2, of all mountains, might have been regarded as an Italian preserve. Between 1938 and 1953 no less than three expeditions from the United States attempted it: two (1938 and 1953) were led by Charles Houston, and the 1939 one by Fritz Wiessner.

The 1938 expedition consisted of five climbers, with an English liaison officer, and there were six Sherpas. The whole outfit was the lightest possible, seventy-five porters took all the gear. Houston's team reached the foot of K2 on 12th June. But a great deal of time was lost in reconnaissance—to no purpose, since the ground had already been covered in 1909 by the Duke of the Abruzzi. On 1st July, Camp I was pitched at about 19,700 feet and the 18th July, after some very hard going and some nasty set-backs, saw Camp VI go up at the foot of the shoulder (23,000 feet). Between Camps IV and V Bill House successfully tackled, for the first time in the mountain's history, that vertical fissure in the rock, about thirty metres high, which constitutes one of the gravest technical difficulties of the whole climb. It is still known today as the Bill Chimney.

At this point the Americans were up against a serious problem: they had got too far away from their base and had given too little thought to the supply line. Could they go on to the summit? It seemed unlikely. Houston and Petzoldt, however, still with the weather in their favour, managed to set up a Camp VII; and on 21st July they got up to 26,000 feet, or thereabouts, from it. Then they made a three-day descent to the Base Camp, fearing a change in the weather, though ironically it remained perfectly serene. Perhaps it was too much prudence that cost them victory, or a magnificent chance of it.

The American Expedition of the following year, under Fritz Wiessner's leadership, was an impressive outfit: five sahibs and nine Sherpa, not to speak of an English liaison officer. The mountain base was reached on 31st May, and the Abruzzi Ridge was rapidly equipped with camps. Ill luck dogged the expedition from the start. The weather, so fair in 1938, turned foul now, and could never be relied on. More than one man went down with sickness and there were ugly cases of frost-bite.

Preparations on the ridge, however, continued in spite of everything, and on 17th July Wiessner, with the Sherpa Pasang Dawa Lama, succeeded in putting up a tent at a little under 26,250 feet (Camp IX). The next day, the pair made a dash for the summit. The climb took bitter toll of them. But the highest point they reached (27,500 feet) still fell a long way short of victory. The two men reached Camp IX again only at 2.30 a.m., the descent continuing far into the night. Pasang Lama lost his crampons too. The pair took a day's rest and made a second attempt on 20th July, but Pasang Lama's lost crampons were vital for ice-climbing, and Wiessner lost time and strength too cutting steps in the snow-covered slopes. They were once more forced back.

Now came one of the worst tragedies in the climbing history of the Himalaya, and it is one on which no full light has ever been shed. When

160

Dawn brings us Mount Payù (21,654 ft.)

The Baltoro Cathedrals of red granite.

53

Mango Gusor (20,632 ft.).

Mitre Peak (19,718 ft.).

56

*Giants of the Baltoro: K2 (28,253 ft.) (54), Gasherbrum IV (26,180 ft.) (55),
and Gasherbrum I, or Hidden Peak (26,470 ft.) (56).*

The Summit of Gasherbrum IV, from Concordia.

58

Sunset over Masherbrum (25,660 ft.) (58), and Chogolisa (25,110 ft.) (59).

59

Night at Concordia.

63

Gasherbrum V (24,019 ft.)

Gasherbrum VI (22,976 ft.)

A strange cloud over Chogolisa (25,110 ft.), from the Base Camp.

Wiessner and Pasang Lama reached the lower camps they found them evacuated and, as far as food, fuel and mattresses went, cleaned right out. At Camp VIII they had met Wolfe. He went down to Camp VII and stayed there, seeing that the leader wished to reorganize things for one more attempt on the summit. But from Camp VI, right down the line to the Base, Wiessner and the Sherpas found all the camps deserted and stripped. It transpired that Tse Thendrup— one of the men in charge of the high-altitude porters—had climbed to Camp VII and from there called up to Camp VIII. Receiving no reply, he had leapt to one conclusion—catastrophe, perhaps in the form of an avalanche, somewhere near the top. All must have perished, he thought. This groundless, superstitious fear of his spread to the other porters, in the lower camps, with the speed of some contagious disease, and there was a real rout. All fled down to Base, taking with them equipment they thought should be rescued for their sahibs.

Now there was no one left at the advance camps except Wolfe, at VII. The days passed, and he did not come down. Rescue operations were organized, but for various reasons it was not until 29th July that three Sherpas—Kikuli, Phinsoo and Kitar—succeeded in reaching his tent. Over a week had now gone by, and Wolfe had sunk into an indescribable state of prostration. The three Sherpas could not persuade him to come down: they did not judge it possible to carry him; and since they had brought no reserves of food up with them they could not stay with him. Therefore they descended to Camp VI again, and bad weather kept them imprisoned there an entire day. On 31st July Tse Thendrup, coming up from the Base again, saw the three men leave Camp VI to make a second climb to Camp VII. But they never reached it. Their fate remains unknown. They must have gone over into the abyss, or else been buried in an avalanche. K2 preserves that silent secret. Wolfe's fate was sealed too. The party made one more attempt to get up to him, but one storm after another weakened their resistance and it was all they could do to get back themselves. Wiessner and his men went down the Baltoro completely aghast.

G. O. Dyhrenfurth, attempting an objective appraisal of these tragic events,[1] ascribes them basically to the team's lack of climbing experience. The expedition had been a private one, recruited largely in the light of what financial contribution each member could make. 'Wiessner was the one first-class climber among the sahibs. That spirit of close co-operation between a number of men, all with ample experience, could not begin to exist.'

After the Second World War the Americans once more returned to the attack, with Charles Houston as leader (1953). The team numbered seven sahibs (among them Pete Schoening) with a British liaison officer. The men were at

1. In *To the Third Pole*.

the mountain base by 19th June. Preparations were then made. The Abruzzi Ridge was equipped with camps and fixed ropes right up to the shoulder (25,394 feet): all eight reached it on 1st August. Victory this time seemed a foregone conclusion.

But then came one of those sudden changes in the weather so typical of the Karakoram. A furious gale got up: clouds lowered and snow fell. Everything might still have gone well enough had not Gilkey, the geologist, been struck by a grave attack of phlebitis. On 10th August the decision was taken to get him down. This operation, however, proved worse than tricky. It took on preposterous difficulties. By the end of the first day the little caravan had managed less than 500 feet.

At one point somebody lost his footing. The next man could not hold him: and five men, forming two separate rope teams, looked like going over the edge. That was the moment when Pete Schoening, with superhuman strength, succeeded in holding them all. They then decided to bivouac the night. Poor Gilkey was belayed with pitons and the rest crossed to a shelf to put up some sort of camp. When they went back for Gilkey they were horrified to see no sign of him. A sudden avalanche had swept the rocks and hurled him into the abyss. He was never found. His shocked and dazed companions made their way on down to the Base Camp through the violence of the storm. It took them five days. George Bell's feet were so frostbitten that he had to be taken right to Skardu on a stretcher.

Such was the record of this mountain, which the Italians were next to tackle. Their expedition of the Italian Alpine Club, led by that veteran of the Baltoro, Ardito Desio, reached the foot of the Abruzzi Ridge on 15th May 1954. It was one of the strongest, without a doubt, ever to have set foot in Asia. It was known that the Americans were preparing for another attack in 1955. Every obstacle had to be overcome, and victory achieved.

'This expedition,' said Desio, 'had been formed to reach the summit—not merely a very high point on the flank.'

Everyone was fired with the same spirit. The finest climbers of the Western and Eastern Alps were called in; only Riccardo Cassin, unable to see eye to eye with the leader, was missing from a distinguished list. The enterprise was generously financed, and preparations were meticulous. If only the weather proved favourable, as it had in 1938 (and was to prove in 1958), victory was not merely a foregone conclusion: it would be a comparatively simple task. Alas, it turned out otherwise. The weather was not on our side. There were frequent savage storms. Victory was achieved, but only at the cost of unprecedented sacrifice.

K2
28,253

26,509

25,300

24,087

22,874

21,932

21,538

K2, with route and camps of the Italian Expedition in 1954

The story of this bid for K2 has been told often, and in detail. There is no
need to go over such familiar ground again.[1] A brief résumé will suffice. The
conquest of the Abruzzi Ridge was continually hampered by wind, cloud and
storms. On 21st June, at Camp II, tragedy struck in the form of a collapsed
lung, a misfortune not unknown at such altitudes: the sufferer was Mario
Puchoz, a redoubtable guide from the Valley of Aosta, and in the arms of
Dr. Pagani, who had rushed up to try and save him, he expired. This was a
terrible blow for everyone. 'It left such a bitter taste in our mouths, and such
black thoughts in our minds, that for a moment the expedition looked like
disintegrating. All our efforts came very near to being wasted, for we were
in two minds whether to press on or give up.'[2]

1. A. Desio, 'The Conquest of K2' (*La Conquista del K2*, Milan, 1954).
2. Achille Compagnoni, *Uomini sul K2*, Milan, 1958.

On 27th July Puchoz was buried among the rocks at the foot of K2, and on the same day 'operations were resumed on the Abruzzi Ridge'.

Throughout the month of July—the whole time against terrible weather conditions—the men plodded on, setting up a line of new camps and furnishing them with rations, fuel and gear.

On 30th July Compagnoni and Lacedelli, already selected very early in the day for the final dash for the summit, were able to advance from Camp VIII (25,300 feet) to rig up one more minute 'Camp', IX—their spring-board, so to speak. In this last phase of operations they had with them such men as Abram, Bonatti, Gallotti and the Hunza porters Mahdi and Isakhan; all these gave of their best, they drained their energies to the point of utter exhaustion, to ensure that the two leaders should lack for nothing. On the night 30th–31st July Bonatti and Mahdi had to bivouac at 26,200 feet with no shelter at all. Miraculously they survived. Mahdi, however, lost a half of each foot by frost-bite.

With 31st July the day arrived for the final venture. Compagnoni and Lacedelli got up with the feeling of extreme weariness. 'A night spent at 8,000 metres without oxygen was taking its toll.' Yet somehow or other they found 'the strength of desperation' to press on. As a result of a series of misfortunes, the oxygen cylinders, from now on an absolute necessity, were some hundred metres lower than the tent. They decided to leave them there and go up without oxygen. But a few steps were enough to convince them that they would never make it. 'Our lungs just emptied, in the same way as the gills of a fish out of water flap down. Our heads were buzzing and our legs gave way.' They went back for the oxygen after all, aided by a glissade. The cylinders weighed forty pounds. If they tried to lift them, they seemed to crush them under their weight. Yet, at the very first inhalation, the pair felt a curious sense of well-being—'as if a current of energy were running through every fibre of my exhausted body', Compagnoni put it.[1]

For a while they climbed and all went well. Then they were tormented by an unbearable sensation of burning in the nose and throat. In three hours they succeeded in reaching a couloir which enabled them to cope with the wall of rock and ice from which rises the peak of K2 itself. The couloir was very tricky, and above them rose 'a monstrous edifice of greenish ice, a cluster of blocks and jagged edges'. They got up right under this dangerous monstrosity, with their hearts in their mouths—not even venturing to speak lest a landslip or an avalanche should be precipitated by the vibration of their voices. Then 'with no less caution than we should have used to walk on dynamite, we crept to the left of the encumbrance until we were at last out of danger from it'.

1. Op. cit., together with all other quotations.

The two of them could now take a breather. The weather was calm again. For a few minutes they enjoyed a 'cosmic spectacle, the sun resplendent against a violet background studded with stars. Sun and stars together! I thought at first I must have fallen victim to hallucination. I took off my oxygen mask and said to Lacedelli, "What can you see?"—"The sun and the stars!" he replied.'

The two men put their masks on again and once more started climbing—through deep, soft snow which 'closed in again after every step, like water'. It was impossible to go on! Compagnoni blacked out for a moment: then started once more. They were trying to get across a stiff slope to their left in order to reach rock which appeared to be free of snow.

We were up against a very steeply inclined sheet of snow likely to slide away at any moment: to this day, I cannot see how it came to hold. It might be thought that altitude, or exhaustion—or a heady, exalted state—had removed our faculty for appreciating danger, but this was not so. We knew only too well that our lives hung by a thread. I was conscious of it to the extent that I had decided, should the wall of snow collapse, to throw myself out as far as possible, clean into the void, rather than smash myself up before reaching it by bouncing two or three times on the rock-face.

Somehow or other the two men reached the clear rock. They were sure to make it now. It was already four o'clock: in the valleys, the shadows were beginning to lengthen, but there could be no turning back. Everything went very well for a time. Suddenly, 'a steel hand gripped me by the temples, my head pounded and thudded and hammered a wave of heat through my whole body. Then I shuddered, transfixed by a searing cold. The oxygen was finished.' A few minutes later it was Lacedelli's turn. The two men were at 27,500 feet.

All the aspects of their situation darted through their minds. Achille and Lino could remember all their briefing, and they were well aware that exertion without oxygen, at this altitude, was suicide. Should they lose their lives through failure to return to Base soon enough, they would be held guilty of unpardonable negligence. To go on would be pure folly. Yet they went on.

'Three steps, and a stop. Three steps, and stop . . . to let the lungs seize upon what little oxygen the air contained.'

It was getting late now. In order not to lose a second they kept on their empty cylinders—a useless burden of forty pounds: the movements needed to get free of them were too complicated. A little farther on came an experience which alarmed them. They had a definite impression that someone was coming along behind. It was Puchoz! He wanted to be with them at the summit. No . . . not Puchoz. A second sensation, 'alarmingly identical' in both men, seized hold of them: it was a woman. 'We confided this to each other with hesitation, disconcerted to find that our minds were on the same track.' This, in point of fact, was no new phenomenon. Occult presences and strange visions had also haunted Frank Smythe on Everest and Hermann Buhl on Nanga Parbat.

In such an atmosphere, so remote from the ordinary plane, at such a stage of utter exhaustion, of violent and outrageous demands upon the power of human resistance, the mad bid came to an end: here was the summit itself. The shadows were gathering in the valleys of the Karakoram. 'We reached it at six o'clock when, our eyes deceived by the long hump which runs between the summit and the foresummit, we thought we had got to the very end of our tether.' And at that very moment of victory the darkening and mysterious landscape below was swallowed up in night.

Those last few steps of all—as every climber knows—are among the greatest moments of the whole ascent. Just as these two men were reaching the summit, a setting sun broke through a gash in the cloud and the air was full of a golden dust—in reality, the smallest flecks of wind-driven snow. 'Under our feet, the going was flat. It rose no longer. I looked round. I looked up. Over our heads, there was nothing but the sky.'

Their first reaction was a gush of tears.

The two men then contemplated the world at their feet, their racked and driven bodies quivering with emotion. Thanks to Achille Compagnoni and Lino Lacedelli, K2 was now Man's dominion. It is not hard to see that this was a solemn moment. To achieve it, men had come from cities in America, from villages in the Valley of Aosta, from the hamlets of Solu Khombu on the borders of Nepal—and men lay dead, too, imprisoned somewhere in the ice and rock. But, if they had fallen by the wayside, there had been others to press on. And the goal had been reached.

The return, as can well be imagined, opened up a whole new chapter of tremendous endurance for these two. Not till very late in the night did they reach the tent that formed Camp IX. Compagnoni's hands were frozen stiff: as stiff as wooden boards

.   .   .   .   .

Broad Peak's story is brief, and happily a peaceful one. But it is not a story one can pass by.

From the epoch of the very first explorers in the Baltoro, this mountain had been surveyed and studied as one of the surest goals for a victorious climb.

Broad Peak (26,400 feet) as seen from the Baltoro Glacier,
with route of Austrian Expedition in 1957

In 1927 Giotto Dainelli prepared a plan of attack—thirty years too soon! For,
in 1957, it yielded results. But in 1927 the plan was set aside: it was not seriously
considered.

The first attempt was made by a German party under Herrligkoffer, in
1954: they got up to 23,400 feet, to be driven back by unbearable cold. They
had picked the wrong time—autumn, after the monsoon: a needless hazard in
the Karakoram, where the monsoon proper can be relied upon not to come
before the middle of July and to be over by the middle of August.

On the 15th May 1957 there arrived at the foot of Broad Peak four
Austrians: Marcus Schmuck, Fritz Wintersteller, and two absolutely superb
climbers—Hermann Buhl and Kurt Diemberger. Their expedition was on the

167

lightest possible lines. Up to the Base Camp they took sixty-eight porters. From then on, they decided, they would cope alone. As in the Alps, so here. . . .

It needed men of this calibre before such a bold and novel technique could be tried out. Kurt Diemberger had three mottoes which summed it up: Minimum equipment; minimum number of camps; minimum furnishing for each camp. If delayed in the last phase of the climb by bad weather, or for other reasons, then the whole team would go right down to Base Camp. The idea was for a very limited stay on the mountain—long enough for a few lightning moves up to the summit, and not a day more.

A first camp was set up at 18,500 feet and a few days later another at 20,700 feet. Climbing was all on a very steep snow slope: going up, hour after hour of sheer donkey-work; coming down, just twenty minutes on the seat of your breeches. Bad weather came for a few days: the climbers retired according to plan to the Base Camp. Thanks to this excellent system they avoided protracted stays at great altitude, which always weaken the mountaineer; and they were not eating food which had to be painfully humped to the heights! Of course we have to bear in mind that Broad Peak, of all mountains, seemed specially adapted to an attempt of this kind: its very configuration promised the Austrians success.

On the 26th May a steady improvement in weather conditions appeared to have set in, and the four got up to Camp III (22,700 feet) at a very fast pace. On the following day, in diabolical cold, they started very early on a dash for the summit. Hour after hour of hard going, now with solar irradiation to make matters worse, brought them at about 1500 hours to the hump between the two peaks. The men took a brief rest and, a little before sunset, reached the summit —or so they thought. They were just about to give expression to their soaring spirits when they realized that farther on—a good deal farther on—there was another eminence of slightly greater height: the very highest point of all. Acknowledging defeat, they retired—not to Camp III but, faithful to the principles of their technique, going down to Base, which they reached in two days. There they rested up, and completely shook off the ill effects of their killing exertions.

A few days later, aided by a run of fair weather, they started off on their second assault. This time they left Camp III before dawn—and again in fearful cold which later changed to oven heat. On the higher part of the last slope, Buhl was not allowed to forget that three years previously, at Nanga Parbat, his feet had suffered from frost-bite. Schmuck and Wintersteller went on in advance, and made the summit by late afternoon. Diemberger and Buhl got part of the way very slowly. Then Buhl had to sit down on the snow, unable to take another step. But he urged Diemberger on. Thus Diemberger too reached the summit. As he came down, Diemberger soon saw Buhl on the snowy slope. He had recovered somewhat, and started climbing again. Diemberger turned back in his own steps and saw his companion safely to the summit. The expedition had had complete success: all four had reached the mountain's highest point.

It was nearly 2000 hours. Around the two men, a day of perfect weather was fading into darkness. It was one of those days bequeathed every so often by the Karakoram—tranquil, luminous, serene. At such moments, even at 26,000 feet, one can be aware of nature's protective hand. The view must have been indescribable. Diemberger recalls a mountain wall plunging to abysses 10,000 feet deep—towards the west—covered with 'snowy, mushroom-like cornices'. A little later 'a vast pyramid of darkness was flung over the desert infinitudes of Tibet, losing itself in the gloom of impalpable distance'—this was the shadow of Broad Peak.[1]

The descent was made in none-too-bright moonlight—right down to Camp III, over 3,250 feet below.

The conquest of Broad Peak was an impressive achievement. But it cannot be taken as the normal pattern of such enterprises. We need only observe the wide distances between the camps—3,300 feet between Base and First, then 1,800 and 1,960 for the rise from First to Second and Second to Third, leaving nearly 4,000 feet between Third and the Summit—to realize that such a venture, with any climbers but those of exceptional ability, would have had little chance of success.

Caravanserai and acclimatization

Soon we had been a week at Concordia. Seven days of hard and highly complicated work. We got ourselves organized pretty well in the middle of the vast plain where glacier meets glacier: we had our own individual tents, and a big one too. At night it gave shelter to the high-altitude porters. By day it served as common-room, reading-room and office.

Office—repeat office! In fact, Concordia, just now, was like a railway station, or perhaps a caravanserai: the greatest part of the work, at any rate for Cassin, the chief, and for me, was ADMIN. That multilingual ADMIN, with all its hurly-burly and its pleasant little surprises, with which by now, alas, the reader must be on highly familiar terms. One of the first things to make an impression on us, when we got up here, was that many of the porters were in no fit state to go on, especially if the weather turned against us. Quite a few

1. K. Diemberger, 'Broad Peak', *The Mountain World*, 1958–9, p. 126.

were suffering from altitude-sickness, or catarrh, foot-sores, intestinal disorders and so on. There were others clothed or shod in no proper fashion for coping with the night cold or a spell of bad weather, right up here, so far from the usual Base Camp site. It is true that the Balti has powers of extraordinary resistance to hardship and cold. In daytime they could often be seen going barefoot over the snow, if only to freshen up their feet; but it would have been too much of a good thing to carry the practice any higher up the mountain, and they themselves knew as much.

All in all, Cassin and Gobbi decided to send down 200 men, keeping 120 of the more fit. Our charts showed us that we had another two days' march to the site we had chosen for the Base Camp. The 120 men would do a shuttle service of three journeys between Concordia (15,000) and Base Camp, at about 17,000 feet, on the Duke of the Abruzzi Glacier. This would give them a chance to get all the equipment up.

One of the earliest problems we had to solve was this: many of the men who were poorly equipped wished to stay on, and many of those sufficiently well equipped to stay on wanted to go down. And they weren't taking any orders, either! They were susceptible, however, to gentler methods of persuasion, and, although they did not proclaim the fact from the housetops, the promise of future favours could always be relied upon to induce them to yield. Here, it will be seen, was the stuff of committee-meeting after committee-meeting. We had to remember, too, that a forty-four-man section had to be set aside to return with one of us to Urdukass to pick up the forty-four packs we had been obliged to dump there.

If I turn to my diary I find entry after entry on these lines:

'15th June: Arrive Concordia at nine. Sun fierce. Glare, snow, black sky. Agenda: ration dole-out for porters, pay-off for 165 going down (six hours' hard labour to this alone!). Ration dole-out No. 2 for 120 going up tomorrow to Base Camp: Ditto for 44 going down to Urdukass with De Francesch. Absolutely done by nightfall.

'16th June: Rise and shine 5 o'clock. 6.30 begin ops. to effect departure of 120 porters. Usual confusion. All move off at last. Bonatti in lead, Gobbi and Oberto bringing up rear.

'18th June: About 12, 120 men begin to trickle in from Base Camp. Ration dole-out: endless work. Cold. Late afternoon and evening—porters cooking chupatty cakes for two days' march. Fuel problems.

'20th June: Up at 5.30. Long, complicated preps. for 120 porters returning to Base Camp (second trip). Before these get off, in march the 44 from Urdukass with Bepi De Francesch. These 44, plus 9 sent back by Gobbi (53 altogether), leaving for Askole; dismissal arrangements, rations, pay—busy till 1300 hours.

'21st June: Porterage problems. 120 men in from Base Camp. Only 60 packs now. Therefore must pick out 60 best men, send other 60 down. A headache. Take it slow. However you work it out, there's always grumbles.'

The truth was that the altitude was now beginning to make itself felt among us all. True, it is better to *be* 15,092 feet up than to put in just a few hours at that height, as can happen in the Alps. Still, acclimatization is a long business. For the first few days you are more nervous, more irritable, more weary and worn than usual: what else can be expected? When, on top of this, you get these unending ADMIN difficulties, you can easily become a case of bad nervous debility.

Down to Urdukass[1]

'16th June 1958. At eight o'clock, Cassin called us together and said: "I've got a none too pleasant job for one of you. Somebody's got to go back to Urdukass with 44 porters to bring the gear up. Dar wants one of us to go along with them. Any volunteers?"

Certainly, the idea of a return journey to Urdukass, when it had taken nearly three days to get from Urdukass up to Concordia, pleased nobody. However, I thought a bit about it and it seemed to lie in the line of duty, so I said "I'll go".

I went off at 11 a.m. with my 44 porters. The next three hours we spent covering ground which, taken earlier in the day, had been covered before in an hour and a half. For two kilos we were sinking into snow at every step, and none of the porters wanted to be trail-maker. We got to the point where we had bivouacked. The porters made tea and stayed till 1430 hours. I said we ought to keep marching till 1800. I took the lead myself (and as long steps as possible!) —and at 1800 hrs. we were at the stopping-place. On 17th, at 9.0 we made Urdukass after only three hours' march. Towards midday I gave out two days' supplies: 200 lb. of flour, 9 tins of condensed milk, a pound apiece, 6 lb. of chick peas, 9 lb. of butter and 15 cigarettes a head, restrospectively (they count on five a day): for two days' full supplies I should also dole out 12 lb. of sugar, tea, salt and matches, but these I hadn't got. They would have to draw them back at Concordia.

While I am writing this, the porters are cooking their chupatty cakes and singing round the fire. It is a very dark night and my thoughts travel far—among my own native mountains, to my home. . . . Better take a turn round the "camp"

1. This section, up to page 173, was contributed by Bepi De Francesch.

before turning in, to make sure everything's all right. At 6 tomorrow, 6.30 at the latest, I reckon to start back for Concordia with the porters and their loads.

18th June. This morning, with my 44 porters, started off from Urdukass at 6.30. Now 1330 and we are one kilometre ahead of the point where we bivvied the first time with the biggest part of the porters: with my present 44 I'm counting on getting still farther ahead before making a stop. Have promised them we go on till 1700 hours only. Up till now, no trouble, only the usual grouses. Whatever you give 'em, it's never enough. These men are like kids, pig-headed ones: primitives. Yet they cry out for pity too, half-naked as they are underneath their rags and tatters. Their turbans aren't much better and all they've got on their feet is a miserable pair of shoes or slippers stuffed with straw. At heart they're good chaps and, for every man-jack of them, working for the Expedition means a fortune. Step by step and stone by stone, we're getting up to Concordia along this endless Baltoro glacier.

At 1400 hours the porters took it into their heads that they wouldn't go another metre: promises proved as useless as threats. They'd made up their minds and wouldn't budge. So I was forced to put up my Pamir tent. I was keen to get on with the journey because there was snow coming, and 8 or 10 inches of it on this moraine would make for very hard going: we had crevasses to face, and besides, I hadn't the rations to hold out for long. I told them again and again that it would snow tonight, better get ahead; if we made Concordia in two days I'd see they got three days' pay . . . but it was all useless. Now we should see. . . .

19th June. At 5.30 a.m. I put my head out of the tent. Snowing. Five centimetres on the ground. Had given the two guides marching orders for 6 o'clock, but they were still asleep. In weather as ugly as this, they didn't want to stir. There was no moving off before 8 o'clock. We were on the march when about 10 o'clock the sun came out. Much to my dismay, the porters stopped. I asked the guides why. They said the porters had stopped because the sun was melting the snow. The bad weather was obviously going to set in again. There were nasty black clouds coming up from the valley. I told them all this with some urgency, but it had no effect. I had to contain my impatience for a halt of a whole maddening hour—in the course of which I saw no snow melt!

A little while after they had at last decided to go on, the storm burst—as I had expected it would. The porters did not stop now to see if the sun was melting the snow: no, they made a halt every hundred metres to pray to Allah that the tempest might cease; it became more violent, and went on for about an hour and a half. If they had listened to me yesterday, 1300 hours today would have seen us safely in Concordia: instead of which, here we were, at the second bivouac point of our outgoing trip. We had scarcely got to it before the porters were clamouring for their rations, and I was forced to tell them that if they wanted to eat they would have to go on to Concordia, where everything was waiting for them, as they well knew by now. All I had with me here and now was the cigarettes, and I didn't want to dole them out for the simple reason that, being unused to smoking, when they did smoke they coughed like the damned, and felt under par.

20th June. This morning, very early, I heard the porters talking among themselves. I looked at my watch. It was only a quarter past four. After a while I went out of my tent. Some little snow had fallen in the night. By the time I had beaten it off the canvas, a dozen of the porters had started off. I got the idea! The thought of wages, cigarettes and food, all waiting for them, had spurred them on—thank goodness! Their aim now was to get to Concordia, draw all their dues, and start back again still in time to be well below the snow zone for tonight's bivouac—because tonight they would no longer have our ground-sheets, only their own miserable coverings.

I was at the head of the caravan, as trail-maker, with only two kilometres to go, when I went into a crevasse hidden by newly fallen snow. I had a biggish pack, which saved me from going right down. I managed to drag myself up out of it. The porters were two hundred metres behind me. Soon after 7.0 hours we arrived at Concordia with the 44 loads.'

Some jottings from my notebook

Dead of Night. An avalanche crashing down, somewhere in the distance. Sinister booming sounds, like a house collapsing. Wide awake. No chance of sleep now. Take a few deep breaths. Can't get enough air. All round, silence—not complete, though. Light hissing of the wind: the tent guys quivering? Who knows? . . . a long torpor. Then an avalanche again, much farther off still, but must be a big one. This time it sounds more like thunder. Storms and lightning. . . . Is it true they have never been known in the Karakoram? Why should it be? Men coughing now. And somebody crying out in his sleep.

Dawn. The first gleam of light in the tent. Somebody coming out from another tent to urinate. Can hear his steps on the frozen snow—then the thin, warm stream boring its little hole, a circle of yellow in the white. Now I've got to follow suit. Outside it's enough to freeze a brass monkey. Just below twenty, by the thermometer slung on one of the guy-ropes of the communal tent. What a spectacle, though, all round! It's a sin to sleep through a dawn like this . . . slip on down-padded trousers . . . but to have to stand outside for the ceremony! Ceremony of the stars palely dying, of ice becoming light, colour, flame. K2 is the very first peak to receive the 'sun's kiss'. Cursed clichés, how true they are all the same! 'Sun's kiss'!—it's exactly that. Meanwhile, behind G.IV there's a cosmic aurora in explosion. The mountain has imprisoned the sun, it's battened down the hatches of its great mountain walls on the sun: the sun is trying to burst free, its howls are those rays that rend the sky. Rock and incandescence of light, at death-grips. Which will win? The mountain seems to tower higher and more forbidding with its green and violet walls. The sun is a shell-burst of flame, ever more powerful, more unquenchable. At last it is over the ridge. Concordia returns to life.

A Couch in the Snow. Night up here is pitiless. Cold prowls its way down the mountain, it seems to steal out of the crevasses in the glacier, a great silent sigh of cold, tensely, relentlessly the same. How do the Balti manage to live through it, out there in the open? One salutes them for it—after admitting, somewhat incredulously, the evidence of one's eyes! One gives them the same admiration as we give to the champions of the sporting world: *they* can do it, but you and I are common mortals, who could never hope to achieve their records. There they are, the Balti: they've walled themselves in with packing-cases, they've spread the good old *tarpals* on the ice, they've taken their clothes off and turned them into a double covering of 'bed' clothes, they've slipped in between them with another *tarpal* over the lot. There was a little snow tonight, some of them are half-exposed, too, powdered with white, like huskies in a polar storm. When the sun comes up, life seems to flow back into them. Half an hour later, they're all awake. Now and again Mauri and I have taken a peep at them, and shaken our heads.

'We ought to be ashamed of ourselves, sleeping snug in a tent, inside a sleeping-bag, and on a rubber mattress too.'

True. But the other way to look at it is—either this, or we shouldn't be here at all! We are just incapable of doing it under the conditions the porters put up with, and we couldn't do it without their help. All the same, for my own part I'll freely confess—it'll be a relief to get up to the Base Camp. Then we can send the ordinary porters down and we shan't have to watch their pitiful antics as they bivvy up for these terrible nights in the open.

From Ice to Oven. In fair weather like this, once the sun is up over the peaks, one passes from a polar cold to the torturing heat of an inferno. In a very few minutes the glare becomes intolerable. During the daylight hours, and especially in the afternoon, it is an ordeal. You don't know where to hide your head from one long, relentless bombardment. The sun seems to have got you in a boxing ring! There's no refuge from its blows. In the tent, it's worse than outside—the conditions are soon suffocating. The orange hue of the tents is perfectly splendid for photographic effects, and it strikes a cheerful and welcome note on dismal, misty days—but, in the sun, that colour is a curse. It gives no protection: it just multiplies the bombardment of the rays. There is only one thing to be done: cover the whole tent with clothes, coats, kit-bags, anything—open both sides to get some movement of air into it—and lie upon your mattress gasping for breath. And the less said of one's skin, the better. Poor skin—what has it done to deserve this? All reddened, it is. Blisters are there already. Now little flakes are beginning to peel and bleed. The sun is a big, delayed-action atom bomb.

The Post. Lo and behold! two men, roped together, advancing along the hilly ridge of the moraine. The couriers! The post! So it works! A bare five days from Skardu. We're not so absolutely remote from the world as it sometimes seems.

Home news. The papers. Mauri shows us a picture of his son Luca. He has reason to be proud. The boy looks healthy and high-spirited, with something about those lively eyes that suggests that mice will play when the cat is away.

A Long Afternoon. The sky is veiled. It is one of those days free from ADMIN business, or any other. The camp is silent and deserted, like a station in a railway strike. Reading in the tent. Free to rest up like this; once the harsh necessities of caravan and camp life release you from their grip, you begin to feel the altitude: a certain languor; the heart beating a little heavily; a hunger for air. Let's hope those red corpuscles multiply fast and induce that state of harmony with novel conditions which we call acclimatization!

Murad the Mournful. Murad the Mournful, donning a military cape like a consul his toga, brings us a fried egg.

Mountain Wolf. Riccardo has gone off alone on a pair of skis. Where? I've no idea. When will he be back? No one can say. 'A Chief shouldn't expose himself to unnecessary danger' you might well say. True, when all's said and done. And yet that's just the way I like Riccardo, that old oak! He and the mountains feel at one together, with no need for words. They need each other. Riccardo and the rocks, Riccardo and the secret recesses of ice, Riccardo and the wind . . . the mountains know a true friend when they see one: Riccardo is no chatterer, no empty-phrase maker. He and the mountains will spend hour on silent hour together, like good-natured giant bears.

News from the Heights. The first porters back from the Duke of the Abruzzi Glacier. They have that devil-may-care air of veterans. The organization sounds first class up there: little hillocks clear of snow in the sun, running water everywhere (in the warm hours) and no danger from avalanches.

End of a Dismal Day. Snow coming down all the afternoon. Desolation—that's the word. In fair weather, Concordia seems less vast. The enclosing presence of the mountains makes itself felt at once. But in foul weather, we are lost in a wilderness of white. Some of the peaks loom vast and distant (they are both!)—like grey, forbidding shadows. A ray of sunlight broke through the clouds towards sunset—while the snowflakes were still falling slowly: seen against the light, like volcano ash. At a lower level, nearer the earth, they suddenly turned white. Every now and then they swirled in a gust of wind. Then there was no snow to be seen at all: the sun had disappeared without the slightest ceremony, and all that remained was a low ceiling of dark, boding sky and a frightful solitude. A pair of big crows hopped about, at a respectful distance from the camp, waiting for night and a few scraps. The cold took a more and more wicked hold. If only one could have held back the night and the darkness, or else fled! This was no place for men. I wanted life again: houses, voices, kiddies, the sound of a train going through the countryside. But those things didn't exist any more. It was as if we had embarked on some abandoned planet for an endless journey through space. The porters' poor little flicker of a fire was enough to make you weep; it was nothing but a gesture in the great cavern of those entombing skies.

End of a Fine Day. Even today we had our afternoon gale. But for once it was a gale with an almost festive touch! Just a minute or two of real, driving wind. Then, cloudlets playing hide and seek among the towers and spires of the mountains. When the sun left us, we didn't know where to look, so fantastic was the scene. Mitre Peak had a vortex of dense cloud under the hooked beak that forms its highest spire, and every so often grey scraps would fly off it, empurpled with fire as they reached the open sky. Gasherbrum held the sun's burning eye till the very last: a Rosengarten of the Baltoro. Clouds wreathed it like garlands: from green violet in the darkness of the mountain shadow to crimson round the peak. And K2! Day lingered longest there: Day, in love with our world, clinging desperately to the giant, putting off that dark moment when it must die in the pallor of space.

And then night. . . . Then came the real night. In its pure, transparent cold, a whole world turned to brittleness, everything in it seemed ready to crash and tinkle into smithereens. Go out of the tent, and the snow would crackle with your every step, against that boundless silence. Far over the tent, that little pin-point of warmth and light—the only thing from horizon to horizon that was human—towered Gasherbrum, a phantom in an empty dark.

At last—the Base Camp!

The weather stayed serene, beautiful. Beautiful to the point of evil: for in the end we began to hate the sun that hailed down its own light from the sky and sent the glare of the snow bouncing up at us from the ground, till we were like burned-out husks of men.

On the first day I got quite a little way upwards on skis. That night we made a stop at the foot of Chogolisa, among some hills where the snow had melted, at least for the present, off moraine-rock. A little farther in, the surface of the Baltoro was all pinnacles and pyramids of snow-crystals—almost ice pure and simple—seventy or eighty feet high: a forest, a Gothic forest, of pointed sails; from afar, a dream-city, one would have said, a background from Hieronymus Bosch.

In the distance, time and time again, we saw the Muztagh Tower. From this point, it took on the aspect of some inaccessible fortress. But it was very far off, and, as I have said, the reality bears little relation to Vittorio Sella's famous telephoto. Chogolisa, on the other hand, was stupendous. The Bride's veils fell like feather-light miracles on to the body of the mountain. Harmony was in her every line: grace interwoven with grace from top to toe. And her colours, with the sun going down, were those of the alcove.

One last burst of energy was called for today. A long, tiring march. We were 16,200 feet up. The Baltoro lay behind us; we were on the broad high-way of the Abruzzi Glacier. Slowly, a mountain of majestic solitude edged into view: Gasherbrum I, Hidden Peak (26,470 feet). To our right, we were dominated by the brimming glaciers of the Golden Throne. Towards three o'clock in the afternoon we rounded a little hill—and there was our Base Camp.

A Mountain—or a Nightmare?

'In the kitchen—like an Army deserter, see?'

I wasn't in on the birth of the Base Camp, but it must have been a moving moment. Gobbi, Bonatti and Oberto were the first to reach this point with their 120 porters (on 17th June); and their choice for the site fell on a handful of moraine-hills in the lee of the wind and out of the path of avalanches, at the meeting-place of the South Gasherbrum Glacier and the Abruzzi Glacier. The site was well placed: there is very little snow on the moraine rubble.

At first glance, one might have thought we were on terra firma. But no, we were on ice: beneath the layers of broken stone lay ice—the ancient, greenish, growling ice which is solid water in mass! The place was a natural choice; indeed, without knowing it, we had finished up on exactly the site chosen by the Austrians in 1956. Here and there we found pieces of wooden board with the legend: 'Austrian Expedition—Karakoram, Himalaya'—not to speak of old empty tins of various kinds, and pieces of packing. One may well think: what a wretched fate—to travel half the globe only to end up in one more pile of litter—worse than that in a public park, or on the Mottarone summit where crowds of Milanese picnic on Sundays. The truth was that in this vast solitude, this desolation scarcely trodden by Man, a pile of litter could be quite a moving sight.

Gobbi, Bonatti and Oberto, with Mauri and Zeni to join them a little later, hadn't been sitting there twiddling their thumbs. They had already got two big tents up; the one extending into the other, they made a most inviting domain. The first, you could say, was rest-room and conference-room; the second, the kitchen—liquid gas, and no bad smell—tidy, clean and eminently practical. All the way round empty cases were stacked up, and these made admirable cupboards for rice, pasta, cheese, tinned meats and so on. A further stack of cases formed a sort of corridor leading to the tent-flap. We could cover these with a groundsheet or two, and there was our palace complete with porch. The individual tents were scattered here and there among the hillocks on flat stretches cleared by the porters. The high-altitude porters naturally had their own communal tent, on the same pattern as our own big ones.

To make the most of the good weather, which was still holding out without a break, Bonatti, Gobbi and Oberto had already gone up the first ice-fall of the South Gasherbrum Glacier and with great difficulty opened up a trail through a labyrinth of seracs and crevasses. At 18,300 feet, in the middle of a wide flat expanse, they had pitched the tents of Camp I. From there they had gone on to clear a good stretch of track up to the precipices of Gasherbrum V. Their reports were on the whole encouraging. Fresh deep snow made progress very heavy work, but all the time we were pressing on slowly towards our mountain's topmost peak.

Our arrival at the Base Camp, however, held one unpleasant shock. Three days before, Carlo Mauri had made a false move while opening a pressure-cooker full of soup: he was badly scalded, and he had an armful of burns. Zeni was looking after him with complete devotion, but Carlo's spirits were low. The pain alone must have been bad enough, and at that altitude any physical shock has its repercussions on the sufferer's morale—not only in the obvious ways but in a hundred little subtle and surprising ways too.

'Just to think,' Carlo almost wept, 'I get up as far as here—and then I slam the door in my own face, like the damned fool I am. I could have gone down a crevasse—I could be lying under an avalanche—I could have fallen off the rock-face and split my head. But no. In the kitchen—that's where it has to happen . . . I might be just an Army deserter, see? Believe me—if I have to go down again, I'll die—die of the misery of it. . . .'

All of us tried by every possible means to put some heart back into our Carlo. We knew for certain that it was ultimately a case of pain and shock to the system, nothing more. But at times it was hard to buck him up. He had sunk low indeed. When Zeni stripped his arm to treat it, we saw a disconcerting sight. There was no pus, but in other respects it reminded us of that terrible foot on the poor devil at Chongo.

The last labour of Babel

That evening, I went through the ration dole-out (to the ordinary porters) for the last time. Next day they were going down. There were just sixty-five left, real veterans, done to a turn in the sun, bearded like cave-men. But a funny thing happened—not that the phenomenon is unknown in such cases—for days we had dreamed of the time when we should be free from all the problems of a caravan; but when the moment actually came for us to cut ourselves adrift from all these men, it held sadness for us, more than relief. Goodbye, old Kasim! ran my thoughts. Goodbye, old, ugly, gnarled Ali Ghulam! Goodbye, Hussein, you old sharper! I shan't see your dirty, lopsided faces and your bleary eyes any more—and, goodness knows why, I'll miss them! Many a time, passing up and down the line of march, we've been exasperated, not so much by your words as by your grunts and groans; maybe we've exchanged a snarling look or two over a tin of ration butter, and we may have called down curses on each other's heads, but just the last few days—well, so many things, big and little and largely unexpressed, have forged a bond between us. And now it is that silent bond that is being broken. Leaves a funny taste in our mouths. Anyway, who knows that we might not meet again in a couple of months? Goodbye, Kasim! And Ali Ghulam. *Salaam*, Hussein! *Kudai Pakra* to you all. *Arrivederci!* Till we meet again!

But in life, as in all the best films, one emotion is always succeeded by its direct opposite. The porters ordinary were so simple, so sympathetic, so transparently honest in their little games; the porters extraordinary, the high-altitude men remaining with us, weighed the balance down again the other way: they were insolent rogues. Our hearts were moved to see the sixty-five go off. We turned our heads, and our hearts rancoured at the sight of those who were left. For this is what happened:

Cassin, Gobbi and the rest—all except Mauri and myself—had already decided to leave later that day (23rd June) for Camp I. There was the chance to make a useful journey, carrying up a variety of gear. The weather had not broken, and it spurred us on. It was impossible to slack off for a moment now. On, on, upwards all the time! Who knew how long we had left? Make the most of it while it lasted! . . . And this was just the moment when the porters, the chosen from among the porters, dug their toes in and wouldn't budge! Because they had already done their foot-slogging for the day?—without packs to carry, at the most just a personal bag of their own things—in conditions far removed from the ordinary porters', and for pay a good deal higher? No, that wasn't really the reason; what they wanted now, and quickly, in addition to all the clothes and equipment we'd given them at Urdukass, were mattresses and sleeping-bags.

Such a request may appear simple and reasonable enough. But coming *now*, as the least expected move on a chessboard, in a highly complicated game played with weights and measures and movements, it introduced unholy problems. Provision had been made, for example, that every camp should be equipped with mattresses and sleeping-bags so that those moving up to it (climbers and porters) should be free to carry food and equipment unencumbered by an additional load. But if more sleeping gear was to be taken up, how were we to get the very necessities of life up to the heights? In conditions of the difficulty we were going to encounter, it was either one thing or the other: it was impossible to ship both. To grant the porters' request—which now came to include down-padded clothes as well—meant an entirely new set of calculations: the whole transport line for the rest of the ascent would be radically altered. Naturally it had been provided that the porters should have free access to everything, just like ourselves. But they demanded a whole set each, and as a gift: clearly they had no intention of handing the material back to us after the Expedition. So it was not only a question of hour upon hour of desk-work—table-work—very considerable sums of money were at stake too.

Discussions began in the afternoon. They soon warmed up and lasted—I know it seems scarcely credible—till midnight. Nor must it be forgotten that at 17,000 feet nerves fray, tempers rise, and, however deep they may be buried beneath the protective strata of the best educations, the pricklier points of personality are apt to come to the top. We began this palaver all sitting at the flap of the big tent. When it got chilly we moved inside. Imagine a parliament in miniature, a parliament of a dozen men shouting, raging, walking out, climbing down, meeting one another halfway—and then starting it all afresh, like a pack of reindeer in a fury on a boundless desert of silence and snow. That evening I saw Cassin in a mood of real ferocity, and at his wits' end. Bonatti too would explode from time to time. Gobbi, always the most self-controlled, succeeded better than the rest of us in putting forward a point of view and giving it a new look to appeal to our adversaries. But you could see he was feeling the strain.

'You must appreciate that the latest move would hold up the whole expedition. We've studied and schemed over this thing for weeks: now you want to throw everything in confusion. The mattresses are there, so are the down-padded clothes. Whoever goes up there will have the use of them. Everything's been minutely organized so that nobody need fear going up without the essentials. . . .'

'That's not our concern. We want the stuff. Just that.'

The fact of the matter remained that all this last-minute delay *was* their concern—and very much so. They knew that the longer they stayed on the mountain, the more money they earned. Nobody said this. But it was always there, and it put a poisonous edge on our relations.

Captain Dar that evening once more took very definite sides against us. Marching at the head of the rebels, with banners flying, was evidently something he took a delight in. The fact that the rebels were his own oppressed kind, and that the oppressors were 'imperialists, bourgeois and foreigners', sent his spirits soaring higher still. The reality of the situation here and now was that we ourselves represented the oppressed party. We had respected every single article in the climbers' code, even though it made demands we had never heard of till we reached Skardu. The whole of the present impasse was due to greed —greed for the possession of that little bit more, which was a whole lot more than anything provided for in the rules.

'Try to make it clear to the Captain'—Gobbi repeated to me—'that where we come from, and all over the Alps, the guide, the porter, the muleteer too, engaged for an ascent or crossing, brings everything—from the rope to the shoes and the ice-axe. Here, we are giving the porters full use of expedition material—and it isn't even ours, remember, it's the property of the Club. Then, when everything's over and done with, something may be given away as a present or reward. But it's impossible for us to go so far as to give away, just like that, a whole lot of highly valuable equipment, in exchange for no special service and no work outside the limits agreed on. And who's going to assure us that the stuff won't be spoiled, neglected or lost—with the result that, just at the moment when it's needed most, it won't be there?'

The poor interpreter! Faithfully he rendered all this word for word in English. Then he duly received the answer and put it into Italian. Every now and then the fur would start flying in unofficial little bits of Urdu or Balti, or even German of the rudimentary '*gut*' and '*nicht gut*' variety. When the storm was particularly fierce, all would turn to the interpreter: their fury was intended to smite their enemies, but it had a most unfortunate habit of stopping at the translator and falling about his head!

I relayed the reply:

'What you say is all very well, but the Captain quotes Article VI of the Agreement: "High Altitude Porters should be provided by the Expedition with the equipment necessary for great heights. . . ." '

'But we are providing the equipment,' said someone, jumping up. ' "Provide" doesn't mean "give away".'

After which the battle shifted to another front. The Captain listened to the words that were put in my mouth, but then his own personal point of view broke through. '*These men are entitled to have what it has been decided they should have. "Provide" means that they must be able to use, whenever they think fit, every bit of high-altitude equipment. Look at yourselves. You have all the equipment at your disposal. . . .'* And now the discussion inevitably took a personal turn.

At last, at long, long last, we found a way out: antagonists always do when they have a mutual interest. The material was to be given, lock, stock and barrel, to the four porters engaged for transport purposes beyond Camp I. This concession would still leave us the proprietors of our very last reserves of equipment. The mutual interest needed no explaining to either side. We were here to climb the mountain, and the Captain, as I have mentioned already, was very keen that the 'Victory Team' should be the one he had a stake in. There was also the porters' side. If they went down now they would be killing the goose that laid the golden eggs. To put it in other words, here was a clear example of an ancient biological law which always holds good: never misuse a living organism you need; weaken it beyond a certain point and it will wither and die, and what use will it be to you then?

The difficulties we had experienced till now—and most expeditions seem to run into them—might be avoided if future leaders and organizers, in their calculations, treated climbers, officers and the first-class porters as a small-scale army and arranged for a standard outfit for one and all. Distinctions in equipment very easily make enemies: they emphasize other distinctions which it might be as well to soft-pedal nowadays. The days of litter-borne milords are over, and surely every traveller with any sense of the deeper values in human relations will be thankful that they are.

A peak for a bridegroom

My companions (with the exception of Carlo Mauri, immobilized on account of his arm) had gone up to Camp I. The ordinary porters had gone down. The Captain was keeping to his own tent. At last! A day of peace and quiet to restore one, after the Calvary of the caravan! The Base Camp had the most beautiful setting imaginable. Without the altitude, it would have been the perfect spot for a rest-cure.

We were in the heart of a rough, rude world, and an alarmingly non-human one. Ice, rock, snow, ice. That was all we saw. The lowest point on the horizon was perhaps Conway Saddle (20,669 feet). Over our heads we had two 8,000-metre (26,250-foot) giants (Gasherbrums I and II) and at least five or six mountains over 23,000 feet (Gasherbrums II and IV, Chogolisa, Golden Throne, Sia-Kangri and the 22,995-foot shoulder of Gasherbrum I). Gasherbrum IV, from here, could not be seen, but we had only to take a few steps to the east and there it was, in one of its most elegant aspects, too—the Southern Cusp view.

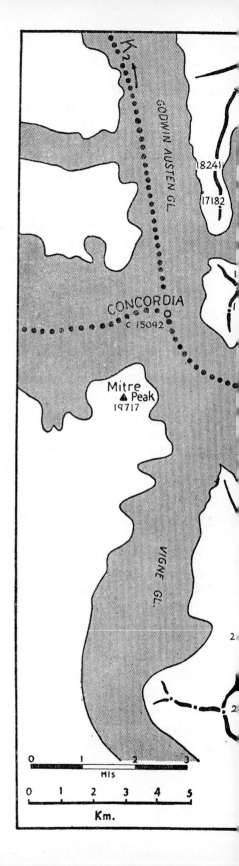

THE UPPER BALTORO AND
THE GASHERBRUM FAMILY

.... Route followed by Expedition

o   Camp

JBC Japanese Base Camp (Chogolisa
ascent)

ABC American Base Camp (Gasherbrum I ascent)

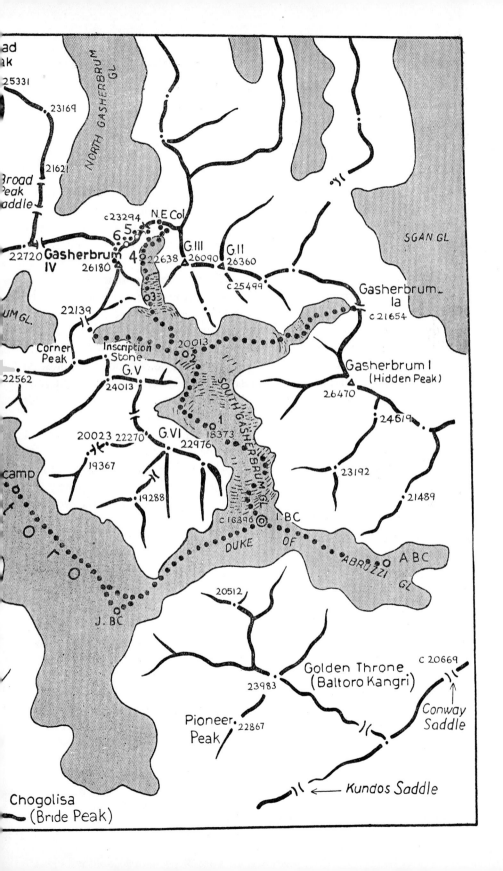

Among these mountains, the one that made an immediate and striking impression was Gasherbrum II. A real Egyptian pyramid—Cheops and Chephren themselves were not more absolutely regular in outline, and the Gasherbrum had just their tawny colouring, too. Chogolisa, looked at from this point, lost some of the grace it had worn when we saw it from the Upper Baltoro. But there was more boldness to it, more spiring thrust. Golden Throne lorded it towards the south with its baroque magnificence: portal and recess, window and balcony—and fantasy and even greater fantasy the higher the eye roamed— each had its glittering facet of ice; it was a mountain of ice, ice to its very bones, its bowels. A strikingly noble sight was Sia-Kangri, one of those mountains which do not so greatly impress at the first audition—excuse the musical parallel!—but which reveal, on closer acquaintance, beauties that are ever new. A mountain that is strong and gentle at one and the same time. Strong in the mighty structure of its ridges of rock, gentle by virtue of those cradled glaciers with their airy grace gathered within its walls. They catch the first stealth of the dawn light, and in the twilight hours the peaks still gleam with a ghostly pallor when day has long plunged down into the abyss. At such moments the usual pattern of light and dark is reversed. A dew of darkness falls from the sky: light creeps upwards along the earth from the horizon. That mantle of ice holds new wonders, carved by still more cunning and devoted hands.

All these mountains, forming one individual whole in a skyline of towering peaks, and a host of others too—the enchanting, unnamed 22,266-foot peak to the north of Chogolisa for one—set us a boundary, hemmed us in: we might have been in some vast amphitheatre, frightening in its austerity and its desolation. When we were at Concordia, we had a link with the world of men: the 'Grand Canal' of the Baltoro was down there, ready, a master highway to take us back to the safety of humankind. But there was nothing like that here. There was no such channel of communication with 'the world outside'. Here, that world belonged to another planet. It was a childhood memory, an old man's tale. There are times when this absolute isolation is a wonderful thing. Blessed with almost a lyrical sense of privilege, you feel you have reached *terra incognita* almost untrodden by other feet; you are advancing into the unknown, an ambassador of the human race. But in other moods you are afraid: a nameless anguish takes root in your heart, and the height plants flesh-and-blood pangs there too, as you struggle for breath.

But for the most part the sheer beauty of the scene made up for this. Ice, rock, snow, sky—these were bosom friends. There was one more: cloud. Cloud too came within the horizons of our little world. There were the ordinary, everyday clouds of no particular shape that sailed along and dropped their shadows on to the peaks. And there were slender little wisps of cloud, like feathers, like gossamer—and metaphysical glories of cloud, up above the loftiest summits. There were clouds that were light, dainty, gauzy and capricious: pretty little gift-box clouds, born to play around the peaks and when their game was over vanishing like unpredictable guests suddenly tired of the party. There were clouds made of anything but that vague white woolly stuff we always associate with clouds . . . in fact, every one of these celestial beings had its own exquisite personality, every one chose a peak for a bridegroom, kissing that brow, resting crown-like on that head.

The Gasherbrum family

We shall soon be taking the road to the heights once more, into the very heart of the clan, but now is the time to make the acquaintance of the six brothers who dominate this region of the Baltoro. The eldest, Gasherbrum I, has solid shoulders and a bull-neck: a magnificent mountain, full of a vigour that does not preclude solemnity, its powerful flanks planted in the wide valleys it rises from. Gasherbrum I is the pride and joy of the Gasherbrum stock. Furthermore, it is a simple-hearted, honest mountain. It never puts on moods. Faithfully it follows the traditions of its august ancestors. Full well it knows that Destiny has reserved for it a place of honour that others may envy. It only desires to fill that place with dignity and decorum. The world does not expect from it the heroic splendours of crazy contouring, or the fantastic touch of a lunar landscape dreaming through the green night's cold. The Karakoram can sleep sound. The Gasherbrum family has a representative here who will never commit an error of judgment, or even one of etiquette; a prince who can always be counted on to put in a smiling and self-confident appearance, without bluster and without false modesty, at the Ceremonial of the Ice-Kingdom, alongside the great monarch K2 and those court dignitaries Broad Peak, Chogolisa and Muztagh Tower.

Gasherbrum II on the other hand has a more shy, retiring nature than the eldest brother—to whom it leaves the handling of all family moneys and the maintenance of the clan's prestige in the eyes of the world. It has no love for ceremonies and receptions, preferring the quietude of study. Perhaps this is why it has a touch of the Egyptian pyramids. Certainly the learned pursuit of archaeology and the erudite researches of the library attract it beyond anything else. Sometimes the world is inclined to laugh, saying it has its head among the clouds: but they are clouds of exquisite shape, which could be shown off in the highest circles.

The third of this brotherhood (26,090 feet) has a less definite personality

187

than the others. To a certain extent it may be said to lean on Gasherbrum II, with whom it has grown up and whose ascendancy it has always felt. All great families have one member who, so far from shining by his own light, will nobly shed it on his elders and betters. But at certain times—and from certain angles— even this third-in-the-line appears to bristle with the desire to assert his own rugged independence. There are certain valleys which he seems to claim rather jealously as his very own, and from which he rises more erect. But the courage and the erectness don't quite last all the way up to the head! And the true lines of his personality are only apparent to one who studies him closely and long.

Let us pass to the fourth of these Gasherbrums. Here is a character for you, with a vengeance. This is a true Gasherbrum, a real chip off the old block— born of the same stock as the other brothers, breathing the same air from infancy onwards—and yet, at a very, very early age, striking out for himself. He must have felt the true sap of superabundance in his veins. Doubtless he was well aware too that even without his family connections he could have made his way in the world. He had no need of parental care and affection. He has faced the world by himself, and it has not taken him long to carve out a place in it which is the envy of all. Look at him from some places—the Baltoro for example—and you see him alone. The bigger brothers are reduced to mere shadows somewhere in the background. Looking at him from the Baltoro, too, you might well pronounce him the mountain par excellence, the archetype of mountains: such is the perfect symmetry of those bold and powerful flanks, thrusting upwards to a peak whose elegance makes it a peak in a thousand. Everything in the picture is force, youth, decision, confidence, courage; yet, at the same time, instinct in this mountain, there is an inborn sense of balance, of wisdom—the wisdom of millennium after millennium in the body of an athlete. This fourth brother never gives a hint of folly, of impatience, of un-justified risk or loss of self-possession. Every gesture, every expression (and isn't that what they amount to, petrified in stone, those walls and ridges and ice-falls?)—every one is a perfect curve. That fourth Gasherbrum has the stuff that dynasties are made of. The rock world that encircles Gasherbrum IV is mere accessory, preface, precinct, extension of that Self.

And then last come the youngest brothers: Quintus and Sextus (24,019 and 22,976 feet). These are the devils, the caymans, of the Gasherbrums. No great family would be complete without such scions. The old folks, sitting at home, may well shake their heads, but the fact of the matter is that the slight air of scandal about these youngsters is not altogether unwelcome. It is something to be added to the scutcheon. Perhaps these two young Gasherbrums have suffered since their early days from the stuffiness of the three elder brothers—

View of entire Gasherbrum group, as seen by the Japanese from summit of Chogolisa.
In the lower right corner, place of Italian base camp

all so correct, so measured, so faultless, always dressed up in their court breeches
—or from the effortless, the unconscious superiority of a Gasherbrum IV, which
they could never live up to. Or perhaps they had been spoiled by an over-
indulgent mother: they were the youngest and she set out to protect them from
brothers who were already grown men. The fact remains that everything
about them suggests an unsuccessful effort after self-assertion, fame, popularity.
Women and horses, fast cars and the gaming tables: here is their counterpart in
rock, in precipices defiant to the point of absurdity, in cornices that are crazily
irresponsible and avalanches that are homicides. Not mature mountains, these.
Not mountains you could trust. They have too many furies to unleash. Ador-
able in many ways, but in so many others—just a scandal in stone.

189

Such is the Gasherbrum family. It has its good points, and it has its bad. A fascinating family. Not one single brother without a surprise up his sleeve. Impossible to be bored with the Gasherbrums. To know them is one unending adventure.

Their story

The first explorers to penetrate into these valleys hemmed in by mountains so mighty and so forbidding were the members of the Conway Expedition in 1892.[1] The only mountain they succeeded in climbing was Pioneer Peak, a secondary peak in the Golden Throne/Baltoro Kangri group; but, in doing so, they got up to a record height (22,867 feet) for that time. The real importance of their expedition lies in the fact that no one before them had gone to the farther reaches of the Baltoro: and they were the first to measure the astounding height of K5 (Hidden Peak)—now Gasherbrum I (26,470 feet).

The two Italian expeditions of 1909 (Duke of the Abruzzi) and 1929 (Duke of Spoleto) did not penetrate far into the Gasherbrum group, but a good deal of photographic material on these mountains was provided by Vittorio Sella, and (more especially) by Ardito Desio and his companions who reached Conway Saddle (20,669 feet) at the head of the Baltoro.[2]

The International Expedition of Dyhrenfurth's in 1934, in which P. Ghiglione took part, made two brilliant climbs—Sia-Kangri (formerly Queen Mary Peak) and Golden Throne (Baltoro Kangri). It also greatly enlarged our knowledge of the glacial recesses among the Gasherbrum group. Dyhrenfurth and Roch, together with the porter Mohamedjan, ascended the Gasherbrum South Glacier, reaching 20,500 feet on the south-west slope of Gasherbrum I (1st July 1934) without suspecting, so far as we can gather, the real vastness of the area (G. Cwm) opening up before them. Their return was hampered by soft snow and the frequent collapse of bridges over the crevasses: they had to bivouac, but fortunately without any appreciable ill effects. A few days before this (26th June) Ertl and Roch with three Balti porters had made a direct attack on Gasherbrum I along the ridge which the Americans were to follow twenty-

---

1. They were: William Martin Conway (later Lord Conway); Lieut. (later General) Bruce; A. D. McCormick, the artist; the guide, Mattia Zurbriggen; and four Nepalese Ghurkas.

2. Conway guessed that this pass could provide important communications between various glacial basins (Baltoro–Kundos): he called it *Probable Saddle*. Professor A. Desio reached it on 27th May 1929, with the guide Evaristo Croux. The Duke of Spoleto, who reached the saddle on 11th July 1929, with V. Ponti, E. Croux and a Balti caravan, decided to rechristen it by the name of the British explorer Sir Martin Conway (*C.A.I.–T.C.I. Alpinismo Italiano nel Mondo*, Milan, 1953, p. 110).

four years later. But they met with an astonishingly steep snow-ridge melting in the sun and decided to come down; days passed, and the porters could not be persuaded to tackle this ridge, so this particular venture had to be written off.

Another direct attack on Gasherbrum I was made two years later by H. de Ségogne. Of all the expeditions mounted in the Karakoram this was the most impressive: the 11 Europeans were followed by 35 Darjeeling Sherpas and 660 Balti porters carrying 14 tons of equipment. At the cost of much strenuous effort the Frenchmen managed to place five camps up by the steep ridge (representing a climb of exceptional difficulty for the times) and they got up to 22,310 feet on 19th June. But the weather worsened and the party had to come down. There was one ugly mishap. Two porters fell 2,000 feet: miraculously they survived with light injuries.

For the best part of two decades the desert silence of the zone was undisturbed. Then, in 1954, Captain Francesco Lombardi, topographer to the C.A.I.'s K2 Expedition, made an excursion to the South Glacier of the Gasherbrum in the course of some work in the Upper Baltoro basin.

Finally, in 1956, a strong Austrian expedition left for the Baltoro to make a bid for Gasherbrum II—the Egyptian pyramid (26,362 feet). The leader was the well-known climber Fritz Morawec. After a good many adventures and vicissitudes, the Austrians placed their Base Camp at 16,750 feet on the Duke of the Abruzzi Glacier—at the very spot where, two years later, we were to set up our own. From that point, when they had got up the first couloir of the glacier, they began to transport their equipment to an 'Advanced Base Camp' in the G. Valley—at the start of the steep, snowy slopes of Gasherbrum II. Towards the end of June, however, there was a long spell of very bad weather, and all had to go down again to the Base Camp proper.

On 30th June, when the party went up to G. Cwm again, they were shocked and dismayed to find Camp I completely buried under a huge avalanche. Fortunately its tents had been abandoned during the bad weather or it might have been the Nanga Parbat tragedy all over again—where it was not a case of a few ice-axes and packing-cases being lost, but of sixteen men being entombed. The camp had been set up at a place which looked safe enough, but the glaciers of the Karakoram are capable of some unexpected behaviour, and they can bury whole plains.

The Austrians thus found themselves in a situation of exceptional difficulty. They had lost most of their food and nearly all the high-altitude equipment. Reluctant to go down again, they decided on a 'blitz attack'—a bold, fast and very lightly mounted assault on the summit.

191

GASHERBRUM III
26,090

GASHERBRUM II
26,360

Gasherbrum II (26,360 feet) with route and camps of Austrian Expedition in 1956.
Point between Camp III and summit shows place of bivouac

In no more than four days—aided, fortunately, by a fine group of high-altitude Balti porters—they opened up a route over very steep snow and ice slopes as far as the 23,000 feet level, and placed two camps. Higher than that, advance preparations could not go. They hadn't the gear, they hadn't the men, they hadn't the food. The summit was 3,280 feet higher. They decided on one rapid bid for it, with a bivouac halfway.

The advance team, comprising Morawec, Larch and Willenpart, left Camp III in the afternoon of 6th July. The snow was so bad that they chose to climb unroped: the man who slipped would go to his doom alone. At 8.30 in the evening they reached the outcropping rock of the 'Egyptian pyramid' and bivouacked there, making the best of it in terrible cold. On the 7th July they were lucky: fine weather. Starting at dawn and plodding painfully on, metre by metre in deep snow, they got to the summit at 1330 hours. The sky was clear: the air—by one of Fate's little ironies—almost like spring! They made a lightning descent. Evening saw all three at Camp III.

Gasherbrum II (26,360 feet) had been the first of the family to bow its head to Man (1956). Now two other brothers were being engaged. Gasherbrum I by Clinch and his Americans, Gasherbrum IV by us.

Jaded appetites

On 26th June I went up to Camp I at last, with Dr. Zeni: our companions badly needed some supplies brought up. The alarm was set for 4.15. By this time one's sleeping-bag has really warmed up: it is a cosy little nest, and dragging oneself out of it is always a painful business. But it is essential to get on the move before the snow starts melting in the sun, otherwise the going is an ordeal. Besides, one has only to peep out of the tent and the splendour of the dawn more than makes up for a slice out of one's sleep. The morning was on the cold side—twelve degrees below. In the kitchen everything was frozen stiff. We heated up some tea and ate our eggs with chupatty cakes. The desire for fresh food becomes an obsession at altitude, and the porters' chupatty cakes or buns tasted much more appetizing than the biscotti we had brought from Italy, at the cost of much toil and trouble and expense. We left the camp at 5.30.

Our route lay up the big lower ice-fall of the South Gasherbrum Glacier. What is an ice-fall? Not every reader will know. A glacier, in essence, is a big, solidified river flowing slowly from high level to low level. When an ordinary river, in its course, comes to a stretch where the bed slopes down more steeply than elsewhere, what happens? If there is an actual drop in the bed, a waterfall is formed. But if there is merely a comparatively steep incline, then you get waves, whirlpools, swirling and eddying, in short, continual turbulence. But water is a fluid. Ice, by contrast, although it may behave in the great surface outline of its movement as a very viscous fluid, remains a solid. When the floor of the valley—that is, the glacier 'bed'—becomes steeper than usual, or falls in steps, the result produced in the ice-mass, which may be several hundreds of metres thick, is a network of fissures, cracks and flaws which are called crevasses. The blocks which remain solid between one crevasse and another are known as séracs.[1]

We had scarcely left the camp tents before we were involved in a most tortuous form of progress—all twists and turns and manœuvres to avoid crevasses, to get over bumps, to edge our way between séracs and so on, which is what movement implies in terrain like this. There are no real difficulties: but danger can lurk in a crevasse, in the movement of a sérac and in a dozen other quarters, and it doesn't do to let the mind wander! Our path was very clearly flagged with bits of red cloth—most useful in fog or bad weather. Not that there seemed any danger of that at the moment. The weather looked like holding splendidly for many hours; enemy number one was the sun. All this uninterrupted sunshine had had one real drawback: it had dissuaded us from taking two or three days' rest—and that would have given us a precious reserve of strength to tackle the mountain with. We had been going on and up all the time, and, to be frank, our organization for the final attempt didn't amount to what it should have done. We had felt all the time that we must not let one single precious hour be lost: the monsoon might be punishing us at any time, and then—goodbye to everything while we sat it out!

The snow now was fine and firm. In order to keep to the rules, Donato Zeni and I had very prudently roped ourselves to each other. One of the great secrets of climbing at these heights is to strike the rhythm which makes for the right balance between your pace and your breathing-rate. There is always the temptation, as soon as one gets started, to strike a pace which is really too fast to be justified. It is far better to stick to one which may seem too modest by far but which soon permits an easy, effort-free breathing-rate. Luckily, Donato's 'rhythm' was the same as mine, and we advanced without too much strain. From here on, all of us used ski-sticks—a real discovery!

Very soon we were in the heart of the ice-fall. A tempest of towers! A San Gimignano of ice. A frozen cataclysm. An earthquake's havoc in the sudden glare of lightning. Standing towers, crumbling towers, crushed towers, towers in pairs and towers in turmoil, phalanxes of towers. And between one and the other of them, between wall and glassy barbican—lanes, streets and twists and turns of streets and narrow alleyways—and through them all 'the route'. There were

1. The French form is generally used.

narrow stretches with galleries and shafts running off them into blue-green grottoes; there were open spaces mutely contemplated by walls in whose layer upon layer of ice the snow-story of ancient winters could be read. One half-expected to find some age-old church in them, or some medieval habitation or fortress. Time after time, here, there, everywhere, channels opened in our path: channels that spiralled their dark way into a mystery world—the glaucous heart itself of this warren of crevasse and fissure, this intricacy of ice. From time to time came growls, creaks, low thunder; and our steps often sounded as if a void stretched below to trap us. At every turn the ice-city offered new palaces, new ruins, new bolt-holes, new cross-roads, new stairways, new galleries. A voyage of discovery—discovery at every step! Riccardo was right the other evening when, coming in from one of his trips up to Camp I, he said to me:

'You'll see for yourself—the ice-fall's a wonderful experience.'

All the while, the sun was getting up. Form and texture, miraculous already, took on the new miracle of light and colour. The sun's rays stole down to frolic among the battlements of ice, embroidery work and filigree of ice; now lighting veins of iridescence in a mass of dark, now plunging like a torch into the amethystine secrets of a crystal alcove. And the green peaks that ringed us round took on their true gigantic scale as we made our ascent: Chogolisa (25,110 feet) a pyramid of dazzling incandescence, in whose peaks still lingered the dark-green hues of night; Golden Throne (23,989 feet) mantled sumptuously in ice; Gasherbrum II (26,360 feet) the Egyptian pyramid, isolated in the sun like some heraldic device.

We made our way slowly, but we kept up the steady pace. From time to time we stopped to exchange a word or two. Here, all round, was the stuff for an unforgettable 'high-mountain' reel. But I knew it would never be made. Even 16mm. equipment, with the camera, tripods, the film itself and the rest of the gear, means a crippling weight—more than I could manage myself—and the porters had other things to carry up just now. My companions were right. This was a difficult mountain, and climbing it was a whole-time job in itself. Better bring back the Summit and no film, than all film and no Summit!

Why is it that, of all the great expeditions which the Karakoram and the Himalaya have seen of recent years, none has succeeded in making any film which really comes to grips with the highest mountains in the world? The answer is simple: the filming has never been taken seriously enough. It is something secondary. Climbing is the thing, not cinematography. There is only one way to produce first-class results; I don't say, of course, that one should centre the whole expedition round the cameras and make the climbing something merely ancillary, that would be absurd. But there should certainly be a 'film squad', parallel to the climbers, but independent. The man with the cine-cameras should be unencumbered with any other activity—photography included. He should film, and do nothing but film, and he should have the assistance of one or two strong and willing companions, with a certain number of porters allocated to him, so that the time never comes when a vital but unfortunately heavy item of equipment happens to be down at the Base Camp at the precise moment when it is needed higher up. It must not be forgotten that, at altitude, work involving the muscles is very tiring. But work involving the mind is more tiring still. It may not sound much to keep a 'film eye' open as one goes along, for the cinematic angles, even if there are no human actors to be 'caught' before they have gone out of the picture. But a few hours of it can prove exhausting. Finally, of course, there must be some provision for all the cinema gear to be looked after with the greatest care. It is vital that it should be shielded from the extreme heat you can get in a tent, and it may be fatal to leave it out in the sun.

Soon, Donato and I came to the point where the glacier flattened out to a certain extent. We were beyond that city of blue glass. We climbed slopes of crystalline snow which danced in a myriad points of iridescence in the sun's slanting rays. We also came across those famous 'cans of the Americans' that Cassin had told us of. We opened one, and found some fruit in syrup. This is what had happened: after setting up a Base Camp a good deal lower than ours, the Americans had done a fair bit of reconnaissance for their ascent of Gasherbrum I. We have already seen that two different approaches were tried in 1934 and 1936. The French tackled a ridge which comes down on to the Gasherbrum South Glacier, above the ice-fall. The Americans had come up to this point, where they had deposited some supplies; at the time, this ridge was the approach they favoured. But they appear to have changed their minds. They took up their Base Camp and transferred it to a much higher level—the foot of Conway Saddle; from there they made the ascent by the Ertl-Roch (1934) route, reaching the Urdok Combe, right under the summit (*see* diagram on page 245). It transpired that the Americans had proposed an exchange between some of their food supplies and some of ours. A good idea. They were short of everything. We could make it possible for them to have a bigger safety margin, to enable them to make their plans on a bolder scale; we were sufficiently well supplied to take the lesser quantity in exchange, and the variety would do us no harm.

It really passes belief how difficult, how jaded and capricious one can become over food at that height. 'We must all be pregnant,' laughed Riccardo. The fact is that at upwards of 17,000 feet you are a normal human being no

longer. You are just a sick man doing his best to survive. Tinned meat is something you can't even bear to look at. Yet every now and again you rout out a
tin of some variety you hadn't seen before, and for a day or two you are a
fanatical devotee of, say, chicken or reindeer-meat or oxtail stew. Fruit in syrup,
tomatoes, anything that tastes liquid and fresh, is most tempting. But there is
no rhyme or reason in any of it. The only rhyme and reason is variety. Any
expedition would possess two enormous advantages if it could (*a*) find some
means—small portable ovens?—of ensuring constant supplies of fresh bread,
(*b*) stock up with the utmost variety in mind. The object is, after all, to make
them eat, these madmen who insist on going to places where human beings
were never meant to live! They will try anything once, or twice if it is really
new. If it isn't, it may well be wasted. For the period likely to be spent above
18,000 feet supplies should be planned as far as possible so that one need never
eat the same thing three times.

The farther up we went, the more gradual the slope became. Our path
even contained a declivity for a short time. Then came a long, gently rising
stretch and at the end of it we saw the two tents of Camp I, *c.* 18,300 feet. How
small and distant they seemed! Step by step, however, we plodded on. And something rather bigger came into view, sealing off the valley—the pyramid of G. II.

It was somewhere here, twenty-four years previously (on 1st July, 1934),
that G. O. Dyhrenfurth, André Roch and the Balti porter Mohamedjan spent a
wretched night in the snow. After being the first men to see the G. Cwm, they
fell victim, on the descent, to soft, wet snow, with the crevasse bridges collapsing everywhere.

'Getting over the crevasses with the light going,' Roch has told us, 'became
a more and more hazardous business, for we could scarcely see the lip we were
trying to jump on to.' Then later: 'We came to a near-horizontal slope, to find
ourselves surrounded by such a maze of crevasses that we resigned ourselves to
spending the night there.' Cowering in some little hole they found in the
glacier, they stayed there with their teeth chattering.

'We had no light, and no matches, and the night was cold. We kept rubbing our feet to keep the circulation going. Mohamedjan, for his part, prayed to
Allah and resigned himself to his fate with Oriental fatalism.'

Fortunately towards midnight the moon rose and Chogolisa was flooded
with its pallor; and by half past one they were on the move again, while '*la clarté
nous touche et fouille de sa lueur blafarde le chaos inextricable au milieu duquel nous
nous sommes fourrés*'. At three o'clock in the morning they managed to reach
the camp. 'This little misadventure,' Roch concludes, 'should be a lesson even
to experienced climbers: the mountains of the Himalaya are still a little bigger

197

than we think, and it is as well to keep one's sleeping-bag within easy reach if the prospects of returning by nightfall are the least bit uncertain.'[1]

Camp I: a sea of crevasse and sérac

Camp I was set up on 22nd June, by Bonatti, Gobbi and Oberto, on an eminence in the glacier. Behind us the valley was closed by the dome of Golden Throne which had been towering up vaster and vaster (a phenomenon often to be noted as one climbs up a valley) till it had finally assumed its true gigantic proportions (*Plate 66*). Above us rose the ponderous Gasherbrum I with its barbicans and buttresses, where rock merged with ice to form a striking counterpoint of black precipice and gleaming slope. From a shoulder near the summit a steep and twisted tongue of ice crawled down: at any moment it looked as if, losing its precarious solidity, it would turn into a swirling torrent: avalanches come frequently from that quarter, and the clouds of powdery snow that follow them hover in mid-air for a long time afterwards. Looking round, we had the grooved and crenellated rampart of Gasherbrum VI which was divided from Gasherbrum V only by a forbidding ridge of bristling, snow-white teeth. Right opposite, the scene was dominated by Gasherbrums II and III (*Plate 62*) and by our own mountain, the Great Fourth. Down here in the valley, all round us lay a choppy sea of crevasse and sérac (*Plate 67*).

Beyond Camp I: fatalists all

Ten vital days had gone by: I had taken no part in them myself, I had stayed at the Base Camp as little more than storeman, reorganizing all our supplies and ensuring the immediate accessibility of any single thing we might need. But while I was down there the advance party, slowly and against mighty odds, had forged upwards to the second ice-fall, thus hacking out one of the key-passages in the first part of the ascent. For G.IV, in actuality, was really two mountains—one on top of the other. Climb I was a dozen kilometres of glacier, less characteristic of the Himalaya than of the Arctic or Greenland; Climb II, though as yet we had no very precise ideas about it, was all rock, ice and snow up the tremendous North-East Ridge—all 3,000 feet of it—finishing up, from 23,000 feet to 26,180 feet.

Now the moment had come for me to go on up. I wanted to take some film, if possible. I wanted a first-hand knowledge of the terrain where the last battle would be fought, where my companions were already coping with every hardship undaunted; and I wanted to photograph everything that could be photographed. And of course I was spurred on too by the desire to see with my

1. A. Roch, *Karakoram Himalaya, Sommets de 7,000 m.*, Neuchatel, 1943.

own eyes the 'forbidden territory' of very high mountains, climbing higher than I had ever climbed before. The weather had not been too good for four days (30th June–3rd July), but on 4th July it was fine once more.

The route up to Camp I we are already familiar with. This time I went up on skis, with seal-skins. I had Haji Ismael and another porter with me. At the camp we were surprised to find one tent chock-full of victuals and climbing gear. I had been sending up supplies by the porters, day by day, in accordance with instructions sent down from above. They had got no farther up than this point. Did that mean that transport arrangements ceased to function here? Or did it imply that the advance party was so far advanced that these supplies would not be of any use to them? We should soon know.

The day before, the weather had worsened again in the afternoon. Ponderous grey hostile clouds had risen sluggishly over the Baltoro—from the west. Harbingers of the monsoon? We had kept to our tent, chatting and snoozing. Outside, all was silence: a strange silence broken by a stranger din—a cawing. I looked out several times, always finding the same mournful chough grubbing patiently in the snow around the tent, hoping for a few scraps. I tried time and time again to throw him some biscotti, I called to him in gentle tones: at least, in human language they would have passed for gentle tones. In crow language they must have been closer to insult and threat than endearment, and the bird kept flying off with a squawk to circle the precipices of G.I.

Evening came and the hard grey tones of the mountain were untouched by any other colour. At such moments, the splendid mountain scene can look lugubrious indeed, and a valley entombed by cloud can hold the vague terror of anguish. It is then that you start thinking of things impossibly far away—ordinary life, your dear ones, your friends.

Eight o'clock brought darkness. We went to bed and to sleep. What else was there to do? You couldn't read for the cold. And, frankly, who would want to?

Next morning, when I stepped outside my tent about five, the air was freezing cold but the sky perfectly clear. Haji Ismael and the other porter, with whom I had come up to the first camp, were still asleep, snoring loud enough to wake the dead, in the tent next to mine. They took some waking. We heated some café-au-lait, breaking up a packing-case to make a fire—our cylinders of liquid gas being all empty—and we dipped some dry bread in it.

Oberto and a porter joined us, coming up from the Base Camp. All five of us set off together for Camp II.

For a long stretch, up past Camp I, we found ourselves covering ground which would have made perfect skiing slopes—without the crevasses and without the altitude. You have to drop 10,000 feet from this height before skiing becomes anything but an exhausting pursuit. For climbing, it is not too bad. You get into a regular stride, and try to harmonize it with your breathing rhythm. But, for going down, it is another story. The irregularity of the movement and the effort required for turns make skiing here a sport de luxe—the deluxe part being the dissipation of that most precious of mountain-riches: energy.

Farther on we came to the South Face of Gasherbrum V. It is encrusted with hanging glaciers and down these come the avalanches—big ones, and quite frequent. They can be of various kinds. Sometimes they are slides of new snow, throwing up a white whirlwind of fine 'smoke' quite capable of suffocating anyone caught in it. Then there are the avalanches formed by fragments of the hanging glaciers themselves. These break off and come crashing down. A terrifying sight. The ice-blocks are like so many boulders. You can often see them down on the plain, still hurtling along for a fair distance, such is the force of their initial rush.

Our route now led across an undulating open space right at the foot of Gasherbrum V (24,019 feet)—and right in the path of these avalanches. It was one of those places where safety-first notions had to go by the board. The resignation of Islam was the better part. Here, we were fatalists all. If several hundred tons of ice, up there hanging in the balance, chose just this moment to break off from the mountain and come sweeping down, then clearly there was only one thing to do about it—enjoy one more minute of all this sombre splendour before being buried for ever. You can take bigger steps, you can even run, to cover the ground faster: but this is a mistake too. At 20,000 feet every extra effort means you have to stop for breath. No, let us have calm, patience, faith. *Insh'Allah*—God Willing—we shall arrive, safe and sound.

Camp II and its mountains

What a grand feeling it is to see one's friends again! There was no need for words between us—at this height, indeed, no one had the energy for a lot of effusive greeting. Just a growl or two was enough! The warmth was in the undertones.

Toni Gobbi and Donato Zeni were at Camp II: they very soon gave us the latest news. Walter Bonatti and Carlo Mauri had already got beyond the ice-wall. The snags were tremendous. Nearly all the porters were down with mountain sickness. Taqi and Mahmud Hussein alone were still able to make themselves useful. Reports of Taqi were extraordinary. He had come out in his real sporting colours, he was always the man ahead. Yes, we had to revise our opinion of Taqi. The loud-mouthed ragamuffin of the plain, the good-for-nothing whose sole purpose in life appeared to be to beg for cigarettes—to smoke cigarettes, and to chew the butts—had become the Balti champion—a Sherpa of the Karakoram! There were no flies on Eric Shipton. It is never too late to learn something in life.

Camp II was situated at some 20,000 feet, very nearly in the middle of a valley of incomparable grandeur, where one had a remarkable sensation of freedom. Once we had heard the main items of news; once we had restored our flagging energies with one of those broths which are the rule up at these heights where one is always more thirsty than hungry; the first thing we did, quite as a matter of course, was to look at the view: to breathe in the splendours which quite certainly we should only see this once in a lifetime, to engrave on our minds a scene which, once it had ceased to stand for the present, would never be anything but a memory. At Camp II, as at Base Camp, we were closed in by peak, crest, high pass; but, whereas down below we had always been conscious of a valley, even a valley that was enclosed, here we were in an amphitheatre open to the sky, to space itself. We might have been in some great debating chamber of Ancient Greece, except that the architectural marvels around us were mountains: it was open only to the south and east. That way one could look along great white manes of ice towards India.

August, solemn, a very symbol of solidity—such was the Gasherbrum I we saw from here. At a mere glance, the traveller might be tempted to dismiss G.I as a conventional mountain, even a dull and uninspired one. The truth is that, like certain simple and unadorned masterpieces of human achievement whose author has utterly refused to gild the lily, it is a giant of serenity, breathing a deep faith in life. Its crests rise and fall with a superbly generous rhythm: the glaciers that mantle its shoulders curl like majestic stoles on to its lower slopes.

Something in the same vein might be said for Golden Throne: this lesser peak closes in the valley on one side, and from the tents we could see only a part of it. But Gasherbrums VI (*Plate 64*) and V (*Plate 63*) were different altogether. G.V, from here, did not show in its most favourable light. It was far too foreshortened—a single wall, ponderous with hanging glaciers, bordered near its skyline with cornices and volutes of snow. But G.VI shone with all its savage splendour—Great Spectre of the Baltoro—pausing on the very brink of our valley, drawing back, the better to spy on us.

G.II and G.III were too close for us to take in the whole picture of either: we could only admire a few of the finer points within our range at their lower levels—a certain touch of the Dolomites, for instance, in the crags jutting out from the glacier. Our own G.IV, however, of which we now saw only the heights, had become much more impressive (*Plate 72*). Down below, it had presented a diamond's splendour and a diamond's bold gleam. In its line one seemed to discern a vast force exploding upwards towards the sky; but the strength was all in that force, not in the stuff of the mountain itself. There, all was grace; from here, all was power: castles, fortresses came to mind. But in the apparent change a large part, one must not forget, was simply due to the play of perspective. The higher reaches of the mountain were more distant than its lower reaches and this detracted from the objective truth of what we saw. This is true of all mountains, and the camera has to allow for it no less than the naked eye. Here everything—including the possibility of optical illusion—was on a bigger scale than usual (*Plate 68*).

Right opposite us I saw too the extremely steep ice-fall (the Italians') leading up to that cwm (its very existence was unsuspected till a short while ago) which is hidden between Gasherbrum III and IV. To find a route up there, to make a trail and fix ropes, had been a very long and exhausting task for the advance party. They had spent whole days with the ever-present threat of avalanches and crumbling séracs.

Camp II: the 'avalanche of 1st July'

Avalanches, to some extent, constituted a threat to us all the time we were on the mountain. At any hour of the day or night we might hear one rushing down. Sometimes the noise of the falling masses sounded like an automatic being fired, or thunderbolts falling near at hand. At others, it was a deep heavy rumble. After a snowstorm or a spell of warm weather, they were naturally more frequent. But not even constant sunshine or an intense frost had much of an effect on their baleful frolics.

Camp II already had a tale to tell where avalanches were concerned. At a rough glance a traveller might have judged the camp-site as one of the safest places in the world. Here we were, in the centre of a very wide valley on the gentlest of slopes, over a glacier without a single crevasse. But the mountains of the Karakoram range can be terrifying; what with the dizzy height of their summits and the steepness of their walls and the masses of ice that accumulate to hang in the balance all the time, they provide, constantly, the ideal conditions for upheavals which would certainly be hailed as cataclysms if they were not confined to regions so desolate. Above the G. Cwm rose the ramparts of Gasherbrum V—4,000 feet of precipice of every shade, on which, poised precariously at various points, were hanging glaciers (one thinks of the Civetta, the Eiger or the Matterhorn)—but all on a vastly greater and more threatening scale than any of their counterparts in the Alps. Right up by the summit, under that long horizontal ridge (24,019 feet), there was a bulging, quite illogical balcony of ice. It drew an immediate glance, a worried one, from all who came this way.

On the night of 30th June: 'An enormous avalanche came down from G.V, giving us rather a jolt in the camp.' This was a phlegmatic entry in Beppi De Francesch's diary. So great was the commotion that Riccardo Cassin, who had been up to Camp III, very soon decided to move the tents to a quarter which might prove safer. It must not be forgotten that in this very valley—though right underneath Gasherbrum II at a site where, perhaps, it was asking for trouble to place a camp—the Austrians' Camp I had been buried in 1956, as we have seen. The ice that came rushing down on to their tents seems to have measured a depth of 'eighteen or twenty feet'. But let us pass to the following account of what happened on 1st July:

'In the morning we were thinking of moving Camp II'—this is De Francesch again—'Cassin and Mauri said it would be better to take the tents higher up. I didn't care for this idea very much myself. Anyway, we got the tents down and started shifting them to a higher level of the valley. Cassin and Oberto went off a few minutes before I was ready. Suddenly I heard a mighty rumble. I looked at the mountain (G.V) and saw an enormous slice (say 650 feet by 250 feet by 200 feet) break off from the highest hanging glacier. I kept my eyes on it all the way down the 4,000-foot wall—and then I saw a huge white cloud coming for us. I ran off its path for a few dozen metres, but the cloud got pretty well on top of me. I threw myself in the snow with my hands over my mouth. A rush of wind and a driving storm of fine snow passed over me. I waited for the ice-blocks, but there was nothing else. As soon as I could feel the wind had gone by, I got up, but I couldn't see anything for snow-dust. Then I made out two standing figures. One was Zeni. One was Mauri. Thank heaven we were safe, anyway. But what had happened to Cassin and Oberto? They were a hundred metres farther on. . . .

'At last we saw them, and nothing much had happened to them. But if they'd been just another hundred metres farther still, they'd have been caught and buried. And to think that the foot of the wall was more than a mile away! We shifted about a hundred metres up towards G.II. However, you can pitch the tents where you like here, the risk is the same everywhere. The only safe place for the camp would be on a peak!'

Such is De Francesch's account of this horrifying incident, and he was in the best position to see what was happening, being a fair way off. But now let us go a hundred metres higher and look at the same scene through Cassin's eyes.

'I heard a rumbling. I raised my head and saw the enormous hanging sérac of G.V come off and plunge down. We were say two kilometres off, but still in danger. This enormous ice-block bashed its way down the steepest part of the ice-wall, carrying everything with it. When the avalanche landed, something like a volcanic eruption went up, for hundreds of yards, and the whole precipitation came bowling along right at us, at crazy speed. I shouted to Giuseppe Oberto to run uphill. The funny thing was that the avalanche went uphill too. We jettisoned our heavy packs and ran the other way. We'd only gone a few steps when we felt a terrible wind. I dug in my ski-sticks. In a second, I was in the middle of a hurricane of snow and I braced myself for the oncoming mass. Luckily it didn't come. I was in the middle of that white swirl more than ten minutes, and it seemed a mighty long time. When it cleared, I looked round, and there was Oberto sitting down absolutely encrusted in snow—completely white—so was I, we had a snow crust on us at least five centimetres thick. I burst out laughing, and saw De Francesch coming towards us. . . .'

At that moment, as at a good many others, we can well say that the Expedition was favoured by the Gods. We might have been their favourite sons. No rose without a thorn, they say! But we did have our roses, and we were thankful.

Elephants on storks' legs

Such ceaseless danger, combined with a physical strain that was killing at this altitude, could not fail to have an effect on us. We would snap like mad dogs, our patience went to the winds, when spoken to we just grunted an answer and then shut ourselves up in a hostile silence. If I admit as much, it is certainly not to try and show up my companions in a bad light. I had the utmost admiration for them, and of course I didn't bear them a grudge in the world. No, I am simply admitting, I am bringing into the light of day, just one aspect—and one of the most important—of this life of supreme hardship. What we were trying to do was to defy conditions which made human life a gamble. In the literature of mountains, we have all had too much of that troop of noble souls advancing to the accompaniment of Alpine songs and waving banners. Rhetoric. Perhaps the truth is not more attractive. That troop really consists of men whose cheeks are hollowed by privation; their beards have grown to an inordinate length; their eyes are haunted; they shout and they swear. And yet . . . in spite of it all, they have their moments when their silence means something more than irritability. They too can be moved, deeply moved, and their spirit can make a brief escape from the bondage of its harness. All in all, they are supremely human. At immense physical cost they plod and clamber on, into the very secret heart of mountains not meant for men, bending nature to their will (to use a Western expression)—or, if you like, being all the while bent by nature to hers (to look at it through Eastern eyes). But whatever they have seen, whatever they have lived—up there—will remain for ever branded into their souls.

It may be worth while to pause here and give a rather more detailed picture, from personal experience and from hints my companions let fall, of what human living really amounts to at these great heights. . . .

Everything conspires against Man. Man is the hated intruder. Up here, Man must be prepared to eat humble pie. He is a worm, and he had better not mistake himself for a mountain eagle. He will have his unforgettable moments; he will gaze on marvels indescribable; there will be times of communion with the very being of things so close that it aspires to ecstasy. All this lies up in the mountains. Its price is misery, suffering, pain and anguish.

Take ourselves, for instance, just now. We had fine weather. It was an atrocious persecution. Clear skies: they were hell. Hell with hardly a cloud. The sun would burst up over the mountains every morning, flinging a thunderbolt of light, and lord its way over an empty sky. Even when it sank at last behind a crest it was still a ball of fire, and the fire would roar at us unseen. In many ways this was our good fortune—whose smiles by now we had come to take quite for granted. We could see where we were going at every step. We had none of that maddening uncertainty that dogs one's time-table in bad weather. Above all, we had the tremendous moral boost of bright sunlight everywhere. But that wasn't the whole story. There was another, crueller, side to it.

For one thing, our continual fear of the weather worsening had pushed us on, at a mad pace, without a minute to breathe, or to rest up and reorganize. The point is that fine weather is the real bad weather! Whereas, if winter comes, spring cannot be far behind. Fine weather gives the command: make the most of it before it breaks. Hence all the rush, and the fatigue and the confusion: for, if it is fine now, bad weather will certainly set in again any minute! It was clear to us by now that our supply line could never keep to the speed of our advance team. We were like a big bicycle race in which the champion has got too far ahead of the rest and the rank and file straggle too far behind. The only difference was that in this case the champions and the rank and file had to keep together, because it wasn't just a victory that was involved, it was survival itself. The rank and file—in our case the porters—were doing their best as a whole, but the number of them that got up past Camp III was two only, and it cost them enough effort. And what was there to be done about it? No more than you can do about the number you have drawn in a lottery. What if the North-East Ridge should turn out to be easy after all? As every climber is well aware, such things have been known to happen. Walls or ridges that look ferociously difficult, by some trick they keep up their sleeve until you get there, can turn out to be quite simple! What if the North-East Ridge should be like this? In that case, it would be sufficient to get up there with no supplies at all—because the Summit could then be reached in one single spurt from the North-East Col.

The sun had to be reckoned with as one unending explosion. This oven-heat Karakoram was something we had hardly expected. No one had said a word about it. There it was like living in a world stripped of atmosphere, a bare, unprotected world, with nothing between it and a pitiless sun. Up there, movement was restricted to before 0900 and after 1600 hours. Between these hours it was inadvisable to stay exposed to that storm of radiation. No amount of hats, or a handkerchief over one's face, or gloves or dark glasses, would withstand it. You were burned up with heat; parched and blunder-headed with it. The only thing to do was to stay inside the tent. But I have already said that our tents were a beautiful orange colour. It was fine for a Kodak. It was purgatory for a camper. We had to drape the tent with sleeping-bags, groundsheets, any clothing we could spare, to make it habitable. The air in itself was not very hot, the thermometer read four to six degrees in the shade.[1] It was the radiation that was so appalling. Inside an unprotected tent, the thermometer jumped to forty-five or even fifty degrees. But by draping the canvas with some care, by opening the 'doors' and the 'windows', one managed to obtain some semblance of an atmosphere in which it was possible at least to lie down hoping for the gradual restoration of a fraction of one's strength.

But, with the evening, the sun had not long gone down before the oven became ice-box. Don't run away with the idea that we had a pleasant half-hour in between! Nothing like it. It was a quick-change act. It was as well to have your down-padded clothing handy as soon as the shadows lengthened—and your gloves, and the hoods the Expedition had provided. The change from ice-box to oven was equally brusque in the morning, but it was not quite the same process. Passing from the great cold of night to the warmth of the sun was a pleasant business. These were the only few minutes of the day when we felt that nature was really welcoming us, inviting us to share her hospitality.

By night, in the normal run, the thermometer went down to ten or fifteen degrees below zero. But we were very well equipped against the cold and I don't think any of us had anything to complain about. We were less prepared for the radiation. But what equipment could we have provided? Black umbrellas? The peasant hats of Indo-China? Certainly, tents of some cooler colour

1. Centigrade.

and more opaque material would have been a boon. On the other hand, perhaps we were forgetting that you cannot have two series of tents, one for fine weather and one for foul. In snow, or on a dismal day, the light diffused by the orange canvas puts some heart into you and makes the most of calorific rays, then rare enough.

This daily change-over from ice-box to oven and from oven to ice-box naturally had dire effects upon our skin. We had our creams and emollients, we were for ever daubing our lips and our cheeks and our hands with them, but all in vain. Nothing could stop the rot. First came the red blotches, then the cracking, then the dead skin. I touched my own face and it felt like tree-bark. I looked at my companions: fried slices of pork. Our beards were a very good protection. If we let them grow, it was no Nibelung cult of the aspect heroic that inspired us to do so. Our eyes suffered too. We had to be very careful not to remain more than a minute or two without very dark glasses: the risk was temporary snow-blindness or conjunctivitis—not a mild attack, either. But, for real martyrdom, the respiratory organs took the palm: the nose and throat above all. The parched air in the end dried up passages which need constantly renewed atmospheric moisture. 'My throat feels like a crack in a wall'—as one of us put it—'you'd think it was all chip and mortar and rubble.' By day, this is not such an ordeal: one speaks, swallows, drinks; one's throat in one way or another is continually refreshed. But, by night, the regular rhythm of breathing turns it to fire. Every now and then you wake up thinking you are suffocating. There is a ghastly sensation in your throat, which really has become 'a crack in a wall'.

The night was hard to get through for other reasons. In the first place, the real effects of altitude are felt more strongly when one stops than when one keeps going. By day, especially on the march, one certainly puffs and blows: there is that continual gasping for air. But there are so many other things to think about; and then, before long, one strikes the right balance between walking and breathing so that one can get along without the feeling of over-exhaustion. But one has only to stop—worse still, lie down to rest—and breathing seems all-important, at times it can become nothing less than an obsession. The height and the lack of oxygen, at such times, make themselves felt in the most distressing—and the most dramatic—manner. You would think that a breathing rhythm sufficiently sustained to keep the organism going would establish itself automatically, but, strange as it may seem, this is not so. Five or six normal breaths—sometimes only two or three—and you feel the need of a deep sigh. This is the part that never becomes automatic, never a reflex act. In so far as it remains an act of the will, it continually reminds the consciousness of the strangeness of the surroundings and all the unknowns of 23,000 feet up. All this applies to the daytime siesta. Multiply it by a hundred for night and sleep. That sigh, every five or six breaths, which is so necessary for even a moderate intake of air—at night, when you are dropping off to sleep, you get the panicky feeling that you will forget it, and you know it will not come automatically. Hence you feel that, if you do not die of suffocation, at any rate you may find yourself in extremities through oxygen shortage.

Night is also the time when another of these 'altitude anxieties'—a more subtle one now—comes into its own: the psychical side. Sleep becomes a precious boon which everyone yearns for, but very rarely does it prove an unmixed blessing. By day, one is irritable and nervous, one suffers from forgetfulness and indecision, one can be as easily affected as a child—and as tearful! But by night the hidden fears take over, the unacknowledged anguish prowls abroad, the white solitude assumes its grisly terror. Anywhere higher than Camp I—at II, III, and IV—these vague fears of imminent disaster find something to grip on—the avalanches. To every growl, every creak resounding through the valley, the sleeper responds with a secret start. The idea of being crushed beneath tons of ice is horrifying and it is more than an idea, or it is one that goes with a sharper pang of fear, since it is an ever-present possibility. Not a night passed but, to the best of my belief, the haunting shadow of Nanga Parbat flitted across everybody's mind: sixteen men buried, at twenty minutes past midnight, in one of those colossal avalanches which can come crashing down without warning and follow no known rule as they come. Then there were those sinister growls and creaks, the shivering of ice: was a crevasse opening up underneath us? For, in a half-waking state, one's fears wore another face: the sudden rushing darkness of the avalanche ceased to terrify; what haunted one now was the picture of one of those gulfs opening in the glacier itself: all the horrors of the bottomless pit and the meandering shaft and gallery, beneath the entombing ice, from which one would never escape.

So the night runs slowly out, a sequence of anguish after anguish, each taking a different form. There are long spells of mere torpor, which do little to dispel fatigue but do bring a certain sense of peace. Then comes some sudden noise—it may be the growl of an avalanche, it may be a movement down in the ice, or it may be just a catch in your own breath—and you are awake again, staring into the dark. Then the very seconds seem leaden-footed, and you sigh for the distant and inestimable boon of day.

Fortunately, as I have already said, we were quite well protected against the cold. Why is it only in the last few years that Man has been able to climb the world's highest mountains? The French began with Annapurna (26,411 feet) in

Up in the heights: Golden Throne (23,989 ft.)
and Camp 1 (18,250 ft.)

Gasherbrum IV (26,180 ft.) from Camp II (c. 20,000 ft.).

The high sector of G. Cwm.

70

The moon over Conway Col (70); Base Camp and Sia Kang-rì (24,350 ft.) after sunset (71).

71

Camp II (c. 20,000 feet).

73

The first ice-fall (74) and Camp III (21,000 ft.) (73).

74

75

76

77

The ice palisade.

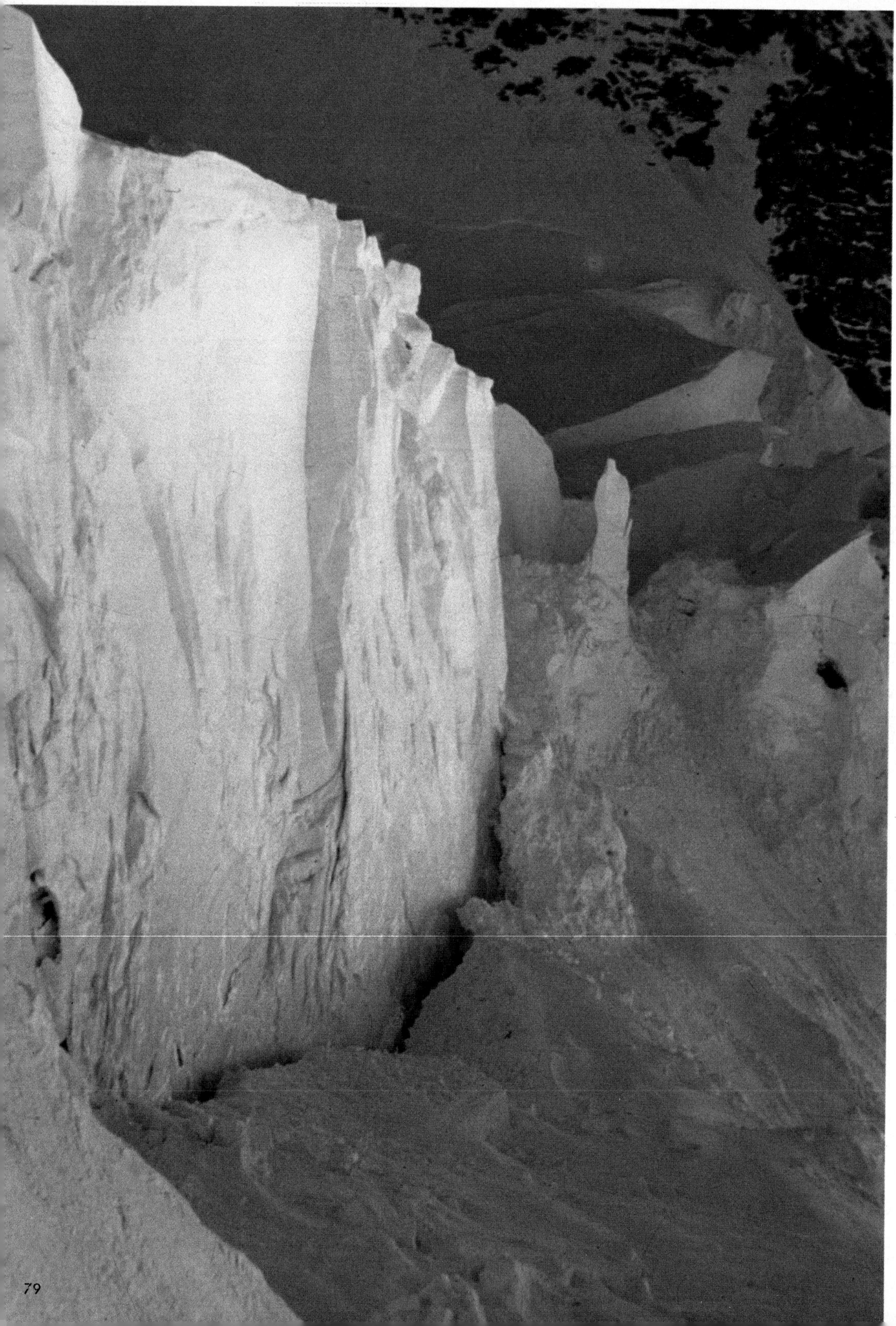

The final pyramid of Gasherbrum IV from the North-East Col (23,100 ft.).

80

81

82

The Baltoro, like some vast frozen river, from the north summit of Gasherbrum IV.

85

The Gasherbrum summit (85);
The pyramid of Gasherbrum IV from the slopes of Gasherbrum III (86).

86

1950 and today (1960) only one of the supreme peaks remains unconquered. The decade from 1950 to 1960 may well be known to the future, in the history of world exploration, as the 'Decade of the Ice-Colossi'. There are organizational and psychological reasons, there are technical and political explanations for this phenomenon, but we must not forget that a decisive part in these victories has been played by some very humble things. Among these I number the rubber mattress and the down-padded clothing. Up there, we slept on ice, true, but a simple pneumatic mattress—of the kind seaside holiday-makers use as a raft—creates a stratum of air separating the sleeper absolutely from the ice: he is suspended, so to speak, on a layer of gas. On top of that, we were dressed in down quilting, and we could tuck ourselves into a quilted sleeping-bag. For those rare moment when we could overcome all the obstacles to sleep, all those obscure anxieties, tent and sleeping-bag together really did make an extraordinarily snug little nest! We would reach our prospective site with night already falling. Everything around us had the same appalling inhospitable air. The feeling would come to us that we were mere mortals, wretched, fragile creatures in a battlemented world of ice and cold, and that we could not hold out for very long against a hostile world . . . the tents would go up, and there would be our tiny alcoves: places where we could find protection, and survive. All this happened in a few minutes. Every time I saw it happen, I seemed to be watching a little miracle. But it was a miracle that sprang from some very simple and unassuming items of equipment, after all.

Then dawn would come, and sometimes there would be a sunbeam in the tent. Delicious, healing moments! Time to get up. To pull oneself out of the bag, to look for one's shoes in the hope that they weren't frozen—and start the major operation of putting them on! A job that needed a lot of will-power at this altitude, a lot of time, a lot of effort and a lot of pauses for breath. But then—the magnificent moment when one could look round the tent-flap and stroll out into the dawn! This was one of those times worth living for. Here were the mountains again: the one world that was real. You were no longer trying to walk those tight-ropes between fear and the dream, memory and dread. The spirit had the living senses to hold on to now, the daytime senses that were in contact with splendour, and reality as well.

Then one had to think of food. What, was it necessary to eat already? Yes. That was another of the bleak sides of this grey life: the almost total lack of appetite. There were so few things one could manage to get down, and they were nearly all liquid or semi-liquid. Tinned meat—one glance and you wanted to vomit. Cheese, chocolate and preserves you took like medicine, pulling a wry face. As for soup, cups of café-au-lait with dry bread, dried fruit soaked in hot water—these you could just swallow. Some things would have been worth their weight in gold: fruit in syrup, tomato juice, syrups. We consoled ourselves for the lack of them (all except the fruit, of which we now had a few tins) with *karkade* and tea, which we drank by the pint. Drinking was more than merely useful as a substitute for eating: at this height, with the air so dry, it was highly necessary. You had to be very careful indeed not to dehydrate yourself past a certain limit, and for that reason it was as well to watch the colour of your urine: too much orange was bad, and a reddish tinge was dangerous. Several expeditions had had unexpected cases of phlebitis, apparently caused by an evaporation-rate in the body uncompensated by the intake of sufficient liquids.

When reveille brought a fine morning, it was generally followed by marching orders, for which we gathered our strength. After a meal which we took for the most part as a hygienic exercise or a mere 'calory-reinforcement' we would collect our gear, kit up the material needed aloft, and leave the tents. The act of climbing, in these celestial places, was profoundly against nature. The weight of one's body grew and grew, out of all proportion. We were elephants on storks' legs. We advanced with infinite effort, a few hundred feet an hour. But, before long, everyone struck the right pace-to-breathing ratio and was therefore able to look round and admire the sublime light-changes among cloud, rock and coating ice as the day deepened. Coming down, strangely enough, was always simple and easy!

Reveille is a sad business, however, when there is cloud, and it is worse with high wind. If these two enemies are in league together then it is infernal. The jaws of the warm, snug sleeping-bag are still open—but woe betide you if sloth should drive you back between them! Time will take on a slow, strange rhythm in your mind, and your soul will fill with alarm and despondency. Every so often the wind blows up strange howls, shrieks: for all you know, it might be an avalanche coming down right on top of you. You are like a man sheltering from a storm under a tree, with lightning striking the wood. The banging and billowing of the tent, with the gale pounding away at it, thunderclap after thunderclap, begins to tear at the nerves. As far as the inside of the tent goes, the less said the better. In the most favourable conditions, one's socks display a remarkable propensity for getting near the marmalade and the butter has a delightfully playful habit of plastering the ice-axes, hammers and crampons. During spells of bad weather the squalor and confusion reach mythological depths. And if on top of everything the wind is so strong that one cannot leave the tent when nature calls . . .

Ah, now you're just trying to turn our stomachs, you may say. Nothing of

210

the kind. Would you have fine phrases? These mountains of Asia, in their very vastness and remoteness, imprint themselves on the soul of the man who once sets foot on them, because they touch him at every human level: they bring him a mystic ecstasy at one moment, they remind him of his animal nature at the next. And through them he comes to know everything from nameless terror to the joys of scientific discovery.

Woman—and salads

In the dreams that visited us by night we saw, laid bare, many of our most secret desires. Dream Number One, the most frequent and the most gratifying, ever welcome above all others for its voluptuous appeal to the senses, was of salad. Ah, green lettuce leaves divine! Succulent lettuce, endive so tender, verdant growths, symbols of life! Memory of field and meadow, cool and blessed shade! Flesh of red tomatoes, earth's supreme gift, jewels of the vegetable world, rare and impossible privilege of the immortals! Sometimes our dreams would take us through the countryside where in row after endless row, with the rich and dewy green of arum-lily shoots themselves, salads of every shape and form, of every consistency and variety of taste, would sprout up, one after another. We would drench them in olive oil and sprinkle them with vinegar or lemon. At other times we would be sitting at table with presentable, well-turned-out people: we had napkins, glasses, plates! But what really interested us was not so much our fellow guests as an endless festive procession of green dishes and fruits and the juices of fruits: chlorophyl visions, green shades of botanical gardens and some celestial Buddhist feast.

In Dream Number Two beside the salad bowl there was Woman. But in no erotic sense! With our whole being nearly drained away by the twin processes of evaporation and sublimation, we had no interest in flesh. No, our longing was a longing for tenderness, for soft and soothing voices: not for woman but for womanhood. Up at this height, everything inanimate had the stark bleakness of the stars themselves: everything human was rough and rude and tremendously male. Snow, ice, rock and space; sky, with its celestial mechanics of war and its august gestures of peace. And, in the humbler sphere, the ice-axe and the piton, the beards and the beastliness, the grunts and the sweat. The woman of our dreams was a smile, a low and pleasing voice, a hand that stroked one's brow; nothing more.

'God, what a hole!'

The progress made by my companions in this upper world, so harsh and so preposterous, really had something superhuman about it. How much, I came to appreciate when I myself saw the places they had battled for and breathed the thin air they had breathed. As if great altitude alone was not sufficient of a trial they had experienced several days (especially 1st and 2nd July) of weather so bad that they had been chained to their tents, with the snow piling up outside. And after that—when the fine weather returned and they could emerge—every step spelled exhaustion, even along a route that had already been cleared, for all their efforts had been rendered useless by a fresh carpet of white.

It would take too much space, and exhaust the most indulgent reader's patience, to record all the various movements of climbers and porters during these last few days. There had been one long coming and going over the slopes and the boundless expanses of the South Gasherbrum Glacier. From the Base Camp to the North-East Ridge was a 6,400-foot stretch, from 16,900 feet to 23,300 feet. Beyond lay the mountain's grimmest battlements. Our achievement fell into two phases. The first was the opening up of a route as far as the 'Italians' Ice-fall', with the placing of three camps—Camp I, 22nd June; Camp II, 25th June; Camp III, 29th June. Then, from 29th June to 6th July, a bitter battle was fought to discover, mark out and then equip a route over the Ice-fall. Towards the end of this latter period, Carlo Mauri's arm had nearly healed, and he had gone up to the advance party—replacing Oberto, who was forced down by continual intestinal trouble.

Cassin and De Francesch meanwhile, with frequent help from Zeni and some from me, were transport officers with the job of keeping the porters at it with the necessary supplies, so that the advance party could push still higher and yet be able to rely on a very long line of communication. Cassin certainly had not spared himself: more than once he had racked himself out with work. From some points of view, it might have been better for Riccardo to stay at some fixed central point (say Camp II) directing the Expedition's complex operations. But he was always the one to set the example, never avoiding the donkey-work. Like a general in battle, too, he had to follow every movement through his glasses, and a chief's right to adopt whatever methods seemed to him likeliest to lead to success was inalienable and sacrosanct.

Many a time, all this responsibility, all these decisions to take, and all this sheer hard work, must have meant a heavy load for Riccardo. On leaving the Base Camp on 24th June he went up to Camp I and 'a sun that cooked you' to find himself involved with the porters in one of the worst 'negotiations' of all. From Camp I on, every single load that went up the mountain was as vital as a move on a chessboard. Take Load A—ropes and rations—to go from Camp I to Camp II, or, let us say, from Camp III to Camp IV. If it was due today, it must go up today. Tomorrow was not the same thing. An entire pattern, a whole

24,700

23,600

22,800

20,800

Gasherbrum IV (26,180 feet) from Camp II. Between Camps III and IV, the 'Italians' Ice-fall'; between Camps V and Summit, great rocky ridge

elaborate structure was upset. The six porters, by a fatal misunderstanding, had, on one occasion, taken up from Camp I their own gear and their own rations (both useless, because they themselves would be returning to Base) instead of gear and rations for the advance party. The climbers were naturally furious. The porters' reaction was the usual threat to abandon the Expedition.

Riccardo's diary, for this particular period, is full of entries which give some idea of the immense strain. For 24th June I found: 'The last part of the journey down to Base Camp was hard going indeed. Very warm, enough to cook the skin: snow and ice-dazzle too. Sinking into the snow all the time on less steep slopes.' On 25th June Riccardo went up to Camp I again with supplies. For the return journey 'went down roped with two porters, but we had made a late start: soon very tired—I fell into two crevasses, could not see that the snow bridges were going. Fortunately managed to wriggle out. Not so easy with one of the porters in the same boat. He went right in. I got him out, luckily with no harm done: it was one of those super-treacherous crevasses, narrow at the top but widening out below.'

On 26th June Cassin returned to Camp I to find De Francesch newly down from Camp II with the news that Gobbi, Bonatti and Oberto, worn out with the effort of making a trail through deep snow, could not get down for the supplies which were so vital but had failed to reach them. Here was a grave set-back. The plan of attack needed revising completely.

The 27th June brought heavy snow. While the advance party were immobilized in the the tents of Camp II, Riccardo and two porters were climbing together with brutally heavy packs. 'I wanted to try my skis,' Riccardo wrote, 'but it was a weary business. However, I covered two-thirds of the ground on them. But then the snow got so thick I decided to abandon them, and went on with the porters.' Two days later (29th June) as the party was going up from Camp II to set up Camp III, some altercation started. 'Then it became apparent that we hadn't got our rations. Made an ill-tempered start. Very difficult going, the route covered in snow.' The morning's argument between Bonatti and Riccardo started afresh. Luckily 'Gobbi intervened, crying. Walter very sportingly offered me his hand. All's well that ends well.' The fact was that the effort, exhaustion and never-ending tension were becoming more than flesh and blood could stand. And yet . . . somehow or other, we were managing to ride out the storm. Not united and smiling, as we should have had to appear in an official photograph, but true down-to-earth human beings, desperately involved in a venture that turned us into stupendous beasts.

On 30th June: 'We left Camp II rather loaded up, about six [Cassin, Oberto, Zeni]. Fine, clear weather, but not cold. Made Camp III about eleven—a bit worn out myself—joining Toni Gobbi and Walter Bonatti, who were working away till late last night on the Ice-fall. They came out to meet us. Toni took my pack: surprised at its weight. They told us the way out of the Ice-fall wasn't funny: a lot of new snow, and a dangerous likelihood of slides. Drank some tea, put up the tent and rested. Very warm under canvas, though. Atmosphere suffocating. But it was Hobson's choice. Couldn't stay out in the sun, and the dazzle is terrible here—the snow, being always newly fallen, is intensely white. After a while Bonatti brought us some first-class broth: devoured it greedily with one or two other things. Then took a nap. Towards 1600 hours, gave a hand to Bonatti and Gobbi—off to have one more try at the Ice-fall. They got another two hundred yards, but the weather worsened and they had to give up—also, through poor visibility, fog dimming the moon. They got back to the tents at 2100 hours and told me the whole story. The passage seems to be on the dangerous side, but there's no possibility of any other. I said Oberto and I would do the next stint, and decided to get off early. Got up at three, everything prepared beforehand.'

The next morning, however, heavy snow meant further changes in the programme. Cassin and Oberto, followed later by Gobbi and Bonatti, went down to Camp II to fetch up more supplies for Camp III. This was 1st July, 'the day of the avalanche'. The party got down, but not back. They stayed at Camp II.

Bad weather again on 2nd July. 'Snowing in the morning: continued all day. But not cold. Talk, discussions. Might have been some singing too, but nobody was in a good humour. In the evening we went to bed, hoping for better conditions.' A forlorn hope. 'When I woke [this was the morning of 3rd July] the tent seemed to come down very low over us. I prodded it in several places—the same all over—shook the canvas and felt the snow sliding down. I got up and saw that it had snowed more in the night than on the previous day. We had to work hard to get the tent clear of snow. The others woke up and nobody said anything. Just a muttered "Good morning". I saw Toni sitting in the open tent-flap with a scowl which looked as if it was branded on, and his beard did nothing to sweeten his expression. In one hand he had a packet of rusks and in the other a pack of marmalade. But he didn't know whether to eat or not. Meanwhile another head came round the tent-flap. It was Carlo [Mauri]. In his good old Lecco patois, he grunted: "God, what a hole! . . ." '

Camp III—a balcony of fear

Mountains possess incredibly diverse personalities at different moments. The mountain that glitters with sunshine is scarcely the same when it retires in high dudgeon under mist and cloud. And Camp II the next time I saw it—was it the same place as that 'hole' of a week before, where my companions had passed those dismal hours Riccardo had so graphically described?

It was one of those atrociously beautiful days of the type we knew so well. Gobbi, Zeni, Oberto and I stopped under canvas gasping for air for the duration of the solar bombardment. The porters too had rigged up a sort of shelter with some groundsheets and ski-sticks. The camp, seen from those short distances which had to be traversed from time to time for one's vital needs, wore the aspect of a seaside resort on a Sunday afternoon when, in addition to the summer holiday-makers, the peasants too will turn up from the neighbouring villages, with their carts and their rugs and their hampers of

GASHERBRUM VI
22,970

The G. Cwm, with itinerary and location of Camp II.
somewhere near Gasherbrum

GASHERBRUM V
24,013

...nd Gasherbrums V and VI are visible. View is from
...ween Gasherbrums I and II

provisions. The reality was rather different, as I have said before. This splendid place specialized in subtle tortures: its dry and frozen air burned the throat, the scorching sun seared eyes and skin, and in its super-heated tents one ran the risk of suffocation, just like moth-grubs shut up in a trunk.

The hours crawled, slower than those of night itself. Each of us had some mania: we would lie down for a while, then we had to get up, leave the tent, take a look across the valley, drink tea, scratch our head, urinate, say something that never got an answer, start making notes in a notebook which was subsequently thrown away. . . . G. Cwm, cloistered by mountains of dazzling marble with its cobalt sky that seemed at the same time a metal bowl and an immense emptiness, could appear a sublime place—which it was supreme privilege to visit—or the grimmest of prisons. My kingdom for a field, a meadow, a little pathway, a house among the trees and the shouts of children at play! Here, there was nothingness. We were like butterflies impaled on a board for all eternity, on pins from which there was no escape.

'I wonder,' mused Toni, 'I wonder if we'll manage to get back to Italy by the end of August. I should like to do a bit of mountaineering.'

Many a true word . . . ! For this was no mountain we were on. It was a science-fantasy of a mountain, it was the chemistry of the stars, it was a land of glass measureless to Man: such was the stuff of this mad experiment.

At long last, towards four o'clock, the shadows began to lengthen and G. Cwm was no longer an oven of gleam and glisten and heat. In the mountains which dominated it you could begin to make out the faint beginnings of stereoscopic depth and enchanting translucencies. Gobbi and Zeni now started for Camp III. We watched them from afar as they plodded their slow way up, bowed down under heavy packs of supplies. The ski-sticks with which they helped themselves along gave us the illusion that they had skis strapped to their feet.

The route from Camp II to Camp III was all open ground and from either end you could take in the whole stretch at a glance, up or down. We followed Toni and Zeni the whole way up. By Camp III they had left a third of the Ice-fall behind them. Toni's pace was extraordinarily regular—and gave a hint to his personal make-up. While Riccardo was all heart and impulse, rock-man, man-flower, man-star, man translated into nature's primordial force or manifestation, Toni was all head: he was brain-man, man of caution—and wary conserver of all his energies. Such a combination of personalities in our two chiefs would have given the whole lot of us a fine, forceful leadership had circumstances (alas for all this fine weather that persecuted us!) been more favourable to the notion of a team acting in concert as a team should. We were lucky, too, in the two young champions we had forging ahead. That

218

balance of qualities, so apparent in the two veterans, was only a shade less clearly visible in them.

'Oberto made a first-class minestrone—then to bed.' So ends the entry in my diary for 8th July. Side by side with the extremely definite, clear-cut personalities of Cassin and Gobbi, or Bonatti and Mauri—all of them cast in different metals, but in metals equally strong, equally bright—side by side with these, Beppe Oberto and Bepi De Francesch cut a poor figure. They were the quiet ones, the silent men of the Expedition. But, when you came to know them a little, underneath that surface you found what you expected to find—a mind capable of subtleties and fine shades, a good warm heart, a readiness to go out and do the job and say nothing about it, and well-springs of generous feeling. Oberto had been indispensable to the Expedition for those first few days of the attack on the Ice-fall; after that his stomach had begun to trouble him, and now he had to be careful about it. It was a pleasure to be where he was. He got us our meals (incidentally, he was the best cook we had), he set about doing everything he could to make everybody comfortable, as if he felt he was one of a band of brothers. If a tent wanted propping up, you could be sure it wouldn't sag much farther once it had come to Oberto's notice. It was as if his bad stomach gave him some sort of guilty conscience: when he was up and about, he pitched into everything with a will—to redeem himself in our eyes!—as though he needed to make up for all the time he had to spend lying down. De Francesch was up aloft now. I could well imagine him trudging on like a pack-horse, with bowed head and never a word—up into a white and dazed world whose walls spired out of the nothingness of space itself.

The 9th July was another day of solar fury at Camp II. In the later afternoon, Oberto and I went up to Camp III (20,800 ft.); I went on skis, Beppe on foot. When the shadows of night began to fall, they came with a sudden, furious cold. Sun still streamed over the high G. Cwm from the mouth of Col 22,139 ft. (*Plate 69*). Opposite us were Corner Peak, a slim spire in a foam of ice, and the Inscription Stone, a barrier-cliff in rock of every colour, with the strange emblem of the 'Flying Woman' suggested in a patch of dark, reddish violet.

The trail rose only very gradually. For long stretches at a time the going was quite flat—at first across the path of that huge 1st July avalanche, whose visible traces were still to be seen and still made us shudder; then over an eminence dividing two minor hollows in the glacier. When we came to the beginning of the last rise—fairly steep in parts—I left my skis behind in the snow. Slowly, as we climbed, the splendours of the dying day marched with us. The snow beneath our feet darkened with shadow, almost with night itself, from Gasherbrum IV, flecked with colours that were mere sighing memories of

219

colours, frail evanescences that defied a name. The blue of the sky turned to some celestial azure, the distant peaks were touched by the level sun with a rose-red haze, gauzy with suggestions of the rainbow and the alcove. There were crevasses that made us think of cradles, and séracs that looked like toy boxes of biscotti for some giant dolls' house. Two worlds, infinitely distinct, for one magic moment crossed each other's orbit. Ahead of us, across the valley, the horizon was shut off by the bristling precipices of Gasherbrum V. Not for nothing do these ramparts face north: theirs is the pitiless splendour of ice. For months at a time, the dark arrogance of this North Wall is lighted only obliquely by the sun's radiance, if at all. But the rays of sunset lingered long over the peaceful dome of Gasherbrum I. And, soon after they had gone, over to the east rose that band of purple, to be seen only at great heights, where the lower atmosphere, dark with shadow, merges with a still-luminous, translucent, upper layer.

What a deep frost at Camp III! Our steps rang out on the ice as we approached. There were two tents. One was for Taqi and Mahmud Hussein —who gave us a royal welcome. We shared the other. I took some photographs. Oberto made the minestrone and we drank it off in great haste before letting it cool. Camp III had a fantastic setting, and a frightening one. It stood on a small snow-ridge, a balcony overlooking G. Cwm—and half the Karakoram too—right as far as K36 (Saltoro Kangri). It was on the median line of the Italians' Ice-fall and a third of the way up it. The panorama was spellbinding: mighty mountains, huge valleys that joined up like thoroughfares in some metropolis of the Gods; everything on a vast yet harmonious scale. But when you looked up you saw another panorama, and one you shuddered at: awe-inspiring in every sense. A stack, a vast battalion of ice-blocks, each one the size of a house or the size of a palace, was ranged immediately over our heads. Behind that battalion there were other battalions, and beyond them others yet, till the eye lost sight of them—right up to the last rampart that closed off the Ice-fall—an almost sheer cliff, of forbidding height, in colour a livid blue. What a horrible, frightening place—'What a hole!' Ravine and cliff would have made it baleful enough if everything around us had been of rock and stone; but it was all ice, unstable, impermanent ice. We were encamped on the broken crest of a wave in an ice-river, solid enough now . . . and till when? What if it pleased to unburden itself of some of its immense weight of ice, and send it hurtling down? In that case our one gleam of hope, for what consolation it might be worth, was that an eventual avalanche would follow the grooves flanking the little rise where our camp had been pitched. But rise and groove were dwarfed by those ice-blocks. A serious avalanche, of the kind that could happen here, would sweep away everything, ourselves included.

The daylight hours were perfectly calm; but with darkness a wind that was dry and bitter cold began to blow in fits and starts from the heights, howling down the glacier's grooves and channels as it came. A roar came from the séracs with every squall that bulldozed its way down between them. An avalanche for sure, this time! How did one sleep, in all this? One eye open, and both ears, all night! 'Was that wind—or is this it?'—the question rose, in such dramatic terms, every few minutes. How I envied Oberto's gift of sleep —the sleep of the just! Before going down into his sleeping-bag, he observed: 'Well, if we get an avalanche, there's nothing we can do!'—and, secure in such ghastly insecurity, he serenely closed his eyes and fled to his Macugnana pasturelands and his Monte Rosa ridges. The porters went on cooking their chupatty cakes till the most unearthly hours, chattering away and in the end singing the song whose little wail of a chorus came again and again with the word *mendok*, flower. Then they quietened down.

Perhaps I slept a little. After that, in the great silence between one howl of wind and the next through those canyons in the ice, I went out of the tent for a while. You must never look at your watch at such times. Your ignorance of the hour makes the dawn seem a little closer. Let the hour remain a forbidden secret. The empty, measureless night, a prey to the wind, to the insubstantial shadows between the séracs and the ghostly sheeted peaks, filled my heart with terror and wonder. I did not know whether to cry out or to pray. The stars blazed, founts of light of every colour: a firework display frozen into the secret of perpetual fire. Over Gasherbrum V hung Scorpio, motionless. How strange and out of place it seemed here: the constellation that stood for summer and warm nights and the tang of ripening fruit and sighs of love and sounds of distant gaieties! Speed on your way, Scorpio, you have no business there. This is homeground for Sirius, Sirius bristling with his savage darts of pure light. But not for you. The ice and desolation of a winter without end are not for your soft beams.

At the foot of the Wall of Ice

Oberto and I were astir at the earliest possible hour. We had the Ice-fall to climb, and it was best to get started before the sun softened the snow, possibly encouraging some avalanche in the process. Now it was cold. The sky looked immutably clear.

Camp III had been one of the key-points in the first phase of operations. Now it amounted to just two tents for arrivals and despatches. But for many a long day and longer night it had been the advance party's refuge. From Camp III they had gone up to find a route over the great Ice-fall and to equip it. And it was here, a few days before, that Riccardo Cassin had picked the Summit team, the team for the very last stage itself: Bonatti–Mauri.

We left the tents of Camp III at 5.30. In the distance there were peaks even now gleaming with sun but here we were in shadow, and in shadow we should remain until about 9.0, when the first rays crept over the ridges of Gasherbrum III. Snow and ice mirrored the ghostly tints of the sky: they seemed the very essence of pitiless cold. We went up very quickly indeed, to the place from which rose those tumbled heaps of séracs. In their midst there was one whose fortress walls rose absolutely sheer—fifty yards of pallid glaucous green above our heads. The trail here was so steep that all we had for steps was a grip for the toes of our boots. It was just at this point, where one advanced with one's heart in one's mouth, that we felt a shock of movement accompanied by a subterranean growl and followed by the evil creaking of ice. Goodbye! This must be it! Oberto gave me a look. For a long minute we stayed absolutely motionless—as if our ridiculous human weight could have the slightest influence on thousands of tons of ice in slow motion, on the brink of crashing down. What could we do? Nothing, absolutely nothing. We should be less than ants in the earth under the plough (*Plate 78*).

Farther on, the trail continued as steep as ever, but for a fine long stretch we were out of immediate danger. We climbed slowly now. Even at that height, if one is careful to keep the pace a steady one, with correctly timed breathing, it is possible to make fair progress—even pleasurable progress. The snow was very good, holding up like cement under the foot—not like the first few times Bonatti, Gobbi and the others came here, when half a metre of fresh powdery snow must have made for infernal conditions. The sun climbed higher and higher. Soon it shone on the prodigious face of Gasherbrum V, from which avalanches fell frequently, flying spumes of white smoke. We now passed isolated séracs like old ruined towers, we gazed down crevasses which turned into veins of blue in the depths of the glacier, we saw natural arches of snow with battlements and gewgaws of ice, or else long glistening icicles. Soon now, taller and more threatening than any other visible thing, there rose up against us the vertical ice barrier that closed the Ice-fall. A diaphaneity of glass, a Niagara of alabaster (*Plate 79*). The nearer we approached, the more clearly could we make out a number of towers or projections, already in part detached from the main body and certain to drop in the fullness of their time. Thus, after a brief respite, we were once more in forbidden territory where any moment could be our last.

On a tiny flat expanse up in the centre of the Ice-fall Bonatti and Mauri had set up one little tent, which they called Camp IIIA. They passed two

nights there (4th and 5th July). They had to mark out a route out of the
Ice-fall, and for this purpose it was obviously of great practical convenience
to be able to remain on the spot. This may have justified the choice of such a
site, but nothing else did. What an accursed place it must have been to sleep
in! Under the ever-present threat of falling ice, with all the creaking and
growling of a glacier in its lethargic motion. Even men with nerves of steel
deserved a medal for that. The only sign of Man's presence visible now was
a marker to help us find the tent.

We went farther, right up to the Wall of Ice—a bulwark some 300 feet
high (400, according to Toni: he may have been right, it was difficult to arrive
at an exact figure). We passed directly underneath the ugliest and the most
fantastic of all those towers: a slender pinnacle of ice, tall as a belfry, supported
by some greenish blocks which looked as if they would roll over at the slightest
provocation. It was like walking through a minefield. We hardly dared look
up at the tower, and the reason may well have been some childish fear of
making it fall by looking! Who knows?

Fortunately we were soon out of this treacherous place: a steep climb with
an excellent snow surface got us up to the first rock of Gasherbrum IV. Pure
Dolomite! Oberto led and we were roped. Higher up we found the fixed ropes
with which we tried to equip all passages of particular difficulty (*Plate 77*). I
thus came to have some faint idea of what was involved in climbing at great
altitude, when every effort seems to cost the climber the very last of his
breath. The sun had meanwhile burst over the ridge of Gasherbrum III. In the
grateful heat of the new day we crossed a crevasse whose ice-walls were almost
vertical—and we were out. We sat on a level stretch of snow and rested. Down
towards the bottom we could see Taqi and Mahmud Hussein climbing slowly
with their packs. The dot behind them was Haji Ismael.

Camp IV: the Combe à Vaches

Beyond the Ice-fall lay quite unexpected terrain: only our friend Edoardo
Buscaglione had prepared us for its existence. We had seen his extraordinarily
detailed topographical charts (which have still to be published). Among all
these preposterous, ice-curtained mountain-walls; these ramparts of stone; these
pointed peaks and razor-edged ridges; here was a little valley, a sunny little
place that made you welcome. In gentle curves it rose gradually towards the
ridge which runs between Gasherbrum III and Gasherbrum IV. So peaceful
and so sheltered was it here that one was half surprised not to find a colourful
crowd of week-end skiers, all in the middle of a hubbub of loudspeakers and
orange-vendors and sweet-stalls. True, there was no red-awninged platform

223

from which the judges decided the winner of the Ladies' Skiing Cup, but you would not have been altogether astonished to find one!

Toni's idea of it was different.

'Summer in the mountains!' he exclaimed (as if summer was not just at its very height! But then, it was always winter here.) 'Can't you see the meadows and the Alpine flowers and the cows? For me, this is La Combe à Vaches.' And that was what we christened it. Little haven of peace, little land of milk and honey, it is good to remember you on those bleak heights!

Halfway across the Combe, sheltered by a cluster of fallen ice-blocks, were the tents of Camp IV. We were at 22,800 feet now, at a camp-site where we felt quite at home. It was a good deal better than the lower ones. From the Ice-fall to the camp much of the track was almost flat: these slopes at the foot of the East Wall of Gasherbrum IV contained nothing very abrupt just now. It was here, I am not sure why, that all of us became more or less conscious of the first real effects of great altitude. At every few steps one wanted to sit down, ready to drop—a hundred years old. And now we began a phase of existence which might have been called our automaton period. If we went on, it was only because we were impelled by the obscure remnants of a sense of duty —duty towards the whole organization of which we formed part, duty to friends that waited at home for 'good news', duty towards one another. For a memory of similar sensations and a parallel state of mind I have to go right back to the war and a concentration camp. Those too were days when hunger, cold and misery almost forced us to succumb. Now we had come to grips once again with the bare essentials of life. We were creatures almost reduced to bone, tooth and nail, grappling with the glassy treachery of ice purely to save ourselves from plunging into the abyss.

The marvels we saw around us were only passively recorded now. Their real enjoyment was for some future day, when they would be taken out of storage from some memory cell in the brain. In crossing the flank of the Combe, while we made for the tents of Camp IV—which seemed to grow more distant with every step, as if bewitched—what new discoveries we made! Gasherbrum III, for example, seen from here, was no longer the big clumsy hump which had dominated Gasherbrum Valley. It swept down on the Combe à Vaches with a glorious façade the colour of bread straight out of the oven. It was a true castle, a crag, possibly the highest crag in the world. Nothing I have ever seen round the 26,000-foot mark carries such a suggestion of the Dolomites.

At last we reached Camp IV, where we found Cassin, Toni Gobbi and Bepi De Francesch. What poor shape we were all in—bearded, swollen-faced, the skin peeling off our cheeks . . . we looked like shipwrecked men; we had crossed perilous seas and found land, but it proved no refuge, it was only one more stop in a weary pilgrimage to heaven knew where, from God knew whence. The simplest task up here made one gasp for breath again and again; one had to break off to rest. Some of us refused to speak when spoken to, and others refused to listen. One man had headaches, another vague feelings of nausea. One talked in his sleep, another would flare up for nothing. Tell us the simplest and the all-important thing, and it would go in one ear and out the other. Camp IV was a hospital, a home for nerve cases.

'Don't speak to me,' I told Dr. Zeni. 'I am just at that tragic point between retarded childhood and precocious senility.'

Now we heard the latest news of Bonatti and Mauri. Two days before, they had reached a point on the North-East Ridge (c. 23,600 feet) and found a small flat sector which would take a tent very well. The next day they had pitched it, and there was Camp V. Today, we learned, they were making an attempt to reach the Summit. These were moments of great tension for everyone of us. We were all the time looking at the weather, dreading any sign of it worsening. Fortunately, it still held: only a few light clouds during the afternoon or evening marred a perfectly clear sky. Every now and then we heard a shout from Bonatti or Mauri. The distance was considerable, but with certain favourable conditions you could make yourself heard at Camp IV from the North-East Ridge.

Advance—its problems and logistics

The welcome I myself received at Camp IV was not one of the warmest: and, if my companions gave me no more, they were perfectly right. One more mouth to feed was a problem up here, even with appetites reduced to nothing. Things were critical: one soon grasped that. In fact, we were repenting at leisure now, for making the most of the fine weather and forging ahead in such haste. We had failed to consolidate our supply line. If the North-East Ridge turned out to be a simple matter, then no great harm had been done. From the little one could gather, though, the possibility of reaching the Summit in one single spurt from Camp V seemed to be ruled out, however bold a bid was made for it. Height, distances and difficulties were too great. Victory could only be achieved as the last operation in a methodical campaign—point by point, chimney by chimney, traverse by traverse—over the whole of the ridge, parts of which would need pitons and fixed ropes. These stretches could then be covered with comparative speed and safety and from them we could get on to the strange ground. The Peak itself in the end would then be in fairly easy range, enabling us to reach it and make the descent again all in one day without the risk of bivouacs.

But such a 'Campaign of Occupation' presupposed a non-stop pipeline from the Base, and this had begun to show signs of too much strain and interruption. There were too few high-altitude porters; of the six we had two or three were constantly ailing, or so much under the weather as to be of no practical use. And once we had exhausted the supplies at Camp II we should have to set up queens, pawns and knights and start afresh from the stores down by the Duke of the Abruzzi Glacier, playing a fresh game of chess with the mountain.

At Camp IV, as early as 8th July, Cassin made this note: 'Going over our stocks, I saw that we were very short: we took up one pack to the Black Rocks (on the N.E. Ridge, proposed site for Camp V). Here we have just the remains. I made a pot of coffee-with-milk. The crumbs of the rusks and biscotti sent up will have to do for Bonatti and Mauri when they get down from the N.E. Ridge.' On the evening of 9th July Gobbi and Zeni came up to Camp IV 'bringing no provisions, only a little tea and sugar. We eked this out, night and morning too.'

I had promised Gobbi that I would send up twelve packs of provisions by four porters from Camp II; but one man fell by the wayside, and Haji Ismael, climbing under very considerable stress, staggered into Camp IV under the weight of the cinecamera, which he had brought up by mistake instead of the rations. This set-back depressed me a lot. Everybody was going to think that I had given a merely useful article priority over a vitally necessary one. It was a genuine case of misunderstanding on the porter's part. I had asked Ismael to carry up the machine *snang-la* (the day after tomorrow), not *diring* (today), and not to carry up the machine till he had got back from carrying up the food.

Cassin, Gobbi and I—the three seniors—finding ourselves together in one tent, got down to a counsel of war, there and then. I myself was taking part in it not strictly as a climber but rather as an 'extra'; in so far, too, as I was last man up, I was perhaps able to make my contribution to the debate. I felt it to be perfectly natural that all my companions should aim at reaching the Summit: mountains were either their profession or their great vocation in life. One certainly didn't come so far to be content with Point So-and-So or Camps IV or V. I felt the same sense of frustration myself. Yet it was easier for me to turn my back on the chance of success: the whole of the rest of this excursion, with its full complement of new countries, new peoples and mountain glories, had been ample riches, and I was well aware that with the very high altitudes my usefulness with the cameras would not be so very great. I could get better results lower down. On the score of all this, it was not so hard for me as it

226

would have been for the others to put into words something which everyone felt, and no one liked to acknowledge to himself.

'The position is very simple really,' I said. 'There are too many of us up here. We cannot all get to the Summit. We can't all be the advance team, and we've got to be absolutely firm with ourselves over it. The detailed arrangements you must decide, but what we've got to do is get down to Base Camp as fast as possible and take up the chain again from there.'

Cassin and Gobbi seemed to agree. Gobbi produced one of those magic notebooks of his chock-full of figures, sums, lists and formulae, and got down to some long and complicated calculations. At last he asked Cassin if it might not be better to start as soon as possible—right now—for the Base Camp. Cassin said yes, and a little while later Gobbi left us, thus giving one more example of personal sacrifice for the sake of the Expedition's chances.

Cassin and I decided to go down next day. Oberto was to go as far as Camp II to pick up pitons and snap-links and take them up to Camp III, from which point Zeni and the porters would see them up to Camp IV and Camp V, on the ridge, with all possible speed. So the machine was turning over once more. All that remained now was to pray to the Gods of the Baltoro that this wonderful weather would hold for at any rate a week, and that the two men who formed our advance team should be filled with patience and understanding. If, at this supreme moment of the dash for the Summit, a failure in communications left them stranded without food, and without the equipment they needed, they would most certainly gnaw off their hands!

The sun sets on the North-East Ridge

On 10th July I had come up from Camp III to Camp IV all the way along the Ice-fall. It was Cassin's suggestion that I should now go with him and Bepi De Francesch to the North-East Ridge. This was after I had taken a few hours' rest and eaten a minestrone and a tin of reindeer meat (by the law of caprice that reigned up here it turned everyone else's stomach and to me it tasted divine, while the ham the others were feasting on made me feel sick). I was feeling completely done, and I should have liked to take twenty-four hours off from climbing. But I soon saw that this would be impossible. The food at this point was too scarce for one to stay put here. In other words, it was the ridge now—or never.

So I loaded myself up with photographic and filming gear, took a pocketful of sugar and urged on the old bones in the trail of Riccardo and Bepi. We left the tents at 1630 hours, when the sunlight had passed its full ferocity. We were all very tired, and we went forward in Indian file, bowed down and silent, making Siberia of the Karakoram, the perfect representation of 'Three Prisoners in Flight'.

The snow on which we could so easily have lain down to rest covered slopes that grew steeper all the time, and our pace slowed up accordingly. The last pitch was such hard going that I thought we should never get over it. Two hours it took us to get up 600 feet!

Yet we made it. And what a moment that was—yes, even here, in these conditions. To get to a ridge, and then with every step to discover the world on the far side of it! Fresh chains of mountains, ice, clouds, sky and peaks till now unglimpsed, valleys unknown. Such moments more than made up for everything—the anguish of the nights, the hard hours of the ascent, the atrocious sun, mirrored in the blinding faces of the séracs. Once more one knew that sense of gratitude, of supreme and unmerited privilege. We put down the packs that had all but broken our backs and took a short rest. Opposite us now was the last pyramid of Gasherbrum IV—not improved by foreshortening and flattening. The North-East Ridge, on closer acquaintance, proved to be jagged with rocks, rose-red in the light of a setting sun, with fantastic cornices of snow and blue ice-cliffs (*Plates 80, 83*).

From high up above we were now seen by Walter and Carlo, and they shouted down a mighty welcome. It is incredible how even a landscape like this can lose something of its desperate bleakness at the sound of a human voice. We hoped that the pair of them up there in their eyrie would find our presence here as heartening as we had found their call! A little while after this, Cassin and De Francesch left me for Camp V—sited at a point where the ridge began a steep rise. Instead of going along with them I clambered up a rocky point on the north of the ridge to take some photographs. Half an hour before I had really felt fit to drop, there and then, on to the snow. Now, I seemed to have surprising reserves of energy to unleash. That extra 300-foot climb was wearing, true, but I did it. I even managed to hoist myself up on to the knife-edge of the ridge itself, to stand poised over 10,000 frightening feet of nothingness, and the Valley of Shaksgam.

The sun was setting now. The air was perfectly still and translucent. The very temperature was quite pleasant. *You are over 23,000 feet up, in the heart of the Karakoram.* Yes, I told myself this, more than once, but I still couldn't believe it. It seemed mere fantasy. But it wasn't fantasy. Here, in very truth, were K2 and Broad Peak, with the sun sinking behind them. Seen from Concordia,

Broad Peak had appeared to us as a heavy, a bulky mountain. From here it was a proud fortress of snow-girt ridge and fine-tapering pyramid, plunging 10,000 feet down to the North Gasherbrum Glacier. Towards the west rose a thicket of upswording peaks—the jagged peaks and pinnacles of the Lower Baltoro. Not far away, Muztagh Tower and Masherbrum were clearly defined.

To the south, the Combe à Vaches, inserted between the precipices of G.III and G.IV, looked like a balcony, a hanging garden over Chogolisa; G.V and G.VI and Golden Throne—all of them a playground for the last precious rays of a level sun, and a haunt of violet shade (*Plate 82*). Right over me rose the ramparts of G.III, lit with true Dolomite fire. But it was the view to northward that held the longest, lingering spell, not only with the beauty of chain after chain of mountains bathed in an orange glow that floated on the purple seas of night, but with the fascination of the unknown as well. This was one of the least-explored regions of the face of the earth. Here marched the unmapped boundaries of Pakistan, India, China and Russia. Asia's heart. The land that saw Marco Polo and Genghis Khan (*Plate 81*).

Confronted by such far-flung grandeur, one's mind turns to human intimacies: I found myself thinking of distant friends, of the climbing companions of Europe's mountains, or Japan's. I wanted to share with them this fabled silence. And was it today that Yuki, my daughter, reached the age of nineteen? Yes, today! And, against all likelihood, I imagined her with a throng of friends all in light summer clothes, blowing out the candles on a birthday cake. . . . Away with it, fool! Those things no longer existed. Here, we were alone, cut off, cursed survivors of a world terraced in rock, condemned to ice— and the sublime.

The sun was going down fast now, its last rays glancing off the neighbouring crests of K2. The mountains glinted like pieces of coral, the valleys faded into night. A band of violet darkened the horizon. Ice blazed with electric sheens and mirrored the infinitudes of space. The sudden evil cold was coming down. It was time to flee this spot. I could already see Riccardo and Bepi coming down again. I made haste to join them. We got back to the tents of Camp IV in the dark. It was bitter cold. We were almost drunk with fatigue, with a vague hunger, with misery. But the heart can hold its secrets, and no one could rob us now of ours.

So near—and yet so far. . . .

Red-letter days these, all along the line: from the Base Camp right up to the heights. The splendid weather held. Something like frenzy had touched us all. We had to wring the last ounce out of these hours of sunshine for there might be no more. In the briefest possible space of time we had to get fresh supplies up to the advance team and we ran into ever-increasing difficulties with that inferno of precipice, peak and cornice: the North-East Ridge.

On 10th July Walter and Carlo had made a first attempt on the Summit. Leaving the tent that formed Camp V at dawn, they began to open up a route along a snow-covered rib that rose towards the rocks. It grew steeper all the time, and narrower, with cornices that had to be collapsed before the pair could advance without danger. Seen from the North-East Ridge, and likewise from the lower level of the Combe à Vaches, this tricky pitch looked like nothing more formidable than a hump in the expanse of the ridge itself. In reality it was a razor's edge whose true nature could only be seen from above (*Plate 95*). Then it showed plainly as a sort of rising wave of rock and ice frozen to immobility as it reached its apex. It had been christened Cornice Crest.

This first dash for the summit by Bonatti and Mauri soon taught them one thing—that the idea of 'getting there and getting down again in one day' was just an idle dream. What they had to tackle was terrain they had to work at like Trojans, metre by metre. And how long would the weather hold out? Would the vital necessities—pitons, rope, snap-links, fuel—reach them in time? Such doubts must have gnawed at them continually; they were already racked out with superhuman effort, and on top of that there was the great altitude to tempt them into moral collapse. That can happen, at these heights, very suddenly. There must have been heavy moments when they felt we had abandoned them to their fate. Yet all along the line from camp to camp we were doing our level best to keep them supplied. We were separated from the Base Camp by a very long journey, and to cap everything the last stretch of the climb held difficulties none of us had reckoned with.

There was, however, one great point in our favour: we were all of us well (with the sole exception of Oberto, whose stomach trouble was proving obstinate). We were also extraordinarily lucky to have had no accidents either among climbers or porters. And when you looked at the séracs and the crevasses which seemed to lie in ambush for their prey; when you thought of all the journeys we made through such terrain, up the mountain and down; you were bound to feel that Fate was keeping a brotherly eye on us!

On the evening of 10th July De Francesch and Cassin got up to Camp V and made contact with Walter and Carlo.

'Bonatti and Mauri scarcely heard us coming'—runs Bepi's account—'they were glad to see us because they knew we'd be bringing food. That day they'd eaten nothing but a few pep tablets. They told us they'd done about a hundred metres on Cornice Crest and the going was terrible. There were stretches where they had to go on all fours and they needed pitons and rope galore, and two more climbers to help them get the ropes fixed right up to the end of the Black Rocks—25,000 feet.'

On 11th July Bonatti and Mauri once more made a start from the tent at the earliest possible moment. They covered the ground opened up the day before quite rapidly, and then they did one more 100-metre stretch over virgin territory. It makes all the difference in the world to have been up once already, especially over snow and ice: to find a trail ready and waiting, with sure footholds over the rock cleared of ice and fixed ropes for the difficult or dangerous pitches, gives the climber a fine feeling: but a still finer one comes from the fact that this time he knows the going. He has a psychological sense of possession: the mountain, or this particular stretch of it, is his. This is the real value of having been there once. You have tackled it, you have conquered the unknown.

The unknown element of G.IV came after Cornice Crest and a diminutive col: it turned out to be a series of small peaks or crags running all the way up the pitch and defying us to pass. This entire sector of the mountain was of brown granite. Although it seemed to offer good holds, the stuff was far from solid rock: it was very easily broken and would crumble away into nothing. Bonatti and Mauri found themselves snow-and-ice men at one moment and pure rock-climbers at the next.

On the first crag, Bonatti tackled a chimney about a hundred feet in height; so closely did it resemble the well-known one on the Abruzzi spur of K2 that he wanted to give it the same name—the 'Bill Chimney'. But, while this represented one of K2's major difficulties, it was just one more tricky pitch on G.IV, a good deal easier than some. After a long and bitterly hard stint, Walter and Carlo turned back exhausted to Camp V. They had barely conquered the first of the crags.

So Bepi too, with Zeni this time, assumed the humble role of porter and climbed with rations and gear from Camp IV to Camp V. 'This morning,' he records, 'Zeni came up from Camp III with two porters. They had brought five incomplete ration-packs, one rope, twenty pitons (both ice and rock). Why do the rations have to arrive tampered with? They're made up well enough at Milan. Yet as they get higher the very things that tempt your appetite (and there aren't many up here) seem to vanish from the containers. The fruit in syrup goes, and the dried fruit, and some of the biscotti and other tit-bits. . . .' Certainly there was nothing wrong with the packing back in Italy, but it seemed

South Summit   North Summit

○ BLACK BLA
○ BLACK TO
○ SNOW CO

LAST TOW
○ CAMP VI
○ III TOWER
○ GREY TOW

○ I TOWER
○ CAMP V

N.E.Col

Terminal Pyramid of Gasherbrum IV (26,180 feet) from face of G.III

to have occurred to no one in the packing station that the plastic bags were transparent: the porters had learned just where to put their hands for those little items which, for them as well as for us, '*gusto mucho*'.

'At 1530 hours,' Bepi goes on, 'I left Camp IV for Camp V with Zeni: we carried two sets of rations (with gaps), two ropes, pitons, a rock hammer and two cradles. Up there they say they must have two more hands on deck: but there's nobody here except Zeni and myself. Cassin has gone down because he's under the weather, and we've no idea how to get all the stuff we'd have to take up there—two tents, liquid gas, another four ropes and our own equipment. It would take at least three trips. The four ropes they want just aren't here, they'd have to come up from Base. If we only had some good high-altitude porters! Bonatti and Mauri seem to reckon on placing a Camp VI very high up,

The four major Gasherbrum Peaks, as seen from summit of Broad Peak by the Austrians of the 1957 expedition. On the ridge of Gasherbrum IV, the route of Italian expedition is marked (. . .), showing location of Camps V and VI

say 1,000 feet from the Summit. The weather holds, and this would be just the time to do it.'

This was the first mention of a possible Camp VI. The fact was that the terrain was turning out to be more extensive, more complicated and more hostile all the time. One highly difficult and dangerous pitch followed another,

233

exhausting both the physical and nervous energies of the two leading men. The Summit seemed to become daily more distant, more inaccessible.

On 12th July Walter and Carlo, clenching their teeth and summoning hidden reserves of energy from nowhere, left their tent (Camp V). They went up over the crags they had already covered—already tamed!—during the past day or two. Then came Grey Turret. Its conquest took them hours and hours and left them utterly spent. Above them now thronged a confused mass of crags, snow-slopes and razor-edges. On the left they had a plunge of several hundred metres down to Camp IV and the Combe à Vaches. To their right the rock-face dropped away into a bottomless pit whose eventual floor was the North Gasherbrum Glacier. They were moving forward and upward all the time with nothingness on either side of them. To their practised eyes, used to weighing up obstacles in the Alps, some of the perpendiculars in front of them looked possible. But the demands they made on muscles and lungs, at this altitude, were fantastic. The short stops after every exertion became perforce longer and longer. Soon, the slightest effort meant that they had to pause, even without a chance to sit down. From below, the entire ridge might well appear to amount to nothing more than a line of conjunction between two mountain-faces. The truth of it was a whole anthology of every climbing difficulty, known and unknown. To give some examples—the razor-edge arête, the traverse that called for the most delicate manœuvres, the overhang, the sheer face and the chimney, all of them with Grade IV pitches. Never before, at such height, had such risks been taken. Muztagh Tower may have opened up a new era of climbing in the Himalaya, but, at the altitude at which G.IV began to bristle with difficulties, the summit of Muztagh Tower had already been reached. Very slow, but very sure, conquering one obstacle only to be faced with the next, Walter and Carlo made their way up.

The 13th July dawned with one more of those flawless skies for which mountain men would often give their very souls. But our own team could scarcely stir. They were tired out to the marrow of their bones, their throats were on fire, their eyes bloodshot and painful—and then they were short of everything; food and fuel were reduced to a minimum (and in these places, where drinking is more important than eating, no fuel means no water); they needed far more pitons, rope, cord, before they could get on with the job. What must have been the thoughts, the state of mind of those two lonely men, up there in their heavenly inferno, a hell of splendid spectacle and cruel torment, as they waited for the hours to go by, forced to squander the inestimable treasure of a perfect day? For such a case we should need the services of a machine which has still to be invented, even in these days of so many machines

—a psychograph, to register *'the flow of thought'*; for to take up pencil and note-book, at that altitude, would involve a superhuman effort of will-power.

To make matters worse, Bepi and Zeni were in poor shape too. 'Zeni and I,' wrote De Francesch on 13th July, 'started for Camp V with a load of about 55 lb. We tried to get up as far as possible, but after a hard hour's trudge we were forced to give in, feeling finished. We returned to Camp IV.'

14th July. A day of record activity. Would it be the decisive day? Walter and Carlo felt all the better for their rest. They got off to an early-as-possible start again, determined to put an end to all the torment and the uncertainty and see the job through. Little by little, panting not with exertion alone but reduced by hunger too, they had covered Cornice Crest, they had reached the small col, and then embarked on that endless series of knife-edge and rock-face, cliff and overhang, conquering First Turret, Grey Turret, Mule's Back. They had pressed on over untrodden snow and crags that rose ever steeper and more defiant, right up to Last Turret, with its maddening smooth-walled vertical chimney (*Plate 103*) and Snow Cone—a slippery spring-board on to nothingness, which from the North-East Ridge had appeared to be the highest point of the whole mountain. Alas, once the climber had put this behind him, the true Summit was revealed, in all its discouraging distance. Between that and these two men lay obstacles never suspected—for instance, a minor ridge as sharp as a knife, crenellated throughout its entire length with tight-packed cornices of that strange Karakoram snow which at one moment can be as hard as baked or frozen mud and at the next can powder to nothing like fine ash. To try and bivouac anywhere in this region would be madness. Once more the decision had to be taken to go down again. Yet it had been a red-letter day: nearly 300 metres of terrain opened up for the first time. By now it was clear that the Summit could never be conquered without a Camp VI, placed some-where very high up on Cornice Crest.

De Francesch (who was feeling none too well) and Zeni at last (on 14th July) got up to the North-East Ridge with supplies. That evening the four men gathered in the tiny tent which formed Camp V.

'Bonatti and Mauri told us,' wrote Bepi, 'that they had got to within 1,150 feet of the Summit.'

Such distances and such differences in altitude as I give at this stage scarcely seem to represent serious figures. Just here and now, however, they were sufficient to create a barrier capable of defeating the total strength of our entire Expedition, and the audacity and iron will of some of the outstanding champions of the Alps.

235

Wild beasts that roam . . .

In the meantime Gobbi and I had gone down to Base Camp. From Camp II onwards, we made the descent by ski, over snow that was hard and compact. Cassin had paused at Camp I. The whole question of getting food supplies and gear up to the mountain was now reviewed and put on a new methodical basis. All the same, the high camps meant a long and difficult trek and we had too few porters. The only two still working were Taqi and Mahmud Hussein. They had taken the greatest strain, and they were now beginning to feel it. Of the remainder, one after another was going down sick, and when you sent a load from Point A to Point B there was no guarantee that it would get there on the same day. So we were still in the hands of Fate—or the moods and humours of a Rustam or a Ghulam.

The 11th, 12th, 13th and 14th of July had been days of the most intricate organization throughout the lower camps. It would be tedious to go through all the movements of such a time-table! Oberto, Cassin and Gobbi had stuck to it like human pack-horses, humping weights that were enough to kill them, and persuading the porters by prayer, promises and precepts to go and do likewise. Gobbi, after making the descent from Camp IV to Base (22,800 feet to 16,200 feet) went up again in three days (13th, 14th, 15th July) to Camp IV—a truly extraordinary feat, especially for a man of forty-four.

Now for the first time oxygen came into the picture. We had eighteen cylinders of a type specially designed with high-mountain work in view. As a general principle, my companions were against the use of oxygen, and the experience of a good many expeditions does tend to indicate that up to 26,300 feet it is something you can do without: G.IV was just under the critical figure. The view generally held—with some justification—was that the cylinders were an encumbrance and any advantage they might afford was cancelled out by their weight. But here we were, faced by difficulties we had not foreseen even in our blackest moments: perhaps it was as well therefore to resort to our secret weapons. So a few cylinders were despatched to Camp I. An aspect of oxygen that everybody knew about was its value during sleep. The sleeper breathing air with a slight oxygen enrichment woke more refreshed than he would have done without it. The French had proved that in the course of their Makalu Expedition.

The time-table of our movements over these few eventful days was further complicated by the fact that Captain Dar, suddenly wearying of the Base Camp, decided to take his faithful Ali and make a quick upward tour. He left the valley on the 10th July. He was at Camp III on the 12th. From there he went up to Camp

IV, going down alone in a single day to Camp II. This was prowess indeed, especially when one considered that Captain Dar had had no real high-mountain experience at all. It was only a pity that his ascent had to coincide with the most delicate moment of a logistic crisis.

Here we are touching on a thorny subject, and it has come up in a good many expeditions before. The accompanying officer not only wishes to fulfil his role of 'intermediary between the foreigners and the Pakistani' but, very reasonably and understandably, he wants to go back to his regiment with a certain experience of climbing to his credit. This will be highly useful to him in a mountainous country which has as yet very little knowledge of its mountains and very little technical equipment in the field. If the accompanying officer turns out to be a grand seigneur—like Colonel Ata Ullah, appointed to the K2 Expedition—it will not need to be explained to him that the problems involved by such a tremendous climb are such as to rule out absolutely any 'instruction classes'. Should the mountain offer reasonable—as apart from desperate—difficulties, he may take part in the attack; this happened, as we shall see, with the Americans in the case of G.I. When you get the unfortunate combination of a mountain bristling with difficulties and an accompanying officer with great ambitions, then you are in for some perfectly magnificent misunderstandings.

One slight climbing incident deserves recording over this period: Toni Gobbi fell into a crevasse while he was advancing alone, on skis, along the South Gasherbrum Glacier. Once more, the invisible angel of good fortune, so constantly with us, came to our aid. Plunging down only a few metres, Gobbi was saved by a soft cushion of snow—the crevasse being mercifully closed by a second, subterranean bridge! He came to no harm at all. If we'd all been in a good humour, if we could have brought with us intact the light-hearted mood of the Alps, we should have drunk to his health. But just here and now we were wild beasts that roam the forest. The mountain had become a phantom, dogging us into the most secret strongholds of the night. The mountain was a nightmare.

Storm without end

On 15th July there happened what had to happen, if the Weather Gods of the Karakoram were not to be proved out of their right mind: a change, definitely for the worse. Up in Camps IV and V the advance parties held out every minute they could. But at last they had no option. There was only one thing to do—take their courage in both hands and go down to Base. Everything had to be reorganized—logistics, up-and-down movements of men and supplies, in short, the entire expedition. Then, after two or three weeks, a second attempt on the Summit could be made.

'Here we are at Camp V,' Bepi recorded on 15th July. 'Bonatti, Mauri and self. Weather has changed. It's nasty. There's a terrific wind that seems bent on carrying off our tent. We're right out in the open here, with no protection at all. . . .'

For 16th July, the entry was this: 'Bad weather with a vengeance today. Driving wind and snow. . . .'

At Camp IV Cassin wrote:

'Weather worsening all right. Impossible to leave the tent for this morning's gale. Beginning to get worried about our four friends on the North-East Ridge. Can't even go out of the tent for one's most intimate needs. All day the same: the night too. . . .''

Had it not been for these conditions, 'the programme would be this . . .' wrote Bepi, during the actual gale, up at Camp V. 'Bonatti, Mauri, Zeni and I decided to attack the Summit together, bringing up a tent. The idea was to place a small camp at the highest point Bonatti and Mauri had reached, and go on from there, all four. The four of us could make lighter work of bringing up the tent, etc., over Cornice Crest. Am certain that had the weather held only two days more, the Summit would have been ours. As it is, who knows how things will go? . . .'

17th July was hell let loose. 'This morning'—it is Bepi taking up the tale again—'we decided to go down to Camp IV. The storm never let up. A metre and a half of snow has fallen, on one side of the tent we had to clear off the snow five times, or it would have been swamped. Started down at 10.0. Scarcely got two yards when we sailed off in an avalanche that started under our feet. Managed to stop myself after a couple of yards, so did Mauri, or we'd have gone with it 1,500 or 1,800 feet down! Bonatti afterwards went on, roped, but ten yards was enough. He turned back, saying it was impossible in so much wind and snow, with visibility so bad you couldn't make out what was only a few metres in front of you. He'd put it mildly. With the wind driving the snow into your eyes you couldn't see a thing! Went back to the tent, wondering what comes next. Decided we had to get down at any cost. Roped up again. I went as leader. The hardest part was getting down to the ridge proper, both because the going was so steep and because of avalanches too. I went leader because I knew the path better than the others, having done six transport jobs from IV to V and seven from the ridge to V. In three-quarters of an hour we got to the ridge, and two hours later made Camp IV. Found Cassin there, recovered somewhat, and Gobbi. Weather still ugly. Decided to quit this camp too. For myself, it seems a pity. I feel fit and up to anything.'

On the 18th they were all at Camp III. For a short while it looked as if the weather might be on the change. The wind had dropped, the mountains had the white gleam of new snow; but a few hours later: 'Change again—gale

Inscription Stone, at the head of the South Gasherbrum Glacier, with its 'Flying Woman', a dark brown patch of rocks many hundred feet high in the light-coloured limestone of the mountain

raging.' It was the monsoon. There were two factors in our favour: the remoteness of the Indian Ocean, and the existence of some chains of mountains between us and the plains of India and Pakistan. This meant that monsoon storms reached us late and soon blew out—they were over far quicker here than in Nepal, for instance. Moreover, between one storm and the next there was always a distinct patch of fine weather. But there was a fundamental change in the air, not a doubt about it. It was much more humid now, and heavier, with less temperature-difference between day and night. At the Base Camp the thermometer went down to two or three degrees below freezing point at night, and in daytime jumped to eight or ten above—even with a clouded sky.

All that remained for us now was to go right down, and no half-measures, right down to Base Camp on the Duke of the Abruzzi Glacier.

Days of Success

A table laid for nine

ONCE more—all together at the Base Camp! There was no doubt about it—the mountain had beaten us. Nine men ate to get their strength back, they read the papers and the letters that had come from Italy, they wrote home, they made notes—but mighty long faces they pulled! An expedition is not quite the sort of spree that so many people seem to think it is. The real thing is a far cry from the glowing colours in which popular imagination paints it. As different as chalk from cheese, or real war from all those altar-of-patriotism heroics. Just now, this particular expedition was a Calvary: an amalgam of hardship, hurt pride and repressed rage.

One of the porters came in to shout the news to Dar and me: '*Tharing-ne mi mangmo ongwet!*'—'A long way up there—many men coming . . .'

With our hearts in our mouths we scrambled up on to the little rise over the Base Camp; and *up there*, among the séracs of the glacier, beneath a sky that hung low and heavy and dropped a few sluggish flakes of snow, we saw seven of our party and a few porters descending slowly, stumbling every now and again, roped in groups against the lurking dangers of the crevasses. A scene of tragedy. The ragged tail of some disastrous rout, some defeat that was not quite on a material plane, rather one that involved the spirit. No, we hadn't a moment's doubt now about the tidings our companions were bringing. So much so that we never even asked them: 'Have you done it?'

Their bearded faces were drawn and blistered by the sun, there was weariness in them and a sort of self-disgust. Cassin was unrecognizable. All that effort, physical and moral, all that responsibility for our lives and our success—the weight of it must have been more than one man could bear. A few days earlier, at Camp IV, he had made this entry in his diary: 'I can see plainly now that at upwards of 23,000 feet I can't do all that I would like to do. Am going down to Camp III or II . . . I can't ask too much of myself. I've been away from Base now since 24th June, with only one day's rest at Camp III. I've got to admit too that I'm pretty near fifty. . . .'

I knew Riccardo: if he'd put words like that on paper, it meant he was at the end of his tether and could not have gone on. Not just then.

But it is simply extraordinary what a few hours' rest, a wash and brush up, can do even for men who've seen the worst of the hardest battles. That evening, round the table in the big tent, before nine brimming bowls of smoking minestrone—with a steady-burning liquid-gas lamp for a light, and one's Sunday best in the way of clothes—a jersey or a jacket unpacked from one's kit to replace the rags and tatters we'd grubbed about in up aloft—that evening, my companions were new men, their appearance was human, civilized, and at times definitely cheerful. It was fine to be all together again; and in the end we did enjoy a short spell, at any rate, of really high spirits. We relaxed.

Going down to Base had restored to us one thing we had been sorely deprived of in the higher camps: our appetites. The restoration was particularly noticeable in the young 'uns. Walter and Carlo wolfed the dried bread in milk and coffee, and rice-minestra they devoured. Between meals, they kept their strength up with a non-stop progression of biscotti, dried meat, ham and cheese. Riccardo and Toni too, for that matter, did some serious eating. Donato Zeni, on the other hand, always a figure of slight mystery—we knew him for a champion on Dolomite rock, but we were surprised to find him also an absolutely first-class mountaineer 'Western style'—Donato appeared to take his nourishment in the form of subtle little dishes and transparent drinks, arousing in the rest of us a certain respect for his qualities as the miracle-man of the snows. We were our own cooks. After a series of disastrous experiments with paid ones, perhaps it was better so. We all took turns in the kitchen, in theory, but not in fact. Nearly all the cooking was done by Oberto and Carlo Mauri, and incidentally we could not have been better pleased. They were artists at pastry-making, both for sweets and meat pies.

Our conversation might turn to every topic under the sun; but every so often the compass-needle swung round, and back, to its real magnetic north—the mountain. We could feel its invisible presence all the time. It was always there, just outside the tent. A boundless and terrifying power, with which we should all have to settle our accounts. Walter and Carlo would often tell us details about their days among the crags and cornices of the ridge. 'That would be a pretty good climb even at 10,000 feet,' said Walter. And Carlo took up the tale: 'One day, when we were going up, we did six hours' hard—and at the end

Q

of it we felt drained of the last drop of energy—clearing snow-cornices to get just a few metres. Then we went back to Camp V and it took us twenty minutes.'

'At the moment,' said Walter, 'we're in a highly advantageous position on the mountain. And we're in a highly disadvantageous one too: we're tired and worn. But, on the credit side, we've got five camps rigged up all along the line, we've got a good sector of that ridge fitted up with pitons in the worst places, with 600 or 700 yards of fixed rope. If you ask me, five or six days of good weather is all we need; we could get from Base Camp right up to the Summit.'

'Let's hope an avalanche doesn't bury one of the lower camps,' some pessimist observed. But all of us were in better heart now. Even a disaster on those lines, I felt, wouldn't have proved too much of a set-back now.

That first evening ended with the last thing one would have expected—music. Before leaving Italy, I had asked my daughter Dacia to prepare some tape-recordings of classical music, with the idea of putting them on the machine. But which of us had ever had—I won't say the time, but the slightest desire to listen to music? Till now, the Expedition had been a dire battle with men and things and nature, it had left its rough, uncivilizing mark on us all. Our one recourse against exhaustion, against anxiety, against conflicting spirits was—sleep. But this one evening proved an unexpected haven of peace: a clearing in that wild forest.

The tapes were discovered by Donato Zeni, the most passionate music-lover among us and certainly the most well-informed too (he was an accomplished pianist), and suddenly, there was Vivaldi, with the Four Seasons, keeping company with the clouded giants of the Baltoro. God, the power of music! The walls of ice, in which we seemed to have been immured for so long, fell down. The world came back to us over their ruins. There were other things, things that had lost their existence for us ever since we had lived in this Kafka-like segregation, week after week. There were other thoughts, other horizons. There were homes, children, women, kisses, flowers. Divine discovery that they should still exist!

I went out of the tent for a moment. Golden Throne appeared vaguely through the mist which had now risen and half blocked out the sky. Great love can sometimes turn into great hate. 'Mountains,' ran my thoughts, 'to-night I hate you! Ask me not why. I cannot explain, I can only feel. You want none of us, mountains? But what do we want of you?'

> To hear the winds of Boreas fling forth
> From out their iron gates and rush to war——
> Is to hear Winter. . . .[1]

1. From one of the four 'introductory' sonnets which precede *Le Quattro Stagioni*.

But up there lay the land of eternal winter. Never would they know spring or autumn—those grim walls of ice, those proud, horrific peaks: those places not made for Man.

Waiting to go

Early morning.

One opened the tent, and there, right opposite, rose Sia-Kangri, Golden Throne, Chogolisa, all agleam with fresh snow. Accursed mountains, who can hate you for more than one brief moment? We are your slaves, O Queens, all over again. How could it be otherwise? We leave home and family and far-off loves, the world of men and the world of the reasonable Gods, to come and worship you.

No time for more than a word or two now. No time for thought or sentiment. Only action. The Base Camp was as busy as a beehive. There were cases to be prised open and new ration-packs to be made up; rope and cord to be measured out; items of worn-out clothing to be replaced . . . Bonatti and his Summit-team were hard at it studying a plan of attack in which nothing should be left to chance and not a single contributory movement—with all allowances for the mountain and the human factor too—left unmade.

Toni Gobbi turned the table into a desk, and there he sat for about two days, working far into the night. With such problems, one starts from the highest point: to get sixteen high-altitude packs up to Camp V, with fuel and climbing gear too, how many supplies and how much fuel would it be necessary to send up to IV, how much to III, II and I? All of us, with Cassin in the lead, and of course Bonatti and Mauri not far behind, had helped to elaborate the scheme for the final assault. But it has to be said for Toni Gobbi that he was the one who got down to it with paper and pencil, and turned all our talk into a time-table. In the ordinary, everyday, low-altitude world, this would have been child's play. But it must not be forgotten that even in the Base Camp, at over 16,000 feet, we were still in that world of sublime elevation where anything, anything at all, was a better fate than mental effort. Better to hump half a house from A to B than to decide between A and B; better to climb among the craziest séracs than to solve the simplest problem. Mental energy was the very first thing to evaporate in this thin air. Once reach a certain point, and the higher you climbed the nearer you came to the automaton stage. On this score, I claim that Toni Gobbi's contribution to our second attempt and eventual success was vital.

What we had to do now was to find some secret elixir to fire the porters, too, with sufficient fervour for an intense—and, one hoped, a brief—spell of

243

effort. Taqi alone was awake to the sporting nature of our enterprise, if one can call it that. He was proud of having got up to 23,600 feet. The rest now looked on him as a demigod. He had grown a long beard which suggested the Wise Men of the East. It would have scared anyone who encountered him alone at night. That intolerable air of the smartee, with a hint of the Mafia, which had characterized him down in the valley, he had now totally lost.

Our plan for the second assault envisaged—starting from the word go, or the moment X—eight days' preparations and eight days' attack. During Phase 1 the following material had to reach Camp IV (22,420 feet): 4 loads (16 high-altitude rations) plus 3 loads (ten cylinders of liquid gas) plus 1 load (1,150 feet of rope for use on the ridge), total 8 loads. Each one of us would take command of one camp and check the work of the porters: I was put in charge of the Base Camp—Camp I stage, Oberto Camp I—II, Zeni Camp II—III, Gobbi Camp III—IV.

This may seem very simple but it involved the old, old problem of transport through uninhabited regions, the man who carried the loads from one camp to the next had to eat, and he had to melt ice before he could drink. Therefore it was necessary to allow for five further loads for the maintenance of those carrying up the supplies. Three loads had to go up to Camp II and two to Camp III. Finally, every camp commandant who wanted to go higher when his particular job was finished understood that he must carry rations up with him in order to be self-supporting, and not a burden on the organization.

In Phase 2, the attempt on the Summit, three teams were to operate from Camp IV upwards, when no aid would be forthcoming from the porters (with the possible exception of Taqi). First off, the eight loads would be taken up to Camp V. Then a Camp VI would be placed and from it the advance team would make the final dash. Should they fail, they would return to Camp VI to be re-supplied from Camp V until another attempt was made.

After that first moment of weariness and confusion—almost of resignation —we were all brimming with enthusiasm to conquer this mountain that seemed to hold us at arm's length. We went into every detail of our plans and dotted every i of them. We spent entire hours looking up at the sky, watching for the return of that fair weather which would enable Cassin to pronounce the words, 'Boys, tomorrow morning is X-hour!'

The Americans on G.I

In the meantime we had news of the American victory on Gasherbrum I. It had come on 5th July. We were very pleased about it, but we had to admit to certain more rueful feelings too. Either we were a pack of good-for-nothings,

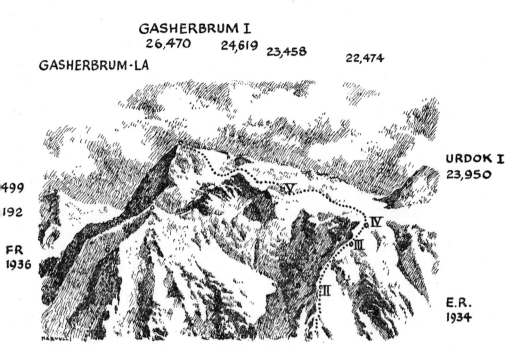

GASHERBRUM I
26,470   24,619   23,458   22,474
GASHERBRUM·LA

URDOK I
23,950

499

192

FR
1936

V

IV

III

II

E.R.
1934

Gasherbrum I (26,470 feet), with the route and camps of the American Expedition
in 1958. To the left (FR 1936) highest point reached by the French Expedition of
1936; to the right (E.R. 1934) highest point reached in 1934 by Ertl and Roch of
the International Expedition

or else our mountain was a real devil. Not much of a consolation either way!
Let us see how our friends got on in an assault so rapidly crowned with a
brilliant success.

In Gasherbrum I an expedition had what might be called a possible, an
accessible mountain. This had been known for a long time. It was clear that
the French, in 1936, had chosen an unnecessarily difficult route. Moreover,
they had fallen back at the first sign of bad weather without pausing to reflect
that in the Karakoram the monsoon seldom if ever comes with the merciless
force it can display in the storms of Garhwal, Nepal, Sikkim or Bhutan. As
for the International Expedition of 1934, led by G. O. Dyhrenfurth, it ascer-
tained the existence of many points which would greatly enhance the chances
of any assault which was not dogged by bad luck.

By 10th June the Americans were ready for the last lap. As we have
already seen, they decided not to try the spur attempted by the French in 1936

but to revert to the Ertl-Roch approach of 1934. Nick Clinch jokingly called it 'Roch's Rock'. The problem with this mountain has always been one and the same: to overcome the barrier of precipices at comparatively low altitude, in order to gain the high glacial plain—the 'Urdok Cwm', to give it Dyhrenfurth's own name.

The first 6,000 feet proved, in fact, to be the Americans' hardest pitch. Before the high-altitude porters could get up to Camp IV (22,420 feet) they had to rope the very steep snow-slopes and the trickiest rock passages, and they needed no less than 5,300 feet. From Camp IV onwards, with the Urdok Combe, the worst of the climbing part, strictly speaking, was over and done with. It was now simply a question of advancing through deep powdery snow over long, gentle—but, at that altitude, exhausting—slopes, right up to the final pyramid. On 30th June they were able to place the tents of Camp V at about 23,800 feet. After that they were confined to them, and to their sleeping-bags, for two days—our own experience—while storm raged over the Karakoram.

The final dash for the summit was made on 5th July by Pete Schoening and Andy Kauffman, in beautiful but intensely cold weather. Refreshed by a night of oxygen-aided sleep, they left camp at five in the morning. The thermometer stood at twenty degrees below, but there was no wind: it was the heavy powdery snow that made the going so difficult. Schoening improvised some snow-shoes out of strips of plywood from the packing-cases, fixing them on to the points of his crampons!

The saddle between Point 24,538 and the summit was reached at about 1000 hours. Both men were on oxygen now, but frantic efforts were still needed to get through the snow, and the very last dregs of their energy seemed to have gone by the time they had crossed the last level pitch, confronted the pyramid and hoisted themselves up on to the crest. It was all a slow and painful process. At long last, however, the two men stood on the summit itself—at three in the afternoon. Here, they were welcomed by the same beneficent sunlight, the same almost Riviera-like air, as had greeted the Austrians in 1956 on Gasherbrum II. 'For one glorious hour Pete and Andy absorbed the view from the highest summit ever climbed by Americans. Then reluctantly they started down.' Nick Clinch and his party of 'raw students' (as he called them) could well be proud. Their eager, high-spirited attempt, made with no fanfares and an empty purse, had come off.

But the descent brought them their share of disaster. It had hardly begun before the oxygen ran out. By the time the pair got to Camp V thirst and sheer exhaustion had very nearly been too much for them. On one foot,

Kauffman had four frozen toes. The next day they made their weary way down to Camp IV, encountering Nick Clinch, Dr. Nevison and Bob Swift as they went. The doctor fortunately was able to put Kauffman's foot right without resorting to amputation.

The Americans had barely reached their Base Camp before they had the choice of a fresh batch of porters. These were the men who had gone up with the Japanese Chogolisa Expedition. In their return, therefore, they made very quick time indeed; so that one of the lightest expeditions ever mounted in the Karakoram also turned out one of the fastest. Skardu—the summit—Skardu in just two months!

Sons of the Expedition

The weather refused, so to speak, to put its cards on the table. The sky was often blue, but there was something heavy about the atmosphere which still made one wonder what it might have up its sleeve! No longer was it the electrically dry air which Central Asia seemed to fling off southwards in masses. The atmosphere was that of the monsoon—a monsoon which, for all the vapours it might have lost in crossing the Himalaya, still remained quite heavy with humidity. It was not very cold. The thermometer kept to round about freezing point and by day there were spells, if not of sultriness then of something approaching it.

In the meantime (on 22nd July) the post had come in. From the Base Camp you could see for kilometre on kilometre, all moraine, right up to that enormously wide glacier stretch where the Duke of the Abruzzi joined up with the Baltoro. It was here that the Japanese had placed their Base Camp. If anyone was coming up to us, therefore, he was visible hours before his arrival—first as an infinitesimally small point, easily confused with a rock or the dark smudge of a crevasse. Then as a small ant, until at last he became a toy soldier that had started marching! That was how we saw the two couriers who came up from Askole every ten or twelve days. One man brought the post from Skardu to Askole; there it was taken by two men who got up to Base Camp in four days of forced marches. One of the two was generally that hulking giant, the son of the *lambardar* of Askole. He would arrive with a great horse-grin across his face and pitch into the food set before him like a starving cat. Then he would join in the porters' nightly singing and start back before dawn. A mountain wolf, and the least tamed that ever came my way! A cave-man, born 20,000 years out of his time.

The post came in a poor, thin little post-bag of green canvas, with a padlock. The post official and Riccardo Cassin had a key apiece. As soon as it

247

spilled its multicoloured contents on to the stones, a little crowd gathered to pounce down on them, everyone scanning the envelopes for a hand that was dear to him. Into this life of weariness and peril and absurdity the post brought just one grand moment. Mauri was always showing us new photographs of his Luca. Cassin, Gobbi and Oberto would tell us the latest about their children. These 'children of the Expedition' were eleven in number, I think, according to our calculations. Eleven slender threads; eleven links with home across glacier, desert, sea and storm; eleven telephone wires that hummed suddenly 'live' with love and warmth at the least expected moments—in the silent depths of night; in a gale; while one of the fathers was boiling up a bit of rice in a saucepan, or tying his shoes.

The papers and magazines reached us with the letters. Then for a few hours a window was opened on to the 'outside world'—to us, up here, another planet. We received the air-mail edition of the *Corriere della Sera* and *Time* and the *Pakistan Times*. There were days when the news looked really ugly. War seemed horribly close. All right then, stop thinking about it! We had enough on our hands with our own problems. And somehow or other, with all our seven and a half tons of gear, we hadn't a radio. Thus, we not only had to do without weather forecasts, a piece of bad news left us on tenterhooks for ten or twelve days waiting for the sequel. We had little field-radios which could transmit and receive within a range of two or three miles. Why these found favour with none of us I do not know.

When all was said and done, the hours passed swiftly enough at the Base Camp. Such was our desire to get our strength back that our great treat was sleep—or if not that, then lying idle in the tent, like old hunting-dogs at the fireside, with a complete rest-up both for the muscles and the grey matter in the mind.

X-hour and afterwards

Then came an evening with just that limpid sky we had known before the monsoon. X-hour was almost striking! The second assault had virtually begun.

Next morning Oberto and Zeni went off at the earliest possible hour with six porters. Two days later Gobbi was to follow. Twenty-four hours after that it would be the moment for Cassin and De Francesch to move off; and lastly, when the first four camps were occupied, Bonatti and Mauri would leave Base and go up to V on the ridge, in four days. In a musical metamorphosis, this assault plan would have been a study in counterpoint: an identical motif taken up time and time again by different men and at different moments, each separate theme interwoven with the rest to form a whole. And in the same way

248

as the most practised of musicians have still to reckon with one unknown quantity—the public—so we had to reckon with one uncontrollable factor: the weather. We could only hope to continue as fortune's favourites, even beneath such uncertain skies.

Fine weather—and great obstacles

Everything went off according to plan.

There is no point in stressing things everybody knows. But one of them was forced on our attention now, once again: the vast difference between climbing in the Karakoram and climbing in the Alps. The Alps stand for the realm of individual enterprise, of swift, unencumbered movement, of snap decisions, even caprice if one prefers it (privileges, for better or worse, of free men). But out there nothing was possible without the strongest and closest teamwork; without meticulous plans that imprisoned individual movements and individual will-powers in a collective motif; without all the irksomeness (hard to bear at times) of discipline, of marching orders, of observing the calendar and the clock. All that alone was enough to weigh down our spirits. As one of us had put it: if we could only get back home before the summer finished, we might still manage to get in a little mountainwork!

I was still at the Base Camp in charge of stores and had to stay there till all the supplies had gone up. I had spent some of the most enjoyable days of the Expedition down there with Bonatti and Mauri. We made brief excursions with a camera and spent hours talking about Patagonia, K2 or certain hair-raising feats in the Alps.

Mauri, rather in the same way as Riccardo, was an elemental force of nature! With the difference that Riccardo's greater age had brought a leavening wisdom to his character: blessed by now with an infinite experience of mountains and men, he was full of respect for the one and understanding for the other. Carlo, by contrast, still had the lightning impetuosities of more innocent years. If he was hungry, his was a Homeric hunger. If he loved, he would brook no obstacle. That sea might swell with tempests of hate, or it might lie strangely becalmed. Carlo could be a spellbinding companion, or a menace, according to the winds that chanced to be blowing through his soul. Everything was open about him. There was no suspicion of mystery. He never bore a grudge. In a certain sense, his was the spirit (and the physique!) of the *Chevalier sans peur et sans reproche*.

Walter Bonatti was a horse of another colour altogether. A closed book and a complicated one. In some deep recess of his personality he concealed a terrifying, a superhuman force. It almost frightened him too, sometimes.

You could be his mate for weeks. You had a companion whose manner was consistently kind and sometimes exquisitely thoughtful. And then, a veil of steel might come down between him and the world. Perhaps life had been hard to Walter, in some secret fashion, way back in the long ago and far away of childhood. His first reaction to anything at all could easily be one of suspicion: 'Why d'you say that?' 'In what spirit do you ask me this?' And then, though not very often, a miracle could happen and there would be another Walter, all his defence-mechanism laid aside, all openness and friendliness. Over the course of these few days, somehow or other, this miracle happened. They were days of serene friendship.

Walter and Carlo! The welding together of two such radically opposed personalities resulted in a team no mountain could resist. The one was forcefulness, backed up by reason and caution, audacity within fine limits—feline audacity, almost. The other was boldness, the headlong rush, well-nigh unbridled force. One man completed, integrated, the other. They were the firmest of friends: the two of them a solid front, not only against the mountain, against rock and ice, but against life too. Carlo was something of a bridge between Walter and the rest of humanity. Walter—for whom Carlo had a veneration he may not even have wished to acknowledge to himself, but which soon became apparent when you were with them—Walter represented form, style, expression for the upthrust of Carlo's primordial energies. It was only fitting that these two should form the Summit-team. Not only were they better climbers than all the rest of us. They represented the perfect synthesis of personality, whose like all the other combinations and permutations of which our group was capable could not have reproduced. It was Riccardo's fine intuitive sense which had combined them. Riccardo scarcely ever failed when he picked his men.

One evening had a charm all its own. We had another tape-recording of certain songs of the Incas. With our tent filled with the music of distant Bolivia and Peru and Chile and the Argentine, Walter and Carlo, far-away looks in their eyes, told me about South America—the countries they had seen, the friendships they had made, the mountains they had climbed. Then in some fashion the talk veered nearer home, and Walter described, factually and exactly, a ski-crossing of the Alps from Friuli to Piemonte that had always seemed to me to belong to legend. He really ought to publish some record of it. With him, we went through some of those wooded valleys of the Carnic Alps that no one would ever see, though the very names left a feeling of nostalgia in the heart; we lived through moonlit nights up on the pass and storms which had all but marked the skier's last hour. And there were the glaciers, flying white manes of snow in the gale, up there beyond the Matterhorn. We went to bed very late that night: at 9.30. Ah, the mountain! Sometimes we spoke of it as of some distant love. But were these mountains? Or what were they? All we could wish for, but remote indeed from such mountains as we had learned to know! Sometimes they appeared just as Great Obstacles. Yet every day brought its few glad moments, when we could believe in them again, and in our repentant selves.

City of séracs

On 1st August I returned to Camp I with Haji Ismael and Rustam. We left Base at 5.30. Clear sky; cold; excellent snow. After a while, however, things did not seem so good. How different conditions were in the first ice-fall! Two weeks of the monsoon had ruined it. It was a leviathan, rotting. Where once there had risen towers of white with battlements still whiter, where snow and ice had fused in soft translucency, where the life-force was clear and crystalline, all that remained was a sorry scene of putrefaction. A herd of giant elephants, alabastered in ice, might have come here to die—and to rot. Everywhere the ice was old ice, dirty ice, pock-marked ice. The séracs were a cross between the rust of scrap-heap motors and the grey pulp of brains. Every now and again one came to a crevasse that seemed some monstrous vagina, or else one squirmed at an eye half-closed with sores. Insects vast as dinosaurs sprawled on piles of bones. Giantesses of that foul ice gave birth to monsters of ice. Here was a Chamber of Horrors, a Louvre of nightmares.

We climbed on, and the city of rotted séracs was left behind. The mountain was a mountain once more. At Camp I we did not find a living soul. Soon the sun beat down with fury and it was impossible to go on. Then the sky darkened and the sunlight turned grey. But by now it was too late. We spent the night at Camp I, all of us huddled in one tent against the cold. The odour of *tsong* (dried onions) from Haji Ismael and Rustam was potent. Part was given off by the skin of the body itself, the rest came in exhalations from above and, alas, from below. Out in the wilds like this, you have to get used to everything. In the course of the night, avalanches rumbled and rumbled as if we were caught in the middle of some invisible war. Under the encouragement of a warm and more humid atmosphere, they went plunging crazily down. The big, shuddering ones that sounded like a landslide; the ones with the slight dry rustle that put one in mind of fire breaking out; the treacherous, deadly ones that slid down with a mere whisper threatening to suffocate and bury in silence. . . .

In the morning I went out of the tent at dawn. After a night of gas attacks

by *tsong*, what a joy it was, this vast, pure, virgin mass of Karakoram air—
a universe that might be only five minutes old! The clear sky, and the vigorous
cold again, with the thermometer at ten degrees below. We made a fire out of
a wooden case (there was nothing here, and no liquid fuel) and heated some
milk. Then we went on upwards. At the foot of Gasherbrum V the plains were
strewn with avalanche debris which could not have fallen long before. Here the
route was easier but dangerous. Fortune did not desert us. We made Camp II
before ten. All was deserted here too. We lay up in a tent during the hours of
fiercest sunlight; in the late afternoon I started off for Camp III, arriving with
the sunset.

'Down there it's fine, but up here it's torment'

At Camp III I found Cassin. He gave us a very warm welcome indeed: we
were carrying cylinders of gas, rations and the post. Regarding the post: 'I'll
get it up to IV tomorrow morning,' said Riccardo. 'Then Gobbi can take it
up to the ridge. I'm certain there's nothing like news from home to give their
morale a boost up there.'

The attack was on now, no mistake about it. Between Camps II and
V, eight climbers and four porters were all pulling together for the final
victorious effort. Decisive days, these. 'If you ask me, it won't be long now.
It may only be a matter of hours.'

Riccardo himself, however, was rather down in the mouth: once more,
he was feeling none too well. He had absolutely worn himself out over the
last few days, to make sure that this time victory shouldn't elude the youngsters
at the top. I glanced at his journal. I soon saw that the 'reconquest of the
Camps' hadn't been such a walk-over as I had thought. '27th July—Base to
Camp I. Left at 6. Arrived 8.30. We were a bit loaded—beyond the limits
we'd allowed for! What with our own clothes and the radios and other stuff,
the load got pretty heavy in the end.'

'28th July. Camp I to Camp III. Must do two stages today if we are
to keep to programme. When we'd got loaded up we found we were still
a gas cylinder short each, so we humped that too, to keep up with Gobbi's
calculations. Made fair speed to Camp II, heads cooking gaily in the sun.
Found Oberto and Zeni already there four days, for despatch of supplies
and gear. Had a drop of tea and went off again before the snow got too
soft. But so often it did: very exhausting trek by the end of it, sinking
absolutely. Arrived on the tired side—specially me. Had something to drink
but only a spot of Emmenthaler cheese to eat. Couldn't sleep. Only dream!

'29th July. Camp III to IV. When we got up I started staggering—head going round. Weather looking none too settled. Went off all the same. Gobbi and two porters with us. Gobbi went empty-handed, as trail-maker. Snow fairly soft, especially under the Italians' Ice-fall. I kept behind Gobbi all the time. Had a struggle keeping on. Head spinning badly. At Camp IIIA felt the need to lighten my load. Toni took the ration-pack off me, and on we went. De Francesch in the lead now, right up to the Ice-wall. Toni stopped off, since he was due to go back. Useless for him to go on to Camp IV. He gave me back my ration-pack. Went on, through worsening weather. Got to the camp worn out and feeling really done. Dived into my tent, after closing De Francesch's on him. He was so spent he hardly knew the storm was filling the tent with snow. Tried to get my breath. Blowing harder outside. Tents completely covered with snow.

'Made an effort to get up and brew myself some strong coffee, to see if it would pull me together. Made Bepi some too. Didn't feel much better for it, though. Bepi cleared both tents of snow. Very decent of him. In mine everything seemed to be going round. There were two tents at Camp IV and we thought we'd be better off with one apiece.

'Wind all night. Snow too. But in this camp the snow is a puzzler—it only needs a wind and it'll snow even with a clear sky. The wind always comes from the Ice-fall—i.e. from below, and brings the snow with it. My theory is that the wind, always blowing pretty strong up the mountain, takes the surface snow up off the glacier—in this way keeping its weight down so that it doesn't go spilling downwards. With an ice-fall that wasn't so steep, helped on by a basin of any size, it would slide down much more. Couldn't sleep a wink all night. Bepi said he hadn't got much sleep either. Some consolation!

'30th July. Camp IV. Got up feeling completely numbed. Gale still blowing. Staggered out of the tent to obey calls of nature. Tried to get both tents clear of snow—both buried on the right side like the first evening here. Then made a drop of coffee, but an effort to get any down. The stomach seemed to want to refuse everything. A job to keep it down when it gets there. A bit later, I had another try with a spot of *Karkade*—and all day tried to swallow a bit of this and a bit of that. By evening, feeling slightly better but still staggering. Managed to get some sleep in the night. Funny, the first time I came up here I stayed three days and kept well: I even managed to get three loads up to Camp V. This time I must have come up in too much of a hurry.

.   .   .   .   .

253

'30th July. Camp IV. Bepi, though you wouldn't think so to look at him, is crazy on astronomy. He's always out with his big glasses when it's a clear sky, watching the moon and the stars. He knows the names and all about them and can tell which is which. The planets, constellations, everything. He's our Astronomer all right. When the weather is bad, he'll explain it by a change in the moon. This is the first quarter, he'll say, or the second, after that, you'll see, it'll be different. He's always willing to be weather prophet. Only since we went down on 19th July, even if good weather was holding at the Base Camp, the peaks were always clouded, morning and evening. In fact, as I write, I've only got to look down the mountain and it seems fine, but up here it's torment. "Well, my dear Bepi, it's a change of the moon today, but it still seems to be pretty nasty. What sort of astronomy's that?" "You're right, I can't make it out," he replied, all seriousness. His excuse is that it's the monsoon season. Every now and then we look out of the tent to see if there's any sign of Walter and Carlo. But it'll soon be night. Perhaps they've had to put off their starting time.

'31st July. Camp IV. Eight o'clock, snow and gale. I had cleared the tent, but it's covered again now. Am feeling better, but not at my best yet. Have more appetite, but my head's still spinning and I feel weary. . . .

'At ten o'clock, Bepi told me they were coming along, six-strong: Bonatti, Carlo and four porters. In this trip they'd brought up everything needed for the second attempt. I had to go down, however. I don't feel I could be of any use, so it was better not to be a burden on the Camp's food supplies, etc., and go back down to Camp III. Carlo and Walter hoped to start tomorrow and couldn't relax. But I felt far from A1. Decided to go down to Camp III with the porters. Bonatti and Mauri asked me to send up Gobbi and Oberto soon.'

The two black feathers

Up above our heads, in the Combe à Vaches and on the North-East Ridge, our other companions were meanwhile reoccupying the abandoned camps. De Francesch was at Camp IV on 29th July. Bonatti and Mauri went up there on 31st July. Gobbi and Oberto on 1st August.

The weather was unsettled, and it looked as if it was going to be bad. Gale—as we saw from Cassin's journal—was frequent. In spite of all this, the men received a strange visitor. 'In the afternoon, it clouded over,' Bepi De Francesch recorded. 'At three o'clock, I had a visit from a bird I had managed to see, till now, only in the distance. I was in the tent. I heard some funny noises, not just the usual ones you get with wind and snow, and I knew that in the other tent [Bonatti's and Mauri's] there was nobody stirring. Then it occurred

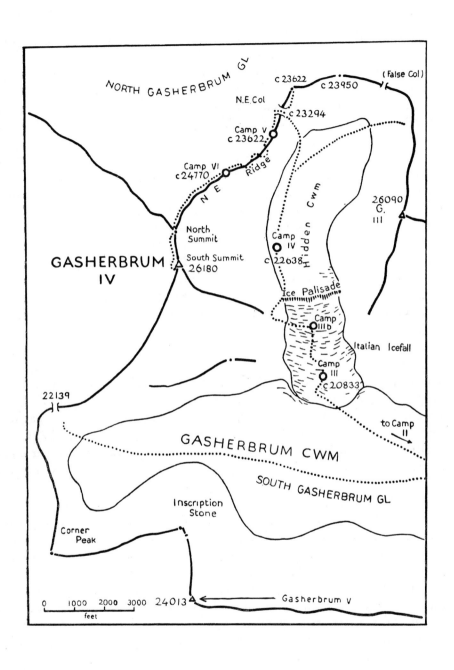

NORTH GASHERBRUM GL

(False Col)

c 23622   c 23950

N.E. Col

c 23294

Camp V
c 23622

Camp VI
c 24770

N E Ridge

Hidden Cwm

26090
G.
III

North
Summit

GASHERBRUM
IV

South Summit
26180

Camp
IV
c 22638

Ice Palisade

Camp
III b

Italian Icefall

Camp
III
c 20833

22139

to Camp
II

GASHERBRUM CWM

SOUTH GASHERBRUM GL

Inscription
Stone

Corner
Peak

0   1000   2000   3000
feet

24013

Gasherbrum V

to me some bird might have been driven near the camp for a bit of food, by the storm. I opened the flaps. But when I got outside he was already a long way off, up by the crags. I got a view of him in a gap in the cloud. He was one of those black, fearsome birds you see round these parts. He hadn't stayed long, but even so he'd put his beak through a double-plastic container, opened a package of Ovomalt and wolfed half of it; and the only visiting card he'd left was two black feathers.'

On 2nd August: 'About seven,' De Francesch's diary continued, 'we left Camp IV, five strong (Bonatti, Mauri, Gobbi, Oberto, Self), all heavy laden with a few days' supplies for Camp V. For 700 feet Walter was trail-maker. I followed, and then led as far as the ridge. We stopped for a good half-hour, then went on up to Camp V, 300 feet higher. Bonatti was worried because the little super-K2 tent couldn't be found and the Pamir was too heavy to take up to form Camp VI on Cornice Crest. I felt fit and well. With no hesitation, I said the Pamir was a good bit bigger, he and Mauri would be much better off in it than in the little one, and that I was going to bring it up myself. "You mean that?" he said. "Yes, of course!"—which sent my companions' spirits up considerably.'

A tent at the Last Turret

The 3rd, 4th, 5th and 6th of August. Days of decision: a finale to a bitter struggle over two months. Luckily, the weather was with us again. All of us were well up on the mountain now, to give all possible aid to the final assault. Bonatti, Mauri, Gobbi and De Francesch were at camp V; Zeni at IV; Cassin at III; Oberto and I at I. Taqi and Mahmud Hussein, with two other high-altitude porters to help them, kept going between Camp II and Camp IV. Every moment counted. It was now or never.

On 3rd August, in the solitary tent that composed Camp V, the alarm went off for Bonatti, Mauri, Gobbi and De Francesch at 4 a.m. Twenty-three thousand feet up means miserable nights, and it takes a long time to come to life in the morning. Every single thing means effort. A decision to make? It may be a very simple one, but up there it becomes a colossal burden. Which shall I do first—tie up my right shoe or eat a dried apricot? Shall I load the camera with colour-film or not? Shall I go to the left or right past the tent? To the left there are two cylinders to stumble over, but on the right there's deep snow. Something like Cassin's picture of our friend 'sitting in the opening of the tent with a packet of rusks in one hand and a tube of marmalade in the other, not knowing whether to eat or not' was to be seen twenty times a day. Continuous lack of oxygen had reduced even men who were not exactly

Two men, and a sky of stone:
approaching the Summit

Hard going among the rocks.

A very steep snow slope.

90

91

A hard stretch back from the north wall towards the crest.

93

Toni Gobbi, Bepi De Francesch, and Donato Zeni (supporting party to summit team) carrying loads to Camp VI (24,550 ft.)

97

98

Evening and sunset on the North-East Crest: in the background, Gasherbrum III (26,090 ft.).

100

101

102

Never before have such difficulties been tackled at such heights.

10,000 ft. over a valley of ice.

105

The last of the rock - but not of the difficulties.

106

12,30 hrs. on August 6th. 1958; Walter Bonatti and Carlo Mauri on t

...mmit of *Gasherbrum IV (26,180 ft.) with the storm about to burst.*

At the Base Camp on the Duca degli Abruzzi Glacier. Reading from left to right: Riccardo Cassin, Captain A. K. Dar, the Pakistani liaison officer, Giuseppe Oberto, Doctor Donato Zeni, the Expedition's medical officer, Walter Bonatti, Fosco Maraini, Toni Gobbi. In front row: Bepi De Francesch, Carlo Mauri.

weaklings to mere shadows of themselves. They were men no longer. They
were memories. But something hidden, deep and primordial, spurred them on.

A good two hours passed before the men were ready to go. At six they
left the tent. They were loaded like pack-horses: thirty-two pounds is a killing
weight at that altitude. They carried a tent, 1,100 feet of rope, a small container
of liquid gas, pitons, snap-links and rations. 'The teams,' wrote Bepi, 'were—
Bonatti and Mauri ahead, Gobbi and De Francesch following. (Since one of
us was a Western Alps mountain guide, and the other a guide in the Eastern
Alps, we decided that one should lead over ice and the other over rock.)

'The ascent began over snow,' runs Bepi's record. 'Then we passed on to
rock, with very difficult patches. Over 23,000 feet one step forward means breathing in and out three or four times. At 23,100 feet on the ridge I took my pulse
—138 in the first minute. My normal rate never exceeds the fifties. Climbing
over rock with Third or Fourth Grade difficulties, with a kit-bag of thirty-five
pounds, means exertion hard to picture. I have done Sixth Grade climbs and
never made anything like such demands on myself. Here, you take a few
steps forward, or climb a few feet up, and you just lay your head against the
nearest rock and take fifteen to twenty breaths. So it goes on. Hold by hold,
and breather by breather! That's Cornice Crest.'

Three thousand feet down the mountain, at Camp II, we followed them
metre by metre. Bonatti and Gobbi had red jerseys which stood out with
extraordinary vividness against the chocolate colour of the rock, the whiteness
of the snow and the deep blue of the sky. At 8.45 Bonatti reached the little dip
between Cornice Crest and the Turrets (*See* sketch on p. 258). At 11.21 I saw
him tackling—very, very slowly—'Bill Chimney' and the First Turret.
Toni Gobbi was to write later: 'The ascent was an indescribable ordeal—a
strain so gigantic that it seemed at any moment everything inside our heaving
"breath-boxes" might go. Yet for all that, there was still one side of us—a
professional side struggling to survive—that relished these difficulties, for they
were classics that seemed to take us back to some great Alpine ascent; and we
still had an eye for the wonderful view on the East Face of Broad Peak and K2,
and the unforgettable spectacle of a regatta of white "snow sails" down the
Urdok Glacier.'

The sun came down with all its non-stop fury, but just for once I was
immune from it. I got the binoculars fixed neatly and firmly into position on
the tent. I didn't want to miss a moment of a spectacle which was not only
first class from a mountaineering point of view, but also deeply moving from
a human angle. Our companions up there were truly a symbol, if ever there
was one, of Man and the Universe: alone, mysteriously alone. Here was the

R

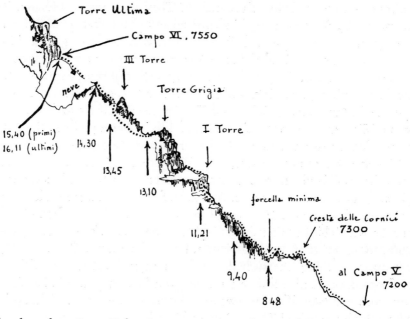

A sketch made at Camp II showing movements and times of the two teams, Bonatti-Mauri and Gobbi-De Francesch. N.E. Ridge, G.IV, 3rd August 1958

spirit, the will to know, to possess the world, to overcome those cruel barriers that tie us to a time and a place, and the weight which pins us down to mere Earth.

Their efforts must have been superhuman. A glance at the little sketch I made, as well as I could, there and then, will show the amount of time they needed for each pitch. From Cornice Crest to Camp VI—a rise of 820 feet—took no less than seven hours. A mere 117 feet an hour! At regular intervals, a figure would advance; stop; remain motionless for a long time; then advance once again . . . you could almost hear that panting for breath—like a death-rattle! Perhaps it was as well that one could not, with the physical ear, or the spectacle would have been unbearable to those of us who watched it from below. Of the men themselves, there was little to say. Bonatti was a god. To watch Bonatti climbing was to see a small, red silhouette advancing—for all the paradox of it—effortlessly: advancing with a decision, a lightness of touch that made him unique. The others by comparison were clay, they were earthy, they were humble human flesh. If I say as much, I am sure my companions will not hold it against me. There are certain talents so outstanding as to be

258

beyond all dispute, certain gifts which must come straight from the Gods. The Greeks of old had the wisdom to hymn them with an ode. We might do the same, and leave it at that. In Walter's class, I could only think of one single name: Emilio Comici. But his climbing was done at 10,000 feet. Who knows how he would have acquitted himself up there? Supreme altitude is a fourth dimension, an unknown for everyone.

In tackling the Grey Turret the two teams were lost to view for some time on the hidden face. Then they reappeared. The sun was beginning to set when they reached the Third Turret: the sky took on those dark-blue depths characteristic of fine afternoons. Now I could see the men clearly outlined on the pitch under an overhang that would mean a particularly strenuous climb. Even Walter seemed to be having a hard time of it. He disappeared once more on to the face opposite Broad Peak. From this point on there were some very tricky bits. Gobbi, who knew every climb in the Western Alps as few others did, had his mind cast back now more than once to his experiences as an Alpine guide. Cornice Crest (we learned from his subsequent notes) reminded him of the 'more delicate stretches of the S.E. Ridge of Mont Maudit, and the steeper ones of the Peuterey route to Mont Blanc'. The various chimneys encountered among these Turrets brought back 'the famous one of the Ryan-Lochmatter route, on the Aiguille du Plan'. The far side of Grey Turret 'by its delicacy, if not its difficulty, recalled the South Ridge of the Aiguille Noire'—and the immensely long traverse that followed 'struck me as a faithful copy of the one before the final assault of the Gervasutti route on the Petit Capucin'. Then, lastly, 'the succession of slopes covered with verglas were every bit as bad as the last rocky terraces of the Via Major on Mont Blanc'.

It was 1540 hours when Bonatti, after tackling the Mule's Back, a long, very steep snow-stretch, came to a stop at the foot of Last Turret. The ideal would have been to climb higher still. A Camp VI beyond Snow Cone would have been an absolute guarantee for the success of the Summit dash. But it was too late. To stop now was the only thing for it. The teams were fagged out. I could see the men moving with a lethargy that was awful to watch. One step forward, or two—and stop. Just now, possibly through some trick of the light, I could see them with extreme clarity, and follow their very gestures. I could see head and shoulders drooping over an ice-axe (I felt I could hear that death-rattle breathing again too). I could see them sway back against rock ledges or on a steep snow-pile just as if they were wounded. To goad oneself on, in a state like that, even for a few metres, would have needed an effort that defies imagination.

At 1611 hours the last man of the second team got to what appeared to be a minute open space at the foot of the Turret. As in a film, I followed the opening of the tent. I imagined the relief of a few moments' rest. Strength, or some of it, returned. 'As a proof that we were not yet done,' Toni Gobbi recorded later, 'we celebrated the placing of Camp VI with a fine pipe.' I thought of the boundless satisfaction my companions would feel. I envied them beyond words for being so close to victory. I envied them beyond the power of words to tell for every one of those minutes they spent up in the eagles' haunts; for what they saw; for the companionship, passing strange, that would rise between them and those rocks, between them and those sheer walls of frozen green, between them and those rugged crags, as old as the world, so near the stars, untouched till now by Man.

'I could be none too sure of ever coming back to these heights,' Bepi wrote, as if confessing a secret. 'So I left a statuette of the Madonna of Lourdes, entrusted to me by my wife with the words, "Bepi, I'm giving you the Madonna of Lourdes to take with you, to leave at the highest point you reach, to honour Her and invoke Her blessing for the mountain."'

In the evening Toni Gobbi and Bepi De Francesch went down again to Camp V. They were overtaken by the dark. But then the moon rose to cast her mysterious light on crag and precipice. It was ten o'clock by the time they reached their lonely tent.

'Here, a welcome surprise awaited us,' Toni Gobbi wrote later. 'We found our post and rations. They had been brought up by Cassin and Taqi who had come up from Camp III and gone down again to IV.'

The Summit seen from Black Turret

On 4th August the sun rose in a clear sky. The air was very cold: eleven below at Camp II certainly meant twenty or twenty-five below at Camp VI. Our Gasherbrum wore a halo of cloud around the Summit. Up there, it would amount to something more than a halo: it would be a serious episode in the weather, perhaps a frightening one. Being still all eagerness to do my whack where supplies for the higher camps were concerned, I got off to an early start for Camp III with Haji Ismael, Ghulam Hassan and Mahmud Hussein. At Camp III I found Bepi Oberto, who had come down from Camp IV.

Bonatti and Mauri had braved the cold and that halo of cloud. They had started off from Camp VI at the earliest possible moment, taking with them a good 1,100 feet of rope for fixing on the higher stretch of the pitch. Once more they crossed Snow Cone, with its ice-sheeted walls plunging straight down into the abyss; once again they crossed that crest which is piled up with treacherous rocks in much the same way as a wobbly table might be piled up with heavy books—and no less likely to spill, being held together by snow that was at the same time as crisp and as unstable as the white of egg in a meringue. Lastly they tackled Black Turret. A tortuous gully, followed by an exposed face with a Grade 5 traverse—at that altitude representing the extreme limit of human endeavour—occupied them for a long time and took the last of their strength. When they set foot on Black and White Rise, where the black crags came to an end and the marble-like limestone of the Peak could definitely be said to have begun, they knew that it would be folly to go on. They were at 25,750 feet and it was late. Walter had survived one night's bivouac at about 26,000 feet on K2, and he knew that there were risks one just did not even contemplate—especially at this stage of exhaustion, or prostration. Slowly the two men went down to Camp VI. Once more victory had gone to the arrogant mountain.

Down below, the whole team was keeping an anxious eye on the rocks. 'Our thoughts were up there with them the whole time,' Bepi De Francesch noted at Camp V. 'Will they? Won't they? . . . .' Riccardo Cassin, at Camp IV, had much to preoccupy him now. 'The Peak is ringed with mist. The wind carries it along at speed but cannot disperse it. The visual impression is that the wind is chasing it round and round the Peak. A very cold wind, too. In the ordinary way the down-quilted jacket is a discomfort in the hours of full sun, but today one is mighty glad to have it on. In the tent, once the sun is really up, you need to spread the canvas with padded clothing before you can stay inside. But today you need the flaps closed for warmth. Let's hope Walter and Carlo can still go on, with conditions like this.'

At Camp III Oberto and I spent the day with our noses in the air, in the hope of catching sight of something moving, something human, up there among those crags with their long flying scarves of mist circling endlessly, implacably. All at once Giuseppe shouted: 'There they are! They're coming down from the Summit.' A momentary gap in the cloud had actually enabled him to catch a glimpse of Bonatti and Mauri on the Black Rocks. His eye had not deceived him. It was our interpretation of events that was wrong.

'In the evening, towards 1900 hours, Gobbi made out two black points coming down in the direction of Camp VI [this is Bepi De Francesch at Camp V]. I called up, "You've done it?" "No," they replied. "We got within say 330 feet of the top. Tomorrow—bring us food and pitons." We shouted back, "Tomorrow we'll come—all three." ' The third man at Camp V was Zeni (the Expedition's doctor, too); he had only just got there. Donato Zeni was in fact a climber of the highest class. His efforts and his enthusiasm

261

at this stage were something very fine, which I should like to put on record here.

Once more, in the haphazard fashion of last-minute decisions rather than long and conscious planning, it had come about that a final assault team embodied both the great traditions of Italian climbing: East and West. West stood for ice, and defiant, unyielding peaks, for the Val d'Aosta, Valtellina, Valmalenco; East for rock, for the slender and intensely difficult crags of the Dolomites. In the final days of K2 those who climbed side by side were Compagnoni and Lacedelli, a man of Valfurva and a man of Cortina. Here, it was Bonatti, Mauri, Gobbi, granite men and ice men; with De Francesch and Zeni —champions of air-acrobatics on the rock-face and the pinnacles of the Dolomites.

After sunset, Oberto and I, with Haji Ismael, went down to Camp II. We also were able to make out Bonatti and Mauri getting back without trouble to Camp VI. We saw flickers of light as well, which rightly or wrongly we took to be a signal of greeting: we shouted a lusty answer, hoping to make our voices heard even at this height in the vast tranquillity of the evening. Had this proved the day of days? For the moment, it had ceased to matter. What counted, and set us at ease, was the fact that our friends were alive and well, and safe back in their tent for the night.

A postal service—even in the sky!

5th August. Still fine, still cold. At 6 a.m. the Camp II thermometer read minus thirteen degrees. A cutting wind blew relentlessly from the north. Up there, at the foot of Last Turret, it must have been terrible.

Rather than stay put, kicking our heels, Oberto and I had decided to explore the high G. Cwm, with the hope of reaching Col 22,139 feet: it should have afforded a good view of the Baltoro and the West Gasherbrum Wall. We started at 6.30, making a fair pace over good hard nevé. I had a pair of skis with me, but kept them over my shoulders to get up faster. The vast scale of the valley is something surprising. You would never expect such a size from down below. Long plains alternate with slight rises, or with hollows which mean an occasional slight drop. Over us hung the terrifying ramparts of Gasherbrum V—over 3,000 feet of rock terraced with crazy balconies of an ice transparency. At any moment they might avalanche their thunderous way down. The good lady of Inscription Stone was still flying. Flying—who knew where? She wore an expression of bigoted severity, as if she felt called upon by the sublimity around her to adopt the somewhat strained role of angel. Farther over, Corner Peak rose sharply, its tip a sword into the sky, hilted with creamy incrustations of snow and ice; or it might have struck you as a wedding-cake, iced with glaciers, for some Grade 6 champion's nuptials.

Giuseppe made nimble progress. He was calm and sure-footed. I had only to stop to take photographs, letting him go on, and he would well-nigh disappear into the immensity of the snow. There was nothing very special about this trek we were making. Yet who could describe our emotions in that landscape of mountain and ice which no human eye had seen till now? What a prize for the spirit! A ceremony without ceremonial, without banners, an initiation that was silent and secret. On our right we were dominated by Gasherbrum IV which till now had been hidden by a strange partner. Of like shape, but lower, this curious counterpart rose before it. But now the Gasherbrum peak had struggled free. We had a foreshortened view of a rocky eminence that was quite forbidding. Behind us, we had the magnificent spade-tipped Gasherbrum II (26,360 feet): a gilded incandescence sweeping into the sky.

Our excursion came to a sudden end, though, when we were confronted by a deep and dangerous crevasse which Giuseppe declared to be impassable. We were within 300 feet or a little more of the point we had set out for, which was ringed round with great cornices that might have been made of icing sugar. It was a great disappointment to have to give up. From the lower level of our starting point, we had underestimated the difficulties we should meet and had come equipped with only one ice-axe and one pair of crampons. Had Giuseppe had a more expert companion than myself, or even a better equipped one, he might have got round the obstacle; for the left side of the crevasse, at any rate, contained some rocky holds and ice-fissures by which we could have clambered down to gain the right bank where it narrowed. Point 22,139 feet therefore remains untrodden by human foot, and the interesting photographs of the Baltoro which we had promised ourselves were not for us after all. They will be a prize for bolder, or more fortunate, spirits of the future.

This waiting and waiting for news of victory at the Summit put everyone in a state of nerves. No one could keep still. Cassin, at Camp IV, found, as we did, that he had to keep busy. 'Sooner than sit twiddling my thumbs here,' he wrote, 'I decided to go up to the South-East Ridge of Gasherbrum III to see what there was on the other side. Maraini and De Francesch said there should be a glacier. I found that it ought to be possible to get up on to the West Face by crossing the wall at a point I reached. This would need two, with ropes and pitons: I couldn't make it alone. Still, I got some fine photos of Gasherbrum IV, highly impressive from this side' (*Plate 86*).

Had Gasherbrum IV proved less intractable, the Expedition might quite possibly have climbed Gasherbrum III as well. This remains, even today, the highest virgin peak in the Karakoram. On his return from this interesting bit of solo reconnaissance, Riccardo got to a point right under the North-East Ridge. The calm of evening had come by now, and by shouting hard he managed to exchange a few words with Gobbi, De Francesch and Zeni. 'I gathered that they had come down from VI to V again, and that Mauri and Bonatti were resting today, to make the final attempt tomorrow.'

Gobbi, De Francesch and Donato Zeni had indeed made a second trip from Camp V to Camp VI; in a spirit of absolute self-sacrifice, they had once more, at the cost of great hardship, carried up supplies to the advance team. It was thanks to them that Walter and Carlo could now face the last lap with a certain tranquillity. 'We had with us,' De Francesch wrote later, 'two ration-packs, two of pitons, a cylinder of liquid gas and our own food. We reached Camp VI at 1300 hours. Gathered from Bonatti and Mauri that it's far from plain sailing yet. Their best so far is 300 feet below the Summit mark. But that still left a good stretch of ridge, with many cornices. Reckon to do it tomorrow. I left them a red rocket to fire off if victorious.'

De Francesch and his two companions had also brought the post—direct from Italy, from homes in Courmayeur or Lecco. It had crossed oceans and deserts and the Himalaya, it had travelled by hand through the gorges of Baltistan, up the ice-falls, along the ridge, over a razor's edge with an abyss on either side, right up to the foot of Last Turret, that wild and solitary crag. 'A letter from home with good news in it!' wrote Carlo Mauri. 'In conditions like these, when you've seen nothing but snow and ice around you, and your only roof is canvas or a grey sky—it gives you heart and hope. That little sheet of paper that our dear ones have filled with good news of home and family, those words which tell you to trust, and all will be well—there's our one link with the world.'

For the two Summit-men, that day's wait at Camp VI must have seemed interminable, intolerable. They had now come to pretty well the end of their tether. 'My lips,' Carlo Mauri wrote afterwards, 'were terribly split: ears covered with cracks, and scaly. A few hours' sleep at night with the mouth closed was sufficient to blister the lips together. It was a painful business—in the morning you had to open them very, very carefully. My throat was full of sores. Coughing could mean loss of blood.' The description has a terrible force, an almost despairing ferocity.

Carlo said again: 'We knew that if we failed this time we shouldn't have the strength for a further attempt.' It was tomorrow or never. 'For two days we hadn't succeeded in drinking even a cup of tea. We could breathe only with difficulty. Oxygen masks would have meant extra weight, which we wanted to be free of. At five in the afternoon, we bedded down in the tent to rest. We lay there in silence, staring into the darkness with our eyes open. I thought of my Ginetta and my little Luca, nine months old—I have scarcely had a moment to give him a kiss—back in my home at Lecco. I thought of my friends quietly walking the country roads, or the lights in the windows and the green fields and things growing. I too would like to be sitting in a tavern and drinking one orangeade after another. I'm thirsty—just thirsty—nothing else.'

6th August: Day of the Summit

Oberto and I (on 5th August) spent a long time trying to read a meaning into all the going and coming up on the ridge. From eleven o'clock onwards—that is, from the time we got back from our own excursion—we had not taken our eyes off it. Had they got to the Summit, or not? I maintained that they had, and that the movement arose from Riccardo's wanting to get up as far as Camp VI. Beppe claimed that it involved more supplies for a second attack. He was right! At a late hour, we actually succeeded in getting into radio contact with Taqi at Camp III (one of the very few times when the radio came in useful). In a mixture of English, Urdu and Balti he got his message across: No, the sahibs have not got to the Summit. They urgently need more fuel. Tomorrow morning I will come very early to Camp II to take some. Is there any left?—Yes, one.—Good. *Insh'Allah*—if Allah so wills—I will be there at first light.

That evening was long and grey and we were gnawed by doubts.

But next morning dawned gratefully bright and clear and cold again. At 5.30—there was Taqi! What a grand fellow he had turned out! Remember how odious he seemed down there in the valleys, with his showy, braggart airs? The Expedition owed him a very great deal. Just when things were beginning to be really grim, he came out in his true colours, capable, reliable, cheerful and calm. On this occasion we gave him our one container of fuel (we could get along by making a fire of empty wooden cases) and off he went up to Camp III.

Up there on the heights, 6th August dawned with blood-red splashes across the sky and a haze towards the east. Unpromising! But everything was ready: it would be folly to delay. Today was the day of the Summit, there was no more to be said.

265

'Neither Bonatti nor I could sleep,' run Carlo Mauri's notes. 'We weren't impatient and we weren't too taut, but we wished it was all over!' The tiny alarm on the wristwatch went off at 2.30 a.m., 'but it was scarcely needed,' said Walter Bonatti, 'because both of us had been awake the whole night, though without a word to each other: we were each lost in our own thoughts. Now we just had to wait for dawn, and it was a long wait. How many times already hadn't I peeped out of the tent to see how the weather was shaping—Mauri too. Not a single change was lost on us. We followed every stage. The clouding up you get with the monsoon looked pretty threatening last night. It moved up slowly but terribly surely from the west eastwards, it had covered Gasherbrum IV and there seemed to be more left for Hidden Peak too. At the same time, another cloud formation, on a lower level, had coated up Saltoro Kangri, Chogolisa; and other cloud had gone off over the eastern horizon. Exactly the same omens of bad weather as we had twenty days ago, and they made us tremble! Only De Francesch, who's crazy on astronomy, told us yesterday that the weather was bound to hold out twenty-four hours, "on account of the moon", he said. Late in the evening, a filmy light stole suddenly into the tent, so we knew the moon was rising. But what guarantee of the weather holding out could that give, when the air outside the tent wasn't cold enough and the cloud was still building up menacingly round Gasherbrum IV? I don't think I ever longed for freezing temperatures and wind like that night! My prayer was answered. About one o'clock, cold and wind arrived together, in such violent form as to become one more obstacle. The wind naturally dispersed the cloud, but all the same it left some nasty patches of mist in its place, roughly fish-shaped. Then the moon was blocked out by the mountain and it was dark again. But not for long, for us. The alarm went off at 2.30, we put on our little torches and heated up something to drink. We had lately done very little drinking.

'Nearly 4.30. No sign of the wind going down. We decided to go anyway. Whirling snow outside. We stopped in the tent as long as possible, getting everything prepared. Then the packs were ready. We had everything—food, reserve clothes, pitons, snap-links, hammer. In order to be able to move lighter and faster we ditched the cinecamera and the Leica, but we took along my good old faithful Condoretta, which would have to provide both of us with documentaries for the climb. We roped up, too, but when we came to our crampons we found it impossible to get them on in the crouching position we were forced to assume by the dimensions of the tent. That was a job that could only be done outside, and the frost outside was so heavy that it could well have done our hands serious injury.

266

'At the start, it was still dark, but once I got to the fixed ropes of the "Chimney of Trouble" [*Plate 103*] all I had to do was hoist myself up by elbow grease! At the end of the passage I gave two tugs on the rope to let Mauri know he could start off. He shouted something to me from down at the bottom, but in all the noise the wind was making I couldn't catch it. For good measure, I gave the rope another tug, testing the strain too for safety's sake. A few minutes passed. Then up came Mauri. He seemed furious. He had a crampon in his numbed hands. The explanation turned out to be this: he was just starting up when one of his crampons came unhooked. By pulling at the rope, I had given him no chance to put it on again. Before he could do this, he had to come up to where I was. Whilst we were straightening all of this out, day broke. We were able to get on faster now. Over one snowfield I took up twenty metres of fixed rope and put it in my bag, for use in case of emergency. At 5.30 we were up on Last Turret. We were in perfect form and making superlative time. We later discovered that this was just as well, not only for victory's sake but for our own safety too! With the first sun, the wind gradually died down and the temperature eased up. But that haze put in an appearance again on the horizon.

'At 6.0 we were on Snow Cone. We were one hour out. Other times, it had taken us not less than four. The ropes we had fixed forty-eight hours before were a boon. At 7.30 we were on Black Turret. This was better going than we'd dared hope for. We allowed ourselves a few minutes' rest and then we turned to the attack of the long chain of virgin pinnacles. I was one metre from the top of the first gendarme when I blacked out for a moment. I was demolishing the nth cornice when it collapsed right on to me, without, however, sweeping me off. I was in a sorry plight and got out in a cold sweat. Mauri watched with his heart in his mouth. He had been all set to hold me from Black Turret, and had the rope belayed ready. After traverse after traverse we came to a horizontal, knife-edged ridge. We straddled it and got along it that way, hacking off parts of this 'blade', where it was too brittle and crumbly to be safe, as we went. Then we reached that longed-for little point which marked a clear dividing line between the dark granite we had barely conquered and the white marble splendour which led to the fore-peak of G.IV.

'It was only 0910 hours, but the desire to see what awaited us on the other side was so strong that we found ourselves pressing on without a pause. Rock and snow now merged into one white dazzle, and the sky was a black I had only rarely seen. Higher, higher! We tackled a sharp corner, minor walls, patches of treacherous snow—and now we came to a dark marble fissure

267

tunnelling down on us, about ten metres high. Mauri made the rope fast to a spontoon, ran it out, and I started clambering up. But it was too smooth and too tricky: I couldn't make it. I took off my gloves and went in once more. Twisting and turning, struggling and panting past belief, I got there in the end. Technically, without taking the altitude into account, I think it would be a Grade IV difficulty. We called it "White Chimney".

'Next, we were on an incline with a broken rock surface. It grew easier all the way, till soon we were almost walking. We were able to look west-wards now at the other face of G.IV. The sight we saw was really superlative, worthy of the mountain we were climbing. After about two months, lo and behold the Baltoro again! For the first time we saw it at its full length, and in every detail. A glacier a good eighteen miles long. Seen from here, it seemed coiled beneath us like a long river with a wrinkled surface [*Plate 84*]. Even the highest peaks which we had admired on our way to the mountain seemed quite small, and on the horizon now lay other chains of mountains. Our gaze wan-dered everywhere among them, exploring the hidden features of this mighty unknown world; a reality, but one so fantastic that it gave one a feeling of ecstasy: one felt so infinitely free, suspended in space, as if one had cast off the bonds of nature's physical laws.

'Only a few feet now stood between us and the fore-peak, but with all my eyes and mind I was trying to discover what we still had to master to reach the true summit, the highest point of all, so that, precious as these moments were, they were all but lost on me.

'We were on the fore-summit at ten-thirty—and immediately puzzled by something we had never expected. The Summit appeared to be at least 1,000 feet off. The intervening terrain was a wide, shallow cup, gleaming with snow, like the mighty West Wall which formed the cup's side. Towards the east, however, where the wall plunged down to Camp IV with a 3,000-foot drop, its ridge disappeared into nothingness, and along it there were some appalling cornices that seemed to lick at the sky. But the really surprising part was this: here, we had the impression of being higher up than the actual point which had always been reckoned the Summit of G.IV.

'The so-called Summit also looked a fair way off, and uninviting: and the sky was clouding up as it had done the day before. We were very dis-concerted. Here we were, thinking we'd only got to the fore-peak, and sud-denly discovering that we might have conquered the mountain outright! But since we weren't sure, we couldn't go back on our tracks now.

'The spirit in which we had pressed on, however, was ours no longer. Perhaps we recoiled from facing still more difficulties. Perhaps we felt an

unacknowledged reluctance to do one more pitch all for nothing. I am inclined
to think now that we were behaving in a rather curious fashion. Both of us
were the victims of an interior crisis, and both of us kept silent about it. In a
vague, absent-minded sort of way, we just went on spotting the tents at
Camp IV and the thin traces of our track over the glacier, which we had hardly
been able to make out till now, though we had looked for them from the
cornices.

'Again, looking back, I am inclined to think our silence was no bad thing,
for as it was, before we had confessed any of our doubts, we found ourselves
just automatically plodding on. We had taken the more courageous decision,
and the one that led us to victory in a sort of daze.

'This was the way we started off across the Shining Cup—like two auto-
matons. The going was not too bad at all. But the wind was now an icy
blizzard and it paralysed our movements. And the various strata of cloud
which already circled K2, Broad Peak and some other surrounding peaks now
began to hover round the Summit we were making for; while beyond the
ridge, on the East Face, there was quite a mass-movement of clouds in turmoil.
We had to hurry. Nearer and nearer came the Summit, which outlines itself
in the form of a wall rising steeply to five distinct points. We could not make
out which of them was actually the highest and we kept on looking for an
easy way up the wall. In the end we discovered that by a delicate traverse we
had covered the whole West Face of the mountain. Above us, however, there
remained this last unknown quantity—fifty yards of smooth and well-nigh
vertical wall. Below us, the terrain sloped off into the "Shining Wall"—an
abyss of 8,000 feet with the Baltoro at the bottom. For a moment, I felt
badly discouraged at the thought of having to buckle to and get down to it
once again, but I got over this feeling and just started to climb.

'Mauri followed. We exchanged no views on the situation, but I guessed
that we both took the same view of it! The wall was smooth, compact, yet at
the same time likely to crumble, just like the thin layer of snow which inter-
mittently coated it. We often had to resort to the use of pitons for safety's sake,
and every time we had to recover them, or we should have been left without
any. Everything was a treacherous risk: the rock, the snow, the pitons which
might not hold, and the cold too, for in certain delicate pitches it was necessary
to take off our gloves, and we certainly felt it. We should have liked to take the
crampons off our feet too, but in such a severe temperature we decided not to
—in case we needed them later and wouldn't be able to get them on again.
Technical difficulties were round about the Grade V mark, while the altitude,
the cold and the imminence of a full-scale blizzard made our slow progress

269

exasperating. A desperate struggle between the mountain and ourselves, but we were the winners, and at 12.30 exactly the little pennants of Italy, Pakistan and the C.A.I. fluttered on the Summit itself. Fluttered—no, blew out in the howling gale.

'In spirit, the whole Expedition was with us at that solemn moment of fulfilment. We embraced each other, deeply moved.

'The Summit which we had gained by such a narrow margin takes the form of a short, steep rock-crest, quite bare of snow, owing to the prevalence of extremely strong winds on the West Face, and there is scarcely room for a man to stand up. On the East Face, beyond the rocky crest, there is a flat, snow-covered field, of some size—a striking sight, which appears to be completely suspended in the void.

'We thought we might take some refreshment now, but the only things we wanted were all frozen hard. We stayed up there nearly an hour—and with breaks in the cloud so few and far between we needed every minute of it to get the photographs from every angle. Then, rather anxiously, we made our way down.

'With the pitons we had taken out on our way up, we fixed the twenty-metre length of rope I had put in my bag and went down on it. Then we made two quick descents with doubled rope. All this was rather in the nature of a flight, but soon it grew almost as tricky as the ascent. By the time we were under the fore-summit, we were swallowed up in cloud. A double-cord along the White Chimney: a swift up-and-down the sharp ridges and pinnacles and Black Turret—and then it began to snow, a blizzard of fine, driving, lashing snow. When we reached Camp VI at 1810 hours, it was at its height of fury. A terrible revenge, it seemed to us.

'All we wanted was a drink, and yet more to drink. We were cold all over, right to the marrow of our bones, and we couldn't warm up. It was the cold you get in slackening out after periods of extreme nervous and physical tension, the cold that follows victory. But had we really won through? If it went on snowing like this, how could we get down and rejoin our companions?'

6th August: with Beppe Oberto on Gasherbrum-la

Electrifying days these.

At any minute great news might come from the heights—where two of us, alone—as one is always alone before the ultimate things—battled with the last crags. It was impossible to keep still.

At 6.20 Beppe and I started out from Camp II for Gasherbrum-la, the col we had first seen on the day we reached Gasherbrum Valley, separating as it does Gasherbrum I from Gasherbrum II. It is one of the very few cols in the world to be found between two 8,000-metre (26,250-foot) peaks, and un-climbed: though it presented topographical features of considerable interest. We hoped, however, to avoid our fate of the previous day, when an unex-pected obstacle had beaten us at the last minute.

Early in the morning, while it was still cold (ten below) the snow was excellent and we had no trouble making a good pace. In little more than an hour we were down at the bottom of the valley, and another hour's slow climb brought us to the top of the ice-fall, with no special difficulties on the way. This particular ice-fall offered many parallel features to the 'Italians' Ice-fall' between Gasherbrum III and Gasherbrum IV but proved much easier, and less intimidating. Certain stretches of it were very steep (*Plate 75*); at others, séracs piled up and crevasses interwove with a mad confusion. But there was no ice-wall at the end and the absence of those tortuous and hazardous turrets was more welcome still.

Beyond the ice-fall we discovered—a parallel again with the big gap between Gasherbrums III and IV—a valley with a slight upward curve, and without crevasses. It ran eastwards roughly, rounding the West Wall of Gasherbrum I. It made easy and eventless going for a couple of kilometres—exactly the case with the Combe à Vaches. We reached the col about 9.30, a little out of breath: a hard north wind had made it difficult to get along. On this side of the pass we encountered a big rock ('like a whale' was Giuseppe's description) and we stopped there for a breather. We set a little snow marker and left a bottle bearing our names and the date. Professor G. O. Dyhrenfurth claims the height of this point to be 21,326 feet. From on-the-spot observation, and by comparison with nearby peaks, I should say this is putting the figure rather low: 21,600 or so might be nearer the truth. But, as everyone is aware, the method of estimating height easily lends itself to error, and my doubts about Dyhrenfurth's figure are based only on a personal impression.

The hill, when we set foot on it, turned out to be one of those false passes typical of the Himalaya: though it may appear to be a pass from the distance, it is more of the nature of a balcony or window. On the Shaksgam side, in fact, the mountain wall, coated with a thick foam of snow, plunges down to measureless depths. The view of the mountain landscape to be obtained from here proved quite stupendous: right opposite us were the ramparts of those Shaksgam Dolomites whose existence had been first confirmed by Ardito Desio in 1929. In the distance you could make out unknown giants whose peaks just now, however, were being gathered up into the darkness of a storm.

Eastwards lay some very high mountains: we might well have seen Teram Kangri (24,455 feet), first discovered in 1906 by Longstaff, and believed for some time to belong to the 26,000-foot category. The 'pass' opened towards the east, and above us towered the grim north wall of Gasherbrum I—ramparts of rock and ice of a livid bluish tinge dropping sheer in greater and greater precipices. Down below us we saw the great glaciers—Urdok, Sgan, Nagpo and North Gasherbrum: the perfect images of the 'frozen river'. They were all strewn with pointed flakes of white which from above suggested the scales of an ivory crocodile.

One interesting observation we made was this: the snow-line, on the mountain faces we saw from here, must have been very high up indeed. Mighty peaks rose against a sky bare of snow or ice. The explanation is that the air coming in from the Indian Ocean scatters its last reserves of humidity content over the high crests of the Karakoram. Travelling onwards towards Central Asia it has no further humidity to discharge and only an intense dry cold envelops the rock.

We left the pass at eleven and reached Camp II soon after 1400 hours. The last stretch was killing, what with the heat and the dazzle and the soft snow: this was overlain by a very thin layer of ice which broke under one's feet with the silvery tinkle of frail glass smashing to smithereens. The weather was worsening. Towards 12.30 I managed to get a momentary glimpse of the Summit of Gasherbrum IV in sunlight. On the marble of the south face of the very summit itself I thought I made out a black point. Our two? I said nothing to Giuseppe, out of a fear that he might only accuse me of 'seeing things'. Then once more the Peak disappeared behind cloud.

We talked of this and that for the rest of the day, but all the time only one question haunted our thoughts. Have they done it? We cooked our supper with the last few splinters of a case, a few candles and two old numbers of *Epoca* magazine. A smoky evening, and a slow one. The weather had indeed taken a turn for the worse: very definitely for the worse.

7th–8th August: descent through the blizzard

6th August. Day of Victory. And the day the weather broke.

Late that afternoon, Bepi De Francesch—at Camp V with Toni Gobbi, waiting for the Summit-team to return from the mystery world of the heights —Bepi made a worried entry in his journal: 'It is now 1600 hours. We have seen nothing, know nothing. Have they got there? Will they have had to come down in the blizzard this afternoon? Where will they be now? Our thoughts are up there with them, while the gale plays havoc with our tent. Heavy snow

now. Once Gobbi burst out, "I can hear steps in the snow." I didn't hear any, and said so. Gobbi: "But there's somebody trudging through the snow." This time I said, "If there is, they may get quite near the tent and still not be able to see it with visibility nil, like this." Gobbi took the torch and went out and called, but there wasn't anybody. Only a mighty fierce wind beating against the rocks. . . .'

At Camp IV, which he now shared with Zeni, Cassin, at mid-day on 6th August heard two shouts 'which seemed to come right from the Summit'. But he had to give up the idea of ascending to Camp V: 'At 1900 hours it was snowing hard and went on all night.'

Dawn on 7th August had to struggle slowly through the dark mists of a frightening storm that enveloped the whole mountain. The gale howled and swept the snow horizontally over the rocks. They were encrusted with white: with mineral flowers. It was very cold and the visibility was no more than a metre or two. De Francesch and Gobbi at Camp V, Cassin and Zeni at IV, Oberto and I at II—all of us were full of anxieties for Bonatti and Mauri up there.

'This weather shows no sign of mending at all,' Bepi went on to record at Camp V. 'The tent on one side is completely covered with snow, and we haven't even got the will-power to clear it. We're too anxious for our companions. Where are they? At Camp VI or on their way down to us?'

Then this is Cassin at Camp IV:

'At 7.50 I got up and roused myself sufficiently to go out of the tent to clear the snow off. Wasted labour! The snow went up, swirled round—and there was your cleared patch covered again in no time! You just opened the tent and it was white inside. When I was back in, it dawned on me that the ventilators were not closed and must be full of snow. Very worried now for our companions. We know they're quite well off for food and fuel, but we know they'll be rather done too. Will they have got there yesterday before the storm?'

At Camp II, I noted:

'Weather horrible. Ground mist. Snowing.'

Bonatti and Mauri, after an appalling night, buffeted by the gale, parched with thirst and with the cold eating into them, still had the strength to set off from Camp VI at first light. 'We knew full well,' said Carlo to me later, 'that it would be simply courting death to stay up there. There was a tremendous unknown: the ridge in a blizzard. But we had to brave it.'

What a descent that must have been! There is a realm of experience which can take one so close to annihilation that one shudders to re-enter it. The two of them could never be persuaded to speak of it afterwards. The forces of the subconscious seemed to hold them back, forbidding the very memory to return to those glassy slopes, those crags where the vortices of torment seemed to suck the last grains of consciousness out of the mind. 'The snow in the couloirs and chimneys,' said Carlo, much later, 'swept up vertically into your face, like an explosion.' Anyone who has done any mountaineering will certainly have encountered a blizzard, and he will be well able to imagine the two shadows suspended over a void, in all the driving ferocity of frozen snow, as it fell thick and fast only to be caught up again in whirlwinds before it could reach the ground: two shadows, and the line of the rope stretched horizontally between them. But, here, the altitude was 24,400 feet and these men were seeking a way down all the ice-coated rocks, the crazily tilted slabs and the deep new snows of a ridge 'which would be a considerable achievement in the Alps'—and over abyss after abyss. All this, too, coming as a climax to day after day of superhuman effort above 26,000 feet; after hunger, thirst and sleepless nights.

Then Bepi De Francesch describes events up at Camp V:

'At about ten o'clock, the sound of voices seemed to come from high up on the ridge. Gobbi, outside the tent at that moment, exclaimed: "There they are! They're coming down; I'll go up and meet them. Make some tea!" And with that he took his axe and went off into the blizzard. A few paces, and he had vanished from sight. I made some tea as fast as I could, because the voices struck me as quite close after all. They had to have something hot when they got in. They'd be at the end of their tether. I got the tea ready. No sign of anybody. I put it in the thermos to keep hot. Then I grabbed my axe too and started climbing. After a while I made out a black shape—Toni—higher up. Then two more coming down almost on all fours. It was them! No lull to the storm. . . . At a time like this, what did victory count for? The only thing that mattered was whether they were safe and sound! Then, when they got nearer, they shouted, "We did it!"'

'I was a dozen yards or so lower than Gobbi, and stayed where I was to give them the direction because, as I said, you could hardly see a thing. You could just make out their black forms, the rest was all white. You couldn't tell a slope from a drop, or a hump or promontory from a cliff or a precipice. Everything looked white and flat. The terrible wind snowed up your glasses and nearly carried you off.'

And now, out of the blue came the incident that brought us closer to disaster than any other the whole expedition had encountered. Once again, by great good fortune, our lucky star continued to shine on us, and Bepi, the one who was involved, suffered no more than a few scratches and a bad shaking up. This is his account:

'While Bonatti and Mauri were coming down to me, almost close enough for me to give them my hand, I felt the snow just vanish as if by magic from under my feet—and there I was, shooting down a very steep slope, a good hundred yards. . . .' His companions described the incident thus: 'We saw him disappear as if the storm had swallowed him up. For one moment, he looked just as if he was flying, his head was down and his legs were up in the air. "He'll be killed!" we thought in terror. It flashed through our minds that the glacier down there was full of crevasses. If he didn't smash himself up on a rock, he'd finish up in one of those yawning gulfs. Madonna! Poor Bepi, that was the end of him!'

Let Bepi now take up the tale. 'But, thanks to a merciful God, I came to no harm. I heard them shouting my name up there. I was buried in snow and hadn't the breath to call back. After a while, though, I managed to call out that I was all right.' It took Bepi nearly two hours of terrible effort through snow of unimaginable depth and lightness to get up to the ridge again, and to Camp V. But at long last all four were reunited, and at last everyone had his arm round the other.

'I found Bonatti and Mauri worn out, but the joy of victory lit up their faces.' Then at a later stage, though there was no abatement in the snow and the wind, they made their way down the ridge and the Combe à Vaches to Camp IV. Cassin describes their arrival:

'About 1500 hours I heard voices. I ran out of the tent to see two figures coming through the storm. I managed to make out Gobbi and De Francesch. I asked them for news. They said, "They've done it!" and then, in their wake, I made out Bonatti and Mauri—and ran forward to greet them. We went into the tent. You couldn't stay out in that wind. They told me about "Bepi's flight". He had gone up to meet them, put a foot wrong and slid over a hundred yards down. Thank heaven without hurting himself! He got back on his own. Then they told me about their climb. A mighty hard one. Difficulties increasing all the time as they went up, some parts Grade III and IV. Both of the opinion that no other Himalayan peak is so difficult. Boiled up coffee and milk while we talked. They gulped it down, then ate something and went off to sleep. Three in the tent. All a bit squashed.'

Crevasse encounter

7th August saw Oberto and me at Camp II, with our backs against the wall. The fuel was finished and there was nothing to take its place because we had by now burned everything that was burnable, and our food was reduced to a few crumbs. We had to leave the place. We thought of going up to Camp III: if we did, we should meet all the sooner the men who 'must have done it'. But what if they were running short of supplies too? We decided in the end to go down to Camp I.

I made a record of the trip in my notebook.

'We left at 7.0 with Haji Ismael. Generally, this descent took an hour or just over. This time we needed three and a half. Couldn't see a thing. It was warm. The place was a network of crevasses—dangerous ones. We were roped and I went in the lead, with skis. We got to Camp I soaked and very done. Luckily there were two containers of fuel here, and rations. We sheltered in the tent and slowly managed to get dry. Oberto was very worried over the fate of the others, but I didn't think the picture was as gloomy as all that. Tried to get radio contact between 1700 and 2000 hours, but no use. Slept badly— we had only one mattress, and boards taken from cases.'

8th August was another frightful day.

'All night, snowed without a let-up,' Cassin recorded at Camp IV. 'In the morning, after a drink of hot tea, we decided to go down, even if the weather continued as foul. By dint of some hard effort with the new-fallen snow so thick, we got to the Ice-fall. From there it was easier going with the fixed ropes to the end of the steep sector—then on to powdery snow again— reached Camp III. Here we found three high-altitude porters who'd come up to join in the spirit of things. We ate something and decided to go down to Camp II so that we could spread ourselves a bit more. We had a job finding the camp in the thick mist and when we had found it, the cupboard was bare. We had to go on down to Camp I. Someone swore. . . .'

How right he was to swear. I didn't know what to say in excuse for their dismay at finding an empty and abandoned camp, though it would have been impossible for Oberto and me to stay on there without fuel (and hence water) and without food. We had also entertained the notion of going down to Camp I, getting hold of fuel and ration-packs and then going back up to Camp II. But we were put off by the state of the glacier—with all the bridges crumbling, it was an inferno. We were also under the impression that our companions would skip Camp II, making a quick descent V—II—I. With a shudder, I kept thinking of the fate Bepi had so narrowly avoided. Had some such calamity come about through our being unable to remain at Camp II, the responsibility would have been entirely on my own shoulders. On a glacier, one can never be too careful. The Balti porters were right to

276

raise their cry of '*Saluad*' to the All-Powerful the moment they set foot on one.

'We were tired,' runs Bepi's description of their appalling descent. 'We were absolutely done, and soaked to the skin. No lull in the storm. Visibility almost nil. Snow covering all signs of the camp and markers. . . .'

'It was still snowing,' I wrote at Camp I. 'Towards 2000 hours, when I was outside the tent trying to get some message by radio, I saw a dark patch. It moved! "Giuseppe, they're here!" Oberto came out of the tent with a lamp. He swung it, and we both called out. The others replied. We rushed up, at as much of a run as possible in the soft snow. Just then we heard a shout, "Man down a crevasse!" We all made a beeline for the scene of the disaster. Mahmud Hussein, loaded up like a pack-mule with tent and packs, had gone through a snow-bridge. Luckily he had stuck four or five yards down, held by a sort of ledge of subterranean snow. We got our rope and axes and went to his aid. It wasn't so simple. The crevasse was wide and deep. The snow formation which had saved the victim might go at any minute, sinking down or crumbling to nothing. The ropes we lowered cut into the lip of the crevasse. Mahmud was groaning. It turned out that he had injured a leg. The light from down in the glacier made it look like a trench dug by the gas or telephone men. Bonatti directed operations with a regal calm. At last, Mahmud was hoisted up. Bravo, *bravissimo!* He hadn't let the kit-bag go! We all congratulated him with feeling. Zeni gave him a quick look-over. It was uncertain whether he'd cracked any bones or not. We pressed on to the tent. It grew dark. Only then did we learn the great news, that G.IV had been conquered.'

'At 2230 hours we were still making hot drinks,' said Bepi. Meanwhile, the weather had undergone one of those sudden changes characteristic of these parts. The sky was still clouded, but a killing cold had come from the peaks. I looked among my companions, as a face here and there was suddenly lit up by a flare of gas or the uneven lamplight. What a tremendous thing to have lived through—the ridge and the Summit! These faces made me feel awe-struck. They moved me nearly to tears. My pen recoils from mountain heroics, but it must be said that these were the faces of heroes. What affected me most of all was the reflection that these rags and tatters of humanity, these empty men, these men devoured by snow and ice and blizzard, had begun as men of enormous strength, of colossal physique and iron will. Carlo Mauri was pacing up and down and almost whimpering, as if blow after blow had fallen on his head. Toni Gobbi was the bearded spectre of the fugitive from a concentration camp. His voice was a raucous gurgle in his throat. Bepi—Bepi had a sore for a face, and his arms and legs were inordinately long, like a spider's. Zeni and Taqi were purple. Zeni did not speak words—he sighed them. Cassin was once more all swollen up. Only Walter, only the miraculous Bonatti, seemed to have suffered no ill effects—and more remarkable still, he was in full and undisputed possession of his mental faculties, not only his physical ones. He could smile. His movements were easy. He might have just got in from some tricky little climb beyond the rest-hut: it had given him quite an appetite, and even added to his zest for living. A champion of parts, Walter! There was no denying it, in him we numbered among our company a man who was not as others are, mere flesh and blood and perishable clay.

A bitter-cold night passed slowly, and not entirely sweetly in a tent chock-full of legs and heads and behinds. The morning of 9th August was bright but freezing cold. Clear sky, new snow, sun on the peaks. We all went down to the Base Camp where Captain Dar greeted us with every show of warmth and expressed his friendliest admiration for our two conquerors of the Summit. Mahmud Hussein was limping, but he got 'home' with some discomfort under his own steam. The adventure was at an end.

Flowers on the Glacier—Apricots in the Valleys

'Better I have saucepan—no?'

AT LAST there they were—the porters we had arranged to be sent up from Askole a few days before. Sixty-five of them. The caravan for the return journey was modest indeed by the side of the one for the outgoing! It had begun to snow. The sky hung low over the valleys. The air was cold. At home, we should have been near Bank Holiday time—the Italian Ferragosto—but there were only reminders of a stiff winter here.

Getting the caravan on the march proved a long and delicate business. One thought of Balzac's three elements in the eternal human comedy: passions, persons and things. Our Expedition was certainly innocent of any mysteries of passion. We had gained our Summit, we were all war-weary but happy, all we wanted was to get home to our families as soon as possible. As for persons—well, the men were gaunt, bearded, chap-skinned and hard-used, but otherwise much as usual. It is of things that we have to speak now.

Curious phenomena appeared to obtain that morning, from the earliest dawn-light onwards: miracles of levitation and the absolute annihilation of matter. Ice-axes, ropes, pocket-torches, saucepans, tins, rock-hammers, folding chairs, liquid-gas containers and oxygen cylinders, iron tubing, items of clothing, crampons, penknives, even sleeping-bags and tents. One minute they were there, the next minute they'd gone. It was almost as if the air had hands. For this was the great day of Thing Worship. The annual festival of the Balti. A day blessed by Mercury. The Dance of the Things—big things; middling things; little things; tiny things; new and unused things and old things; plastic things; metal things; wooden things; glass, paper and stuff; common-or-garden

279

things and rare things; brand-new novelties and ancient things full of holes. We laughed at first. How funny, we said. Then we had stronger feelings. Then, in the end, willy-nilly, came desperation.

The facts were simple. The attitude of those good Balti people towards our possessions had undergone a sea-change. It was the rascally Ghulam Hassan who, between grins and gesticulations, acquainted me with the exact position: 'When Sahib climb mountain, we respect everything. Even little pin, useful to Sahib. When Sahib done *keitu*, come down, much stuff no use, eh? We understand. Take stuff no use off Sahib's hands. No use Sahib, much use poor Balti.'

'You could at least wait and let us do the deciding over these so-say useless things.'

'Ah! We went—bad men come take! Better I have saucepan, not him, no? Ha ha! He he!'

In the light of this mournful experience, perhaps we might give this advice to any who may follow in our footsteps in these regions: never, never wait till the porters have come before dismantling the camp. Take down the tents and lock up the valuables while you are still on your own. Leave out only such articles as you may want to give the porters, say, as a reward for good service. What you must not forget is that things we take sublimely for granted in our highly industrialized lands are real treasures out in these very poor countries. A good penknife, a pressure cooker, a small tent, a jacket, a rope—these are possessions that fill one's house. I had almost said, fill one's life.

I do not say this to excuse the Balti, but only to make the point that circumstances alter cases, that there is always the other person's point of view. The fact of the matter was that in an atmosphere of laughter and high spirits we were skinned alive, we were pillaged, we were stripped, we lost not only a great many useful and expensive items, but some of our most intimately personal stuff too. And yet it was partly our own fault. We should have thought of the consequences and put everything back in its case. Confront a Balti with a padlock, and his attitude is the respectful one of 'hands off'. But spill a treasure-chest over the snow of the moraine and you call forth the ancient and deep-rooted human passions for loot and festival. They make a merry blend.

Green tea and algae on the Baltoro

Leaving the spot where our Base Camp had stood—it was now marked by nothing more than a few remnants and a few broken packing-cases among the snow and the moraine-stones—we cut across the Abruzzi Glacier to the Base Camp of the Japanese. At first we were inclined to think that courtesy required us all to look in, but in such weather, some of us scarcely relished the extra journey and went on with the main body of the caravan. When it came to it, there were four of us—Walter Bonatti, Dr. Zeni, Beppe Oberto and myself.

The Japanese had no sooner set eyes on us (at some distance, too) before they started waving for all they were worth. And when at last we set foot on the rise in the moraine where they had placed their camp, all of them gathered round Professor Kuwabara to greet us. They numbered twelve altogether. What a flawless example of the discipline of Nippon we saw! Their camp struck us as being super-equipped. One tent had been set aside for meteorological observations, in another one observed the decencies. There was even a flag-pole. Mind, body and soul, all were catered for. They treated us as old friends and with me spoke their own language. Our exchange of *Rajimemshite* seemed perfectly normal, even if it did take place in the middle of the glaciers.

The snow was coming down faster and faster and the wind blowing up with it. We went into their communal tent and exchanged news. Its chief item was that both expeditions, Italian and Japanese, had gained their objective.

'We did it on 4th August,' said Professor Kuwabara, a likeable, vigorous man who gave little sign of his fifty-four years. 'Here are the men who got to the summit of Chogolisa—Hirai and Fujihira. . . .'

'We got there on 6th August,' I rejoined. 'Here's Bonatti, who got to the Summit of G.IV, with Mauri. . . .'

The whole party was very lively, and the red carpet went out for us. Everyone wanted to shake hands with Bonatti, and several wanted his autograph. Then we had a long chat about the bad pitches both expeditions had struck—over cups of green tea and algae.

Then Professor Kuwabara asked one of his younger companions to fetch a package. It contained a handful of things that had belonged to Hermann Buhl. They had been found in the tent where the great Austrian climber had spent his last night, together with Kurt Diemberger. All they amounted to was a few poor little trifles; and yet, for all of us, European and Japanese alike, they were touching remains. Professor Kuwabara handed them over to our care, so that we could convey them to Hermann's widow in Austria.

The Japanese face Chogolisa

Chogolisa (25,110 feet), one of the most beautiful of the Baltoro mountains, is dear to the hearts of Italians: the Duke of the Abruzzi and his guide attempted it in 1909 and very nearly succeeded.

In 1957, following up their spectacular victory over Broad Peak, Hermann

Buhl and K. Diemberger decided to try out, on this mountain, a 'mobile camp' system which had something crazy about it, and something sublime. They would move with their whole home on their own shoulders—food, a small tent, everything. No porters. No lines of communication. They would be entirely self-supporting and self-contained, except for a few ration deposits to be left here and there among the séracs. Victory eluded them by a hair's breadth: a blizzard forced them back when they had reached the same height, or something not far short of it, as the Italians forty-eight years before.

Buhl and Diemberger had by now reached such a pitch of skill that they tackled the mountain with almost excessive confidence. They were on a crest loaded with immense cornices, all ready to crumble at a touch. They went down it unroped. Very close to the rise between the dome and the summit, tragedy overtook them. Hermann Buhl put his foot on one of those unstable snow-masses and went plunging into the abysses of the North Wall. His body lies still hidden among the Bride's frozen veils.

The Japanese Expedition was slower but surer. It made the orthodox approach. Organized by the Kyoto Academic Alpine Club, it numbered the following: T. Kuwabara (leader), T. Kato (second in command: had taken part in the Manaslu Expedition of 1953), M. Fujihira (Annapurna 1953), M. Yamaguchi, M. Wakizaka (Annapurna 1953), M. Nakashima (doctor to the Expedition), K. Hirai, Y. Takamura, G. I. Watsubo (Swat–Himalaya 1957), T. Haga, Y. Imagawa (interpreter for Urdu), M. Ushioda (cinematographer) and of course a Pakistani officer, Captain A. Wajih.

Leaving Skardu on 21st June with 152 porters, the Japanese placed their Base Camp in the Upper Baltoro on 8th July. Making the best of the fine weather, in a few days they had pitched the tents of Camp I at 18,370 feet, Camp II at 19,350 feet, Camp III at 20,990 feet and Camp IV at 21,980 feet— this last being up on the shoulder of the dome, very close to the spot where Buhl and Diemberger had camped. Not far from the highest point of the dome they placed a fifth camp (22,966 feet) from which, on 31st July, Fujihira and Hirai made a first bid for the summit of the mountain. Much time was lost over the very steep descent between the dome and the summit. At 4.30 in the afternoon, the pair found themselves at an altitude of barely 23,622 feet and they decided to go back.

They now discovered the existence of a much easier passage than the one they had come by. It was provided by a valley which, grooving the south face of the dome, was rather shut in between the latter and Kaberi Peak (c. 22,966 feet). This was a lucky find, and in the light of it the final plan of assault was modified. Camps IV and V, with the help of supporting teams,

CHOGOLISA
25,110
DOME   † B.H.   DA·1909

Chogolisa (25,110 feet), climbed in 1958 by the Japanese, with route and camps.
DA-1909 shows highest point reached by Duke of the Abruzzi and guides in 1909;
B.H. indicates presumable spot where Hermann Buhl slipped and died in 1957

were shifted from the crest down into this small valley, and from the new Camp V Fujihira and Hirai, in excellent weather conditions, made their summit attempt on 4th August. They left at 4.30 with oxygen masks and a supply ensuring two litres per minute. In forty minutes they were down at the foot of the dome: they went up the ridge at its foot, and from there onwards went straight up the crest, following in the footsteps of previous climbers. There was deep snow. Cornices and the threat of slides made for frequently dangerous conditions.

At 1300 hours the oxygen began to thin out, but it never occurred to

283

the two Japanese for one moment to give up. After some hard and heavy going through snow which grew lighter and less stable all the time, they reached the last peak at four in the afternoon. The summit itself is a rocky terrace about 150 feet high and represents a very tricky little climb. The pair got to the top at 1630 hours—only to find it so uncomfortably small and so jutting with sharp points that there was no room for both of them at the same time!

It was 10.30 at night when Fujihira and Hirai got back to the tents of Camp IV. Behind them lay eighteen hours of hard going.

In the meantime, the support teams had not been kicking their heels. They had made two ascents of importance—Kundos Peak (22,155 feet) and Kaberi Peak (c. 22,966 feet). The Expedition could therefore be said to have attained all its objectives.

The tomb of Mario Puchoz

Next day was one that had its counterpart in many an old fable: a day of walking on, and on, and on, walking without an end. We left the camp midway in the Upper Baltoro, towards six in the morning. The air was still very cold, but the sky overcast. We crossed the vast Concordia plain, finding it to be anything but an uneventful landscape. Encounters between glacial-moraine flows had left their mark of upheaval. Here was a stormy sea of unstable hillocks, ice-walls, green lakes and blue gashes whose depths were lost in the bowels of the glacier. It was all up and down, over this, round that and beware of the other . . . a long, wearying, desperate march. Not till ten o'clock were we out of this vale of suffering. At last we had something different under our feet—the more regular whaleback of one of those colossal moraines leading straight to K2.

Trudge, trudge, trudge. . . . Two o'clock, three o'clock, four o'clock—still on the march and beginning to pay for it. But what other way is there of getting a true idea of dimension and distance among these mountains? The mouth of the Khalkhal Glacier drew close to us, then Broad Peak, then the valley of the Savoy Glacier, as we marched on. K2, all this while, was losing that harmony of line, that combination of power and elegance which it had worn from Concordia. It had changed in perspective, too, and not for the better—or the more impressive—in spite of the fact that it took up a good bit of the horizon, and its mighty precipices and fearful ice-falls seemed to weigh right down on us.

A short while before four-thirty in the afternoon, though, we finally reached that rocky spur at the foot of K2 which contains the tomb of the guide Mario Puchoz, who perished on K2 in 1954 (see p. 164). The setting was sublime indeed: worthy of some barbarian king killed in the legendary conquest of distant lands. The spur takes the form of a rock-pile which thousands of years of wind and ice have sculpted into some tortuous shapes—pinnacles, arches, grottoes, all are there. The colour is rust-red. A few tiny Alpine flowers grow on it.

We found a cross, and down below the rock a metal plaque, bearing the names of the victims of K2. We put everything in order there, adding a brass plate of our own, which we had brought from Milan, expressly to commemorate this brief visit we were now making to the tomb of a compatriot and five men from distant lands. It was cold now, with a bitter killing cold. Below us, lost in the gloom of a day whose cheer had gone, lay measureless glaciers and valleys without end. Looming over our heads we felt the mysterious presence of K2.

The place, and the hour too, by their very nature, filled the soul with awe for the great mystery that invests all men at all times. Here were these, fallen in the lands of Allah; for some the Cross, for the others an inscription on stone: *Om Mani Padme Hum.* How small, how meaningless they seemed, these distinctions—before death and tears. What distinction divided the grief of mother or sister in a house in the Val d'Aosta, a village of Solu Khombu, a small house in Iowa?

Our return seemed an unending trek. With night coming down, we reached Concordia. But by now the caravan itself had got as far as Biange, and there would be no refreshment and rest for us till we joined up with the others. Slog, slog . . . from rock to rock, from hollow to hollow, stumbling over stones which in the darkness looked like petrified trees. Every now and again we called a halt, exhausted, and every time our good old Ghulam, loaded with photographic gear, would lie down, roll up into his own Balti blanket and drop off to sleep. When we woke him, he would protest: 'What's that? Sleep now. Finish walk. Enough.' The ferocious cold bit into you, but any old lump in the ice made Ghulam a pillow and he would just curl up like a silkworm in his home-made blanket rug. Ah, to be a mountain Balti!

Slog, slog . . . it is extraordinary, the almost inexhaustible supply of energy that lies within us, to be discovered when needs must; we were finished eight hours ago, six hours ago, four hours ago; it seemed beyond our strength to go on over hump and dip and hillock of ice. Yet here we were, eighteen hours out, and still going with a certain amount of briskness, on the whole. Towards midnight we found ourselves in a desperate maze of crevasse, sérac and yawning gulf, with very small hope of getting out of it till dawn. Ghulam once more tucked himself up in his blanket and went off to sleep. He looked like an over-sized sausage abandoned on the glacier. By a stroke of luck we had a number of 'fire-flies' with us—those miniature pocket-torches which you throw away when the battery is out. Their feeble gleams fell upon an alabastered labyrinth: we made out ramparts of ice—that old ice, pock-marked with holes; blackened cracks, which somewhere down in their deepest depths—as you could tell by dropping a stone—held water; sharp crests, leaping to an upper dark, twisted into the shape of obelisks and arched bridges; narrow, sharp-edged trenches grooved by rivers which flowed in the daytime sun. Bonatti was no longer in our midst. He had gone off to look for a way out. We heard him for a while working away with his axe, cutting footholds. Then silence. We were now resigned to a fate welcomed by Ghulam: we should have to give up, to get what little sleep we could in the cold. Then Walter showed up, on the top of a sort of broad low tower of ice.

'This way,' he called to us. 'I've found the way out.'

Ghulam woke, muttering. He then decided that after all he didn't care for the prospect of remaining here on his own, and got ready to follow us up over a very steep ice-crest. Now someone found a length of cord in his pack. 'Rope the porter,' he said. 'He might slip with that load.' Ghulam was duly roped. As soon as he moved off, however, we saw that we need have taken no special precautions for him! Walter had cut some scarcely perceptible footholds across slopes that dropped into the perilous dark of monstrous crevasses. Ghulam walked up them sure-footed and serene. Ghulam of Surungo; yes—one more Balti who would have made a really first-class high-altitude porter. The problem was finding such champions. What we should really have done in the first place was to invite all the men of Askole—and the nearby villages too—to take part with us in a few rock- and snow-climbs, for the only way to pick out the best is to see them all in action.

At last, at three o'clock in the morning, and more by luck than by judgment, we ended up in two tents—minus mattresses and sleeping-bags. It was due to Bepi that they were pitched at all: at the place where they stood, many hours earlier, he had come upon a group of porters who had fallen well behind the others and had persuaded them to put up this rudimentary camp. In these tents some members of the Expedition spent a few wretched hours, their teeth chattering till dawn. The rest, more sensible, went on to Biange to find the real camp and the main body of the caravan.

The first flower

It is incredible how the morning sun can put heart into the poor traveller at these heights. By night, one might well be voyaging through the strange ice of an abandoned planet. But day comes: the air is sweet, the light a joy, the very ice a living thing, for a myriad streams run off it down the mountain. We had spent the ghastliest of nights among the séracs of the Baltoro. Day brought the first flower, among the stones of the moraine. It was no tiny-petalled Alpine, such as those on Puchoz' tomb, but a big, red, festival bloom.

The return from such a journey as we had made, a venture into the forbidden, the eternal, the sublime, is a far cry from the mere going back on one's tracks. One lives so many things—discoveries, feelings, encounters, all so fresh, so unexpected. Look! Life again, with all its gifts. The little things we had taken for granted, what marvels they seemed now. The first flower! Why, we greeted it like a long-lost brother, there in the good earth of ancient moraine-rock, on the good ice of the glacier.

And then it was the grass's turn. After an interminable, dust-laden trek through moraine, we arrived at Urdukass to find ourselves suddenly surrounded by a meadow. A wondrous thing, I can tell you. A carpet. A green carpet. So fresh. A reward for heroes or gods. . . . Had it not seemed so theatrical, we should have knelt down and kissed that grass; touched it; filled our hands with it; lain in it. And laughed and laughed, like men crazed.

Appetite returned at last, too. Little by little we lived again. Supper at Urdukass was something we enjoyed. Days of endurance, days at breaking point, were over: once more we were beginning to behave like men, and look like men.

A fury of waters

Adieu, Baltoro! Today we bid you farewell, we leave you behind us, measureless old wrinkled worm, prowling and slithering your dark way down to the warmer air—which will kill you and cleave you into a myriad little rivulets glinting in the sun.

How different were the valleys now, a bare two months after we had first passed this way. For then winter still reigned on high, and the ice-dykes were sealed. But now the sun had flung wide the sluices and it was water that avalanched down on to the plain. The sun was the glacier's undoing. It was crumbling away, its rivulets had turned to torrents, its torrents into great floods. And the air was full of a song—the roar of the waters.

Land of apricots

Onward! Every day a new plunge into life, every day a resurrection. What a journey of enchantments! Why, to rediscover them was alone almost worth that hardship. To know what a blade of grass was, or a plant shooting up

287

among the stones; an old gnarled and twisted tree, a birch grove, all murmuring green and silver, at Payù.

How many things that we saw when we reached Askole were 'the first'. The first child, for instance: he came rushing up to one of our porters, shouting for joy. The old wrinkled fellow lifted him up in his arms and his happiness was ours too. The little tot, all the same, was scared of papa's beard and his rough, calloused hands: his face fell, he didn't know whether to smile or cry. Then came the first houses; the first women; the first calves; the awakening of life, life everywhere.

Askole Valley, at this season, is a true realm of dreams. Flowers in every meadow; poplars in the wind; the greenest of green fields; and up there on the heights icy mountains gleaming in the sun, trailing diaphanous clouds of mother-of-pearl. It would be good to linger here, in the valley of legend, before plunging back, like those torrential waters around us, into the asphalt jungle awaiting us down in the plains. Yet some dark nostalgia was at work in our hearts too, urging us ever on.

At Chakpo we found an earthly paradise. Sun, flowers, mountains, rushing streams, a balmy sweet-smelling air and an endless grove of apricots, bowed down with fruit. We wound our way through the green, maze-like paths of the oasis, hat in hand—the hat full of apricots and the other hand diving into it for the precious fruit, which we devoured with all the ecstasy of men denied any freshly growing thing for months. And every time one of those richly laden branches bobbed down over our heads, or in front of our noses, the hats were filled up again with the small, fragrant fruits.

We passed a peasant and felt a little uneasy: all this orchard-raiding had given us a guilty conscience. But he only smiled.

'Go on, eat away,' he told us. 'So long as you just throw the stones under the trees so that we can find them.'

It is, in fact, the kernels which constitute the most precious part of the fruit: from them are extracted the tiny nuts I have already mentioned. The pulp we saw laid out in the sun to dry, vast carpets of an orange-red.

The walnut tree of Biano

Our triumphal march through the apricots seemed to have no end. The Golden Age had come again. Here was the Garden of the Hesperides. Ah, the joy of climbing up into the branches of a tree and letting a now-expert eye rove from fruit to chosen fruit! But there is an old saying: moderation in all things. It was hard to obey with all these riches round us, and the time came when we felt full to bursting point. Not even the furtive and frantic visits we had to make at night to dark corners of the camp could persuade us to eat less fruit.

Many other memories of this journey belong to the same realms of gold. The walnut tree of Biano, for instance: a giant, 1,000 years old. One evening we were welcomed to its shade by a cluster of old men and young men and children. With the simple dignity of a pastoral people, they offered us gifts of eggs, fruits and greenstuff. Then came the hour of song, and the camp-fire. Here was a way of life like no other. The world may collapse, but the walnut tree of Biano and the men who gathered beneath its boughs will surely go on to all eternity, sublimely ignorant of the clash of empires beyond their ken.

A raft to the outside world

Soon we had come to the very last stage of our journey back to Skardu and the outside world. It was fine to be able to start thinking about home and the faces we loved, and our friends. But there was a pang, too, as the time came to leave these valleys to which we should never return. I wanted to stay and savour every passing hour of this life born anew among the apricots and the old walnut trees, and the moonlight and the friendly Balti, but there was little chance. It was on, on, down, all the time: fools fleeing paradise for a land of cement and iron and a deafening din.

At Dasso, the rafts—zak—were waiting for us. On these primitive but thoroughly safe craft we covered, in a few hours, the equivalent of three days' march—some thirty-seven miles of ground. A zak consists of about twenty-five blown-up goatskins, held together by light and flexible slatting. It will take a load of six or seven persons and a certain amount of baggage.

For various reasons of logistics which concerned the rest of the caravan, we left Dasso late in the afternoon, in a pair of zaks. We had hardly pushed off before we had a very bad moment. The current caught us and hurled us out into furious whirlpools and high waves. The zak had no rudder: in those turbulent waters it began to swing round on itself like a cork, completely at the mercy of the current. But the pilots were the most capable fellows in the world: with just a few simple manœuvres they succeeded in keeping the craft quite clear of the rocks—apparent or half-submerged—which were our real danger. Our fears soon vanished and we could settle down to enjoy the changing scene—the sun setting among the mountains, the banks flying past, the foaming whirlpools that formed where currents clashed (*Plate 48*).

When darkness fell, the pilots drew into the bank and pulled the rafts up on shore. We were in the Kashumal region. After one last gargantuan supper of ripe apricots, we put our sleeping-bags and mattresses out under a

T

tree and prepared to get a night's sleep. The moon was up now. The valley glinted with silver.

We should have been very well off indeed, had not some village simpleton found himself drawn to us as if by a spell. He appeared from nowhere, a silent, bare-footed, goitre-throated individual wrapped in a once-white toga. We spoke to him: no answer. We invited him to go away. He laughed. We tried to chase him off. He growled and groaned. There he stayed, still as a statue, and a rather sinister one at that, squatting down, bent on watching us sleep.

He went off with sun-up. We turned back to the river, greeted on the way by a grave patriarch, with all the sorrows of the world inscribed on his noble face (*Plate 12*). Then we got 'on board'. The *zak* continued its journey towards the plain of Skardu, and the outside world.

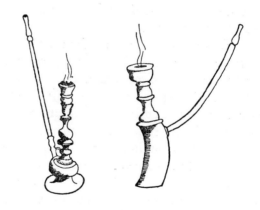

Appendices

1. LETTER GRANTING PERMIT FOR THE EXPEDITION

Immediate

> Ministry of Foreign Affairs
> and
> Commonwealth Relations,
> Karachi

No. EA(i)/13/7/57   Dated the 4th March 1958

The Ministry of Foreign Affairs and Commonwealth Relations presents its compliments to the Embassy of Italy in Pakistan and with reference to the Embassy's Aide Mémoire dated the 27th February 1958 has the honour to state that the Government of Pakistan is pleased to grant permission to Mr. Riccardo Cassin and his associates to carry out a mountaineering expedition to the Peak *'Gasherbrum IV'* during the summer of 1958, subject to the following conditions:

1. The material collected and photographs taken by the expedition shall be made available to the Government of Pakistan before they are printed or published abroad.
2. Only such material as permitted by the Government of Pakistan will be printed or published by the expedition. The rest of the material will remain with the Government of Pakistan.
3. All the exposed films shall be made available to the Government of Pakistan for vetting/scrutiny before they are exported out of Pakistan.
4. Instructions relating to photography of subjects of strategic importance will be strictly adhered to in letter and spirit. A copy of these instructions will be supplied to the expedition on arrival in Pakistan.
5. The expedition will be accompanied by an officer nominated by the Government of Pakistan. He will inform the members of the expedition of the security regulations in force in the areas to be visited by them and these regulations will have to be strictly observed by them.
6. The expedition will arrange to provide necessary equipment, etc., to the porters and the Pakistani officer accompanying it.

7. The expedition will not operate in the 50 miles belt of territory lying on the Sinkiang border north of Baltit.
8. No Pakistani produce shall be taken out of Pakistan without the prior permission of the Government of Pakistan.
9. The expedition will, at no stage, operate into more than one group.
10. The decision to release unique zoological specimens collected by the expedition shall remain with the Government of Pakistan. In case they are retained, photographs and specifications will be made available to the expedition to be utilized by it.
11. Geological and other scientific data collected during the mountaineering expedition will be made over to the Government of Pakistan.
12. The itinerary of the expedition will not be changed even in emergency without prior permission of the Government of Pakistan.
13. Maps, etc., if applied for and issued to the expedition will be returned to the Government of Pakistan before its departure from Pakistan.
14. If any change is contemplated in the composition of the members of the expedition, it should first be approved by the Government of Pakistan well in advance.

It will be appreciated if the Embassy could kindly arrange to have the permission communicated to Mr. Riccardo Cassin and his associates, and supply this Ministry with a list of equipment, etc., to be brought by the expedition to Pakistan, for issuing necessary instructions to the authorities concerned.

The Ministry avails itself of this opportunity to renew to the Embassy the assurance of its highest consideration.

The Embassy of Italy
in Pakistan,
Karachi.

2. INSTRUCTIONS FOR THE USE OF MOUNTAINEERING EXPEDITIONS IN THE GLACIER-ZONES OF THE BALTORO, BIAHO, SIACHEN (KARAKORAM), SUMMER, 1958

1. Six mountaineering expeditions are expected during the summer of 1958 in the region of Baltistan, each having for its objective the mountain specified in the respective official description.

[List follows. Of these six expeditions, only three came to anything: the Japanese (Chogolisa), the American (Gasherbrum I) and the Italian (Gasherbrum IV). A second American expedition under C. Houston (objective K2) failed to take advantage of the permission accorded to it, as did also an English and a German party.]

2. It is requested that all expeditions shall observe instructions issued by the Ministry for Kashmir Affairs (in Rawalpindi) relative to the taking of photographs, the transmission of information and any special knowledge gained to the competent authority, etc.

3. Photographs of general and incidental interest may be taken. It is however forbidden to photograph, without a Permit from the Ministry for Kashmir Affairs, any of the following:

    a. Military installations, military buildings, etc.

    b. Items of equipment for the Armed Forces such as cannon, armoured cars, military transport, aeroplanes, arms, military instruments, etc.

    c. Aerodromes, together with any neighbouring buildings or installations.

    d. Bridges, passes, forts, Government edifices, etc.

4. Agreed conditions and rates for the employment of porters, both high-altitude and ordinary, shall become operative at such time and in such manner as stipulated in the ruling. The exact number of porters required in each category, with their date of engagement, to be communicated to the Political Agent as soon as possible.

Pay-rates for porters have been fixed according to the following scale:

A. Ordinary Porters

    a. from Skardu to Askole and from Askole to Skardu

    b. from Skardu to Arandu and from Arandu to Skardu

    c. from Skardu to Khurkund and return (Kundos zone, Siachen)

Rs. 3/– per day. For forced stops (e.g. crossing of Indus at Skardu or Braldu at Dasso) Rs. 2/– per day.

For the return journey, when no loads will be carried, porters shall be paid Rs. 1/8 per day.

    a. from Askole to the Base Camp

    b. from Arandu to Baltoro

    c. from Khurkund to the Base in the Kapalu zone

Rs. 4/– per day and rations on scale B (hereto appended). For forced stops Rs. 2/8 per day, and rations.

For the return journey to Askole (or Arandu or Khurkund) Rs. 2/8 per day. The days to be counted as equal in number to those taken for the ascent; rations, to be halved.

For ordinary porters, insurance need not be taken up.

B. High-Altitude Porters

    a. from Skardu to Askole and return ⎤
    b. from Skardu to Arandu and return ⎟ Rs. 3/– per day and rations on
    c. from Skardu to Khurkund and ⎬ scale A. For forced stops Rs.
        return ⎭ 2/– per day and rations.

    d. from Askole to Base Camp and ⎤
        return ⎟
    e. from Arandu to Base Camp ⎟ Rs. 4/– per day and rations. For
        and return ⎬ forced stops Rs. 3/– per day
    f. from Khurkund to Base Camp ⎟ and rations.
        and return ⎭

    g. Base Camp to Camp III, at any ⎤
        height not exceeding 21,000 feet, ⎬ Rs. 5/– per day and rations.
        and return ⎭

    h. Camps III, IV, V (not exceeding ⎤
        23,000 feet) ⎬ Rs. 6/– per day and rations.

    i. Camps above 23,000 feet and ⎤
        return ⎬ Rs. 7/– per day and rations.

5. *Insurance.* High-Altitude Porters shall be insured in the sum of Rs. 2,000/– for each man, whether through an Insurance Society, or by the deposit of such sum against each porter, or by an official letter from the President of the Mountaineering Club of whatever country is represented by the Expedition, or in the last resort by a letter from the Expedition Leader himself. All such arrangements to be made with the Political Agent before the Expedition leaves Skardu. Compensation due for injuries shall be made according to the estimates of the Agency Surgeon (Medical Officer of the Baltistan District), indemnities awarded to be proportional to the degree of unfitness involved.

NOTE: Porters still fit, and considered by the doctor of the Expedition to be in good health, and yet refusing to work, shall be paid Rs. 1/– per day.

6. The Expedition shall provide High-Altitude Porters with equipment and shelter required at great height, as also with extra rations, pay, necessities, etc.

7. Ordinary porters proceeding beyond Askole, Arandu or Khurkund to the Base Camp shall be provided by the Expedition with appropriate shelter, snow-glasses, footwear, rations and pay.

8. The equipment issued to the High-Altitude Porters shall be inspected by a representative of the Political Agent before the Expedition leaves Skardu.

9. *Loads to be carried.* Ordinary porters may carry 60 lb. from Skardu as far as Askole, Arandu or Khurkund, this weight to be reduced beyond these points.

10. *Rations.* Certain supplies will be made available at Askole at the following prices:

Flour	⎫	Rs. 26 per mound
Meat on the hoof	⎰	Rs. 1/8 per seer
Meat, slaughtered	⎱	Rs. 2/– per seer
Butter	⎭	Rs. 6/8 per seer

NOTE: Efforts are now being made to insure the availability of the flour at Askole. Confirmation of its availability is awaited.

11. A member of the Police Force shall be posted to Askole (or Arandu or Khurkund) to be at the disposal of the Expeditions in case of necessity, this measure being undertaken in view of the number of Expeditions operating in the same zones. The rations for police personnel, as also special clothing adapted to the cold, to be provided by the Expeditions, the clothing being returnable on completion of service.

12. *Postal Service.* If the Expeditions so desire, arrangements will be made for the forwarding and delivery of letters, etc. For such service, two groups of runners will be needed. The first group will cover the ground between Skardu and Askole (or Arandu or Khurkund) outward and return journey. There would be two runners operating alternately in this sector, paid at the rate of Rs. 30 per return journey. The second group will cover the ground between the outlying villages (Askole, Arandu, Khurkund) and the Base Camps. Here also two runners will be necessary but they will operate together and not alternately. Pay-rates shall be established in the outlying villages (Askole, etc.) taking into account distances to the Base Camp and its particular situation on the glaciers.

It will be necessary for the Expeditions to furnish runners operating between Skardu and Askole (or Arandu or Khurkund) with a pair of stout shoes. Those operating between these points and the respective Base Camps should be furnished with shoes, rations, shelter in the course of the journey and protective aids against bad weather.

13. It is to be hoped that the leaders of the many Expeditions operating this summer in neighbouring regions, and reaching their respective zones of operation by more or less identical routes, will collaborate amicably with one another for the better success of their endeavours.

14. [Lists names of persons responsible in various service-departments.]

Skardu, 30th April 1958   Signed:

HABIB-UR-RAHMAN KHAN

Political Agent, Baltistan

Publisher's Note. The above has been translated from the Italian edition of this book, the original document having been lost.

3. PORTERS' RATIONS

A—High-Altitude Porters

Supplies	Ounces per day	Remarks
1. Flour	24	
2. Rice	8	
3. Fresh meat	6	
4. Butter	2	
5. Sugar	4	
6. Tea	1/3	
7. Tinned milk	4	If fresh, 8 ounces
8. Salt	1/6	
9. Lentils	4	
10. Dried onion	1/4	
11. Powdered condiments	1/6	
12. Vitamin pills		1 per day
13. Cigarettes		5 per day
14. Matches		1 box per day

B—Ordinary Porters

Supplies	Ounces per day	Remarks
1. Flour (*atta*)	32	
2. Butter	2	
3. Sugar	2	
4. Tea	1/4	
5. Salt	1/4	
6. Tinned milk	2	If fresh, 4 ounces
7. Fresh lentils	2	
8. Cigarettes		5 per day
9. Dried lentils	1	
10. Matches		2 boxes per week

4. TABLE SHOWING PROGRESSIVE PAY-RATES FOR ORDINARY PORTERS, OUTWARD AND RETURN JOURNEY, IN RUPEES

	Skardu	Shigar	Kashumal	Dasso	Chakpo	Chongo	Askole	Korophon	Bardumal	Payù	Liligo	Urdukass	Biange	Gore	Concordia	Upper Baltoro	Base Camp
Skardu																	
Shigar	4/8																
Kashumal	9	4/8															
Dasso	13/8	9	4/8														
Chakpo	18	13/8	9	4/8													
Chongo	22/8	18	13/8	9	4/8												
Askole	27	22/8	18	13/8	9	4/8											
Korophon	33/8	29	24/8	20	15/8	11	6/8										
Bardumal	40	35/8	31	26/8	22	17/8	13	6/8									
Payù	46/8	42	37/8	33	28/8	24	19/8	13	6/8								
Liligo	53	48/8	44	39/8	35	30/8	26	19/8	13	6/8							
Urdukass	59/8	55	50/8	46	41/8	37	32/8	26	19/8	13	6/8						
Biange	66	61/8	57	52/8	48	43/8	39	32/8	26	19/8	13	6/8					
Gore	72/8	68	63/8	59	54/8	50	45/8	39	32/8	26	19/8	13	6/8				
Concordia	79	74/8	70	65/8	61	56/8	52	45/8	39	32/8	26	19/8	13	6/8			
Upper Baltoro	85/8	81	76/8	72	67/8	63	58/8	52	45/8	39	32/8	26	19/8	13	6/8		
Base Camp	92	87/8	83	78/8	74	69/8	65	58/8	52	45/8	39	32/8	26	19/8	13	6/8	

This table does not of course take account of stops, various indemnity payments, prize money, etc. An ordinary porter will earn about 100 Rupees (about £7 8s.) for the round trip from Skardu to the Base Camp to the High Baltoro and back.

5. HIGH-ALTITUDE PORTERS IN THE EXPEDITION

(The first six are those retained throughout the entire enterprise)

Name	Father's Name	Village of Birth
Taqi	Mehdi	Satpara
Mahmud Hussein	Haider	Satpara
Rustam	Alì	Satpara
Haji Ismail		Askole
Mohammad	Ghulam	Kuro
Ghulam	Hassan	Kuro
Asad	Mahdi	Satpara
Alì	Haider	Satpara
Haji Alì		Satpara
Ghulam	Mohammad	Kuro
Ghulam	Mohammad	Kuro
Alì	Archun	Askole
Mohammad	Jo	Kapalu
Ismail	Mohammad	Tiakshi

6. THE NAMING OF K2

The following note was handed to the Pakistan Press, by the Minister of Kashmir Affairs, on 13th May 1958, and carried by the daily papers on 14th May:

The Government of Pakistan have invited suggestions for naming the second highest mountain in the world, now known as K-2 in the Karakoram range.

A Press Note issued by the Ministry of Kashmir Affairs yesterday said:

'Few people are aware that Pakistan possesses the second highest mountain in the world. It is Mount K-2, which is estimated to be 28,500 feet high and is situated in Baltistan.

'As a result of the newly aroused public interest in mountains and mountaineering, the incorrect use of the name "Mount Godwin Austen" for this peak has been gaining ground.

'Lt.-Col. H. H. Godwin Austen, F.R.S., was a distinguished officer of the Survey of India, who did topographical work in the Karakorams in the sixties of the last century. But he was not the discoverer of K-2. Before him, in 1856, Lt.-Col. T. G. Montgomery had taken the first theodolite observations that revealed the height and fixed the position of this great mountain.

'No name other than K-2 has ever been officially assigned to this peak. No local name for it is known in Baltistan. In 1888, it was suggested that it should be named "Mount Godwin Austen". But this proposal was not accepted by the Royal Geographical Society in London. It was also rejected by the Survey of India and the Government of India. Other proposals were made at various times to call it "Mount Montgomery", "Mount Akbar", "Mount Babar" and "Mount Albert", but all were rejected. Official maps and records have, therefore, continued to refer to the mountain as K-2.

'On the other hand, certain unofficial cartographers and some of the newspapers persist in the mistaken use of the name "Mount Godwin Austen". Perhaps they find the name K-2 inadequate and unimaginative.

'Since this is a matter of general public interest, Government feel it would be profitable to invite suggestions from the general public for a suitable name for this great mountain, which is the highest in Pakistan and the second highest in the world. The name may be communicated to the Ministry of Kashmir Affairs, Rawalpindi.'

So far, there would appear to have been no outcome to all this, but I mention the matter as worthy of interest.

By a tradition as ancient as man's passion for climbing mountains, the first conquerors of a peak are entitled to give what name they think most fitting to the particular pile of stones, or ice, they have reached at last; for which reason, clearly, Achille Compagnoni and Lino Lacedelli should also be consulted if such a decision is considered.

My personal view is one I have already stated in the text: the name K2, far from being 'inadequate' to the dignity of the mountain, and 'unimaginative', represents one of the happiest victories of chance creation over the congenital inventive shortcomings of men.

Sketches

Maps

Notes on Photographs

NOTE: *The number in brackets at the end of the description is the C.A.I. Catalogue Number for black-and-white negatives.*

1. The great mosque, Shigar, recently renovated. This is not the only mosque in Baltistan to bear some resemblance to the Shah Hamadan Mosque at Srinagar. The pagoda-style wooden spire is of particular interest because it recalls the style of the *chorten* and all similar structures throughout Buddhist Asia, which are both reliquaries and esoteric models of the Universe. Its origin probably goes back to the time when Kashmir and Baltistan were Buddhist countries. In the foreground: two of the Expedition porters, carrying sacks of flour (183).

2. Houses at Askole, altitude 10,000 feet, in the Braldu Valley. They are circular, or roughly so, and built from river-pebbles and mud, or a very thin mortar. Stairs are outside. The man in the foreground is wearing the typical Balti blanket (*kar*), slung round the shoulder in the fashion of a toga (489).

3. A Kashumal interior. The men sit cross-legged on the floor around an open hearth in the centre of the room. Note the iron slab: heated from underneath, it is used to cook the chupatty—buns or cakes of flour made into a paste with water. The first figure, right, and two others of the group on the left, are wearing the Gilgit cap or beret. The others are seen in the white woollen Braldu skull-cap. The structure of the house is very clearly indicated: a wooden framework filled in with mud blocks, and a roof plastered with mud—a very different building style from that found at Askole (196).

4. Weaving wool at an old loom under a tree, at Kashumal (194).

5. Ploughing near Askole. The animals are *zo*, a cross between the cow and the yak. The plough is made of wood with a small metal share (200).

6. A study in stone: weather-worn granite masses between Bardumal and Payù.

7. Fields of grain and a farmhouse at Skardu.

8. Apricots in fruit near Chakpo (at the end of August). The Balti apricot is small but of excellent flavour. Local cultivators are less interested in the fruit than in the stones, from which they extract the kernels. Lightly roasted, these are sold all over Pakistan.

9. A *jula*—suspension bridge—of interwoven branches over the Dumordu, near Korophon. A species of willow provides the raw material for these bridges: the roots are also used.

10. Poplars and mulberries, Tandara. In the background, the mountains forming the eastern boundary to the Shigar Valley: they are the last outcrop of the chain from which rises Haramosh (24,270 feet). The peaks are *c.* 18,000 feet.

11. A typical panoramic view of Baltistan—the Skardu basin, looking north from near the Rest House. Water produces the lush vegetation: its absence, total desert. Up in the heights can be seen the snow and ice which form an inexhaustible reservoir.

12. An old Balti inhabitant of Kashumal. Note the perfectly Europoid features.

13. A boy (Shigar) carrying a small brother (or sister?) on his back—a mode more characteristic of Central or Far-East Asia than the West or South.

14. A girl (taken between Shigar and Kashumal). The jewellery is typically Central Asian—coral and turquoise set in silver, except for the necklace, Himalayan in style.

15. A Balti with undeniably Nordic features: fair hair, blue eyes, Dolicocephalic cranium; above average height. We called him 'The Viking'. An inspired dancer. Such definite Nordic or even blond types are rare.

16. A Balti of the Mongoloid type; although not constituting the normal Balti type, they are quite frequent (perhaps 5–6 per cent).

17. Balti of decidedly southern type.

18. Figure (Maitreya) carved on the Rock of Buddhas, between Skardu and Satpara. Held by some authorities to be of pre-tenth-century origin.

19. Frieze in wood around window of the Shigar mosque. The second (from the inside) motif, the chain of linked crosses, is typically Buddhist: one more testimony to an ancient and important period in the history of this region (191).

20. A little courtyard, as found in nearly all Balti houses—at Surungo, near Askole. The wooden 'hammer-head' pillar-capital is characteristic of a latitudinal zone which runs right through Eurasia, from Macedonia to Japan, with innumerable local variants of style and size (424).

21. Father and son, Askole. The Balti are a rude peasant people, often wild enough in their ways, but they always show a moving tenderness towards children (370).

22. At prayer, turning towards Mecca: evening, Bardumal. The prayer of the Moslem is accompanied by ritualistic gestures throughout, from the bow and the genuflection to the prostration, with head touching the ground (423).

23. Oases, ration-packs, liquid-gas containers, and tents. Askole. Time: a cold dawn. Porters wait, wrapped in their woollen togas. In the old hut (extreme right) are the 'authorities' —Captain Dar and Toni Gobbi. Identity discs are being issued by them (335).

24. Moccasin or slipper-type 'shoes' of skin and crocheted wool (*hlam*). Extremely practical. Give a good grip on rock and excellent protection against the cold—but not against damp (414).

25. Balti porter: characteristic Europoid physique. Is holding the *matu*—an axe-shaped stick which he uses to take the weight of his pack during halts on the march. His turban is by no means common: it generally denotes only those who have made notable pilgrimages (378).

26. Inhabitants of Askole: a group. A much rougher race than the Balti of the lower plains, their resistance to hardship, fatigue and cold is phenomenal. The scene—Payù. In background, an unnamed peak (619).

27. Long evenings, sometimes nearly the whole night, may be spent round the fire—at any rate while fuel can be gathered on the spot. Bardumal.

303

28. The long, long trail: crossing the sandy bed of a former lake which in ancient times filled the Skardu basin. In the distance can be seen signs of the usual afternoon squall. (Between Skardu and Shigar.)

29. The caravan in the snow, in the Upper Baltoro; in background, Muztagh Tower (23,860 feet).

30. A difficult passage. Sand and landslides near Chongo.

31. A tricky stretch of rock near Askole.

32. 33. 34. Discussions at Payù on the day of the 'Payù Revolt'.

35. The whole caravan (about 500 men) assembled on the Payù terraces for Captain A. K. Dar's breakdown of the squadrons into more convenient units, to ease rationing and transport.

36. A dismal evening after a stormy day at Concordia (15,000 feet): group of porters round a poor fire.

37. Soon after sunset: a camp in the Upper Baltoro at 16,000 feet. In background, Muztagh Tower (23,860 feet).

38. Balti porters getting up after a night on the Baltoro Glacier, at Concordia. For their bivouac they spread groundsheets, blankets, clothes, etc., over the ice. They then undress and pile their clothes and whatever else is available on top of them and sleep close together between the two layers. On the morning on which the photograph was taken the thermo-meter stood at zero Fahrenheit!

39. Balti, bare-footed, on the snow. At Concordia (15,000 feet) (1140).

40. 41. 42. 43. *Tok* cooking. The flour is first made into a paste with water; then the Balti takes a dollop of it and wraps it round a burning-hot stone into a rough bun-shape. With the stone inside, it is then heated by the fire. The moment it is cooked it is opened rather like an egg, and eaten. If the flour is wholesome and the cooking done carefully, *tok* are quite tasty (Bardumal) (407, 409, 411, 413).

44. Balti chorus, Kashumal (441).

45. 46. 47. Balti dance, Kashumal. Figure on extreme left is 'The Viking' (436, 438, 432).

48. Coming down the Shigar river by raft. Foreground—head, shoulders and arm of a pilot: opposite us, a whirlpool. The speed of these craft over the more rapid stretches of the river is impressive. They have no rudders and in rough water can spin round like corks. On the return journey the Expedition covered the Dasso–Skardu stretch in these *zaks*. A journey which had taken three days overland was done in a few hours (2091).

49. Mount Payù (21,654 feet) from Liligo. No expedition has yet attempted this mountain (679).

50. The Second Cathedral of the Baltoro (19,245 feet) at sunset. From Liligo (756).

51. The Second Cathedral of the Baltoro (19,245 feet) at sunrise, from Urdukass (767).

52. The Mitre (19,718 feet) from Concordia, lit up by the sun's first rays. The hooked-back shape of the summit is repeated in reverse in another unnamed peak to be seen in the background (816).

53. The first really striking and significant peak to be seen in the course of ascending the Braldu Valley is Mango Gusor (20,632 feet) which towers over Askole. Seen from the

valley of the Dumordu it presents the impressive appearance of a tower covered with ice. It has never been attempted and probably offers considerable difficulties.

54. Giants of the Baltoro: K2 (28,253 feet), early morning. From Concordia.

55. Giants of the Baltoro: Gasherbrum IV (26,180 feet), late afternoon, taken while on our way to Gore.

56. Giants of the Baltoro: Gasherbrum I (26,470 feet), from a crevasse in the glacier near Point (22,139 feet). Climber in foreground is Giuseppe Oberto.

57. The Peak of Gasherbrum IV (26,180 feet). Lit by the sun's last rays. From Concordia.

58. Masherbrum (25,660 feet), from Biange camp, sunset.

59. Chogolisa (25,110 feet), from the Upper Baltoro at sunset. On this mountain, the Duke of the Abruzzi established an altitude record in 1909, climbing up to 24,600 feet. Hermann Buhl went to his death on Chogolisa in 1957. The summit was finally reached by the Japanese in 1958.

60. The first sun-ray peeps round Gasherbrum IV into Concordia.

61. Starlight over Gasherbrum IV. In the vast solitude the only sign of Man is the lighted tent.

62. The pyramid of Gasherbrum II (26,360 feet) which is of extremely regular formation. This peak was climbed by the Austrians in 1956. On the left—Gasherbrum III (26,090 feet) (1134).

63. The wall of Gasherbrum V (24,019 feet), from Camp II (20,000 feet). High up, illuminated by the sun's last rays, can be seen the ice-wall where a breakaway caused the fearful avalanche of 1st July 1958. Remains of the avalanche can be noted at the bottom of the picture (on the plain). What appear to be fragments of snow are in reality ice-blocks six or nine feet high. The avalanche ran a mile or so over the plain from the point where it plunged down from the ice-wall. This wall of rock, ice and snow is nearly 4,000 feet high. Gasherbrum V has never been attempted (1545).

64. Gasherbrum VI (22,976 feet), from Camp II (20,000 feet). Gasherbrum VI has never been attempted (1493).

65. Chogolisa (25,110 feet) from the Base Camp, crowned by cloud of the cirrus type (1273).

66. Golden Throne (Baltoro Kangri) (23,989 feet) from near Camp I. The main summit, not yet conquered, conceals a lesser peak ('V', 23,786 feet) reached by Piero Ghiglione, A. Roch and J. Belaieff, on 3rd August 1934 (1358).

67. Séracs and ice-rivers round Camp I (c. 18,300 feet) (1340).

68. Gasherbrum IV (26,180 feet) from near Camp II (20,000 feet). On right, the 'Italians' Ice-fall'. Top section: against the sky, the North-East Ridge which formed the approach of the advance team (1523).

69. G. Cwm in late-afternoon sunlight, flooding in from Point (22,139 feet) as from a huge window. On the left (high up) 'Inscription Stone' and Corner Peak (lower and more distant). In the foreground, Giuseppe Oberto, with a heavy pack of supplies destined for Camp III (20,800 feet) (1552).

70. Base Camp, with the moon rising over Conway Saddle (20,669 feet). This important pass, which allows communication between the Baltoro and the glaciers of the Eastern Karakoram, was reached for the first time by A. Desio and E. Croux on 28th May 1929.

71. Looking towards Sia-Kangri (24,350 feet) from the Base Camp, after sunset. This lovely mountain was climbed for the first time by various members of the Dyhrenfurth International Expedition of 1934; and again by the Austrians of the Morawec Expedition of 1956.

72. Camp II (c. 20,000 feet) and Gasherbrum IV (26,180 feet). The various colours in the rock from which this mountain is formed can be clearly seen.

73. Camp III (20,800 feet) and Gasherbrum I (26,470 feet), early morning

74. Riccardo Cassin and some high-altitude porters among the crevasses of the first ice-fall of the South Gasherbrum Glacier.

75. Giuseppe Oberto on a steep slope, cutting steps.

76. Haji Ismael crossing a dangerous bridge between Camp I and Camp II.

77. Riccardo Cassin on a very steep rock-face close to the top of the 'Italians' Ice-fall', at about 22,300 feet.

78. Three porters on the 'Italians' Ice-fall'. The vertical nature of some sectors of the climb is not fully suggested in this photograph, in so far as they face the camera. At this point, ice-block and séracs form a wall in places not only sheer but overhanging.

79. The ice-wall, 300–400 feet high, which marks the upper end of the 'Italians' Ice-fall'. Turrets of ice sometimes work loose from this bastion and crash down on to the Ice-fall. Fate was kind to us: a few minor fractures occurred in the ice while we were here, but nothing on a large scale.

80. Gasherbrum IV (26,180 feet) from a small peak north of the North-East Ridge (c. 23,620 feet). The North-East Crest can be seen, with all its turrets. The actual dimensional relationships between the various sectors are greatly falsified by the perspective.

81. Looking north from about 23,620 feet up, at sunset. The picture shows the Shaksgam range (22,310–22,960 feet). A mass can just be made out in the distance: possibly Muztagh Ata, 'The Father of the Snows' (24,386 feet), on the borders of Russian territory. In the left sector of the photograph we are looking towards Sinkiang and China.

82. Looking south from the same point. Clearly distinguishable: Gasherbrum V (24,019 feet) and Gasherbrum VI (22,976 feet). Farther off, Chogolisa (25,110 feet) and, left, Golden Throne (23,989 feet). The band of violet colour across the horizon is typical of fair-weather sunsets at great height.

83. Riccardo Cassin and Bepi De Francesch taking a breather among the snows of the North-East Ridge. The peak seen is Snow Cone (25,426 feet)—not, as might appear, the Summit—above Camp VI (24,700 feet) (1865).

84. One of the world's greatest spectacles: some twenty miles of the Baltoro Glacier, winding like a vast serpent between the Karakoram Mountains; taken from near the Summit of Gasherbrum IV (26,180 feet) on 6th August, by which time the glacier's covering of snow had completely disappeared. The moraines are all showing, each one representing the 'river of stones' from a peak or collection of peaks. Since the mountains of the Karakoram range are formed of widely differing rock, these 'rivers of stones' are of many different colours and textures: limestone white, porphyry violet, granite chrome, basalt black, etc. In the centre of the picture is Concordia (15,000 feet); on left, the Mitre

(19,718 feet) which from here presents the appearance of a mere pinnacle. In background, high up, the crags of Urdukass and Mount Payù (21,654 feet) (2243).

85. The South Peak of Gasherbrum IV from the North Peak. The Summit-team found themselves in some doubt as to which was the higher. Between the two points runs a limestone crest with numerous indentations and turrets (*Plate 105*). In the background, clearly distinguishable: Chogolisa (25,110 feet) and Nameless Peak (22,477 feet) (2242).

86. The pyramid-summit of Gasherbrum IV (26,180 feet) from the approaches of Gasherbrum III (26,090 feet). On right can be seen North-East Ridge and the North-East Crest. Photograph taken by Riccardo Cassin during his solo reconnaissance on Gasherbrum III, 5th August 1958 (1866).

87. Two men alone now, against a highly difficult peak: Walter Bonatti and Carlo Mauri seen in shadow against a rock-wall on the last lap of the North-East Ridge (2184).

88. Bepi De Francesch, photographed by Toni Gobbi, at one of the trickiest places in the hard climb between Camp V and Camp VI (24,770 feet). The support given to the leaders by the Gobbi-De Francesch team (3rd August) and later with the additional aid of Dr. Zeni (5th August) was an indispensable contribution to success. They took a considerable weight of vital supplies from Camp V up to Camp VI. They themselves had no hope of reaching the Summit: their one object was to enable Bonatti and Mauri to do so. These Asian mountains call for collective teamwork. Success is due in great part to those who work away for it in the background. Without their support, the final dash for the Summit would be impossible (2132).

89. A difficult and exposed passage on snow beyond Camp VI at 25,300 feet on Snow Cone (2177).

90. Camp V (23,600 feet) (2148).

91. Camp VI (*c.* 24,700 feet) (2161).

92. It was often impossible to follow the line of the crest. The climber then had to get right out on the most exposed face of the mountain, making his way back to the direct line of ascent through steep couloirs. Carlo Mauri is seen here, photographed by Walter Bonatti, between Camp VI and the Summit (2179).

93. Toni Gobbi in a traverse during one of the two climbs up to Camp VI.

94. The North-East Crest rises with extreme steepness from the North-East Ridge.

95. Cornice Crest, seen from above, could be a Dolomite peak. Height here 24,000 feet.

96. Carlo Mauri on Cornice Crest between Camps V and VI.

97. The same.

98. Suspended on the North Wall of Gasherbrum IV at enormous height over the North Gasherbrum Glacier.

99. Carlo Mauri on the crest between Camps V and VI.

100. Walter Bonatti on the North-East Ridge. In background, Broad Peak (26,400 feet) and K2 (28,253 feet). From this side, Broad Peak looks far more formidable and more imperious than from the Baltoro. Seen from the latter, its aspect is one of cumbrous tranquillity.

101. 102.   Two difficult rock pitches. For long stretches, the North-East Ridge of Gasherbrum IV offers Grade 4 difficulties. Every so often the climber had to tackle an overhang of Grade 5. Such difficulties have never been tackled before at similar altitudes.

103. One of the hardest obstacles in the entire climb: the chimney above Camp VI. At this altitude every effort very soon leads to exhaustion. This passage was one long balancing feat which called for some killing gymnastics.

104. Carlo Mauri reappearing from the abyss, back on the ridge after a traverse: in the far background, violet-coloured shadows fill the valleys of the North Gasherbrum Glacier.

105. One of the last of the difficult pitches, not far short of the Summit. Walter Bonatti leading, photographed by Carlo Mauri (2249).

106. Walter Bonatti at the Summit, 6th August 1958, 1230 hours (2252).

107. Carlo Mauri at the Summit, 6th August 1958, 1230 hours (2253).

108. The eight Italians and Captain Dar at the Base Camp, on their return from Gasherbrum IV, 10th August 1958.

CREDITS

Walter Bonatti, 48, 85, 87, 89, 92, 94, 95, 96, 97, 98, 99, 101, 104, 107
Riccardo Cassin, 86
Bepi de Francesch, 39, 93
Toni Gobbi, 2, 88, 90, 91
Carlo Mauri, 72, 84, 100, 102, 103, 105, 106
Fosco Maraini, 1, 3–38, 40–47, 49–71, 73–83, 108

Bibliography

I am only mentioning some titles. More complete lists are to be found in *La Conquista del K2* by Professor Ardito Desio (English translation by D. Moore, *The Ascent of K2*, London 1955) and in *Der dritte Pol*, by Professor G. O. Dyhrenfurth, München 1960.

ACADEMIC ALPINE CLUB OF KYOTO: *The Japanese Chogolisa Expedition* (Photographic Album), Kyoto, 1959

G. BAND: *Road to Rakaposhi*, London, 1955

M. BANKS: *Rakaposhi*, London, 1959

W. BONATTI: *Piantai il tricolore sulla Montagna di Luce*, 'Oggi', Milan, 18th August 1960

H. BUHL: *Achttausend—Drüber und Drunter. Gedächtnisausgabe mit einem Nachtrag von K. Diemberger*, München, 1954

S. G. BURRARD, H. H. HAYDEN: *A Sketch of the Geography and Geology of the Himalaya Mountains and Tibet* (2nd ed.), New Delhi, 1933

C. CALCIATI: *Al Karakorum. Diario di due esplorazioni*, Firenze, 1930

O. CAROE: *The Pathans, 550 B.C.—A.D. 1957*, London, 1958

R. CASSIN: *Dove la Parete strapiomba*, Milano, 1958

N. CLINCH: *We scaled Doomsday Mountain* (Masherbrum), 'The Saturday Evening Post', 25th March 1961

CLUB ALPINO ITALIANO, TOURING CLUB ITALIANO: *Alpinismo Italiano nel Mondo*, Milano, 1953

A. COMPAGNONI: *Uomini sul K2*, Milano, 1958

W. M. CONWAY: *Climbing and Exploration in the Karakoram-Himalayas* (two vols.), London, 1894

G. DAINELLI: *Paesi e Genti del Caracorùm. Vita di Carovana nel Tibet Occidentale* (two vols.), Firenze, 1924

G. DAINELLI: *Le Condizioni delle Genti* (Vol. VIII of *Resultati Geologici e Geografici della Spedizione Italiana De Filippi 1913–1914*), Bologna, 1924

G. DAINELLI: *I Tipi Umani* (Vol. IX, as above), Bologna, 1924

G. DAINELLI: *Il mio viaggio nel Tibet Occidentale*, Milano, 1932

G. DAINELLI: *Buddhists and Glaciers of Western Tibet*, London, 1933

G. DAINELLI: *Esploratori e Alpinisti nel Caracorùm*, Torino, 1959

F. DE FILIPPI: *Karakoram and the Western Himalaya 1909. An Account of the Expedition of H. R. H. Luigi Amedeo of Savoy, Duke of the Abruzzi*, London, 1912

F. DE FILIPPI: *The Italian Expedition to the Himalaya, Karakoram and Eastern Turkestan 1913–1914*, London, 1932

H. DE SÉGOGNE: *L'expédition française à l'Himalaya*, 'La Montagne', Paris, January 1937

A. DESIO (in collaboration with H. R. H. AIMONE OF SAVOIA-AOSTA, DUKE OF SPOLETO): *La Spedizione geografica Italiana nel Karakoram*, Milano, 1936

A. DESIO: *La conquista del K2, seconda cima del mondo*, Milano, 1954 (English translation by D. Moore, *The Ascent of K2*, London 1955)

A. DESIO: *Libro bianco (In margine alla conquista del K2)*, Milano, 1956

K. DIEMBERGER: *Broad Peak—Chogolisa*, 'The Mountain World, 1958–1959', London, 1959

E. DONATI AND L. LACEDELLI: *I conquistatori del K2*, Milano, 1955

J. E. DUNCAN: *A Summer Ride through Western Tibet*, London, 1904

A. DURAND: *The making of a Frontier. Five years of Experiences and Adventures in Gilgit, Hunza, Nagar, Chitral and the Eastern Hindu-Kush*, London, 1900

G. O. DYHRENFURTH (and others): *Dämon Himalaya. Bericht der Internationalen Karakorum-Expedition 1934*, Basel, 1935

G. O. DYHRENFURTH: *Baltoro, ein Himalaya-Buch*, Basel, 1939

G. O. DYHRENFURTH: *Das Buch vom Nanga Parbat. Die Geschichte seiner Besteigung 1895–1953*, München, 1954

G. O. DYHRENFURTH: *To the Third Pole, A History of the High Himalaya* (translated from the German by H. Merrick), London, 1955

G. O. DYHRENFURTH: *Der Dritte Pol*, München, 1960

O. ECKENSTEIN: *The Karakorams and Kashmir. An Account of a Journey*, London, 1896

I. J. EDWARDS: *The Batura Muztagh Expedition, 1959*, 'The Alpine Journal', No. 300, 1960

J. ESCARRA, H. DE SÉGOGNE, L. NELTNER, J. CHARIGNAN: *Himalayan Assault, The French Himalaya Expedition 1936* (translated from the French by N. E. Morin), London, 1948

M. FANTIN: *K2, Sogno vissuto*, Bologna, 1958

A. H. FRANCKE: *Antiquities of Indian Tibet. Vol II: The Chronicles of Ladakh and minor Chronicles*, Calcutta, 1926

P. GHIGLIONE: *Dalle Ande all' Himalaya*, Torino, 1936

P. GHIGLIONE: *Le mie scalate nei cinque continenti*, Milano, 1942

T. GOBBI: *Gasherbrum IV*, 'Annales 1958 du Groupe de Haute Montagne', Paris, 1958

J. M. HARTOG: *The Climbing of the Muztagh Tower*, 'The Alpine Journal', No. 293, 1956

S. HEDIN: *Southern Tibet. Vol IV: Karakorum and Chang-Tang*; Vol. VII: *History and Exploration in the Karakorum Mountains*, Stockholm, 1922

K. M. HERLIGKOFFER: *Nanga Parbat* (translated from the German by E. Brockett and A. Ehrenzweig), London, 1954

C. S. HOUSTON, R. BATES: *K2, the Savage Mountain*, New York, 1954

K. IMANISHI: *Karakorum, 1955*, 'Sangaku, The Journal of the Japanese Alpine Club', No. 50, 1957

J. JACOT-GUILLARMOD: *Six mois dans l'Himalaya et l'Hindu-Kush*, Neuchâtel, 1904

W. KICK: *Place Names in Baltistan*, 'The Mountain World, 1956-1957', London, 1957

M. KURZ: *Chronique Himalayenne. L'âge d'or, 1940–1955*, Zürich, 1959

T. KUWABARA: *The First Ascent of Chogolisa*. 'The Alpine Journal', No. 299, 1959

T. KUWABARA: *Chogorisa To-cho (The First Ascent of Chogolisa; in Japanese)*, Tokyo, 1959

T. G. LONGSTAFF: *This My Voyage*, London, 1950

G. MAGNONE: *La Tour de Mustagh*, 'La Montagne', Paris, 1956

F. MARAINI: *The Italian Expedition to Gasherbrum IV*, 'The Alpine Journal', No. 299, 1959

F. MARAINI: *A Roman Flag on Saraghrar Peak*, 'The Alpine Journal', No. 301, 1960

K. MASON: *Karakoram Nomenclature and Karakoram Conference Report*, 'The Himalayan Journal', No. X, 1938 (also in 'The Geographical Journal' No. 91, 1938)

K. MASON: *Abode of Snow. A History of Himalayan Exploration and Mountaineering*, London, 1955

G. MONZINO (and others): *La spedizione G. M. 59 al Kanjut Sar*, 'Rivista Mensile del C.A.I.', March-April 1960

F. MORAVEC: *The Austrian Karakorum Expedition*, 'The Himalayan Journal', No. 20, 1957 (see also corrections in No. 21, 1958)

W. NOYCE: Articles on the ascent of *Trivor* in 'The Times', 28th August, 15th September, 5th October 1960

A. F. C. READ: *Balti Grammar*, The Royal Asiatic Society, London, 1934

A. ROCH: *Karakoram-Himalaya*, Neuchâtel, 1946

H. ROISS: *The First Ascent of Haramosh*, 'The Alpine Journal', No. 297, 1958

M. SCHMUCK: *Broad Peak 8047 m.*, Salzburg, 1958

P. SCHOENING: *Ascent of Hidden Peak*, 'The American Alpine Journal', 1959

R. C. F. SCHOMBERG: *Unknown Karakoram*, London, 1936

E. SHIPTON: *Blank on the Map*, London, 1938

E. SHIPTON: *Upon that Mountain*, London, 1943

E. TRINKLER: *Im Land der Stürme*, Leipzig 1930

E. TRINKLER, H. DE TERRA: *Wissenschaftliche Ergebnisse der Trinklerschen Zentralasien-Expedition* (two vols.), Berlin, 1932

G. T. VIGNE: *Travels in Kashmir, Ladak, Iskardo, the Countries adjoining the Mountain-course of the Indus, and the Himalaya, North of the Punjab* (two vols.), London, 1842

P. C. VISSER: *Zwischen Karakorum und Hindu-Kusch*, Leipzig, 1928

P. C. VISSER: *Durch Asiens Hochgebirge. Himalaya, Karakorum, Aghil und K'un-lun*, Frauenfeld und Leipzig, 1935

P. C. VISSER, J. VISSER-HOOFT: *Wissenschaftliche Ergebnisse der niederländischen Expeditionen in den Karakorum un die angrenzenden Gebiete in den Jahren 1922, 1925, 1929–1930 und 1935.* Vol. I, Leipzig, 1935; Vol. II Leiden, 1938; Vol. III R. WYSS, *Geologie*, Leiden, 1940

J. VISSER-HOOFT: *Among the Karakorum Glaciers in 1925*, London, 1926

F. WIESSNER: *K2, Tragödien und Sieg am zweithöchsten Berg der Erde*, München, 1955

F. B. AND W. H. WORKMAN: *In the Ice-World of the Himalayas. Among the Peaks and Passes of Ladakh, Nubra, Suru and Baltistan*, London, 1900

F. B. AND W. H. WORKMAN: *Ice-bound Heights of the Mustagh*, London, 1908

F. B. AND W. H. WORKMAN: *The Call of the Snowy Hispar*, London, 1910

F. B. AND W. H. WORKMAN: *Two Summers in the Ice-wilds of Eastern Karakoram*, London, 1917

F. E. YOUNGHUSBAND: *The Heart of a Continent*, London, 1896

MAPS

——*Survey of India, one inch to four miles* (1:253,440). Especially sheets: 42L, 42P, 43I, 43M, 51D, 52A

——*A New Map of the Karakoram with range and peak names approved by the Karakoram Conference 1937*, Royal Geographical Society, London, 1940

——*Carta topografica del territorio visitato dalla Spedizione di S.A.R. il Duca di Spoleto*, 1:75,000 (three sheets, with Professor Desio's book: *La Spedizione geografica Italiana nel Karakoram*, Milano, 1936)

C. CALCIATI—*Il Karakorum*, 1:500,000; Firenze (I.G.M.), 1928

G. DAINELLI: *Cashmir e Regioni limitrofe*, 1:750,000 (four sheets, with Professor Dainelli's book: *Paesi e Genti del Caracorùm*, 1924)

G. DAINELLI: *Il Bacino di Scardu*, 1:100,000 (one sheet, with Professor Dainelli's book: *Le Condizioni delle Genti*, 1924)

M. KURZ: *Karakorum, Kammkarte*, 1:750,000; Zürich, 1952

F. LOMBARDI: *K2*, 1:12,500; Instituto Geografico Militare, Firenze, 1956

K. MASON: *Shaksgam Valley and Aghil Range 1926*, 1:250,000 (in No.70 of the Geographical Journal, London, 1927)

C. F. NEGROTTO: *Karakorum*, 1:100,000 (partial map in the book by F. De Filippi: *La spedizione di S.A.R. il Principe Luigi Amedeo di Savoia Duca degli Abruzzi nel Karakoram e nell' Himalaya occidentale*, Bologna, 1912)

C. G. PETERKIN: *The Siachen or Rose Glacier and tributaries (Eastern Karakoram)*, 1:100,000 (with the book by F. B. and W. H. Workman: *Two Summers in the Ice-wilds of Eastern Karakoram*, London, 1917)

M. SPENDER: *Parts of the Great Karakoram and of the Aghil Mountains*, 1:250,000 (in Himalayan Journal, Vol. X, 1938)

General Index